Language, Culture, and M

Based on fieldwork carried out in a Mayan village in Guatemala, this book examines local understandings of mind through the lens of language and culture. It focuses on a variety of grammatical structures and discursive practices through which mental states are encoded and social relations are expressed: inalienable possessions, such as body parts and kinship terms; interjections, such as 'ouch' and 'yuck'; complement-taking predicates, such as 'believe' and 'desire'; and grammatical categories, such as mood, status, and evidentiality. More generally, it develops a theoretical framework through which both community-specific and human-general features of mind may be contrasted and compared. It will be of interest to researchers and students working within the disciplines of anthropology, linguistics, psychology, and philosophy.

PAUL KOCKELMAN is Assistant Professor in the Department of Anthropology at Barnard College, Columbia University.

Language, culture and cognition

Editor:
Stephen C. Levinson,
Max Planck Institute for Psycholinguistics

This series looks at the role of language in human cognition – language in both its universal, psychological aspects and its variable, cultural aspects. Studies focus on the relation between semantic and conceptual categories and processes, especially as these are illuminated by cross-linguistic and cross-cultural studies, the study of language acquisition and conceptual development, and the study of the relation of speech production and comprehension to other kinds of behaviour in cultural context. Books come principally, though not exclusively, from research associated with the Max Planck Institute for Psycholinguistics in Nijmegen, and in particular the Language and Cognition Group.

1 Jan Nuyts and Eric Pederson (eds.) *Language and Conceptualization*
2 McNeill (ed.) *Language and Gesture*
3 Melissa Bowerman and Stephen C. Levinson (eds.) *Language Acquisition and Conceptual Development*
4 Gunter Senft (ed.) *Systems of Nominal Classification*
5 Stephen C. Levinson *Space in Language and Cognition*
6 Stephen C. Levinson and David Wilkins (eds.) *Grammars of Space*
7 N. J. Enfield and Tanya Stivers (eds.) *Person Reference in Interaction: Linguistic, cultural and social perspectives*
8 N. J. Enfield *The Anatomy of Meaning: Speech, gesture, and composite utterances*
9 Giovanni Bennardo *Language, Space, and Social Relationships: A foundational cultural model in Polynesia*
10 Paul Kockelman *Language, Culture, and Mind: Natural constructions and social kinds*

Language, Culture, and Mind

Natural Constructions and Social Kinds

Paul Kockelman

Barnard College, Columbia University

CAMBRIDGE
UNIVERSITY PRESS

University Printing House, Cambridge CB2 8BS, United Kingdom

Published in the United States of America by Cambridge University Press, New York

Cambridge University Press is part of the University of Cambridge.

It furthers the University's mission by disseminating knowledge in the pursuit of education, learning and research at the highest international levels of excellence.

www.cambridge.org
Information on this title: www.cambridge.org/9781107689022

© Paul Kockelman 2010

First published 2010
First paperback edition 2014

A catalogue record for this publication is available from the British Library

Library of Congress Cataloguing in Publication data
Kockelman, Paul.
  Language, culture, and mind : natural constructions and social kinds / Paul
Kockelman.
      p.   cm. – (Language, culture, and cognition ; 10)
  ISBN 978-0-521-51639-6
  1. Language and culture–Guatemala.   2. Language and culture.
  3. Mayas–Languages.   I. Title.   II. Series.
  P35.5.G9K63 2010
  306.44097281–dc22
  2009043232

ISBN 978-0-521-51639-6 Hardback
ISBN 978-1-107-68902-2 Paperback

Contents

List of illustrations   *page* vii
Acknowledgements   ix

1   Language, culture, mind: emblems of the status human   1
   1.   Converting desire into pain   1
   2.   Questions, concerns, conundrums   3
   3.   Intentionality: mental states, speech acts, and social statuses   4
   4.   Ethnographic context   7
   5.   Linguistic categories   9
   6.   Expository logic and chapter outline   11

2   Inalienable possessions: what hearts, mothers, and shadows
   have in common   14
   1.   Resonance between relations   14
   2.   The grammatical category of inalienable possession   15
   3.   The semantic extension of inalienable possessions   18
   4.   The pragmatic function of inalienable possessions   22
   5.   Inalienable possession as a discursive category   27
   6.   Ontological classification and individuation, historical and biographical tracing   35
   7.   Possessed-heart constructions and intentionality   37
   8.   Role-enabled and role-enabling reflexivity   41
   9.   Baptism, marriage, and gift-giving   43
  10.   Illness cures and fright   45
  11.   Inalienable wealth and personage in the work of Marcel Mauss   49

3   Interclausal relations: how to enclose a mind by disclosing a sign   52
   1.   Emblemeticity, iconicity, and intentionality   52
   2.   Semantic classes of complement-taking predicates   55
   3.   Morphosyntactic classes of complement-taking predicates   63
   4.   Operator scope and interclausal tightness   65
   5.   Semantics and grammar of possessed-heart predicates: locating psyche   68
   6.   Usage of possessed-heart constructions   73
   7.   The ontology and epistemology of intentionality   80

4   Myths about time and theories of mind: why the moon
   married the sun   85
   1.   Introduction   85
   2.   Temporality as a notional domain   88

3.	Introduction to the system used for describing temporal relations	90
4.	Predicates: inherent aspect and verbal inflection	92
5.	Temporal adverbs and adpositions	97
6.	Temporality: from linguistic encoding to cultural framing	106
7.	Inalienable possessions and the tension between containers and contents	107
8.	Sun and moon as both narrated figures and temporal grounds	112
9.	People and things in relation to identifying descriptions and intentional horizons	116

5   Other minds and possible worlds: when psychological depth is dialogical breadth — 120

1.	Grammatical categories and participant roles	120
2.	Morphosyntactic properties of the modal clitics	121
3.	Semantic properties of the modal clitics	123
4.	Pragmatic properties of the modal clitics	126
5.	Afactive status: *tana*	129
6.	Optative status: *taxaq*	134
7.	Factive status: *pe'*	140
8.	Counterfactive status: *raj*	148
9.	From status to evidentiality: commitment events and source events	158
10.	Meta-stances and subjectivity	161

6   Interjections: why the centre of emotion is at the edge of language — 163

1.	Introduction	163
2.	Grammatical form of interjections	164
3.	The meaning of interjections	167
4.	Extended ethnographic examples	172
5.	Relative frequency of various functions	183
6.	Relation to mind and emotion in linguistic theory	186
7.	Why are interjections so easily analysed in terms of emotion?	187
8.	Meta-language and ethnopsychology among speakers of Q'eqchi'	193
9.	Semantic class of predicates used to gloss interjections	197
10.	The relation between imperatives and implements	200

7   Conclusion: natural constructions and social kinds — 202

| 1. | Methodology as theory | 202 |

Appendix A: Transcription conventions	209
Appendix B: The Marriage between the Sun and the Moon	211
References	237
Index	245

Illustrations

Figures

2.1 The relational function of grammatical categories *page* 25
2.2 Parts of a personable whole and personable nodes in a
social network 26
2.3 Two dimensions of inalienable possessions 27
2.4 Various vectors of influence 35
3.1 Relative tightness of interclausal relations involving mode
events and content events 53
3.2 Operator scope and interclausal tightness compared 66
3.3 Predicate–complement and operator–predicate relations
compared 67
4.1 Kinship relations referred to in text 111
5.1 Unmarked status 124
5.2 Marked status 125
6.1 Situational objects of interjections 169
6.2 Discursive objects of interjections 171
7.1 Semiosis as correspondence 205
7.2 Object as correspondence-preserving projection 206
7.3 Roots and fruits 207

Tables

2.1 Simple noun classes as a function of grammatical possession 16
2.2 Semantic extension of inalienable possessions 19
2.3 Summary of broad distributional patterns of NPs 29
2.4 Overall frequency of simple possessed NPs and inalienable
possessions in text 33
2.5 Possessed-heart constructions 38
3.1 Complement-taking predicates (Transitive Aspectual to
Psych-Action) 56

3.2 Complement-taking predicates (Intransitive Aspectual to
      Intransitive Affectual)   57
3.3 Complement-taking predicates (Jussive to Speaking)   58
3.4 English examples of linguistic terms used in text   59
4.1 Relation between narrated event, reference event, and speech event   91
4.2 Some prototypic functions of tense and aspect in English   91
4.3 Four common adverbs in English   92
4.4 Verbal encoding (inflectional and periphrastic) of temporal features   93
4.5 Temporal features encoded by arguments, adverbs, adpositions,
      negations, and complementizers   98
4.6 Solar-centric constructions   101
4.7 Day-by-day breakdown of narrated events   113
4.8 Techniques of reference and horizons of intentionality   119
5.1 Grammatical distribution and operator scope of the modal clitics   123
5.2 Semantic meaning of modal clitics when contrasted with
      unmarked status and polarity   127
6.1 Situational and discursive objects of interjections   165
6.2 Covert predicate classes: movement and feeling   198

Acknowledgements

I have had many teachers. When I first began anthropology at the University of Chicago, I took courses with Paul Friedrich, William Hanks, and Norman McQuown. I still think of them as standard bearers for the best that linguistic anthropology has to offer. Later, I spent a year at the University of Michigan, where I took language and culture, the first semester taught by Bruce Mannheim, and the second taught by Laura Ahearn. In some sense, my first and most sustained contact with the linguistic anthropology canon came through them. I also took a summer course on Kaqchikel, headed by Judith Maxwell and assisted by Robert Hamrick. They were a model of the kinds of interactions linguists should have with the communities they study. Back to the University of Chicago, my dissertation advisors were John Lucy, Elizabeth Povinelli, and Michael Silverstein. John Lucy taught a course on the self, with a focus on the American Pragmatists, that was fundamental for the topic choice and analytic framework of this monograph. Beth is clearly odd-man-out in this list of teachers: to paraphrase Wallace Stevens, in a world of square hats she wears a sombrero. Michael Silverstein has been called the Johnny Appleseed of linguistic anthropology – and rightly so. I cannot thank these three enough for their ideas, advice, and encouragement. Throughout my fieldwork, speakers of Q'eqchi' living in the villages of Corozal and Chicacnab guided me with pointers and encouraged me with puzzles. Angelina and Alejandro, Humberto and Maynor, Oscar and Adela, stand out for their patience and generosity – and above all for their subtle, analytic minds. Part of this book was drafted while I was a guest in the Language and Cognition Group at the Max Planck Institute for Psycholinguistics, and outlines of several chapters were presented there. Nick Enfield, Stephen Levinson, and Penny Brown gave me particularly helpful feedback. And Asif Agha and John Haviland gave me very useful critical commentary at several important junctures along the way.

In contrast, I haven't had all that many friends – but the few I had mattered immensely to this project: Jessica Jerome, Brett King, and Erik Thogersen; Mike Cepek and Anya Bernstein; Stephen Scott, Paja Faudree, and Walter Little; Alexandra Horowitz and Nick Enfield; Ryan Cheney and Antina von Schnitzler.

And as for my family, why drag them into this?

1   Language, culture, mind: emblems of the status human

1.   Converting desire into pain

The setting is my host's home, sitting around the hearth fire. The protagonist is Maynor, a three-year-old boy known for his angry antics. One morning, he pushes his tiny chair over, narrowly missing the anthropologist's outstretched foot. His ten-year-old cousin, visiting for breakfast, is the only family member who notices. *Ay dios* (goodness!), she exclaims, calling the boy's mother's attention to his misbehaviour, *xten raj li roq' laj Maynor* (Maynor would have hit his foot). Maynor's mother rights the chair and then asks the little boy point blank: *ma taawaj li la* (Do you want the stinging nettle?). Maynor sits back down, shaking his head, eyes on his mother, frowning. The anthropologist moves his foot out of range.

In this example, the girl uses the counterfactual particle *raj* to describe Maynor's action. Without this particle, her utterance could simply be glossed as 'Maynor (has) hit his foot', indicating that in the world of the speech event, the girl is committed to the truth of the narrated event. With the counterfactual particle, however, she signals that she is committed to the truth of the narrated event in a world *other* than that of the speech event. In effect, she says, 'In another world (but not in this one), Maynor hit the anthropologist's foot'.

Building on some ideas from Goffman (1981a) and Jakobson (1990a), we might say that this counterfactual particle serves to distinguish the speech event from what may be called a *commitment event*. In so doing, it allows this little girl to inhabit two roles that are usually indistinguishable: the role of *animator* (articulating an utterance in this world – the speech event); and the role of *principal* (committed to the truth of the proposition expressed by her utterance in another world – the commitment event).

Furthermore, by shifting her commitment to another world with the particle *raj*, the girl invites the inference that in this world (i.e. the world in which she is an animator), she is committed to the negation of the narrated event. This little girl, then, has revealed two opposing yet not contradictory commitments: while in another world Maynor did hit the anthropologist's foot, in this world he did not.

Indeed, the girl's separation into animator and principal invites a separation of Maynor into *actor* (the narrated figure of certain actions) and *agent* (the effecting or intending subject underlying those actions). That is to say, in the world in which the girl is a principal and the boy is an agent, Maynor did carry out an action (hitting the anthropologist's foot). But in the world in which the girl is an animator and the boy is an actor, Maynor did not carry out this action. In effect, the girl's utterance allows a range of interpretations involving attributions of more or less cause and intention: from 'Maynor intended to hit his foot' to 'Maynor tried to hit his foot' to 'Maynor would have hit his foot' to 'Maynor almost hit his foot'.

Lastly, it is important to notice how Maynor's mother interpreted his actions as they were described to her by the girl: Maynor was enough of an agent to be responsible, such that he is culpable, such that stinging nettle as a threat is allowable. Indeed, diachronically, the counterfactual particle *raj* is probably a grammaticalization of *rajb'al*, a nominalization of the verb of desire (*ajok*). Ethnopsychologically, many speakers interpret an utterance involving the clitic *raj* with an utterance involving the verb *ajok*. In this way, just as Maynor's action was subject to public articulation, so this public articulation is subject to a psychological interpretation. With her rhetorical question, 'Do you want the stinging nettle?', Maynor's mother seems to have connected the private desire underlying his action to the public consequences of its possible outcome, thereby pointing out to him how a maternal calculus can transform desire into pain, or wilfulness into sting.

This monograph examines mind through the lens of language and culture. On the one hand, it takes what is most public and uses it to pose questions about what is most private. On the other hand, it takes what is most community specific and uses it to pose questions about what is most human general. Its central goal is to weave together the linguistic and ethnographic details of a particular speech community (in this case, that of the Maya, living in highland Guatemala), and the cross-linguistic and cross-cultural framework in which these details must be rendered (in this case, that of modern cognitive, social, and linguistic science). It aims to develop a theoretical framework within which both community-specific and human-general features of mind may be contrasted and compared.

More specifically, the empirical content of this monograph analyses the linguistic and cultural mediation of mind among speakers of Q'eqchi'-Maya living in the cloud forests of highland Guatemala. It is based on almost two years of ethnographic and linguistic fieldwork, most of it undertaken in a village of some 650 people, the majority of whom are monolinguals. It focuses on a variety of grammatical structures and discursive practices, wherein mental states are encoded and whereby social relations are expressed. These are: inalienable possessions, such as body parts and kinship terms (e.g. the anthropologist's foot, the boy's mother); interjections, such as 'ouch' and 'yuck' (e.g. *ay dios*); complement-taking predicates, such as 'believe' and 'desire' (e.g. *ajok*); and grammatical categories, such as status and evidentiality, which indicate degrees of commitment to, and sources of evidence for, one's claims (e.g. *raj*). These linguistic resources have been chosen because they are discursively frequent, grammatically elaborate, cross-culturally salient, and cross-linguistically comparable. Moreover, they are also locally relevant, subject to rich interpretations by speakers themselves, and thereby caught up in Mayan theories of mind: from childhood inculcation and public ascription, to medical diagnosis and religious prohibition.

2.   Questions, concerns, conundrums

To frame the central concerns of this monograph as a puzzle, we may compare the linguistic and cultural mediation of mind with a similar mediation of natural kinds (say, flora and fauna) or physical properties (say, colour and position). To study these other modes of mediation, psycholinguists and cognitive anthropologists have brought a range of animal pictures, colour chips, and spatial settings to the field, and then compared the linguistic resources used by different groups to describe what they see (Berlin and Kay 1969; Levinson and Wilkins 2006; Lucy 1992a; Tomasello and Call 1997; inter alia; and see the classic early work on kinship by Kroeber 1909 and Greenberg 1966). For example, *penguins are birds*, *this stimulus is yellow*, or *the man is to the left of the tree*. They have thereby been able to pose many important questions, such as: what kinds of lexical and grammatical categories are used by speakers to encode their experience? How do these categories differentially construe the conceptual content and structure of what they communicate? Are there privileged syntactic and semantic resources – for example, resources more frequently used within a community, or more likely found across communities? How do language-specific resources compare to cross-linguistic resources? And how do human-specific cognitive resources, themselves both condition for and consequence of our language ability, compare to non-human primate cognition? In short, what do these results reveal about relatively specific cultural practices, and relatively general cognitive processes?

  The results of this research have been highly revealing. Most generally, there is neither universal agreement, nor radical disparity. Rather, there is often comparable contrast relative to a principled set of dimensions encoding a privileged set of features. Such dimensions and features thereby reveal fundamental facts about our species, *Homo sapiens*: how culture and cognition mediate the relation between language and world. What might we then expect of similar studies, focused now on the linguistic and cultural mediation of mind?

Such a question moves us away from relatively perceptible worldly referents (e.g. domains like flora and fauna, colour and position), and relatively unproblematic linguistic resources (e.g. nouns and adjectives like *cat* and *blue*, deictics and prepositions like *here* and *on top of*). That is, unlike the stereotypic contents of such relatively concrete domains, the contents of mind seem to be imperceptible to onlookers, and hence unable to be touched or tasted, smelled or seen. What could we point to as a standard of comparison? Where do we find an extensional background? What are the objects or events that we might jointly attend to?

Moreover, language seems to be too tightly coupled to mind for such a comparative project. Not only does it most transparently encode one's own mental states (for example, beliefs via assertions, intentions via promises), but its main function is to transform the minds of others. Where wouldn't we find the lexical and grammatical elaboration of mind if the central function of language is to communicate mental states? How can we cut the domain down to a manageable size?

Finally, given these two facts, how do we make sure we do not privilege the analyst's tacit understanding of the salient features of the domain at issue – their folk theory of what mental states there are 'in there' to be encoded, and what linguistic resources there are 'out here' to do the encoding? In short, the problem with studying this mode of mediation is that mind seems at once too close to language, and too far from the world.

To answer such questions, address such concerns, and resolve such conundrums is a central task of this monograph. The next section introduces intentionality, as one key property of mind. It outlines the relation of intentionality to cognitive representations, linguistic practices, and social relations. Section 4 details the ethnographic context in which this research occurred. Section 5 describes the linguistic categories with which this research is concerned. And section 6 outlines the expository logic of the core chapters.

3.   Intentionality: mental states, speech acts, and social statuses

In a tradition that goes back to Brentano (1995 [1874]; and see Brandom 1994; Grice 1989a; Haugeland 1998; Searle 1983), intentionality refers to the object directedness of mental states. Such mental states have propositional contents, or satisfaction conditions more generally. They thereby represent states of affairs in ways that can be correct or incorrect, fulfilled or unfulfilled. For example, just as I may believe that it is raining, I may intend to go to the store. And just as my belief may be incorrect, my intention may go unfulfilled. More generally, the representational nature of mental states means that they are caught up in both logical and causal processes. For example, perceptions are caused by states of affairs, and are used as reasons. Beliefs are in need of reasons, and are used as reasons. And intentions are in need of reasons, and are causal of states of affairs. Thus, just as a state of affairs may cause a perception, which may be used as a reason for a belief, a belief may be used as a reason for an intention, which may cause a state of affairs. In this way, mental states not only inferentially relate to each other (within the mind), they also indexically relate to states of affairs (out in the world).

Crucially, such object directedness is also true of speech acts: just as I can believe that it is raining, I can assert that it is raining; and just as I can intend to go to the store, I can promise to go to the store. Speech acts, then, as a key means of making public our mental states, and transforming those of others, also exhibit intentionality. They too are caught up in logical and causal processes, but now of an interpersonal nature. For example, my mental state, insofar as it stands for a state of affairs, may give rise to a speech act. And my speech act, insofar as it stands for a state of affairs, may give rise to your mental state. More generally, just as I may use your observation as a reason for my assertion, you may use my command as a reason for your action. In short, mental states, speech acts, and states of affairs are inferentially and indexically interrelated – logically and causally connected – both within minds and across minds. Intentionality, then, provides a privileged vantage for studying the relation between language, mind, and world.

Mental states are not only related to speech acts and states of affairs, they are also related to social statuses, and normative processes more generally. Indeed, the essence of John Austin's (2003 [1955]) famous insight is this: assuming the proper words are said, and the proper actions are done, speech acts are only appropriate insofar as participants currently hold (or are taken to hold) certain mental states and social statuses; and speech acts are only effective insofar as participants subsequently hold (or are taken to hold) certain mental states and social statuses. Loosely speaking, an assertion is only normatively appropriate insofar as the one speaking believes what they are saying; and an assertion is only normatively effective insofar as the one spoken to comes to believe what has been said. A wedding ceremony is only appropriate insofar as the two people being married have the social statuses of unmarried, adult, man and woman; and a wedding ceremony is only effective insofar as the two people come to occupy the statuses of husband and wife. In short, mental states and social statuses are the roots and fruits of speech acts: they lead to them, and follow from them. Here, then, is where the intentionality of speech acts and mental states is most clearly caught up in the normativity of social relations, where language and mind are most clearly connected to culture.

While such connections are well known, a more subtle connection comes to the fore if one examines the nature of social statuses. In particular, the anthropologist Ralph Linton (1936) defined a *status* as a collection of rights and responsibilities attendant upon inhabiting a certain position in the social fabric.

That is, the rights and responsibilities that go with being a parent or child, husband or wife, patrician or plebeian, and so forth. And he defined a *role* as the enactment of one's status. That is, the behaviour that arises when one puts one's status into effect by acting on one's rights or according to one's responsibilities. A basic social process is therefore as follows: we perceive others' roles; from these perceived roles, we infer their statuses; and from these inferred statuses, we anticipate other roles from them which would be in keeping with those statuses. For example, just as you can infer I am a waiter by my having brought a menu to your table, you can subsequently expect me to perform other roles – such as reciting the daily specials, or writing down your order – that would be in keeping with this status.

Defined as such, social statuses have a lot in common with mental states. For example, just as inhabiting a social status leads to normative patterns of behaviour, so does holding a mental state – but now patterns of behaviour that are caught up in logical and causal processes. That is, we might think of a mental state (or 'intentional status') as a set of commitments and entitlements to behave in certain ways: normative ways of speaking and acting attendant upon 'holding a belief' or 'having an intention'. And we might think of the public face of such a mental state (or 'intentional role') as the enactment of that mental state: actually behaving in ways that conform to those norms. Thus, a basic process would be as follows: I infer you desire to get well, as an intentional status, insofar as I have seen you behave like someone who desires to get well; and as a function of this attitude (towards your status, having perceived your role), I come to expect you to act in certain ways (and sanction your behaviour as a function of these expectations). For example, just as I may infer what my son wants for his birthday by what he plays with in the store, I may expect him to smile when I present it to him at his party.

Crucially, given that any public behaviour that one evinces may be used by others to infer one's social status, there is much ambiguity: many different roles can indicate the same status; and the same role can indicate many different statuses. As a maître d' may be mistaken for a waiter, curiosity may be mistaken for desire. Hence, the idea of an *emblematic role* needs to be introduced: a role which is minimally ambiguous (so that it stands for only one status), and maximally public (so that we each know that we all know the status in question). As Durkheim (1947 [1912]: 230–1) argued for emblems of tribal and national statuses, such as totems and flags, such symbolic resources both create and clarify group sentiment. While the quintessential emblematic roles of social statuses are uniforms, there exist other relatively emblematic roles, such as actions, accents, and hairstyles. And just as there are relatively emblematic roles of social statuses, there are relatively emblematic enactments of mental states. For example, what a uniform is to a social status, an explicit speech act – such as *(I believe) it's gonna rain* – is to a mental state. Such an utterance may be used to make explicit both a mental state (belief) and the state of affairs it represents (that it's going to rain). In this sense, mental states are no more 'private' than social statuses: each is known through the roles that enact them, and only relatively incontrovertibly known when these roles are emblematic.

Such relatively emblematic enactments of mental states may be called *stances* (Kockelman 2002, 2005a). More broadly speaking, they may be understood as the semiotic means by which we indicate our orientation to states of affairs, usually framed in terms of evaluation (e.g. moral obligation and epistemic possibility) or intentionality (e.g. desire and memory, fear and doubt). The grammatical and lexical categories focused on in this monograph (interjections, complement-taking predicates, verbal operators such as status and evidentiality) have been chosen because they are cross-linguistically available resources, themselves frequently incorporated into speech acts, for making relatively public and unambiguous our mental states. And not only are they used to express our own mental states and transform the mental states of others, they are maximally caught up in the expression and transformation of social statuses – and thus our relations to those with whom and about whom we speak. Stances, then, provide a privileged vantage for studying the intersection of language, culture, and mind.

In short, intentionality – like any other semiotic process (Kockelman 2007c) – is distributed across signs (qua roles), objects (qua mental states or social statuses), and interpretants (qua attitudes). And these are themselves distributed across signers (qua speakers), 'objecters' (qua topics), and interpreters (qua addressees). Within such a framework, some readers may still be tempted to think of mental states and social statuses as powers that are exercised, scripts that are performed, or things that are revealed. However, if I may switch registers for just a moment, they might be best characterized as *imagined virtualities abducted from putative actualizations and subject to unrelenting reification*. (With apologies to Marx, Peirce, and Deleuze.) We will return to these points in subsequent chapters.

4.   Ethnographic context

The data for this monograph are based on almost two years of ethnographic and linguistic fieldwork among speakers of Q'eqchi', most of which was spent in Chicacnab, a village of some 80 families (around 650 people) in the municipality of San Juan Chamelco, in the department of Alta Verapaz, Guatemala. At an altitude of approximately 2,400 m, Chicacnab is one of the highest villages in this area, with an annual precipitation of more than 2,000 mm. It is also one of the most remote villages in this area, the closest road requiring a three-hour hike down a steep and muddy single-track trail. Such a relatively high altitude and remote location provide the perfect setting for the existence of cloud forest. And such a cloud forest provides the perfect setting for the resplendent quetzal, and is home to what is thought to be the highest density of such birds in the world. Because of the existence of the quetzal, and the cloud forest in which it makes its home, Chicacnab has been the site of a successful eco-tourism project fostered by a non-governmental organization, the conditions and consequences of which are detailed in my dissertation (Kockelman 2002).

Alta Verapaz itself, and the Q'eqchi'-Maya speakers who make up the majority of its population, have had an unusual history even by Guatemalan standards. In 1537, after the Spanish crown had unsuccessfully tried to conquer the indigenous peoples living there, the Dominican Friar Bartolomé de Las Casas was permitted to pacify the area through religious methods. Succeeding, he changed the name of the area from Tezulutlan (Land of War) to Verapaz (True Peace), and the Dominicans were granted full control over the area – the state banning secular immigration, removing all military colonies, and nullifying previous land grants. In this way, for almost three hundred years, the area remained a somewhat isolated enclave, relatively protected by the paternalism of the church in comparison to other parts of Guatemala. This ended abruptly in the late 1800s, however, with the advent of coffee growing, liberal reforms, and the immigration of Northern Europeans. Dispossessed of their land, and forced to work on coffee plantations, the Q'eqchi' began migrating north into the unpopulated lowland forests of the Petén and Belize. Within the last forty years, this migration was fuelled by the civil war that ravaged the Guatemalan countryside, with the Q'eqchi' no longer fleeing just scarce resources and labour quotas, but also their own nation's soldiers – often forcibly conscripted speakers of other Mayan languages. In this way, the last century has seen the Q'eqchi' population spread from Alta Verapaz, to the Petén, and finally to Belize, Mexico, and even the United States. Indeed, although only the fourth largest of the twenty-some Mayan languages (with estimates of more than 500,000 speakers), Q'eqchi' has now perhaps the largest percentage of monolinguals, and the fastest growing and most geographically extensive population of any ethnic group in Guatemala.

During my fieldwork, while the majority of villagers in Chicacnab were monolingual speakers of Q'eqchi', some men who had served time in the army, or worked as itinerant traders, spoke some Spanish. Almost all the villagers were Catholic. The village was divided by a large peak with dwellings on both of its sides and in the surrounding valleys. It took about 45 minutes to hike across the village. At one end, there was a biological station kept by the eco-tourism project and used sporadically by European ecologists. And at the other end, there was a Catholic church and a cemetery. In the centre, there was a small store, a school for primary and secondary grades, and a soccer field. The surrounding landscape was cloud forest giving way to scattered housing sites, agricultural parcels, pasture, and fields intermittently fallow. Dwelling sites usually contained a scattering of houses in which resided an older couple and their married sons, all of whom shared a water source and a pasture. Many of the individual families themselves had two houses: a relatively traditional house with a thatched roof where the family cooked and slept, and a relatively new house with a tin roof where they hosted festivals and where older children and eco-tourists could sleep. While all villagers engaged in corn-based agriculture, very few villagers had enough land to fulfil all of their subsistence needs. For this reason, many women in the village were dedicated to chicken husbandry, most men in the village engaged in seasonal labour on plantations (up to five months a year in some cases), and many families engaged in itinerant trade (the women weaving baskets and textiles for the men to sell) and eco-tourism (the women hosting tourists and the men guiding them).[1]

5.   Linguistic categories

Q'eqchi' is a language in the Kichean branch of the Mayan family (Stewart 1980a).[2] Typologically, Q'eqchi' is an ergative-absolutive language: the subjects of intransitive verbs and the objects of transitive verbs are encoded with one set of forms (absolutive case); and the agents of transitive verbs are encoded with another set of forms (ergative case). Moreover, Q'eqchi' is a head-marking language: the arguments of predicates are cross-referenced, via obligatory inflectional affixes, on the predicates themselves.

To give a sense of the morphosyntax and semantics of Q'eqchi', and some of the typological properties of Mayan languages more generally, it is worthwhile exemplifying some of the linguistic constructions that will be of interest in this monograph. While the utterances analysed in subsequent chapters are taken from participation in and recordings of actual interactions which occurred during my fieldwork (as seen in the opening example of this chapter), this one is taken from a myth, recounted more than a century ago. It has been chosen because it clearly and compactly illuminates the relation between linguistic practices, social relations, and mental states. (Appendix B contains the original myth in its entirety, along with an interlinear translation and English gloss.)

[1] Two key ethnographies of Q'eqchi' speakers are Wilk (1991) and Wilson (1995). In addition to these monographs, there are also a number of dissertations and articles written about the history (King 1974; Sapper 1985; Wagner 1996), ecology (Carter 1969; Secaira 1992; Wilson 1972), and migration (Adams 1965; Howard 1975; Kockelman 1999a; Pedroni 1991) of Q'eqchi'-speaking people.

[2] Q'eqchi' is relatively well described by scholars such as Berinstein (1985), Freeze (1970), Sedat (1955), Stewart (1980a, 1980b), Stoll (1896), and Chen Cao et al. (1997).

1)   **a'an_a pe' ki-Ø_a-elq'an r_b-e [in_c-rab'in]_b (chan-Ø-Ø_c sa' x_c-ch'ool)**
Dm F Inf-Abs(3s)-steal E(3s)-RN E(1s)-daughter (say-Pres-Abs(3s) Prep E(3s)-heart)
he must be the one who stole my daughter! (he says inside his heart)

This example is an instance of reported speech, taken from a myth that recounts the marriage between the sun and the moon, and thereby serves to explain the creation of the world. The moon's father, looking into his daughter's room, has just inferred that she eloped with the sun the night before. At the core of this utterance is the verb *elq'ank* (to steal), which is inflected with an evidential prefix (*ki-*) indicating that the event was unexperienced – either inferred by the speaker or reported by another source. This prefix belongs to a larger paradigm, whose members encode semantic features such as future tense, perfect aspect, and imperative mood. Such forms will be the topic of chapter 4.

This verb is also inflected with a person-number prefix (Ø, a zero morpheme), which indicates that the subject of this verb is third-person, singular-number. Here the referent is the sun himself ('he'), cross-referencing the demonstrative pronoun *a'an* in verb-initial focus position. (Cross-referencing is indicated by subscripts.) This pronoun is followed by the factive clitic *pe'*, which indicates that the speaker is committed to the truth of his assertion in *this* world (the speech event). In other words, in contrast to the counterfactive clitic *raj* used in the opening example, the factive clitic *pe'* markedly encodes what is usually assumed (i.e. that the speaker believes what he is saying), and thereby invites the implicature that the speaker was not committed to the truth of this assertion in another world (say, before having checked his daughter's bedroom). Loosely speaking, it indicates that while the speaker now believes this is the case, he wouldn't have believed it before. This simultaneous encoding of one kind of commitment and implication of another allows this clitic to function as both an index of surprise (in speaker-focused usages, as in this example) and an index of doubt (in addressee-focused usages). This clitic belongs to a larger set whose members encode semantic features such as optative status and negative polarity, or epistemic modality more generally. Such forms will be the topic of chapter 5.

This verb is usually transitive, and hence should have two core arguments: an agent (A) and an object (O). However, with the focus construction this verb is in derived anti-passive voice (akin to passive voice in English, but with the foregrounding of the agent and the elision of the object, rather than vice versa). Here the object is encoded using a relational noun that usually functions as a dative construction. And the object of this relational noun is the speaker's daughter, an inalienable possession (*rab'inej*). Unlike the majority of nouns in Q'eqchi', such an inalienable possession loses the suffix *-(b')ej* when possessed. It is part of a larger set of nouns, which includes the words for mother (*na'b'ej*), name (*k'ab'a'ej*), and leg (*oqej*). As will be seen, the number of inalienable possessions that an entity has correlates with their degree of personhood. And the vicissitudes of a person's inalienable possessions, the extent to which they flourish or founder, register on that person as positive and negative emotions. Such forms will be the topic of chapter 2.

Here the possessor of this inalienable possession is the moon's father, himself a character in the narrated event. In other words, there are really three events (with attendant participants) that are being interrelated here. First, there is the original speech event. This one took place in 1909, and involved a Q'eqchi' speaker recounting the myth for a festival on a German coffee plantation. Suffice it to say, the details of such a colonial encounter could be delved into deeply.

Second, there is the reported speech event – as seen by the bracketed content. This is the event in which the moon's father is the speaker, itself at some degree of remove – displaced into mythic time – from 1909. In other versions of this myth, this line is presented using the verb *chank* (to say), in conjunction with a prepositional phrase involving a key inalienable possession, *sa'xch'ool* (inside his heart). In other words, this line would itself be the complement of another predicate (a speech act verb), which would situate the utterance in the father's 'heart', as the father's solitary, self-addressed speech; or even as what the father was thinking rather than saying. Such constructions will be the focus of chapter 3.

And finally, there is the event being narrated in the reported speech event. This is the event of the sun kidnapping the moon, itself part of a much longer narrative. This narrative is rich in causal and logical processes: the motivations for acting and the repercussions of actions; the events leading to emotions; and the actions that emotions lead to. What did the sun have to tell the moon to convince her to leave with him? How did he demonstrate his love for her, and his contempt for her father? What did the sun predict her father would do upon the discovery of his missing daughter, and what did he do to thwart the father's plans? Such a text provides a meta-script, a representation of salient mental states and social relations, as well as their conditions and consequences, their indexical and inferential roots and fruits. Here, then, the portrayal of words and deeds, beliefs and desires, moods and emotions is used to explore and explain a nested set of social relations: not just consanguineal (father–daughter) and affinal (husband–wife), but also colonial (German–Q'eqchi') and cosmological (sun–moon). This will be the focus of chapter 4.

6.   Expository logic and chapter outline

This monograph has six core chapters, each of which analyses a particular grammatical category through the theoretical framework introduced above. In broad strokes, chapter 2 focuses on the relationship between inalienable possessions and personhood. Chapter 3 focuses on complement-taking predicates in relation to ascriptions of mental states. Chapter 4 focuses on tense, aspect, and evidentiality in relation to theories of mind implicit in legends about time. Chapter 5 focuses on epistemic modality in relation to logical operations. And chapter 6 focuses on the relation between interjections and emotions.

The conclusion wraps up the analysis by focusing on mental states as natural constructions and social kinds, a kind of relation between relations that turns on cross-linguistic patterns of language-internal translations. More generally, it makes explicit the methodology underlying each of the main chapters, showing the ways in which analysis must constantly tack between the particular and the general if it is to address the questions, concerns, and conundrums raised above. More intrepid readers, and those desiring a more theoretical introduction, may read it now if they wish.

As will be seen, in each of the main chapters there is a common set of core techniques. First, each linguistic category is analysed with respect to its morphosyntactic forms, semantic features, pragmatic functions, and discourse frequencies. On the one hand, this analysis is done to establish the local contours of a category, and thereby do justice to the particulars. On the other hand, this analysis is a prerequisite for such categories to be cross-linguistically compared, and thereby understood in their generality. This aspect of the project, then, establishes language-specific form–functional domains (particular sets of signs that stand for particular domains of objects) which are themselves instances of cross-linguistic form–functional domains (and should therefore be evinced in any language). In short, language description and linguistic typology are undertaken as complementary pursuits; and linguistics is understood to turn on discourse as much as grammar, function as much as form.

Second, while much of the focus is on the referential and expressive functions of these forms – their ability to point to and provide information about objects and events which seem to be psychological in nature – much attention will be paid to their non-referential and non-expressive functions: in Austin's terms (2003 [1955]), the host of other things people do with words; in Jakobson's terms (1990b), functions such as the phatic, the conative, and the poetic. Broadly speaking, the issue is to analyse how such linguistic forms, and the utterances which incorporate them, mediate social relations as much as cognitive representations, social statuses as much as mental states.

Third, while language is often taken to be a primarily symbolic medium (the relations between signs and objects are arbitrary, or based in convention), the focus here is as much on the iconic and indexical nature of language. Following Peirce (1955), this means the ways signs and objects are related by virtue of having qualities in common; and the ways signs and objects are related by way of spatial–temporal contiguity. In part this is done to understand the ways meaningful processes are motivated: how diachronic processes give rise to synchronic products, and how grammatical structure is the precipitate of discourse practice. And in part this is designed to make context – situational, discursive, and cultural contiguities – central to the analysis.

Fourth, a key move throughout is to see how speakers interpret signs from one form–functional domain (say, interjections) via signs from another form–functional domain (say, complement-taking predicates). That is, one important source of data is language-internal interpretations, loosely corresponding to what Bloomfield (1984 [1933]) called secondary responses, what Jakobson called the meta-linguistic function (1990b), what Silverstein (1995 [1976]) called meta-pragmatics, and what Lucy (1993a) called reflexive language. By having language turn back on itself, for example, we may analyse how speakers understand the pragmatic functions of one domain in terms of the semantic features of another domain, or the social relations transformed by one kind of utterance by means of the cognitive representations implicated by another (and vice versa). In this way, each of the chapters is related to the others as both sign to object and interpretant to sign.

Fifth, each chapter pairs a grammatical category with a psychological theme. Such themes are not meant to limit the analysis, but rather to sharpen the focus. In particular, many of these categories are stereotypically associated with a given domain: for example, myths and time, interjections and emotion, inalienable possessions and personhood. On the one hand, then, I want to do justice to the intuitions underlying the stereotypes, showing the ways in which they are motivated. On the other hand, I want to undermine the intuitions, showing the ways in which they are inadequate to the empirical details.

Finally, a word of caution regarding the title of this monograph: Language, Culture, and Mind. While at times I will indeed work to bring three seemingly autonomous and well-defined domains into relation, I will usually be content to disentangle a few threads from the mangle of meaning.

2   Inalienable possessions: what hearts, mothers, and shadows have in common

1.   Resonance between relations

In the broadest sense, inalienable possessions are things that are inherently possessed by human beings and other highly animate entities, such as arms and legs, mothers and fathers, hearts and names. Such things may be semantically characterized as relatively inalienable parts of relatively personal wholes. In this chapter, the relation between inalienable possessions and human possessors is analysed across a variety of domains, ranging from grammatical categories and discursive practices to illness cures and life-cycle rituals. While this relation is figured differently in each domain, a strong resonance between such relations is shown to exist across such domains. For example, the gain and loss of inalienable possessions is related to the expansion and contraction of personhood. This resonance is used as a means to interpret Q'eqchi' understandings of personhood in relation to classic ideas from William James and Marcel Mauss: on the one hand, a role-enabled and role-enabling nexus of value-directed reflexive capabilities; and on the other hand, the material, social, and semiotic site in which this nexus is revealed.

In the rest of this chapter, the complex relation between inalienable possessions and human possessors is analysed. The first four sections focus on linguistic domains, moving from grammatical encoding, through pragmatic function, to discourse patterning. It is argued that there are two key criteria underlying inalienable possession, whether as grammatical category or discourse pattern: first, whatever any person may be strongly presumed to possess (identifiability); second, whatever such personal possessions are referred to frequently (relevance). Inalienable possessions, then, are quite peculiar entities. On the one hand, we take their existence for granted (as mutually known by speaker and addressee). On the other hand, we worry about their condition (only speaker knows, and yet informative to addressee).

The next three sections show how inalienable possessions allow one to account for valuable objects, evaluating subjects, and the modes of evaluation (qua stances or mental states) that relate them – thereby showing their intimate connection to reflexivity, as a defining characteristic of personhood. The last two sections treat inalienable possession in terms of life-cycle events such as baptism and marriage, and illness cures for *susto* (fright), focusing on the transformation of status relations by means of the circulation of inalienable possessions.

While it will be argued that no one of these domains is primary, the grammatical category of inalienable possession is introduced first, and is subsequently used as an analytic lens to examine inalienable possession in other domains. In the conclusion, the relevance of this category for anthropological theory will be discussed by focusing on its relation to Mauss's notions of inalienable wealth (*immeuble*) and personage (*personnage*), as interpreted by later theorists such as Annette Weiner and Charles Taylor.

2.   The grammatical category of inalienable possession

In Q'eqchi', seven classes of (non-derived) nouns may be distinguished as a function of the morphological changes their members undergo when grammatically possessed (compare Stewart 1980a).[1] These classes have been ordered as a function of the degree to which they are morphologically marked when non-possessed.

As may be seen in Table 2.1, members of the first class are (almost) never possessed. This class includes relatively abstract words like 'motherhood' (*na'b'ejil*), and words with unique referents such as 'sun' (*saq'e*) and 'moon' (*po*) – though the latter can be possessed in certain constructions to refer to the menstrual cycle.[2] In chapter 4, when the myth of the marriage between the sun and the moon is analysed, these last two words, and their personified referents, will play key roles.

Members of the second class of nouns gain the suffix *-Vl* when possessed (where *V* is a vowel). For example, if *tz'uum* means 'skin', *in-tz'uumal* means 'my skin', and if *b'aq* means 'bone', *in-b'aqel* means 'my bone(s)'. I have only found four terms in this class: *tz'uum-al* (skin), *b'aq-el* (bone), *ich'm-ul* (vein/artery), and *kik'-el* (blood). Another term *metz'ew* sits on the edge of this class: non-possessed, it may mean either 'strength' or 'muscle'. And this polysemy is differentiated when possessed, as it may occur either with a suffix *(in-metz'ew-il*, or 'my muscles') or without (*in-metz'ew*, or 'my strength'). Notice that this class has, in some sense, the opposite morphological pattern of

---

[1] Given the relative infrequency of tokens for some of these classes, it is not always easy to determine whether the exceptions are idiosyncratic, perhaps due to performance issues or even dialectal and idiolectal variations.

[2] Usually this would be done with a construction like *w-e po* (E(1s)-RN moon) 'month of mine'. Also, some speakers prefer constructions like *in-pohil* (my monthliness). This word, then, might plausibly be put in class 2 (when its meaning is extended to refer to menstruation, rather than to the moon per se).

Table 2.1. *Simple noun classes as a function of grammatical possession*

Formal features of each class	Examples	Semantic extension	Relatively marked if possessed
1) 'Never' possessed	*saq'e (sun)* **x-saq'e (its sun)*	*Uniques and naturals:* sun, moon, earth	↑
2) Gain suffix *-Vl* when possessed	*kik'* (blood) *in-kik'el* (my blood)	*Extended bodily substance*: blood, bones, nerves, skin	
3) No change when possessed by humans Gain suffix *-Vl* when possessed by non-humans	*xe'* (root) *in-xe'* (my root) *x-xe'el* (its root)	*Metonymic possession*: road, tortilla, animal, basket, etc.	
4) No change when possessed	*chiin* (orange) *in-chiin* (my orange)	*Unmarked category:* Most nouns	
5) 'Suppletive' possession	*kab'l* (house) *w-ochoch* (my home)	*House and home*	↓
6) Lose suffix *-(b')ej* when possessed	*na'b'ej* (mother) *in-na'* (my mother)	*Inalienable possession*: Kin terms, some body parts, clothing, place, name	**Relatively marked if non-possessed**
7) 'Always' possessed	*r-a' (its leg)* **a' (leg)*	*Most body parts*	

inalienable possessions: the noun is morphologically marked when possessed. And members of this class are frequently referred to in non-possessed form. The suffix in question (*-Vl*) is also used in other derivational constructions to mark more abstract (or relatively less bounded) referents. Broadly speaking, this class may be semantically characterized as extended bodily substances.

Members of the third class undergo no changes when possessed by humans, but they gain the suffix *-Vl* when possessed by non-humans. For example, if *chakach* means 'basket', *x-chakach (li winq)* means 'the man's basket', and *x-chakach-il (li wa)* means 'the tortilla's basket'. Semantically, members of this class are difficult to characterize, but they include words such as *chakach* (basket), *wa* (tortilla), *xul* (animal), and *b'e* (road). Notice that when the possessor is non-human, the semantic relationship is not one of physical or legal possession per se, but rather part-to-whole, shared-locale, or means-to-end. That is to say, the basket does not belong to the tortillas; the basket is where the tortillas are kept. Similarly, we can speak of the 'town's road' or the 'tree's animal'. For this reason, members of this class may be semantically characterized as metonymic possessions. (Many possessions are, of course, metonymic rather than physical or legal; what is special about this class is that it is morphologically sensitive to the distinction.)

The fourth class of nouns is the largest and least marked. Aside from being prefixed by a possessive pronoun, its members undergo no changes when possessed. For example, if *tz'i'* means 'dog', *in-tz'i'* means 'my dog', and if *maal* means 'axe', *in-maal* means 'my axe'. Given the ontological range over which members of this class may vary, there seems to be no underlying semantic domain to which it corresponds. This, then, is the unmarked class of nouns – the largest in size, and the least specified in meaning.

The fifth class has only one member, which is highly frequent, and involves suppletion: *ochoch* (almost always possessed) may be glossed as 'home'; and *kab'l* (almost always non-possessed) may be glossed as 'house'.[3] In addition to humans, many animals may be said to have homes. This is especially true of domestic animals, or companion species, such as cats, dogs, pigs, chickens, turkeys, ducks, and cows.

Members of the sixth class of nouns lose the suffix *-(b')ej* when possessed. For example, if *ko'b'ej* means 'daughter (of woman)', *in-ko'* means 'my daughter', and if *ch'oolej* means 'heart', *in-ch'ool* means 'my heart'. These words are pragmatically odd when not possessed, insofar as they usually have generic reference. That is, if you use these words in their non-possessed form, they rarely refer to specific hands or daughters – but rather to hands or daughters in general. Think, for example, of sentences like 'arms are for hugging'. Because these nouns usually appear in possessed form, and because they are morphologically marked and pragmatically odd when non-possessed, they have been referred to as *inalienable possessions*. As will be discussed in the next section, this class includes most kin terms, many body part terms, and the words for name, place, family, and clothing.

Members of the seventh class are (almost) always possessed. This class includes the majority of body part terms such as '(his/her) navel' (*x-ch'ub'*) and '(his/her) chest' (*x-maqab'*) – unless they are involved in butchery.[4] Like class 1, this class is difficult to specify, in that it turns on the word 'always' which would be difficult to confirm. Nonetheless, it is useful to consider it as

[3] In Tzeltal, there is also a suppletive possession: the word for tortilla (Penny Brown, personal communication).

[4] I would include here all body parts, composed of non-derived roots, which undergo no morphological changes when possessed. Note that this is not a grammatically derived set; rather, it is a notionally derived set using my own common-sense idea of what a body consists of. It includes the following words: *xik* (ear), *u'uj* (nose), *peekem* (forehead), *ulu* (brains), *ismal* (hair), *mach* (moustache, beard), *kux* (neck), *tel* (shoulder, arm), *maqab'* (chest), *ch'uukum* (elbow), *tu'/su* (breast), *pospo'oy* (lung), *kenq'* (kidney, bean), *ch'ub'* (navel), *it* (butt, anus), *yupus* (anus), *mi'/b'o'/b'oy/ch'ima* (vagina), *b'irk'/pirk'* (clitoris), *naq'* (testicle, pit), *kun/pirich/tz'ik* (penis), *a'* (thigh, leg), *tzelek* (skin), *map* (joint), *ixi'ij* (nails, claws). It must be emphasized that, in comparison to other body part terms, especially inalienable possessions, these words are infrequently used. Other parts of the body not listed here may be referred to using combinations of body parts, usually involving at least one body part which is an inalienable possession (often as a possessor of another body part). Frequently used constructions include *x-tz'uumal -e* (lips, literally

a limit class. Some linguists would consider this class inalienable possessions as well: those words which are always possessed. And the technical term for distinguishing this class from the preceding class is inabsolutive inalienable (class 6) versus absolutive inalienable (class 7).[5]

While the focus in what follows will be on inalienable possessions of the strict sort (those which gain the suffix *-b'ej* when non-possessed), several of the classes just discussed are *quasi-inalienable possessions* in that they overlap semantically or pragmatically with the main class. For example, extended bodily substances (class 2), suppletive possession (class 5), always possessed nouns (class 7), and many possessed nouns which have been derived may be understood as difficult-to-alienate parts of human possessors. As will be seen, however, they occur less frequently; they are more likely to be found in alienated, non-possessed form; and their possessors are less likely to be human.

3.   The semantic extension of inalienable possessions

Table 2.2 lists all the inalienable possessions (IPs) in Q'eqchi'.[6] As may be seen, there are five different subclasses. First, listed under (1) as *Body parts (spatial relations)* are those inalienable possessions that have a grammatical role as not only a noun denoting a body part but also a relational noun or preposition denoting a spatial, temporal, or grammatical relation. There are around five such terms. *Ix-(b')ej* (back) is also used in the adposition *chi r-ix* (in back of, after). It is also used to refer to the shells and fur of animals, as well as the bark of trees. *U-hej* (face) is also used in the adposition *chi r-u* (in front of, before). *E-hej* (mouth) is also used in the adposition *chi r-e* (at the edge of, during), as well as marking dative case. *Sa'-ej* (stomach) is also used in the adposition *chi x-sa'* (inside of) and, even more frequently, as the preposition *sa'* (at/in). And *yii-b'ej* (waist) is also used in the adposition *sa' x-yii* (in the

---

'mouth's skin'), *r-u'uj uq'* (finger, literally 'hand's nose'), *x-naq' -u* (eye, literally 'face's pit'), *x-kux –uq'* (wrist, literally 'hand's throat'), and *x-b'aqel -jolom* (skull, literally 'head's bone'). Other constructions include *x-kaalam e* (cheek), *r-ixmal u* (eyebrow), *r-uuch e* (tooth), *x-na' uq'* (thumb), *r-u'uj aq'* (tongue), *r-u'uj oq* (toe), *r- u'uj tu'* (nipple), *x-naq' u* (eye), *x-naq' kun* (testicles), *x-map uq'* (wristbone), *x-map oq* (ankle bone), *x-b'aqel xolol* (trachea), *x-b'aqel kux* (neckbone), *sa' uq'* (palm), *sa' tel* (arm-pit). Like kinship constructions (e.g. *my brother's wife's nephew*), body part terms often show up in constructions involving embedded possession.

5 There are also a number of derived NPs, usually nominalizations of other form classes, that interact with possession.

6 This means all the inalienable possessions I ever came across in my fieldwork – requiring that a noun be found in both its non-possessed form (with a suffix *-b'ej*) and its possessed form (without the suffix). It may be that other NPs will turn out to be inalienable possessions, but because I only saw them in their possessed form, or did not encounter them in my research, I cannot know for sure. However, given the fact that one characteristic of IPs is their relative frequency, I have some confidence that there are not too many more.

Table 2.2. *Semantic extension of inalienable possessions*

Q'eqchi' word	English gloss
1) Body parts (spatial relations)	
yii-b'ej	waist (in the centre of)
u-hej (uub'ej)	face (in front of)
e-hej	mouth (at the edge of)
sa'-ej	stomach (inside of)
ix-ej	back (in back of)
2) Body parts (appendages)	
uq'-ej	hand
oq-ej	foot
jolom-ej	head (hair)
tz'ejwal-ej	body (penis)
xolol-ej	throat
ch'ool-ej	heart
3) Non-body parts	
aq'-ej	clothing
na'aj-ej	place (of body, home, field)
k'ab'a'-ej	name
komun-ej	family (community, class)
4) Marginal members	
[ketomj] (ketomq)	domestic animals
[awimj]	seedlings
[anum-ej]	spirit [Spanish *anima*]
[tib'el-ej]	body
[muh(el)-ej]	shadow, spirit
[musiq'-ej]	spirit-breath
[awab'ej]	leader, president, governor
[ojb'ej]	cough
[eech-ej]	possessor
5) Kinship terms	
yuwa'-b'ej	father
na'-b'ej	mother
alal-b'ej	son (of male)
rab'in-ej	daughter (of male)
yum-b'ej	son (of female)
ko'-b'ej	daughter (of female)
yuwa'chin-b'ej	grandfather (either side), godfather
na'chin-b'ej	grandmother (either side), godmother
ii-b'ej	grandchild, great-grandchild
as-b'ej	elder brother
anab'-ej	elder sister (of male)
chaq'na'-b'ej	elder sister (of female)
iitz'in-b'ej	younger sibling
ikan-b'ej	uncle (FBr, MBr, FSiHu, MSiHu)
ikanna'-b'ej	aunt (FSi, MSi, FBrWi, MBrWi)
b'eelom-ej	husband

Table 2.2. (*cont.*)

Q'eqchi' word	English gloss
ixaqil-b'ej	wife
hi'-b'ej	son-in-law (DHu)
alib'-ej	daughter-in-law (SWi)
b'alk-ej	brother-in-law (SiHu of male)
echalal-b'ej	brother-in-law (SiHu of female), sister-in-law (BrWi)

centre of'. In short, words for certain body parts provide a handy domain for the grammatical encoding of spatial and temporal relations.[7]

Second, listed under (2) as *Body parts (appendages)* are those inalienable possessions that refer to relatively discrete body parts. There are six such terms: *uq'-ej* (hand), *oq-ej* (foot), *jolom-ej* (head, hair), *tz'ejwal-ej* ('body', or more vulgarly, 'penis'), *xolol-ej* (throat/neck), and *ch'ool-ej* (heart). Notice that these terms pick out the whole person (body), the five pieces farthest from the centre (limbs, head, and neck), and the innermost part of the person (heart). As will be discussed in section 7, the heart enters into a large number of frequently used grammatical constructions that refer to mental states such as memory, jealousy, estrangement, desire, worry, and belief. Thus, constructions involving this inalienable possession provide a handy domain for the metaphorical elaboration of mind.

Third, listed under (3) as *Non-body parts* are those four inalienable possessions that denote neither body parts nor kinship relations. The term *aq'-ej* (clothing) may refer both to any particular article of clothing and to the general class of clothing, including both the locally made *traje* worn by women and the second-hand American clothing worn by men. The term *na'aj-ej* (place) has three standard referents: the space of an individual's body or a group's bodies; the homestead (including house, garden, latrine, chicken coop, pigpen, and surrounding grounds); and the cornfield (usually limited to one's current *milpa*, but at times extended to include the extent of one's agricultural property). The term *k'ab'a'-ej* (name) refers not only to first and family names, but also to basic-level terms such as 'dog', 'tree', and 'house' – that is, the names of things. Last, the term *komun-ej* (family) is a loanword, coming from Spanish *comunidad* (community), which is now grammatically assimilated to Q'eqchi'. It usually refers to consanguineal kin (as a class), but it may be extended to include affinal and ritual kin, as well as all village members.

Listed under (4) as *Marginal members* are peripheral inalienable possessions. Included are the words *ketomj* (domestic animals), *awimj* (seedlings),

---

[7] As discussed in Kockelman (2009), just about any IP can be used like a relational noun in the right context, and so this distinction between class 1 and class 2 should be understood as relative, not absolute.

anum-ej 'evil spirit' (from Spanish *anima* 'soul'), *tib'el-ej* 'body', *muh(el)-ej* 'shadow, soul', and *musiq'-ej* 'breath, soul'. The first two of these words are phonetically odd (the combination /mj/ is rare), so that it looks like these used to be inalienable possessions but are not any longer, yet still bear a morpho-phonemic trace; and the last three are inalienable possessions for only some speakers (or perhaps in some dialects). There are also a few terms that end with /(b')ej/, but which do not seem to be inalienable possessions: *sa'b'ej* (stomach ache: compare *sa'ej*); *ojb'ej* (phlegm, cough, chill); *jolomb'ej* (head ache: compare *jolomej*); *tuulej* (witchery), and *we'ej* (hunger). The noun *awab'ej* (leader) also has the correct morphology, and certainly shares a con-ceptual resemblance with other inalienable possessions; however, it often occurs in non-possessed form and does not lose the suffix when it occurs in possessed form. In the text to be considered, two of these marginal members – *muh(el)-ej* and *musiq'-ej*, or shadow and breath – were not included in token counts of inalienable possessions, but are included in the discussion of their distribution. In short, just as certain inalienable possessions are coming into Q'eqchi', others are falling out of Q'eqchi'. This is in no way, then, a fixed or stable category.

Lastly, listed under (5) as *Kinship terms* are those inalienable possessions that make reference to particular social relations. Such terms are unique insofar as their referents are simultaneously inalienable possessions and inalienable possessors. They are ordered, from top to bottom, according to the follow-ing semantic feature hierarchy: consanguineal before affinal, lineal before collateral, ascending before descending, first generation before second gener-ation, elder before younger, and male before female (Greenberg 1980; Kroeber 1909). All these terms are underived, or simple roots, with the following excep-tions. The terms for grandparents are derived from those for parents: compare *yuwa'-b'ej* 'father' and *yuwa'chin-b'ej* 'grandfather'. The term for 'wife' (*ixaqil-b'ej*) is derived from the term for 'woman' (*ixq*). The term for 'elder sister' (*chaq'na'-b'ej*) is derived from the terms for 'mother' (*na'-b'ej*) and 'equal/ companion' (*chaq'*). It may be loosely translated as 'mother equivalent'. The term for aunt (*ikanna'-b'ej*) is derived from the terms for uncle (*ikan-b'ej*) and mother (*na'-b'ej*). And a term for 'in-laws' (*echalalb'ej*) is derived from the term for 'son' (*alal-b'ej*) and the bound form *ech-*, which marks relations. As may be seen, the majority of these terms take the suffix *-b'ej* when non-possessed. Terms for cousins (same generation collaterals), and nieces and nephews (first-order descending collaterals) are built, through recursion, from these basic terms. For example: 'my cousin' is *ralal wikan* or 'son of my uncle'. And 'my niece' is *xko'wanab'* or 'daughter of my (elder) sister'. Terms for step-kin are derived from terms for non-step-kin using the term 'second' (*x-kab'*). For example, *x-kab' in-na'* refers to 'my second mother'. Ritual kinship rela-tions (godparents) are referred to using either the terms for grandparents, or the

Spanish loanwords *kompaal* (compadre) and *komaal* (comadre), which are not themselves inalienable possessions for many speakers.

It should be stressed that although members of the grammatical category of inalienable possession have a suffix in common, *-(b')ej*, so that they could be identified merely by hearing them, practically speaking they almost always appear in possessed form. Indeed, it is partly for this reason that native speakers cannot enumerate the members of this category; and published grammars, if they discuss this class at all, usually account only for kinship terms and some body parts (cf. Stewart 1980a). Quite importantly, then, inalienable possession – be it as a form class in the language, or as a set of referents in the world – is *not* a category that speakers will thematize, characterize, or reason about (Kockelman 2007c). For this reason, much of this chapter will be at pains to motivate its local salience in terms of non-linguistic practices.

4.   The pragmatic function of inalienable possessions

Inalienable possession has so far been described as a grammatical category that is particular to Q'eqchi'. As is well known, however, such a language-specific category may be related to the cross-linguistic category of inalienable possession (see the edited volume by Chappel and McGregor 1996; Kockelman 2009). Broadly speaking, this category may be formally delineated as follows: inalienable possessions are relatively marked (morphosyntactically) when non-possessed; and this contrasts them with alienable possessions, which are relatively marked (morphosyntactically) when possessed (Haiman 1985; Nichols 1992). Attempts to fix the semantic scope of this category – say, via implicational universals – have been inconclusive (Nichols 1992). Suffice it to say that the category often includes body parts and kin relations, part–whole or spatial relations, and culturally important possessed items (names, domestic animals, shadows, soul, etc.). Other frequent items include exuviae, speech, footprints, mental and physiological states, and pets.

Nonetheless, just as the semantic features underlying kinship terms relate to each other via implicational universals, we may predict that so too does the inalienability of various classes of kin. For example, if affinal kin terms are inalienable (*my brother-in-law*), so are consanguineal kin terms (*my brother*); if descending kin terms are inalienable (*my daughter*), so are ascending kin terms (*my mother*); if collateral kin terms are inalienable (*my uncle*), so are lineal kin terms (*my father*). (Such contrasts assume that we are holding other dimensions constant.) The logic of this hypothesis is partially grounded in what we already know about feature hierarchies via Greenberg (1980) and Kroeber (1909): what kinds of kinship terms are more or less likely to be out there in the first place. And it is partially grounded in what we should expect regarding the deducibility of kinship relations: the degree to which we may predict the existence of a possession from knowing the nature of its possessor. That is, if you know someone is a person, how certain can you be that he or she has a parent (versus has a child), has a father (versus has an uncle), or has a mother (versus has a mother-in-law).[8] Indeed, we might generalize this idea from kinship relations to all potential inalienable possessions (such as body parts, hair, clothing, names, tools, shadows, and so forth) under the rubric of *emblemeticity*, as discussed in chapter 1. In particular, one might be tempted to hypothesize that the more a possession is prototypically a necessary and sufficient criterion for personhood (all people possess it, and only people possess it), the more likely it is to be inalienable.[9]

However, it is unlikely that the linguistic phenomenon of inalienability turns on logical inference in any explicit sense (qua necessary and sufficient conditions). Rather, it is best to recast the issue in terms of deictic inclusiveness, mutual knowledge, or identifiability: the degree to which a speaker can assume that an addressee can identify a figure (qua possession) given a ground (qua possessor). To clarify this point, it is worthwhile considering the pragmatic function of kinship terms, as one important kind of inalienable possession.

In Q'eqchi', a word like *ko'b'ej* (daughter of woman) encodes a range of features: it indicates that the possession, or referent, is female; that the referent is in a first-generation, consanguineal, descending relation to the possessor; and that the possessor is female. That is, it encodes information about the figure (referent, possession), about the ground (possessor), and about the relation between the figure and the ground. As is well known from the work of Hanks (1991), deictics also encode information about the figure, ground, and relation. However, whereas deictics specify the relation between a narrated event and a speech event (or E^n/E^s in Jakobson's system (1990a)), kinship terms specify the relation between a possession and a possessor, where the possessor is (prototypically) a person. In other words, kinship terms are functionally equivalent to deictics, but rather than have the speech event (and its participants) as their indexical ground, they have a human possessor.

To be sure, the human possessor may always be encoded by a pronoun, which is itself a type of shifter, and so the relation established may be $P^n/(P^{n'}/P^s)$. Compare *the man's brother* and *my brother.* In other words, the relation at issue is two-fold: first, how the possession relates to the possessor ($P^n/P^{n'}$); and second, how the possessor relates to the speaker ($P^{n'}/P^s$). In short, we might say that kinship terms establish a relation between a narrated part (qua figure

[8] Indeed, we may also predict that the younger a referent, the more likely they will have an inalienable possession predicated of them (rather than presupposed): *does he have a name yet* (asked of an infant), versus *what's his name* (asked of an adult).

[9] Crucially, then, any whole with a discrete number of parts could have a special kind of possessivity assigned to it. What is so crucial about inalienable possessions is that their ground is the person – perhaps the most frequent kind of referent in the narrated event; and really the only kind of participant in the speech event.

or possession) and a narrated whole (qua ground or possessor); and the narrated whole may itself be a participant in the narrated event which is specified relative to a participant in the speech event. Indeed, just as verbs of speaking may shift the indexical grounds of deictics, such that the shifters in the reported speech are specified relative to the reported event of speaking, so too may embedded kinship terms shift the referential grounds of inalienable possessions. Compare, for example, *I will do it* and *John said, 'I will do it'* with *my wife* and *my brother's wife*.

These points may be generalized, thereby allowing us to compare inalienable possessions with prepositions and deictics. (See Figure 2.1.) In particular, all these linguistic resources have a similar function, in that they involve a relation (R) between a relatively foregrounded entity (f) and a relatively backgrounded entity (g). Deictics relate a narrated entity to a speech event (E^n/E^s). Prepositions relate a narrated entity to another narrated entity ($E^n/E^{n'}$). And inalienable possessions like kinship terms relate a narrated entity to a narrated person (E^n/P^n).

In the case of *deictics*, the backgrounded entity is the speech event, and hence it is indexed (but not referred to). The foregrounded entity is minimally specified, usually turning on place (*here*), time (*now*), or identification (*this*) – though it can be augmented: *this boy, here in America*, etc. Deictics, then, point very broadly: whatever is proximal. And the relation is often subject to a small variety of distinctions, often turning on a proximal/distal distinction: *here/ there, this/that, now/then*. In short, for a deictic like *now*, R=proximal, f=time, and g=(time of) speech event.

In the case of *prepositions*, both the foregrounded entity and the backgrounded entity may be referred to, usually by an NP, and thus may be as finely specified as one wishes: *the man is behind the red barn*, etc. These slots may also be filled with deictic elements, and thus be specified relative to the speech event: *he was to the left of that.* R(F,G)=R(r(f,g),r(f,g)) or $E^n/E^{n'}=E^n/E^s//$ $E^{n'}/E^s$. And the relation is encoded by a potentially large, but not open, set of prepositions (along with a copula construction): *behind, in front of, on top of*, etc. In short, for a construction like *the man behind the tree*, R=*behind*, f=*the man*, and g=*the tree*.

And, in the case of *inalienable possessions*, both the foregrounded entity and the backgrounded entity may be referred to (as with prepositions, and in contrast to deictics). However, unlike prepositions, the relation is much more constrained: essentially, there is a distinction between alienable possession and inalienable possession; and, within the category of inalienable possession, there is the distinction between physical possession (governing body parts, often part-to-whole) and social possession (governing social relations, often node-to-network). The referent is subject to a much larger set of distinctions than deictics (qua various types of body parts and types of kinship relations), but a much smaller set of distinctions than prepositions (which can have essentially

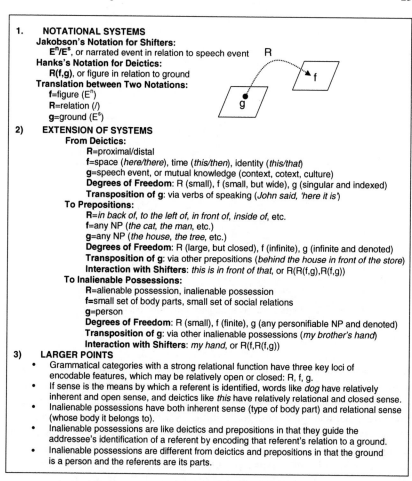

1. **NOTATIONAL SYSTEMS**
   Jakobson's Notation for Shifters:
   E^n/E^s, or narrated event in relation to speech event
   Hanks's Notation for Deictics:
   R(f,g), or figure in relation to ground
   Translation between Two Notations:
   f=figure (E^n)
   R=relation (/)
   g=ground (E^s)

2) **EXTENSION OF SYSTEMS**
   From Deictics:
   R=proximal/distal
   f=space (*here/there*), time (*this/then*), identity (*this/that*)
   g=speech event, or mutual knowledge (context, cotext, culture)
   Degrees of Freedom: R (small), f (small, but wide), g (singular and indexed)
   Transposition of g: via verbs of speaking (*John said, 'here it is'*)
   To Prepositions:
   R=*in back of, to the left of, in front of, inside of*, etc.
   f=any NP (*the cat, the man*, etc.)
   g=any NP (*the house, the tree*, etc.)
   Degrees of Freedom: R (large, but closed), f (infinite), g (infinite and denoted)
   Transposition of g: via other prepositions (*behind the house in front of the store*)
   Interaction with Shifters: *this is in front of that*, or R(R(f,g),R(f,g))
   To Inalienable Possessions:
   R=alienable possession, inalienable possession
   f=small set of body parts, small set of social relations
   g=person
   Degrees of Freedom: R (small), f (finite), g (any personifiable NP and denoted)
   Transposition of g: via other inalienable possessions (*my brother's hand*)
   Interaction with Shifters: *my hand*, or R(f,R(f,g))

3) **LARGER POINTS**
   - Grammatical categories with a strong relational function have three key loci of encodable features, which may be relatively open or closed: R, f, g.
   - If sense is the means by which a referent is identified, words like *dog* have relatively inherent and open sense, and deictics like *this* have relatively relational and closed sense.
   - Inalienable possessions have both inherent sense (type of body part) and relational sense (whose body it belongs to).
   - Inalienable possessions are like deictics and prepositions in that they guide the addressee's identification of a referent by encoding that referent's relation to a ground.
   - Inalienable possessions are different from deictics and prepositions in that the ground is a person and the referents are its parts.

Figure 2.1. The relational function of grammatical categories

any NP). And finally, in contrast to both prepositions and deictics, the ground is prototypically a person.

Inalienable possession, then, is doing the work of identifiability (just as deictics and determiners do), but the figure and ground in question are not a narrated event and a speech event, but rather a narrated possession and a narrated possessor (which itself can be specified relative to the speech event). That is, they are like prepositions and deictics in that they guide the addressee's identification of a referent by encoding that referent's relation to a particular ground; but they are different in that the ground is a narrated person. Broadly speaking, if we think about *sense* as the means by which we identify a *referent*, then open-class categories have a relatively large degree of inherent sense (e.g. *dog*) and

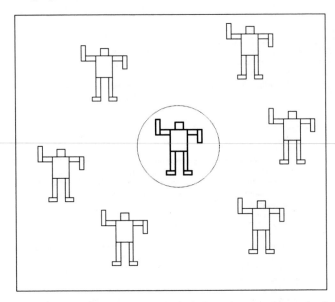

Figure 2.2. Parts of a personable whole and personable nodes in a social network

a relatively small degree of relational sense, and deictics have a relatively large degree of relational sense (e.g. proximal to speech event) but relatively little inherent sense. Inalienable possessions have both inherent sense (e.g. which type of body part) and relational sense (e.g. whose body does this part belong to). They locate a type of part relative to a type of whole with a large degree of precision, as opposed to an indefinite/definite contrast (*a ball* versus *the ball*) or a proximal/distal contrast (*this ball* versus *that ball*). While linguists, at least as far back as Bloomfield (1984 [1933]) have treated possessed NPs as definite NPs, the ways in which they encode fine-grained distinctions of identifiability have not been considered. As may be seen in Figure 2.2, there are parts of a personable whole and personable nodes in a social network. Thus, if circle-qua-self is ground, any of the parts or people are frequently relevant and easily identifiable figures.

What inalienable possessions grammaticalize, then, is not so much necessary and sufficient criteria of persons, but rather those parts (body parts, kinship relations, etc.) of a frequently invoked ground (person) which the speaker may assume the addressee may identify given the existence of the ground. Moreover, anything that can be construed as similar to such a ground (anything 'person-like') may be used as a ground: *at the back of the car, in the face of opposition, at the foot of a mountain*, etc. That is, when we shift the ground from a person to something else, we construe that something else in personal

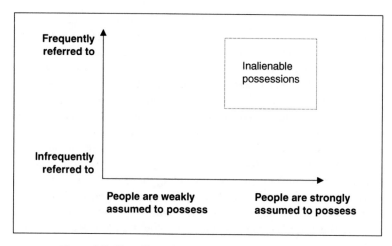

Figure 2.3. Two dimensions of inalienable possessions

terms. (See Brown (1994) and Levinson (1994) for a discussion of this fact in Tzeltal.) More generally, we may always invert the hypothesis of emblemeticity introduced above: the more inalienable possessions something has, the more like a person something is.

In short, the category is really this: 1) *whatever any person may be strongly presumed to possess*; 2) *whatever such personal possessions are referred to frequently*. They are funny entities in this way: on the one hand, we must take their existence completely for granted; on the other hand, we must frequently make reference to them. While their *existence* is symmetrically accessible to speaker and addressee (such that they may be assumed once a person has been invoked), their *state* is known only to the speaker and judged to be relevant to the addressee (such that they may be asserted). In short, as per Figure 2.3, we may hypothesize that inalienability scales with strength of presumption, and frequency of reference.

Such criteria turn on relatively localized cultural practices (what it means to be a person, what is frequently referred to), as much as more general cognitive processes (what parts constitute a person as an inferential frame, such that a whole can prime its parts). And hence membership in this class, be it as discourse pattern or grammatical category, is subject to principled variability.

5.   Inalienable possession as a discursive category

Inalienable possession may be considered a discursive category as much as a grammatical one. Indeed, if one examines inalienable possession from the standpoint of discourse patterning instead of grammatical encoding, its cross-linguistic existence becomes more obvious and its cognitive relevance becomes more transparent. Du Bois (1980), looking at the use of definite and indefinite articles in English discourse (that is, the difference between *the* boy and *a* boy), noticed that once a person has been introduced in a narrative, that person's body parts, hair, and clothing may be immediately referred to without first having to introduce them using an indefinite article. That is, body parts, hair, and clothing form part of a *frame*, whose discursive reactance is the fact that its members are able to be formally marked as definite on initial mention. In terms of the last section, we may say that the speaker assumes that the addressee assumes that entities belonging to the category of 'person' usually come with bodies, hair, and clothing. Thus, a construction like 'there was a woman who had a name/leg/mother' sounds odd, while a construction like 'there was a woman whose name/leg/mother was Anne/broken/dead' sounds fine.

Following the discussion in the last section, this discursive category, itself probably the reactance of a putative cognitive or cultural frame, should be extended from body parts, hair, and clothing to include kinship relations, homes, and names (and whatever else members of a particular speech community frequently presume to necessarily belong to a person). More generally, as long as one understands the reactance of this category to be about discourse patterning (rather than grammatical encoding), and as long as one takes into account the various formal means by which the identifiability of referents may be marked (extending well beyond the range of definite and indefinite articles), such a frame is almost certainly a widespread phenomenon. Indeed, we might expect the nouns that make up this category to have several more features: 1) they would usually be possessed; 2) they would usually have human possessors; 3) they would usually have generic reference when not possessed. Finally, as a discursive phenomenon rather than a grammatical one, such a pattern would turn on relative frequency rather than absolute form – and hence would be a relatively fluid category that might vary as a function of genre, content, speaker, and so forth.

While this discursive category would require an essay in itself (see Kockelman 2009), a brief examination of a Q'eqchi' text should suffice to show the relative overlap, but lack of isomorphism, between it and the grammatical category of inalienable possession. Moreover, with the understanding that today's grammatical categories are often yesterday's discourse patterns, it is worth studying examples of narrative from previous eras. As Hawkins puts it: 'Grammars are "frozen" or "fixed" performance preferences' (2004: 10). Insofar as Q'eqchi' was an unwritten language, this is of course impossible. However, the myth introduced in chapter 1, which will be discussed at length

Table 2.3. *Summary of broad distributional patterns of NPs*

		Tokens	Old vs. New	Resumptive	Animate vs. Inanimate	Zero vs. NP
NPs and	**A-role**	124	100% vs. 0%	0%	98% vs. 2%	87% vs. 13%
PNPs	**S-role**	235	71% vs. 26%	3%	64% vs. 36%	55% vs. 45%
	O-role	120	51% vs. 36 %	23%	29% vs. 71%	35% vs. 65%
	Adp-role	260	26% vs. 48%	26%	23% vs. 77%	20% vs. 80%
	IP	57	7% vs. 63%	30%	33% vs. 67%	NA
	PNP	211	4% vs. 69%	27%	13% vs. 87%	NA
	SPNP	100	3% vs. 74%	23%	8% vs. 92%	NA
Possessions	**KS**	19	11% vs. 37%	52%	100% vs. 0%	NA
	IP	57	7% vs. 63%	30%	33% vs. 67%	NA
	BP	34	6% vs. 74%	20%	0% vs. 100%	NA
	SPNP	100	3% vs. 74%	23%	8% vs. 92%	NA
Possessors	**P of KS**	19	89% vs. 5%	6%	100% vs. 0%	100% vs. 0%
	P of IP	57	68% vs. 9%	23%	87% vs. 11%	65% vs. 35%
	P of SPNP	100	68% vs. 12%	20%	85% vs. 15%	72% vs. 28%
	P of BP	34	53% vs. 12%	35%	82% vs. 18%	56% vs. 44%

IP – inalienable possession; PNP – possessed NP; SPNP – simple possessed NP; BP – body part;
KS – kinship

in chapter 4, provides tokens of over one thousand nominal arguments, distributed across a wide range of grammatical, semantic, and pragmatic contexts: and so relative frequencies may be compared.

Table 2.3 summarizes some broad distributional patterns of the NPs found in this text. There were 1,016 nominal arguments in the text, 482 of which were merely cross-referencing affixes without overt NPs to accompany them. Of these arguments, 124 occurred in A-role (agent of transitive verb, ergative case), 235 occurred in S-role (subject of intransitive verb, absolutive case), 120 occurred in O-role (object of transitive verb, absolutive case), and 260 occurred in adposition (Adp-) role (119 as the possessor of a relational noun, 141 as the argument of a preposition).[10] These numbers are shown in the first four rows of Table 2.3. As may also be seen, cross-cutting these categories, there were 211 possessed NPs (PNPs). And, within this category, 57 PNPs were inalienable possessions (IPs) and 100 PNPs were simple possessed NPs (SPNPs) – a category which not only excludes inalienable possessions, but also gerunds and reflexive particles.

[10] Sixty-one NPs were either formally unlicensed NPs of clauses (46) or formally unlicensed arguments of NPs (15). And, of the remaining 215 nominal arguments, 211 were possessors of NPs, and 4 were semantically empty – having clauses as their arguments.

Looking now at the horizontal categories (information status, animacy rank, and overtness of expression), a number of well-known patterns should strike the reader's attention (compare Dixon 1994; Du Bois 1987; Greenberg 1966). First, as one moves from A-role arguments, through S-role and O-role arguments, to Adp-role arguments (which include both the possessors of relational nouns and the arguments of prepositions), the referents of these NPs go from old to new (or thematic mentions to first mentions), and the animacy of referents in these roles goes from animate (e.g. deities, people, animals) to inanimate (e.g. living things like trees, organic things like feathers, or inert things like rocks).[11] Moreover, the percentage of nominal arguments expressed as full NPs (versus a bare cross-referencing affix) increases accordingly. As has been argued by Du Bois (1987), A and S contrast with O, as actor to undergoer; and S and O contrast with A as new (focus) to old (topic). Here we can see how this trend carries over to adpositions and, ultimately, possessions. Indeed, given the fact that possession is marked with ergative case (like A-role arguments), it is not surprising that possessor-role arguments are relatively active and topical. These patterns thereby provide a useful baseline relative to which the behaviour of IPs and PNPs may be compared.

In particular, Table 2.3 also shows how inalienable possessions (IPs), simple possessed noun phrases (SPNPs), and possessed noun phrases (PNPs) are distributed with respect to information status and animacy rank. The point, then, is to see how PNPs are distributed with respect to all NPs, and then to see how IPs are distributed with respect to PNPs. In particular, the trends just mentioned carry over as follows. First, as we move from A-role arguments to SPNPs, we move from thematic reference (old) to first reference (new). That is, possessed NPs usually have new referents on initial mention: they are treated as identifiable on initial mention (in the context of their possessors, which are usually already established topics). And while IPs are therefore at the bottom compared to nominal arguments in general, they are above other PNPs and SPNPs. Second, IPs are more likely to be animate (33%) than any other kind of possession (mainly due to the contribution of kinship terms). Finally, possessed NPs are, of course, always NPs – and hence the 'not applicable' (NA) entered in the last column. In some sense, though, they might be understood as 100 per cent full NPs (versus zero NPs). Thus, possessions continue the trend whereby the further away one gets from A-role, the less likely a zero form occurs – and, more generally, the less topical and more focal an argument is. In

---

[11] The A-S-O diagonalization does not extend to adpositions because these encode a variety of semantic roles. For example, -e often licenses what would otherwise be an O-role argument in anti-passive constructions; -b'aan often licenses what would otherwise be an A-role argument in passive constructions; -uchb'een often licenses a necessarily human-animate 'companion'; and locative constructions often have inanimate or old entities as their grounds, or reference points, and animate or new entities as their figures.

sum, compared to all nominal arguments, possessed NPs are at 'the bottom' of the three key clines (information status, animacy rank, and explicitness). And, compared to possessed NPs, IPs are at 'the top' of 'the bottom'.

Some other patterns should also be pointed out. First, IPs are *relatively frequent*. Out of 211 possessed NPs in the text, 57 were inalienable possessions, and 100 were simple possessed noun phrases (SPNPs). The remaining PNPs were gerunds (36 tokens) or reflexives (18 tokens). In other words, 27 per cent (57/211) of all possessed NPs are IPs. Indeed, 6 per cent (57/1,016) of all nominal arguments in the text were inalienable possessions. In short, members of a finite closed-class category (IPs) are doing much of the work of a potentially infinite open-class category (possessed NPs, and NPs more generally).

As befits their name, IPs in this text were *always possessed*. 100 per cent (57/57) were possessed compared to 21 per cent (211/1,016) of all nominal arguments being possessed. Indeed, some 60 per cent of NPs are not even possessable, being zero forms, proper nouns, deictics, and so forth. However, if we focus on possessable NPs (consisting of IPs, gerunds, and common nouns), then 53 per cent (211/395) of possessable NPs are possessed. In other words, IPs are indeed relatively inalienable: IPs are unmarkedly possessed and other NPs are unmarkedly non-possessed. Moreover, insofar as IPs are always possessed, they always license other NPs (as their cross-referenced possessor). So, another way to read the above fact is that, in comparison to other NPs, IPs frequently license other nominal arguments.

This fact should be coupled to a related fact that may be seen from the distribution of IPs across grammatical relations: inalienable possessions are themselves *often non-licensed*. In particular, 2 per cent (1/57) of IPs were in A-role. Twenty-three per cent (13/57) of IPs were in S-role, and 16 per cent (9/57) of IPs were in O-role. Nine per cent (5/57) of IPs were the arguments of adpositions (qua possessors of relational nouns). Twenty-eight per cent (16/57) of IPs were the arguments of prepositions, and 9 per cent (5/57) of IPs were extra NPs of clauses. And 2 per cent (1/57) of IPs were extra NPs of NPs.[12] These last three categories are important, for the NPs in question are *not* licensed by a cross-referencing affix on a predicate. In other words, 39 per cent (22/57) of IPs were not formally licensed. Moreover, IPs are also the most frequent heads of relational nouns and prepositions (recall Table 2.2) – and so this trend is essentially grammaticalized (Kockelman 2009). In short, relatively speaking, *IPs license other NPs and are not licensed as NPs*. Loosely speaking, they are more like predicates than arguments, more like heads than dependents. This should make sense given their pragmatic function, as discussed in the last section.

[12] To phrase this another way, 1/124 A-role arguments were IPs, 13/235 S-role arguments were IPs, 9/120 O-role arguments were IPs, 21/260 Adp-role arguments were IPs (5/119 as possessors of relational nouns, and 16/141 as arguments of prepositions). And 6/61 extra-role arguments were IPs.

As may be seen by the bottom third of Table 2.3, possessors tend to have a complementary distribution to possessions: they are at the high end of all the clines. Relatively speaking, such possessions are more like O-role or Adp-role arguments (first mention, inanimate, full NP), and their possessors are more like A-role or S-role arguments (old, animate, and zero expression). Possessors of IPs are very similar to possessors of SPNPs. As may be seen in Table 2.3, their differences come out in animacy: inalienable possessions in this text very frequently had animals as their possessors (shells of turtles, hides of goats, features of birds, and so forth); and the possessors of SPNPs were more likely to be organic (parts of living entities). Notice, then, that it is *not* the case that the possessors of IPs are more likely to be persons (human or deity) than the possessors of SPNPs; indeed, they are more likely to be animals – all of which, however, were personified in this text as speaking and thinking creatures.

Finally, it is worthwhile comparing the semantic distribution of IPs and simple possessed IPs (SPIPs). As may be seen in Table 2.4 (which should be compared with Table 2.1), many SPIPs are similar to IPs – and are often found as IPs in other languages. For example, among the most frequent SPNPs are instruments (blow-gun, bag, axe, cargo, mirror, bed, and so forth). In addition, there are companion species (dog, goat, deer), psychological states (fear, feeling, sleepiness), parts of (non-human) wholes (tip, foam, leaf, past, piece, juice, remains, corner), and body parts (leg, chest, arm). There are four tokens belonging to marginal members of inalienable possessions (shadow, breath) and suppletive possessions (house, home). Most of the PNPs had humans as their possessors, but not all. For example, there were words like 'corner (of a mirror)', 'voice/sound (of animals)', 'smell (of flowers)', 'smoke (of something burnt)', 'feathers (of a bird)', 'threads (of a tree)', 'juice/pollen (of a flower)', 'leaf (of a plant)', and 'shadow (of house)'. As mentioned, certain words like *ixej* (back) had a relatively shifter-like tendency: depending on the animal in question, the referent was different: feathers (birds), fur (mammals), bark (trees), back (humans). Crucially, aside from the unmarked possessions (class 4), inalienable possessions are by far the most common class in terms of lexical types. And, indeed, inalienable possessions are the highest class in overall token number. *Thus, while inalienable possessions are relatively similar to other possessed NPs (in comparison to all NPs) in terms of animacy rank, information status, and grammatical relation, they are relatively different from other possessed NPs in terms of their frequency.*

To briefly summarize the foregoing sections, there is a particularly strong resonance between three domains: first, what is assumed to be a relatively cross-cultural ontological presumption (what parts constitute a person as a whole, say, as a cognitive frame); second, a relatively cross-linguistic discourse pattern (what speakers frequently assume to necessarily belong to any discourse

Table 2.4. *Overall frequency of simple possessed NPs and inalienable possessions in text*

Class type	Gloss	PNP	Tokens
Extended bodily substance (2)	blood	*kik'il*	2
Extended bodily substance (2)	strength	*metz'ew*	1
Metonymic (3)	smoke	*sib'el*	2
Metonymic (3)	sign	*eetal(il)*	2
Metonymic (3)	gourd	*seel*	1
Metonymic or unmarked (3 or 4)	road	*b'e*	2
Metonymic or unmarked (3 or 4)	foliage	*mul*	2
Metonymic or unmarked (3 or 4)	thread	*noq'(al)*	2
Unmarked (1), compound	blow-gun	*puub'che'*	4
Unmarked (4)	bag	*champa*	3
Unmarked (4)	axe	*maal*	3
Unmarked (4)	cargo	*iiq*	2
Unmarked (4)	tip	*u'uj*	2
Unmarked (4)	mirror	*lem*	2
Unmarked (4)	cry/voice	*yaab'*	2
Unmarked (4)	bed	*ch'aat*	2
Unmarked (4)	goat	*yuk*	2
Unmarked (4)	feeling	*eek'*	2
Unmarked (4)	thirteen	*oxlaju*	2
Unmarked (4)	fear	*xiw*	2
Unmarked (4)	foam	*woqs*	1
Unmarked (4)	work/task	*k'anjel*	1
Unmarked (4)	corner	*xuk*	1
Unmarked (4)	self/alone	*junes*	1
Unmarked (4)	sleep	*wara*	1
Unmarked (4)	corn	*b'uch*	1
Unmarked (4)	jar	*kuk*	1
Unmarked (5)	leaf	*xaq*	1
Unmarked (4)	post	*oqechal*	1
Unmarked (4)	piece	k'aj	1
Unmarked (4)	juice	*ya'al*	1
Unmarked (4)	word	*aatin*	1
Unmarked (4)	dog	*tz'i'*	1
Unmarked (4)	deer	*kej*	1
Unmarked (4)	huipil	*po'ot*	1
Suppletive (5)	house	*kab'l*	1
Suppletive (5)	home	*ochoch*	4
Inalienable possession (6)	**back, feathers, skin, hide**	***-ix***	9
Inalienable possession (6)	**face, seed**	***-u***	8
Inalienable possession (6)	**father**	***-yuwa'***	6
Inalienable possession (6)	**daughter**	***-rab'in***	5
Inalienable possession (6)	**heart**	***-ch'ool***	5
Inalienable possession (6)	**hand**	***-uq'***	4
Inalienable possession (6)	**wife**	***-ixaqil***	3

Table 2.4. (*cont.*)

Class type	Gloss	PNP	Tokens
Inalienable possession (6)	**body**	*-tz'ejwal*	**3**
Inalienable possession (6)	**place**	*-na'aj*	**3**
Inalienable possession (6)	**grandfather**	*-mama'*	**2**
Inalienable possession (6)	**uncle**	*-ikan*	**2**
Inalienable possession (6)	**foot**	*-oq*	**2**
Inalienable possession (6)	**husband**	*-b'elom*	1
Inalienable possession (6)	**stomach**	*-sa'*	1
Inalienable possession (6)	**throat**	*-xolol*	1
Inalienable possession (6)	**clothing/feathers**	*-aq'*	1
Inalienable possession (6)	**name**	*-k'a'b'a*	1
Inalienable possession, marginal (6)	shadow	*mu*	3
Inalienable possession, marginal (6)	windpipe	*b'eeleb'al musiq'*	1
Unmarked or always possessed (4 or 7)	remains	*ela'*	1
Unmarked or always possessed (4 or 7)	first/above	*b'een*	1
Always possessed (7)	leg	*a'*	2
Always possessed (7)	chest	*maqab'*	1
Always possessed (7)	arm	*telb'*	1
Always possessed (7), relational noun	companion	*uchb'een*	1

topic that falls within the local category of person); and third, a relatively cross-linguistic grammatical pattern (what words are grammatically marked when non-possessed).

Just so there is no misunderstanding, no claims are being made here about which of these domains is primary (if any) – and nothing in this chapter turns on such a claim. (I would hypothesize, however, that the grammatical category is ultimately the result of the discursive category; and the discursive category is ultimately the result of both relatively widespread cognitive processes and relatively localized cultural practices. See Figure 2.4.) What is at issue is the resonance across disparate domains (in the foregoing sections, grammatical and discursive; in subsequent sections, ritual and practical) in the ways in which the relation between inalienable possessions – as signs or objects – and human possessors is figured.

However, that said, there is no reason to believe that the vectors of influence cannot go in other directions. For example, the existence of a grammatical category or discourse pattern may give rise to a cognitive frame or cultural practice. Indeed, many interpretations of Whorf's ideas focus on the ways grammatical categories might influence cognitive frames. More generally, a relation between inalienable possession and personhood may be evinced in several ways (the vertices in Figure 2.4), each of which may be influenced by

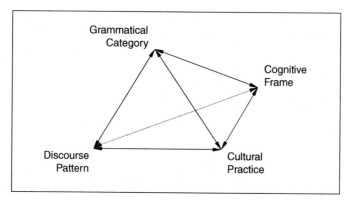

Figure 2.4. Various vectors of influence

the others (the vectors). The issue here is not to answer this question, but merely to highlight one way in which it is much more complicated than it seems. In particular, just as a grammatical category may be the result of a discourse pattern, a discourse pattern may be the result of a cognitive frame; and thus if we attempt to ascertain the degree to which a grammatical category gives rise to a cognitive frame, we may unwittingly treat a distal cause–effect relation (cognitive frame > discourse pattern > grammatical category) as an immediate and inverted cause–effect relation (grammatical category > cognitive frame).

To mitigate against such a potential error, psycholinguists would need to rule out the competing hypothesis, by not finding the following kind of effects: 1) words which are part of the grammatical category, but not part of the discourse pattern, are not part of the cognitive frame; 2) words which are part of the discourse pattern, but not part of the grammatical category, are part of the cognitive frame.

6.   Ontological classification and individuation, historical and biographical tracing

So, having delimited several domains in which the relation between inalienable possessions and human possessors is figured, three general theoretical points may be made – to be substantiated in subsequent sections – regarding the relationship between inalienable possessions and personhood. First, note that inalienable possessions *ontologically classify*: possessing such objects (as types), be it physically or discursively, is almost a necessary and sufficient condition for being fully and prototypically human. Such ontological classification is part and parcel of emblematic signification: possessing such objects, as a role, provides relatively incontrovertible evidence to others – in the sense of being minimally ambiguous and maximally public – that one occupies the status of person (Kockelman 2007b; and see Agha 1998; and Turner 1980). Loosely speaking, all of the objects are possessable only by persons; and each person possesses all of them. To be sure, some non-human entities possess some of these objects (for example, animals, mountains, houses, and gods), and some human entities do not possess all of them (for example, the dead, destitute, immature, and ill). Such exceptions, however, only confirm the rule: these liminal entities have limited social capacities. That is, the number of such objects individuals possess correlates with their degree of personhood.

Second, inalienable possessions *ontologically individuate*: such objects (as tokens) are uniquely identifiable with particular individuals during all stages of their lives. Such ontological individuation is also part and parcel of emblematic signification, but now of various sub-statuses within the status of person: man or woman, young or old, Q'eqchi' or Ladino, Hermelina or José. Of course, the same inalienable possessions may be possessed simultaneously by several individuals (for example, a married couple has a house, field, and children in common). In such cases, however, these co-possessing individuals are often treated as a single social person. To be sure, individuals gain or lose particular inalienable possessions during their lives (for example, in baptism one acquires clothing and a name, and with illness one loses one's name and shadow). In such cases, however, the acquisition, loss, or retrieval of these objects – in, for example, life-cycle events and illness cures – is the site of elaborate ritual. In other words, if there is a notion of the essence, permanence, or continuity of a person (say, a self, soul, personality, or *daemon*), inalienable possessions provide its ground.[13]

Third, and intimately related to classification and individuation, inalienable possessions *historically and biographically trace*. On the one hand, the history of a group may be seen through the types of inalienable possessions that it holds. Note, for example, how colonialism affects indigenous styles of dress, choices of names, arrangements of houses, techniques of body, and organizations of kin. Inalienable possessions, then, reveal a palimpsest of historical change. On the other hand, the biography of individuals may be seen through the particular inalienable possessions that they hold. Notice, for example, that such possessions form a site for the accrual of experience – scars of wounds,

---

[13] The nineteenth-century British historian of law Henry Sumner Maine was the first theorist to focus on the relation between inalienable property and personhood, thereby providing the legal framework within which Mauss's ethnological theories germinated (Kockelman 2007b). In addition, with his classic distinction between status and contract, or socio- and individual-specific modes of personhood (qua role-inhabitance via property rights), he inaugurated the key distinction between community and society (or non-capitalist and capitalist social relations) that has proved so fruitful to scholars focused on cross-cultural and culture-specific modes of selfhood – though usually unacknowledged by them (see, for example, Holland 1992; Shweder and Bourne 1984; Spiro 1993).

memories of events, storage of possessions, displays of wealth, habits of body, and genealogies of kin. In sum, if types of inalienable possessions are a condition for being human and the palimpsest of group history, their tokens are a condition for personality and the armature of individual biography.

7.   Possessed-heart constructions and intentionality

In Q'eqchi', the word for heart (*ch'oolej*) refers to the central part, or source of life, of animate entities. In this capacity, not only people have hearts, but most living things – including plants (referring to the root or bulb) and guns (referring to the charge mechanism). Indeed, the expression 'to extract someone's heart' (*isink ch'oolej*) means 'to kill'. And the derived verb *ch'oolanink* – literally 'to heart someone' – refers to caring for, maintaining, or feeding another living entity. This last predicate may be used in the context of animal husbandry or nurses' work in hospitals, but it is most often used in the context of parents caring for young children, women caring for chickens or people caring for domestic animals more generally, or mature children caring for elderly parents. That is, it is used to refer to social reproduction or maintenance in its most basic sense: *caring for those inalienable possessions who are also inalienable possessors*. The heart, then, is the source of life, and 'to heart something' is to care for its life.

But besides being the source of life, hearts are also the site of mental states. For example, just as other body parts may have the adjectives *sa* (delicious, rich) and *ra* (bitter, spicy) predicated of them to mean 'pleasureful' and 'painful', respectively, so may the heart. (For example, *ra li woq'* may be glossed as 'my foot hurts'.) However, in the case of the heart, such constructions are best glossed as 'happy' and 'sad', or 'feel good' and 'feel bad'. That is, pains and pleasures of the heart indicate basic positive and negative feelings or moods. But whereas most body part terms are predicationally restricted to pleasure and pain (that is, they can have only *sa* or *ra* predicated of them), the heart is implicated in a further set of grammatical constructions, which mark mental states such as desire, memory, belief, and jealousy. (See Table 2.5).

Although a detailed linguistic account of these constructions – and mind, intentionality, or stance more generally – will have to wait until chapter 3, a number of basic characteristics may be enumerated. As a function of these grammatical constructions, the heart is explicitly marked as having physical qualities such as colour, size, position, and shape; that is, as a semantic role, the heart is treated as a theme which is subject to various states. For example, under (4a), to have a red heart is to be jealous; to have a foreign heart is to be estranged; to have a tame or soft heart is to be humble; to have a fast heart is to be smart; to have a straight heart is to be honest or loyal; to have a hard or soft heart is to be brave or timid; to have a two-sided heart is to be insincere; to

Table 2.5. *Possessed-heart constructions*

Construction Class	Q'eqchi' predicate (plus English gloss)	English gloss of entire construction
1) Subject of Intransitive Verb		
a) Activity	*yook* (to be doing)	'to want (CF)'
	poqnak (…)	'to worry'
b) State	*wank* (to exist)	'to be interested'
	maak'a' (not to exist)	'not to be interested'
c) State-change	*ch'inank* (to become small)	'to regret'
	kiib'ank (to become doubled)	'to be conflicted'
	po'k (to become broken)	'to be dissuaded'
2) Adposition of Intransitive Verb		
a) State	*wank* (to exist)	'to remember'
	kanak (to remain)	'to remember'
b) State-change	*naqk* (to drop)	'to remember'
	sachk/sachok (to become lost)	'to forget'
	chalk (to come)	'to agree'
	alaak (to be born)	'to decide'
3) Adposition of Transitive Verb		
a) Activity	*k'a'uxlank* (to think)	'to plan, intend'
	yehok (to say)	'to think'
	chank (to say/go)	'to think'
	… Ø … (elided verb)	'to think (incorrectly)'
4) Theme of Adjective		
a) Simple adjective (state)	*sa* (tasty, painless)	'happy'
	ra (bitter, painful)	'sad'
	kaq (red)	'jealous'
	lab' (malicious)	'malicious'
	ab'l (foreign)	'estranged'
b) Simple adjective (trait)	*tuulan* (tame)	'humble'
	seeb' (fast)	'smart'
	tiik (direct/straight)	'honest/loyal'
	q'un (soft/malleable)	'humble'
	kaw (hard/strong)	'brave'
	kach'in (small)	'timid'
c) Derived adjective	*kiib pak'aal* (two-sided)	'insincere'
	junaqik (unitary)	'concerted'
d) Positional adjective	*k'ojk'o* (seated)	'content'
	tuqtu (levelled)	'content'
	xaqxo (standing)	'animated'

have a unified heart (when engaging in some activity) is to do that activity in a concerted fashion; to have a seated or levelled heart is to be content; and to have a standing heart is to be animated or excited.

Moreover, as a semantic role, the heart is now treated as being the agent of actions, the experiencer of events, the undergoer of changes in state, and the locale of movements. For example, under (2b), for something to drop into, or remain inside, one's heart – as a place – is to remember (something); to have something become lost inside one's heart is to forget (something); to have something come into one's heart is to agree (to do something); and to have something be born inside one's heart is to decide (to do something). Under (1a), for one's heart to undertake an activity – as an instigator or agent – is to desire to do that activity without actually doing it. Under (1b), to say someone has, or does not have, a heart (i.e. to predicate explicitly of someone what is normally presumed) is to stress their interest or lack of interest in something. Under (1c), for one's heart to become doubled – as an undergoer, theme, or patient – is to grow conflicted; to have one's heart break down is to become dissuaded; and to have one's heart shrink is to become regretful. And under (3a), to think inside one's heart – as a hidden place – is to plan or intend to do something; to say something inside one's heart is to think something; and to characterize a proposition as having 'been in one's heart' is to indicate that one believed its contents erroneously.

In this way, possessed-heart constructions mark seemingly abstract mental entities in terms of concrete physical processes. That is, such constructions provide a meta-language for interpreting mind, and modes of evaluation more generally, that is itself grounded in everyday physical intuitions.

This marking of mental states via possessed-heart constructions also has important pragmatic consequences. As will be seen in the chapters that follow, such constructions provide a semiotic resource for reflection (attributing mental states to oneself, for example: 'I believe that …'), transposition (attributing mental states to others: 'Susan believes that …'), and embedding (taking first-order mental states as objects of second-order mental states: 'I believe that Susan believes that …'). This is quite important: such an ability to reflect, transpose, and embed mental states is a condition of possibility for the reflexive modalities of personhood that often fall under the headings of introspection, empathy, and choice (Lucy 1993a; Taylor 1985a, 1989; Tomasello 1999). That is, not only may speakers use them to predicate properties of mental states, they may also use them to predicate mental states of people. They are thereby a condition for speakers to thematize, characterize, and reason with that domain of abstract entities we like to refer to as mind (Kockelman 2006: 104–14, 2007c).

Concomitantly, just as inalienable possessions function as relatively emblematic roles of social statuses (such as person), possessed-heart constructions function as relatively emblematic roles of mental states: they may be used to make relatively unambiguous and public our stances towards states of affairs, and thereby secure relatively intersubjective recognition of them (Kockelman 2006: 86–90; Brandom 1994; and see Austin (2003 [1955]) and Silverstein (1995 [1976]) for related arguments regarding speech act verbs). Possessed-heart constructions therefore provide a resource whereby speakers may make relatively good inferences about others' mental states, and provide relatively good evidence for their own. It is only somewhat paradoxical, then, that the most private of inalienable possessions is the most semiotically elaborated for public discussion.

These constructions will be treated in detail in chapter 3. For the moment, one example should suffice to show the ways in which such possessed-heart constructions figure in everyday discourse, and hence the ways in which speakers disclose their own and each other's mental states. In the case of *ch'inank ch'oolej* (class 1c), the adjective *ch'ina* means 'small', and the derived intransitive verb *ch'inank* means 'to become small'. When the grammatical subject of this predicate is a possessed-heart (i.e. '*my heart* has become small'), the construction may be glossed as either 'to regret (having done something)' or 'to change one's mind (about doing something)', depending on whether the event at issue has already occurred or not. Let me offer three examples of its usage.

First, after I had been living with one man's family for a while, the man's older brother suggested that I could move in with his family if my heart ever shrank about living in his younger brother's home. When I asked him what he meant, he explained that if his brother were ever to mistreat me (*tatixhob'*), such that I 'regretted' being there (*entons aran xch'inank laa ch'ool chi wank*), I could move in with him. When I asked him what it meant for a heart to shrink, he said that it was when one was no longer happy about staying there – literally, 'one's heart is no longer pleasureful' (*ink'a' chik mas sa saa ch'ool chi hilank*). Notice, then, this man's use of this possessed-heart construction to evince empathy, to try to persuade me, to disclose a potential route my motivations could take, and to offer a reflexive gloss on the nature of this motivation.

Second, in speaking to her friend about a piece of land (*xna'aj rochoch*) that her father was going to buy for his newly married son's home, a woman described her father's heart as shrinking with regard to buying it (*xch'inank xch'ool chixloq'b'al*) when he heard that the soil there was of poor quality. In other words, this man 'changed his mind' about buying the land. In the same context, she used a similar construction to explain that her father 'regretted' having sold his land many years earlier (*xch'inak xch'ool chixk'ayinkil lix ch'ooch'*), for his family had grown large since then.

Third, one man discussed how those who don't go to community-wide labour-pools regret it when their names are mentioned as not having helped out (*xch'inan inch'ool naq xwab'i naq xye chaq lin k'ab'a' naq maa nin'okenk ta*). In such a situation, the shame that one felt before one's community (*xinxutaanak chiruheb' lin komun*) caused one's heart to shrink, or caused one to regret not having participated. Notice, then, that both of these last two examples turn on inalienable possessions as the object that one's mental states are directed toward: one's field and home (*na'ajej*), family members (and kin more generally), and name (*k'ab'a'ej*). As will be discussed in the next section, this is typical: the objects of one's mental states very often involve one's inalienable possessions. And this makes sense: that which causes changes in one's mental states is that which matters most to one, is that which inherently belongs to one, is that which *is* one.

8.   Role-enabled and role-enabling reflexivity

Inalienable possessions, while usually difficult to price – and hence often the last stand of non-commoditized goods – nonetheless bear an intimate relationship to value: flesh-and-blood bodies produce value through their labour; mature limbs measure value through their strength and size; possessed hearts register value through their changes in state; mental states are oriented toward inalienable possessions as their valued ends; and only social persons may hold, exchange, or enforce values. Indeed, those three inalienable possessions that can be priced – homes, fields, and clothing – are not only the most expensive objects in the village, they are also the key indices of social prestige and economic wealth (and hence key causes of estrangement and jealousy, as will be seen below). In this way, if inalienable possessions may not be bought or bartered, stolen or sold, it is not because they have too little value, it is because they have too much.

But not only are inalienable possessions values in this basic sense, they are also the key means by which evaluating persons are delimited. For example, above I discussed the ways in which inalienable possessions ontologically classify and individuate, on the one hand, and biographically and historically trace, on the other. Moreover, the last section showed how mental states – those relations between subjects and objects – were couched in terms of various properties of the heart, a particular inalienable possession. In other words, inalienable possessions may be used to delimit evaluating persons, valuable objects, and the modes of valuation (or mental states) that relate persons to objects. That is, inalienable possessions provide a single ontological domain wherein subjects (qua persons), objects (qua values), and the mental states that relate them (qua possessed-heart constructions) may be delimited. Two ramifications of this fact may be illuminated: *motivation*, or the identification of a person with his or her inalienable possessions; and *empathy*, or the identification of a person with another inalienable possessor.

First, insofar as people value inalienable possessions, and insofar as inalienable possessions delimit what counts as a person, inalienable possessors may identify with their inalienable possessions. That is, the mental states that inalienable possessors, or people, have toward their inalienable possessions are inherently reflexive: a subject relates to an object that is just the subject at one degree of remove. This understanding allows us to make a first-order approximation of the motivations underlying human interaction, one philosophically inaugurated by William James (1893), and ethnographically echoed by Nancy Munn (1992): in the causal direction of social world to social person, the waxing or waning of a person's inalienable possessions registers on them as positive or negative feelings – for example, as a pleasureful or painful heart. And in the causal direction of social person to social world, most mental states underlying a person's everyday actions are directed at caring for his or her inalienable possessions.

To phrase these ideas in a more precise semiotic idiom (Kockelman 2005a: 278–84, 2007b), motivation, as a basic kind of value-directed reflexivity, turns on fostering the expansion, and staving off the contraction, of others' attitudes (qua interpretants) towards one's personhood (qua object or status) as evinced in or caused by the gain or loss of one's inalienable possessions (qua signs or roles).[14] Desire, then, is not directed at 'maximizing' inalienable possessions, but rather at securing and sustaining intersubjective recognition of them (Kockelman 2007b). Indeed, the *heartiness* of one's inalienable possessions is the quintessential metric for gauging the strength and extent of one's social relations – which is all value ever was anyway.

In short, a materially, socially, and semiotically constituted category of objects allows one to assess the mental states of individual psychology. Or, to phrase this in terms of meaning rather than mind, we may turn to Heidegger's characterization of the irreducibly reflexive nature of human beings: 'Each of us is what he pursues and cares for' (1988: 159).

Second, inalienable possessions are necessary conditions for empathy – one's ability to know, and even experience, the mental states of others. For empathy is arguably most enabled when empathizer and empathizee have personhood, mental states, and values in common. And, as seen above, inalienable possessions provide just these resources – including the ability for people with distinct modalities of personhood, value, and intentionality to partially establish or gauge those differences. But such ontological equivalence is not enough. What is also needed is for people to be socially equivalent: either *close* (say, having social relations in common), or *similar* (say, having social roles in common). For example, in the case of closeness, two people have the same inalienable possessions as tokens – say, the same parents, home, and field; whereas in the case of similarity, two people have the same inalienable possessions as types – say, both have distinct parents, homes, and fields. And inalienable possessions provide the resources for just that: the closeness and similarity of any two people (or sentient entities more generally) may be gauged by

---

[14] Note, then, that if we replace personal status with property rights, inalienable possessions with alienable possessions, attitudes with recognition, and ritual events with contractual agreements, we get Hegel's theory of civil society; so the basic ideas carry over, with suitable modification, to market economies.

how many inalienable possessions they either mutually or comparably share. (Compare Evans-Pritchard (1940) and Sahlins (1972) on the gauging of structural distance.) This is the reason that kinship relations are unique: kin are the only inalienable possessions that are also inalienable possessors. Indeed, the expression for compassion among the Q'eqchi' is the inalienable possession *qas qiitz'in*, literally 'our older siblings, our younger siblings'. That is, siblings are those inalienable possessions that are closest and most similar to their inalienable possessors.

In short, one might set aside the pronoun 'I' as the key social and semiotic site in which a subject is both figure and ground, both referred to and indexed, and look rather at inalienable possessions as constituting both the intentional subject, or person, and intentional object, or value – as well as the intentional relations (possessed-heart constructions), and modes of comportment (care, or 'hearting'), that unite them.

However, before one can care for one's inalienable possessions as an irreducibly self-reflexive process, one must first either acquire them by way of life-cycle events such as baptism or marriage, or recover them by way of illness cures. As will be seen in the next two sections, all such events of acquisition and recovery involve ritual processes whereby fully social people induct socially immature people further into the role of person, or induct physically impaired people back into the role of person. These sections detail, then, the relatively circumscribed ways inalienable possessions circulate; and how such circulation is related to the expansion and contraction of personhood.

9.   Baptism, marriage, and gift-giving

Among the Q'eqchi', gifts (*maatan*) are given during the two key contexts in which inalienable possessions are ritually acquired: baptism and marriage. I will briefly discuss each of these in turn. Children are baptized (*kub'ilha'*, literally 'to water-lower') at around age four months. To be the godparents of their child, parents choose a married couple, usually with adolescent children of their own. In most cases, this same couple will be the godparents for all the parents' subsequent children, though, with each child, they are formally asked again. Usually the godparents reside in the same village but are not related to the parents. Indeed, it is explicitly thematized as an injunction that the godparents of one's child must be *qas qiitz'in*, literally 'our siblings' but in this case meaning fellow Q'eqchi' (or those with whom one shares compassion), but not *aakomun* (one's consanguineal relations) or *aawechalal* (one's affinal relations). In this way, godparents are liminal people – somewhere outside of family but within ethnicity.

The single expectation of godparents is that they will give a child his or her first set of clothing and provide meat for the Q'eqchi' party that follows the

Catholic baptism. This set of clothing is worn by the child the first time it is publicly revealed, during the church ceremony in which it also acquires its name. (Until then, babies are swaddled if brought to church.) This first set of clothing is new, store-bought, distinctly nontypical (i.e. not indigenous), and highly impractical. For boys, the outfit involves a hat (*punit*), shoes (*xaab'*), socks (*kalsitiin*), a shirt (*kamiis*), pants (*wex*), and even a tie (*korbaat*). For girls, the outfit involves a Ladina dress (*bestiiy*), rather than a huipil (*po'ot*) and skirt (*uuq*). In most cases the child quickly outgrows the outfit and never has another opportunity to wear it. In sum, the child is no longer just a physical body possessing limbs and consanguineal kin: parents provide a child with godparents; a church service provides a child with a name; and godparents provide a child with clothing. Beside birth, then, baptism is the first life-cycle event wherein the ritual accrual of inalienable possessions allows the child to be presented to the community as a social person.

Let me now turn to marriage (*sumlaak*). Spouses are usually chosen from among Q'eqchi' living nearby, either from the same village or from villages that buy and sell in the same inter-village markets. Among such people, the key restriction on choice of spouse is that the young man and woman do not have the same first family name. In other words, couples must consist of individuals who have no ascending male relatives in common. (In this way, inalienable possessions – names – are used to delimit the field of potential spouses.) After the church ceremony, in which the exchange of wedding vows is officiated by a Catholic priest, there is a wedding celebration at the home of the groom's parents. At this celebration, there are two types of gifts given. First, a wife is metaphorically understood to be a gift given to the groom by his father-in-law and brothers-in-law. And second, elaborately wrapped ceramic bowls (*sek'*) are given to the couple by newly created in-laws, godparents, and ascending consanguineal kin (especially married siblings). Such bowls are not to be used for the couple's everyday eating. Rather, they will be used only to serve food to family, affines, and ritual kin on subsequent ceremonial occasions. In this way, while a church service, officiated by a Catholic priest, provides a couple with in-laws (and each other with a spouse) and a full family name for their children; in-laws and family members provide a man with his wife; and godparents, in-laws, and siblings provide a couple with serving bowls. In addition, marriage sets the stage for a couple to have children of their own, as well as a homestead and milpa-field. No longer just two passive social people, a married couple becomes an active social person in its own right, able to provide for itself in the domestic economy, and able to host other social people on ceremonial occasions.

Notice, then, the intimate relationship between life-cycle events and inalienable possessions (compare Conklin and Morgan 1996; Lamb 1997). At birth, an individual arrives in the world with body parts and consanguineal kin, and his or her social presence is limited to household interactions. At baptism, an individual acquires a name, clothing, and ritual kin, and is now able to be hosted as an individual social person by more than his or her immediate kin. Simultaneously, fictive kinship relations are articulated (between godchild and godparents, and between parents and godparents). In short, with the accrual of inalienable possessions attendant on baptism, a child can be object of inter-household sociality, but not subject. At marriage, two individuals acquire affinal kin and serving bowls – as well as the immediate promise of a home, field, and family of their own. And they are now able to host others as a larger-than-individual social person. Simultaneously, affinal relations are articulated. That is, a married couple can finally host others as social persons (i.e. can be subject of inter-household sociality). Last, arriving full circle, once a house, field, and children are acquired, a married couple may be both elected to the civil religious hierarchy and selected to be godparents of another couple's children, thereby able to engage in the key ritual that inducts others into the role of person. In other words, they can be active participants in two key sites for the disclosure of village-wide values.

Inalienable possessions are thus uniquely involved in the giving of gifts, the articulation of social relations, the disclosure of value, and the expansion of personhood. In this way, life-cycle events turn on the accrual of inalienable possessions and, simultaneously, the accrual of new statuses and hence new capacities to act as a social person, ranging from an infant's baptismal ability to be talked about by, and paraded before, other villagers, to a couple's parental ability to disclose village-wide values in public discussion. In this way, inalienable possessions are a key site for the transition from bare life to political life; and thereby a key lens through which such transitions should be theorized.

10.   Illness cures and fright

Among the Q'eqchi', *xiwajenaq* refers to a locally recognized illness that arises from being frightened by unexpected entities or events. In broad outline, this illness is pervasive throughout Latin America and is often called *susto* (fright) (cf. Adams and Rubel 1967; Gillen 1948; O'Nell and Selby 1968; Wilson 1995; inter alia). Depending on the severity of the fright and how quickly one undertakes actions to get well, both the symptoms and the cures can be very different. Despite this heterogeneity of pathology, all versions of this illness fall under the local term of *xiwajenaq*; all involve inalienable possessions in their cause, symptoms, and cure; and all turn on the contraction and re-expansion of the victim's personhood.

The mildest cases of *xiwajenaq* involve unexpected encounters, either with ferocious animals, such as dogs or bulls, or with angry, drunk, or sick people (usually strangers). In particular, one may be frightened by a person's movements while riding the bus into town, or while walking through other villages to nearby markets. One may be frightened by an animal while walking alone through the forest, away from one's home. If a particular cure is not undertaken (to be described below), one may succumb to an illness with one or more of the following symptoms: a loss of strength in the limbs (*maak'a' chik lix metz'ewil laa woq laa wuq'*); a loss of consciousness, or 'thoughts' (*maak'a' chik laa k'a'uxl*); nausea (*chalk laa xa'ow*); and a fever (*tiiq laa jolom*). In particular, one is said 'to lose one's heart'. Given that the heart is the locus of mental states, to lose one's heart is tantamount to losing one's ability to intentionally relate to the world. Thus, a key symptom of *susto* in this village may be phenomenologically characterized as a general listlessness – a slowing down of thought processes, a dampening of desires, a blunting of feelings, a detexturization of personality traits. (In this way, not only does one's personhood contract, but also one's ability to feel, be conscious of, or purposely stave off this very contraction.) In most cases, the severity of these symptoms slowly increases, such that in its most progressed state this sickness results in the total incapacitation of the victim: fever, nausea, unconsciousness, immobility, and non-intentionality. One's ability to think or move, to eat or talk, to feel or want, is impaired. If left uncured, such an illness results in death.

In order not to succumb to this illness, the victim or the victim's family must cut a swatch of fur (*rix*, literally 'back') from the animal, or clothing (*raq'*) from the person. Having obtained this inalienable possession (fur, *ixej*, or clothing, *aq'ej*) from its owner, the victim must burn it, usually over his or her own hearth, in order to inhale the smoke. In most cases, the truly tricky part of this cure is first finding the owner of the offending animal, or the family of the offending person, and then enlisting their help in catching the animal or convincing the person. In other words, the crux of the cure involves securing the swatch of fur or clothing in question by requesting (*tz'amank*) it from its owner, or its owner's owner. In the least severe cases of *xiwajenaq*, one addresses the owner of an inalienable possession – a form of interpellation – thereby securing both an inalienable possession and the owner's acceptance of responsibility. In short, besides being necessary combustibles for the inhalation cure, inalienable possessions are also pledges of their owner's responsibility for frightening the victim.

Let me offer an example that illustrates a household-internal cause, and thereby illuminates some of the tensions that arise with virilocality and the acquisition of affinal kin. A young woman moved into her husband's father's house following her marriage. Her husband had a slightly younger brother, who was ready to get married himself. This brother, however, was the youngest son in the family, and the father, just now beginning to feel weak in his old age, would not yet give the younger brother permission to marry because he needed his help in planting. For these reasons, the younger brother was said to be envious, or 'red hearted' (*kaq ch'oolej*), of his older brother (indeed, of his older brother's more extended personhood), and this jealousy caused him to be estranged, or 'foreign hearted' (*ab'l ch'oolej*), from both his older brother and his sister-in-law.

Now, several months after this young woman gave birth, and while still living in her father-in-law's house, her baby stopped breast-feeding, fell sick, and eventually died. The parents blamed the younger brother for the illness, saying that the baby had been frightened (*xiwajenaq*) by his jealousy and estrangement. They requested that the brother give them a swatch of his clothing so that they could carry out the cure. The brother, however, refused, saying that the illness was not his fault (*maak'a' inmaak*). To this day, the younger brother denies his jealousy and estrangement; and the couple blames him for the death of their child.

The ambivalence of this encounter should be stressed. On the one hand, this couple was able to use the younger brother's jealousy and estrangement as an excuse to start building a new house of their own before they had conceived a second child (usually a couple doesn't leave the groom's father's house until they have a child of their own) – that is, they could hasten the expansion of their own personhood. On the other hand, while the younger brother was jealous of and estranged from his older brother, he also wanted him to stay as long as possible, since his own workload on his father's field was lessened with his brother's help; that is, his brother helped him in the burden of caring for, or 'hearting', his father. In this way, *xiwajenaq* can occur in familiar domestic contexts, and even the least severe of its forms are deadly if left untreated (especially with infants, whose extent of personhood is so limited, and whose hold on personhood is so tenuous).

The most frequent cause of severe forms of *xiwajenaq* is falling. This is so because one is liable to leave behind in the place (*na'ajej*) where one fell one's name (*k'ab'a'ej*) and shadow (*mu* – not an inalienable possession in all dialects of Q'eqchi' [*muhej*], but frequently found as an inalienable possession in other languages). Unless one retrieves one's name and shadow, one will quickly succumb to a severe form of the illness described above. The retrieval of a shadow and name can be done by the victim, or by the victim's immediate family in cases where the illness has already progressed and the victim is too weak to move. Such a cure first involves going back to the place where one fell. There, one breaks off the branch of a nearby tree or bush, and then uses this branch as a whip (*tz'uum*), first to swipe the ground (*taak'e xlob' li ch'ooch*), and then to swipe one's own back (*taarab' chaq chi tz'uum chaawix naq tatchalq*), all the while calling one's shadow back by calling out one's own name.

For example, supposing that the victim was named Angelina, the call would go as follows: *yo' Angelina yo'o', matkanaak* (live Angelina, let's go, don't stay). Notice, then, that one uses one's full first name. Notice that one's name stays attached to one's shadow, such that one calls one's shadow using one's own name. And notice the pun between *yo'* (an imperative form of the verb *yo'ok* 'to live') and *yo'o'* (a suppletive form of the irregular verb *xik* 'to go', in the hortative mood). In accounts of this cure, speakers say one is both calling one's shadow (*taab'oq laa mu*) and calling one's name (*taab'oq laa k'ab'a'*). In this way, sickness or death is associated with one's name and shadow remaining in the place where one fell, and health or life is associated with these items returning with their (original) owner. In a parallel fashion, just as the possessor of a name is split between the locale of a fall and the individual who fell (such that only the person to whom the name first belonged, or that person's immediate family, can use this name to call back the shadow), the lashes of the branch fall on the ground where one fell and the back of the one who fell. In sum, self-interpellation in conjunction with self-flagellation in the immediate locale where one fell ill brings back one's name, and the shadow to which it is attached, thereby effecting the cure. Unlike the less severe cases of *xiwajenaq*, in which one addresses another person in order to obtain his inalienable possessions, here one addresses one's self in order to regain one's own inalienable possessions.

There are also more severe cases of *xiwajenaq*, also often involving falls, that are interpreted as a form of retribution. In particular, the interpretation of such events is that one's shadow-name has been grabbed by the local telluridian deity (*Tzuultaq'a*, literally 'mountain-valley', a character we will return to in chapter 4), because one has failed to show the proper respect. Such sinful or disrespectful behaviour usually involves foregoing some ritual action for the *Tzuultaq'a*: not lighting candles or copal, not praying or sacrificing, not making a pilgrimage to a cave or mountain, not showing enough respect for maize, engaging in jealousy or maliciousness towards kin, or being drunk or adulterous. In other words, one may suffer *xiwajenaq* as a function of poor moral decisions: fully functioning personhood requires decision making based on shared, and easily explicable, moral grounds. Put another way, the inferences that people make to discover the causes of their illnesses uniquely disclose a number of local village values, while articulating particular ethical characteristics of themselves and other people: what moral people should and should not do (qua deontic modality, or mood); and what actual people have and have not done (qua epistemic modality, or status and evidentiality).

In sum, inalienable possessions are directly related to various conditions and entailments of personhood, such as health, responsibility, interpellation, morality, and value. Depending on the severity of an illness, relatively alienable inalienable possessions are used either to effect a cure or to pledge one's responsibility for having caused an illness (including one's own illness): hair (*jolomej*, *ixej*) or clothing (*aq'ej*) is either burnt to be inhaled, or formed in the shape of the victim's body (*tz'ewajej*) to be buried as a substitute. Symptoms involve losing one's basic capabilities as a person, one's most precious possessions: shadow and name, health and heart, and even life itself. In this way, one's possession of certain inalienable possessions, or one's extension of personhood, is tenuous, turning on one's adherence to local ethical norms. And when such possessions are alienated, such that one's personhood contracts, only a maximally explicit and self-reflexive form of interpellation, involving personal disclosure of moral violations, effects the cure.

11. Inalienable wealth and personage in the work of Marcel Mauss

We may conclude by discussing two otherwise unconnected concepts in Marcel Mauss's work: first, the notion of *immeuble*, or inalienable wealth, as discussed in his essay *The gift* (1954), and as theorized by Annette Weiner (1985, 1992); and second, the notion of *personnage*, or personage, as discussed in his essay 'A category of the human mind: The notion of person; the notion of self' (1979), and as theorized by Charles Taylor (1985a, 1985b).

Mauss borrowed the notion of inalienable wealth (*immeuble*) from medieval French law, in which it referred to landed estates, in contrast to confiscatable objects (*meuble*) such as personal possessions (Mauss 1954; Weiner 1985). He used these notions in a number of ethnographic contexts to distinguish between everyday articles of consumption or distribution and valuable family property that is severely constrained in its circulation (in particular, Samoan fine mats, Kwakiutl and Tsimshian coppers, and Maori cloaks). In Weiner's wonderful reinterpretation of both Mauss's text and the ethnographic context, she argues that such forms of inalienable wealth have 'the power ... to define who one is in an historical sense' (1985: 210). This is so because these objects act as vehicles 'for bringing past time into the present, so that the histories of ancestors, titles, or mythological events become an intimate part of a person's identity' (*ibid.*). Insofar, then, as such uncirculating forms of inalienable wealth are bound to a person's identity, they provide a means of creating value while minimizing exchange.

Notice that while inalienable possession departs from inalienable wealth in substantial ways, it nonetheless bears a family resemblance that is worth elaborating. First, these categories only partially overlap: while homes, agricultural fields, and clothing are arguably forms of inalienable wealth, names, kinship roles, mental states, and body parts are only tenuously so. (Yet notice that Mauss and Weiner do emphasize titles, ancestors, and memory.) Second, while the inalienability of inalienable wealth is juridical or moral, the inalienability of inalienable possessions is often physical or ontological (though one reason to relate the two categories is to elide such distinctions). Third, while inalienable wealth mainly consists of artefacts (human-made material objects in the strict sense, such as clothing), inalienable possessions include biofacts (such as body parts), sociofacts (such as kinship roles), semiofacts (such as names), and psychofacts (such as mental states) – though clearly all of these categories overlap, and I invent them purely for making theoretical distinctions. Fourth, whereas for Mauss inalienable wealth is primarily linked to the personification of things (via the *Hau*, often interpreted as the compulsion to return a gift), inalienable possessions may be best understood as the 'thingification' of persons – in the sense of part–whole relations (assuming this is a social, semiotic, and material process). And last, while inalienable possessions do indeed have a substantive role in identity, acting as material aids for invoking historical context, they also have a much larger functional role having to do with certain value-directed reflexive capabilities of persons.

By personage (*personnage*), Mauss wanted to call attention to what he considered a widespread practice wherein a finite number of roles, usually marked by names or masks, were inhabitable by members or clans of a bounded society, in the context of ritually replaying the reincarnation of ancestors (Mauss 1954; Allen 1985). In discussing this aspect of Mauss's work, Taylor luminously explicates the relationship that names have to being an interlocutor (as a key means for recruiting individuals into the role of speaker and addressee); the relationship that interlocutorship has to disclosing values (as a shared discursive perspective for articulating significant features of the social world); and the relationship that disclosed values have to human agency – one's ability to choose which desires one desires (and thus acts upon), relative not to instrumental values such as efficiency or cost, but to local cultural assumptions regarding what it means to be a moral person (Taylor 1985a, 1985b). Taylor, then, while noting a substantive aspect of personhood in the notion of value, also includes a functional aspect of personhood in the notion of reflexive desire, or choice. And while noting the importance of choice in being a person, he locates it in the social and semiotic context of public discourse, rather than the individual and psychological context of self-consciousness.

As captivating as this formulation is, it is incomplete. A more detailed examination of inalienable possession helps to reveal exactly what is missing. First, the condition for interlocutorship is not just being named, but also being related, housed, clothed, embodied, and enminded – that is, being a social person in all its local modalities (hence this chapter's emphasis on inalienable possessions as constitutive of personhood).

Second, the relationship between agency and interlocutorship requires a third component, subjectivity, wherein one is simultaneously indexed ground and denoted figure of discourse, both articulating significant features (as a speaker or hearer) and articulated as a significant feature (as an object or topic) – hence the emphasis on life-cycle rituals and illness cures, in which people induct other peoples and themselves (back) into the role of person via interpellation.

Third, desire is only one of many possible mental states toward which we may take an evaluative stance, and thereby engage in choice; for just as our desires are at issue, so are our beliefs, fears, sorrows, disgusts, hatreds, doubts, and joys – hence the emphasis on the panoply of mental states such as estrangement, jealousy, care, fright, and so forth.

Fourth, any evaluation of our mental states presupposes some understanding of them: we must know something about our mental states if we are to act self-reflexively upon them (hence the emphasis on illness as a key site in which we and others become conscious of, or gain representational agency over, our mental states; and on possessed-heart constructions as a key means by which we articulate, or make public, our mental states).

Fifth, we are just as likely to take such an evaluative (good/bad) or epistemic (true/false) stance toward another's mental states as we are towards our own: empathy is surely as important a human capability as choice (hence the emphasis on closeness or similarity of inalienable possessions as conditions of possibility for empathy with their inalienable possessor).

And last, just as personhood is a condition for the disclosure of value in discourse, discourse is the condition for the disclosure of what we value about persons (hence the opening sections of this chapter, which tried to grammatically and discursively motivate the general category of inalienable possession).

In short, rather than overemphasizing second-order desire, or choice, we must realize that the reflexive capabilities of personhood are manifold. Building on Mauss's work, these scholars offer an account of personhood that turns on a small number of inalienable possessions: Weiner focuses on certain substantive aspects of personhood by paying attention to inalienable wealth and social roles (or identity); and Taylor focuses on certain functional aspects of personhood by paying attention to names and mental states (or choice). But just as inalienable wealth is only one possible kind of inalienable possession, choice is only one possible reflexive capability of persons: the true extent of inalienable possession and personhood remains to be determined. Such theories thereby provide only a starting point for understanding the conditions for being substantively and functionally a person. Hence, the task of this chapter has been to offer an account of various aspects of Q'eqchi' personhood through the lens of inalienable possession: on the one hand, a role-enabled and role-enabling nexus of value-directed reflexive capabilities (itself subject to expansion and contraction); and on the other hand, the material, social, and semiotic site in which this nexus is revealed (itself subject to gain and loss). As will be seen in the chapters that follow, inalienable possessions show up again and again in the creation and clarification of personhood, value, and intentionality.

3   Interclausal relations: how to enclose a mind by disclosing a sign

1.   Emblemeticity, iconicity, and intentionality

The interclausal relations hierarchy is a cross-linguistic pattern whereby the 'closer' two events are construed semantically, the 'tighter' two verbs are bound grammatically. Take the following two sentences: 1) *Dave believes that John was a warlock*; 2) *Janet wants to become a witch*. Each of these sentences has two verbs, the first of which refers to a mental state (believe, want), and the second of which refers to a state or state-change (be, become). And each of these sentences might be understood as representing two events: first, there is the event of Dave's believing or Janet's wanting; and second, there is the event of John's being a warlock or Janet's becoming a witch. Crucially, just as sentence (1) involves two relatively distinct clauses (each verb has its own subject, and is inflected with a different tense: Dave and John, present and past), the state of affairs represented by this sentence seems to involve two relatively unrelated events (believing and being). And just as sentence (2) involves a single clause (the two verbs share a single subject and tense inflection: Janet, present), the state of affairs represented by this sentence seems to involve two relatively related events (wanting and becoming). In short, the more a state of affairs is construed as involving two separate events (causally and logically), the more the construction representing that state of affairs is encoded with two separate clauses (morphologically and syntactically). (See Figure 3.1.)

The interclausal relations hierarchy is thus a profound instance of diagrammatic iconicity: the relation between two signs, qua predicating elements, has properties in common with the relation between two objects, qua predicated events (Givón 1980; Silverstein 1993; Van Valin and LaPolla 1997; and see Peirce 1955; Vendler 1967). The grammatical 'distance' between the signs maps onto the semantic 'distance' between the objects.

Given that propositional modes are often denoted by complement-taking predicates (e.g. *I believe* or *I want*), and given that propositional contents are often denoted by the complements of these predicates (e.g. *that he is a lawyer* or *to go to the store*), this invites the hypothesis that relatively lexical signs of mental states may be grouped and ordered as a function of their tightness: the

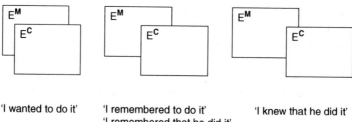

'I wanted to do it'   'I remembered to do it'   'I knew that he did it'
                       'I remembered that he did it'

Figure 3.1. Relative tightness of interclausal relations involving mode events (E^M) and content events (E^C). Here the mode event is the event of *wanting*, *remembering*, or *knowing*, and the content event is the event of *doing*. Constructions involving *want* are relatively tighter than constructions involving *remember*, which are relatively tighter than constructions involving *know*.

degree to which the mode event (E^M), qua event of wanting or believing, and the content event (E^C), qua event wanted or believed, constitute a single event; or the degree to which the complement-taking predicate and the complement are expressed in a single clause. In other words, a key means of classifying, scaling, and ultimately translating the lexical expression of mental states is the degree to which the mode event and content event are mutually implicated – be it grammatically (morphologically and syntactically) or semantically (logically and causally).

For example, Talmy Givón (1980) has argued that English complement-taking predicates may be ordered as follows (moving from looser to tighter constructions): *say* and *tell* > *think, know, believe, doubt, learn* > *decide, agree* > *like, hope, expect, love, hate* > *plan, intend, try*. This list goes from predicates that may take full clauses, to those that may take both full clauses and infinitives, to those that may only take infinitives. This form–functional iconicity may also be generalized across languages (Van Valin and LaPolla 1997: 478–9), using the following hierarchy of possible constructions: unrelated events > sequential events > simultaneous events > conditionals (*if–then* constructions) > reported speech (*say*) > cognition (*know, think*) > propositional attitude (*believe, consider*) > perception (*see, hear*) > jussive (*ask, order*) > purposive (*go, come*) > psych-action (*forget, want*) > aspectual (*start, continue*) > causative (*let go, push open*). As one moves from the top to the bottom of this list, constructions incorporating such predicates represent states of affairs that are more like two events to states of affairs that are more like one event.

In short, by attending to the grammar of certain linguistically encoded signs of mental states (and speech acts), one has a way of accounting for the genus of intentionality itself (complement-taking predicates), various species of intentionality (complement-taking predicates grouped as a function of the types of complements they may take), and the scaling of intentionality itself (how much causal and logical overlap there is between a propositional mode and a propositional content).

This last point has broader implications insofar as understandings of intentionality (as a putative psychological phenomenon) are often grounded in, if not derived from, these overt linguistic encodings. In particular, complement-taking predicates are perhaps the most emblematic signs of mental states – making both the propositional mode and the propositional content maximally public and minimally ambiguous. Moreover, as a function of this emblemeticity, they are also perhaps the most accessible to introspection and communication. In this way, such predicate–complement constructions are not only used by speakers to make explicit their own and others' mental states, they are also used by philosophers and psychologists to analyse what they take to be the fundamental properties of mind. For example, Brentano's original definition of intentionality (1995 [1874]) was couched in terms of complement-taking predicates in German; and Searle's (1983) more recent work on intentionality draws evidence for its claims from linguistic facts. That is, properties of language are used as a means to understand properties of mind – either implicitly, in the case of Brentano, or explicitly, in the case of Searle. In neither case, however, are such properties of language understood in terms of linguistic principles. In short, philosophers, psychologists, and lay-folk alike are often only minding language when they talk about mind.

The focus of this chapter is the interclausal relations hierarchy in Q'eqchi'. On the one hand, then, this involves a radically different set of predicate–complement constructions than English and other Indo-European languages. On the other hand, because of their iconic nature and cross-linguistic applicability, these predicates – and the covert classes which organize them – may be systematically compared to those in Indo-European languages. In chapter 2, when possessed-heart predicates were introduced, we got a first look at some of these constructions. Here the entire system will be fleshed out, and the particular role such possessed-heart constructions play will be shown. Crucially, such an account of the interclausal relations hierarchy in Q'eqchi' is not just important for the nature of complement-taking predicates (as one kind of stance). Rather, such predicates are also used by speakers themselves to gloss, in local ethno-psychological and meta-linguistic terms, the meaning of other kinds of stances, such as interjections and verbal operators. Such constructions thereby provide a key means for actors and analysts to interpret other types of signs used to stand for mental states. In other words, such constructions not only function as signs (of mental states), they also function as interpretants of other signs (of mental states). This hierarchy is thus both an object of analysis and a means to analyse other objects, as will be seen in later chapters.

Sections 2 and 3 treat the semantic and grammatical instantiation of this hierarchy in Q'eqchi'. Section 4 treats diachronic processes of grammaticalization which relate verbal operators (e.g. grammatical categories such as aspect, mood, tense, evidentiality, and status) and complement-taking predicates. It also prepares the ground for chapters 4 and 5, in which such verbal operators are analysed in depth. Section 5 returns to a topic introduced in chapter 2: possessed-heart constructions, now understood as a species of interclausal relations. A crucial property will emerge from their semantics: mental states are unmarkedly understood as relatively coherent. For example, beliefs are true, perceptions are veridical, and intentions are satiable. Section 6 exemplifies practices whereby speakers of Q'eqchi' use such constructions to ascribe mental states to other people, gloss the meaning of other mental states, and generally describe the roots and fruits of mental states as scripts. As will be seen, contrary to widespread claims that Maya do not refer to the mental states of others, the Q'eqchi' frequently ascribe modes of intentionality to themselves and each other. Finally, section 7 summarizes the key ways that these mental-state predicates confer propositional content upon propositional modes, and thereby construe mental states as both objective and subjective. On the one hand, mental states may be a focus of scientific investigation, or a topic of cultural articulation; on the other hand, they seem fundamentally different from stereotypic objects, like rocks and trees, which seem available to the senses, persistent in time, and cohesive across space. The issue in this chapter, then, is not just 'what are the means by which mind is most explicitly revealed?', but also how such modes of disclosure affect how we – as linguists and lay-folk, analysts and actors – enclose mind, construing it as a special kind of thing, or particular type of process, that may be studied.

2.   Semantic classes of complement-taking predicates

Tables 3.1–3 classify verbal predicates in Q'eqchi'-Maya as a function of the types of complements they may take. Column (1) lists nine relatively cohesive classes of such predicates, along with a genus-level semantic definition. Column (2) lists all the Q'eqchi' predicates that belong to each class for which I have discourse tokens. Column (3) provides a simple English gloss for each predicate. Columns (4) and (5) indicate whether such a predicate may take a non-finite, nominalized, or full-clause complement. If applicable, the complementizer (Ø, *chi*, or *naq*) and controlling argument (Agent (A), Subject (S), Object (O), or Possessed Body Part (PBP)) are also indicated. English examples of these linguistic categories are shown in Table 3.4, and section 3 will explain them in greater detail. Finally, the various classes of complement-taking predicates are ordered from the bottom of Table 3.3 to the top of Table 3.1 by reference to the morpho-syntactic tightness of their complementation patterns. In particular, predicates at the bottom enter into constructions that look most like two separate clauses; and predicates at the top enter into constructions that look most like a single clause.

Table 3.1. *Complement-taking predicates (Transitive Aspectual to Psych-Action)*

Class	Q'eqchi' predicate	English gloss	Non-finite, nominalized	Full clause
1. Transitive Aspectual				
	choyok	'to finish'	Ø (A)	
	raqok	'to finish'	Ø (A)	
	kuyuk	'to endure'	Ø (A)	
	b'aanunk	'to do'	Ø (A)	
	kanab'ank	'to desist from'	Ø (A)	
	chanab'ank	'to desist from'	Ø (A)	
	yoob'ank	'to begin'	Ø (A)	
	tikib'ank	'to begin'	Ø (A)	
	tz'aqonk	'to take a turn at'	Ø (A)	
	yalok	'to try'	Ø (A)	
	yeech'ink	'to offer'	Ø (A)	
	tzolok	'to study (how)'	Ø (A)	
2. Psych-Action				
a. Desire, need, intention	*ajok li ru*	'to need'	Ø (A)	*naq*
	ajok	'to want'	Ø (A)	*naq*
	rahink	'to love/desire'	Ø (A)	*naq*
	atawank (li ru)	'to desire'	Ø (A)	*naq*
b. Transitive affectual	*sa/ra ilok*	'to like/not like to'	Ø (A)	*naq*
	sa/ra ab'ink	'to be glad/sorry to hear'	Ø (A)	*naq*
	sa/ra eek'ank	'to feel good/bad about'	Ø (A)	*naq*
c. Fear and shame	*xiwank*	'to be scared'	Ø (A)	*naq*
	xutaanank	'to be ashamed'	Ø (A)	*naq*
d. Heart predicates	*alaak sa' ch'oolej*	'to decide'	Ø (Adp, PBP)	*naq*
	chalk sa' ch'oolej	'to agree'	Ø (Adp, PBP)	*naq*
	naqk sa' ch'oolej	'to remember'	Ø (Adp, PBP)	*naq*
	wank sa' ch'oolej	'to remember'	Ø (Adp, PBP)	*naq*
	kanak sa' ch'oolej	'to remember'	Ø (Adp, PBP)	*naq*
	sachk sa' ch'oolej	'to forget'	Ø (Adp, PBP)	*naq*

So having classified and ordered verbal predicates in Q'eqchi' as a function of the types and tightness of the predicate–complement constructions they allow, let me now discuss some general semantic features organizing the predicates themselves.

As may be seen from column (1) in Tables 3.1–3, complement-taking predicates have been grouped into nine basic semantic classes. Class (9) consists of *speaking predicates*: to ask, to promise, to reply, to say, it is said. These take

Table 3.2. *Complement-taking predicates (Intransitive Aspectual to Intransitive Affectual)*

Class	Q'eqchi' predicate	English gloss	Non-finite, nominalized	Full clause
3. Intransitive Aspectual				
	raqe'k	'to be finished'	*chi* (S)	
	ixtaak	'to insist on'	*chi* (S)	
	okenk	'to assist in'	*chi* (S)	
	ok	'to begin'	*chi* (S)	
	ruuk	'to be able'	*chi* (S)	
	yook	'to be doing'	*chi* (S)	
	b'ayk	'to be delayed in'	*chi* (S)	
	k'aayk	'to be accustomed to'	*chi* (S)	
4. Purposive (Movement)				
	xik	'to go'	*chi* (S)	
	chalk	'to come'	*chi* (S)	
	k'ulunk	'to arrive/come'	*chi* (S)	
	hulak	'to arrive'	*chi* (S)	
	kanaak	'to stay'	*chi* (S)	
	elk	'to leave'	*chi* (S)	
	nume'k	'to pass by'	*chi* (S)	
	wank	'to be (located)'	*chi* (S)	
5. Intransitive Affectual				
a. Bodily states	*lub'k*	'to tire of'	*chi* (S)	
	tawaak	'to tire of'	*chi* (S)	
	titz'k	'to get exasperated'	*chi* (S)	
	jiq'e'k	'to choke upon'	*chi* (S)	
	q'ixno'k	'to grow angry/hot'	*chi* (S)	
	tiqwo'k	'to overheat/anger'	*chi* (S)	
	josq'ok	'to become angry'	*chi* (S)	
b. Fear and shame	*xutaanak*	'to be(come) ashamed'	*chi* (S)	
	xiwak	'to be(come) afraid'	chi (S)	
c. Heart predicates	*yook ch'oolej*	'to want'	*chi* (S, PBP)	
	poqnak ch'oolej	'to worry'	chi (S, PBP)	
	ch'inank ch'oolej	'to become regretful'	*chi* (S, PBP)	
	kiib'ank ch'oolej	'to become conflicted'	*chi* (S, PBP)	
	po'k ch'oolej	'to become dissuaded'	*chi* (S, PBP)	
	wank	'to be interested'	*chi* (S, PBP)	
	maak'a' ch'oolej	'not to be interested'	*chi* (S, PBP)	

full-clause complements, where the complement is a token of direct (or indirect) reported speech. Notice that *patz'ok* (to ask) may also take non-finite and nominalized complements, either without a complementizer or marked by the complementizer *chi*. It could rightfully be in class (2) or (7). And notice that *yehok* (to say) is also listed as a jussive predicate in class (6), where it is best glossed as 'to tell to do', as in 'to order'.

Table 3.3. *Complement-taking predicates (Jussive to Speaking)*

Class	Q'eqchi' predicate	English gloss	Non-finite, nominalized	Full clause
6. Jussive (Manipulative)				
	minok ru	'to force'	chi (O)	
	tenq'ank	'to help'	chi (O)	
	seb'esink	'to scare someone'	chi (O)	
	k'ehok	'to put to'	chi (O)	
	k'aytesink	'to make accustomed'	chi (O)	
	teneb'ank	'to oblige'	chi (O)	
	q'ab'ank	'to calumniate'	chi (O)	
	seeb'ank	'to hurry/urge'	chi (O)	
	taqlank	'to send'	chi (O)	
	b'oqok	'to call/invite'	chi (O)	
	ajok	'to want'	chi (O)	
	yehok	'to tell [to do]'	chi (O)	
	chaqrab'ink	'to order'	chi (O)	*naq*
7. Perception				
	ilok	'to see/look'	chi (O)	*naq*
	ab'ink	'to hear/listen'	chi (O)	*naq*
	eek'ank	'to feel/sense'	chi (O)	*naq*
8. Propositional Attitude (Cognition)				
a. Unmarked	*na'ok*	'to know'	Ø (A)	*naq*
	k'a'uxlank	'to think'	Ø (A)	*naq*
	kaqalink	'to be envious'		*naq*
	na'link	'to know'		*naq*
	tawok ru	'to understand'		*naq*
	paab'ank	'to believe'		*naq*
	oyb'enink, yo'onink	'to expect'		*naq*
b. Heart predicates	*k'a'uxlank sa' ch'oolej*	'to plan/intend'	Ø (A)	*naq*
	yehok sa' ch'oolej	'to think'		*naq*
	chank sa' ch'oolej	'to think'		*naq*
	... Ø ... sa' ch'oolej	'to think (incorrectly)'		*naq*
9. Speaking				
	patz'ok	'to ask'	Ø (A), chi (O)	*naq*
	sumenk ru aatin	'to promise'		*naq*
	chaq'ok/ chaq'b'enk	'to reply'		*naq*
	yehok	'to say'		*naq*
	yemank	'it is said'		*naq*

Table 3.4. *English examples of linguistic terms used in text*

Full-clause complement: 'that he killed the messenger'
Non-finite complement: 'to kill the messenger'
Nominalized complement: 'the killing of the messenger'
Full-clause complementizer: 'that' (*naq*)
Non-finite complementizer: 'to' (*chi*)
A-role control: 'I want to go to the store' (agent of transitive verb controls action in complement)
S-role control: 'I came to go to the store' (subject of intransitive verb controls action in complement)
O-role control: 'I saw him go to the store' (object of transitive verb controls action in complement)

Class (8) consists of *propositional attitude predicates* that are either relatively simple lexemes (to know, to think) or possessed-heart constructions (to say inside one's heart). As introduced in chapter 2, several possessed-heart constructions turn on a verb of speaking; and the addition of the adposition (in one's heart) often displaces the locale of speaking (from out in the open to inside one's heart), as well as shifts the coherence of one's assertion (from true to false). Recall Table 2.5. As may be seen from Table 3.3, the predicates *na'ok* (to know), *k'a'uxlank* (to think), and *k'a'uxlank sa' ch'oolej* (to think inside one's heart) may also take non-finite and nominalized complements, without a complementizer. In each of these cases, the meaning of the predicate changes. In particular, *na'ok* is best glossed as 'to know how' when used with a non-finite or nominalized complement. And *k'a'uxlank* is best glossed as 'to intend' or 'to think about (doing)' when used with a non-finite or nominalized complement. These predicates could rightfully be in class (2).

Class (7) consists of *perception predicates*: to see, to hear, to feel. All of these are states, and the grammatical subject is in the semantic role of experiencer. As will be seen in the discussion of class (2b), each of these is also used as a transitive affectual predicate.

Class (6) consists of *jussive predicates* (or manipulatives): to force, to urge, to send. The predicate *ajok* (to want) is listed both here and in class (2a). In this way, *ajok* may take three distinct types of complements: full-clause complements; A-role-controlled non-finite and nominalized complements; and O-role-controlled non-finite and nominalized complements. *Patz'ok* (to ask) is the only other predicate that may take such a wide range of complements. The predicate *chaqrab'ink* (to order) may also take full-clause complements, marked by the complementizer *naq*. Other predicates in this class are not so 'jussive' or 'manipulative' in their semantics. For example, the negative implicature predicate *q'ab'ank* may be glossed as 'to calumniate' or 'to falsely accuse [someone] of [the action denoted by the complement]'; and the positive implicature predicate *seb'esink* may be glossed as 'to frighten someone while [they are engaged in the action denoted by the complement]'.

Class (5) consists of *intransitive affectual predicates*: to become scared, to become tired, to become dissuaded. These predicates mark the feeling or desire of the narrated participant relative to the action denoted by the complement. This class has been broken into three subclasses: bodily states (5a), fear and shame (5b), and possessed-heart constructions (5c). As mentioned above, the two predicates in class (5b), *xutaanak* (to be or become ashamed) and *xiwak* (to be or become scared), have transitive versions that are listed in class (2c). And class (5c) has the following possessed-heart predicates: to change one's mind or regret (*ch'inank ch'oolej*: for one's heart to become small); to become conflicted, in the sense of gaining a conflicting desire (*kiib'ank ch'oolej*: for one's heart to become two); to become dissuaded, in the sense of losing a previous desire (*po'k ch'oolej*: for one's heart to break down); to want something, without chance of getting it (*yook ch'oolej*: for one's heart to be engaged in an activity); to worry (*poqnak ch'oolej*); to (not) be interested in something (*wank/maak'a' ch'oolej*: to (not) possess a heart).

Class (4) consists of *purposive predicates* (or movement predicates): to go, to arrive, to pass by. All mark the movement or position of a narrated participant as the means to achieve an end (the state of affairs denoted by the complement). These are the most frequently used complement-taking predicates in my data. While they seem to have little to do with intentionality, they are in some sense the supreme locus of intentions (or purposeful behaviour): they indicate that some form of movement was done as a means to undertake some action. There are two other frequent ways to mark purposive constructions in Q'eqchi', using the full-clause complementizers *re naq* (in order to) and *xb'aan naq* (because of). Unlike purposive constructions built out of the nonfinite and nominalized complementizer *chi*, which only occur with movement predicates, the full-clause complementizers *re naq* and *xb'aan naq* can occur with any relatively agentive predicate.

Classes (1) and (3) consist of *transitive and intransitive aspectual predicates*, respectively: to stop, to begin, to continue. Most of these predicates describe the temporal profile of a state of affairs: beginning, ending, continuing, etc. Some intransitive predicates, however, also mark deontic possibility (*ruuk*: to be able), assistance (*okenk*: to assist in), and habituation (*k'aayk*: to be accustomed to). And some transitive predicates mark turn-taking (*tz'aqonk*: to take a turn at) and attempting (*yalok*: to try).

And lastly, class (2) consists of *psych-action predicates*: to want, to remember, etc. They describe a mental state underlying the possible action of a narrated participant. Class (2a) predicates involve desire, need, and intention. Class (2b) consists of transitive affectual predicates. Each of these predicates consists of a verb of perception from class (7), along with either the adverb *sa* (pleasurable) or the adverb *ra* (painful). In effect, such constructions indicate a particular modality of knowing, and a judgement as to the positive or negative quality of what is known. Class (2c) consists of the two transitive predicates involving fear and shame, which have intransitive analogues in class (5b). And class (2d) consists of the following possessed-heart predicates: to remember (*naqk sa' ch'oolej*: to fall into one's heart); to forget (*sachk sa' ch'oolej*: to become lost in one's heart); to decide (*alaak sa' ch'oolej*: to be born in one's heart); to agree (*chalk sa' ch'oolej*: to come into one's heart); to remember (*wank sa' ch'oolej*: to exist in one's heart); to remember (*kanak sa' ch'oolej*: to remain in one's heart).

It should be emphasized that these classes of predicates are primarily based on the types of complements their members may take, and hence the name used to refer to each class is not necessarily appropriate for all members. In other words, the classes themselves are often rather fuzzy, so that not all members are best captured semantically by the class name. For example, the propositional attitude predicates of class (8) include *kaqalink* (to be envious), and the jussive predicates of class (6) include *q'ab'ank* (to falsely accuse). There are also several subclasses distinguished by the formal properties of the verbs themselves rather than by the types of complements they take. For example, heart predicates in subclasses (2d) and (5c) are separated from the other members of their class because they involve a possessed-heart term (*ch'oolej*) in their constructions. Likewise, transitive affectual predicates in class (2b) are separated from the other members of their class because they turn on a verb of perception along with a value adverb in a relatively consistent way. Lastly, fear and shame predicates in classes (2c) and (5b) are separated from the desire, need, and intention predicates in class (2a), and from the bodily state predicates in class (5a), because they show up in two places, once as intransitive predicates and once as transitive predicates.

With these caveats in mind, these classes may now be semantically compared with the cross-linguistic ordering of complement-taking predicates (described in the previous section) as a function of the relative tightness of their complementation patterns.

In particular, we may focus on those classes of complement-taking predicates which stereotypically denote mental states, thereby functioning as stances: psych-action (class 2), intransitive affectual (class 5), perception (class 7), and propositional attitude (class 8). These are covert grammatical categories (Whorf 1956a), distinguished by the kinds of complements they may take or, in the case of subclasses (transitive affectuals, heart predicates, etc.), the form of the predicate itself. They do not correspond to distinctions that speakers of Q'eqchi' would explicitly make, nor are there any superordinate lexemes that would pick out these four types, or six subtypes, of intentionality – nor even the genus of intentionality itself. (Though, to be sure, they may speak about desire (*ajom*), thought (*k'a'uxl*), feeling (*eek'*), sensation (*eek'ank*), and so forth.) Nonetheless, these types and subtypes may be compared with the 'European American Social Science Model of Mind' (D'Andrade 1995; and see Lillard 1998), whose five parts are lexicalized in English as perception, thought, feeling, wish, and intention. Thus, the covert categories of Q'eqchi' accord with, but are not isomorphic to, the classes within the interclausal relations hierarchy, a cross-linguistic form–function domain. Moreover, they are comparable to, but not identical with, a western ethnopsychological typology. In short, a key way to group and order mental states, be it within a single language or across multiple languages, is by reference to the grammatical and semantic properties of the stances that make mode and content events relatively explicit.

To conclude this section, let me hypothesize that a cross-linguistic grammatical pattern (qua product) is itself the result of a cross-linguistic pattern of grammaticalization (qua process). And this cross-linguistic pattern of grammaticalization not only brings diachronic process to bear on synchronic product, but also discourse practice (*parole*) to bear on grammatical structure (*langue*). In particular, one way to understand the interclausal relations hierarchy is this: in any narrative or ongoing discourse, the more the arguments (e.g. subject, object) and operators (e.g. tense, aspect) of one predicate may be assumed to be the same as the arguments and operators of a preceding predicate, the less they need to be overtly encoded. In other words, the degree to which one may take for granted certain features of one event given one's knowledge of certain features of another event (and the causal–logical relation between the two events), the less one has to distinctly encode those features. (Recall an analogous discussion in chapter 2: once a person has been introduced into a narrative, the speaker may assume the addressee assumes that the person comes with various parts – and so these need not be explicitly predicated, but may be implicitly presumed.) Constructions representing mental states carry within them speakers' assumptions about causal and logical relations between mode events and content events: the degree to which one event (say, of becoming angry or going to the store) can be inferred or predicted from another event (say, of being robbed or desiring apple pie). Just as mental states are relatively different from social statuses insofar as they are causally and logically grounded, we see here in the grammatical expression of intentionality the embodiment of this causal and logical grounding.

In short, discourse practices, whereby speakers sequentially enchain predicates referring to causally and logically interrelated events, grammaticalize into morphosyntactic patterns, which evince the interclausal relations hierarchy. Such a process of grammaticalization should be found in any language, and it turns partly on: 1) features of communication (e.g. the more two events are causally and logically implicated, the more the arguments and operators of one carry over to the other, such that they can be left out of encoding);

2) features of cognition (e.g. simultaneous maximization of information bene-
fits and minimization of encoding costs); and 3) features of culture (community-
specific event structures that are frequently referred to, conventional scripts
that constrain what counts as normatively valid causal and logical implication).
Such a hypothesis thereby ties together ongoing process and emergent product,
cross-linguistic patterns and language-specific particulars.

3. Morphosyntactic classes of complement-taking predicates

As introduced in chapter 1, there is a set of implicational universals on display
in Tables 3.1–3. In particular, with reference to the semantic classes enumerated in section 1 (from unrelated events to causatives), members of semantic
classes which are higher on the hierarchy will be involved in complementation
strategies that are at least as tight as, if not tighter than, members of classes
which are lower on the hierarchy (Van Valin and LaPolla 1997: 483). For
example, psych-action predicates will always be encoded with constructions
that are as tight as, or tighter than, constructions used to encode perception
predicates. While the morphosyntactic details of complementation will differ
across languages, this implicational relation should hold in any language. In
this section, Q'eqchi'-specific complementation strategies are described in
detail. Non-linguistically inclined readers may skip this section; and readers
interested in the full details should see Kockelman (2003).

Columns (4) and (5) list the types of complements and complementizers that
members of each class of predicates may take. The complementizer *chi*, akin to
'to' in English, occurs with non-finite and nominal clauses (column 4), and the
complementizer *naq*, akin to 'that' in English, occurs with full clauses (column 5).
A zero form (Ø) indicates that a predicate takes a complement without a complementizer. Letters in parentheses indicate that the non-finite complement is
controlled by either the agent of a transitive predicate (A), the object of a transitive predicate (O), the subject of an intransitive predicate (S), or a possessed
body part (PBP) in the role of agent, subject, object or adposition (Adp). Each
kind of predicate–complement construction is exemplified below:

1) **n-Ø-x-naw naq ink'a' x-in-war**
   Pres-A(3s)-E(3s)-know Comp Neg Perf-A(1s)-sleep
   he knows that I have not slept

2) **x-in-lub' chi k'anjelak**
   Perf-A(1s)-tire Comp work
   I got tired of working

3) **n-Ø-inw-aj xik sa' li k'ayil**
   Pres-A(3s)-E(1s)-want go Prep Dm market
   I want to go to the market

4) **x-in-r-il chi b'eek**
    Perf-A(1s)-E(3s)-see Comp walk
    she saw me walking

5) **x-Ø-naq sa' in-ch'ool chalk**
    Perf-A(3s)-drop Prep E(1s)-heart come
    I remembered (literally, 'it has dropped into my heart') to come

Example (1) shows the cognition predicate *na'ok* (to know [something]) with a full-clause complement occurring with the complementizer *naq*. The complement verb is inflected for perfect aspect (*x-*) and first-person, non-plural-number (*-in-*), independently of the tense-aspect and person-number affixes on the main verb. It occurs with the sentential scope negation particle *ink'a'* and is cross-referenced by the absolutive affix (*-Ø-*) on the main verb as the third-person non-plural O-role argument.

Example (2) shows the intransitive affectual predicate *lub'k* (to tire) occurring with a non-finite complement and the complementizer *chi*. As is evident from the interlinear gloss, the complement verb is inflected for neither tense-aspect nor person-number. Although the complement is not an argument of the main verb, the S-role argument of the main verb, marked by the first-person absolutive affix (*-in-*), is shared with the complement verb as the latter's unexpressed S-role argument. This construction is thus an example of S-role control.

Example (3) shows the psych-action predicate *ajok* (to want) occurring with a non-finite complement without a complementizer. Again, the complement verb is not inflected for tense-aspect or person-number. Unlike example (2), however, the complement is cross-referenced by the absolutive affix (*-Ø-*) on the main verb as the third-person non-plural O-role argument. In this way, the complement is an argument of the main verb; and the A-role argument of the main verb, marked by the first-person ergative affix (*-inw-*), is shared with the complement verb as the latter's unexpressed S-role argument. This construction is thus an example of A-role control.

Example (4) shows the perception predicate *ilok* (to see) occurring with a non-finite complement and the complementizer *chi*. Again, the complement verb is not inflected for tense-aspect or person-number. Importantly, although the complement is not an argument of the main verb (hence the predictable presence of the complementizer *chi*), the O-role argument of the main verb, marked by the first-person non-plural absolutive affix (*-in-*), is shared with the complement verb as the latter's unexpressed S-role argument. This construction is thus an example of O-role control.

Example (5) shows the possessed-heart construction *naqk sa' ch'oolej* (to drop into one's heart, to remember) with a non-finite complement without a complementizer. Again, the complement verb is not inflected for tense-aspect or person-number. The complement is, however, cross-referenced by the absolutive affix (-Ø-) on the main verb as the third-person non-plural S-role argument. The possessor of the heart (or perhaps the possessed heart itself) is shared with the complement verb as the latter's unexpressed S-role argument. This construction is thus an example of possessed-body-part control.

The following criteria are used to order these classes with respect to tightness (from bottom to top). First, the more operators (such as tense, aspect, and mood) and arguments the main verb shares with its complement, the more the construction looks like a single clause and the tighter it is. Thus, constructions involving non-finite complements (which are not independently inflected for mood, aspect, or tense) are tighter than constructions involving full-clause complements (which are independently inflected for such categories). For this reason, classes (7) through (9) are ordered below classes (1) through (6), and class (2) is ordered below class (1).

Second, the complementizer *chi* is absent when the complement is an (erstwhile) argument of the main verb (its subject or object) and present when it is not. Thus, constructions involving non-finite complements without the complementizer *chi* are tighter than constructions with it, and classes (3) through (7) are ordered below classes (1) and (2).

Third, when a non-finite complement is not an argument of the main verb – as in the case of classes (3) through (7) – constructions involving O-role control are less tight than those involving S-role control. This is because in S-role control the privileged syntactic argument of the main verb is shared by the complement verb, whereas in O-role control the privileged syntactic argument of the main verb is not (see Van Valin and LaPolla 1997: 460). For this reason, classes (6) and (7) are ordered below classes (3) through (5).

And finally, classes of predicates that may take more than one kind of complement are ordered by reference to the tightest kind of complementation patterns they are implicated in. Hence, even though verbs in class (2) may take full-clause complements just like verbs in classes (7) through (9), verbs in class (2) may also take non-finite complements without the complementizer *chi*. For this reason, class (2) is ordered directly below class (1), whereas classes (7) through (9) are ordered at the very bottom of the hierarchy.

4.   Operator scope and interclausal tightness

Before continuing, I want to discuss the relationship between complement-taking predicates and verbal operators – as another exemplary locus of intentionality that will be treated in the next two chapters. It is well known that verbal operators (such as aspect, mood, polarity, tense, status, evidentials, and illocutionary force) evince a form–functional iconicity, whereby their semantic scope is diagrammatically iconic to their morphological order (Bybee 1985; Greenberg 1963; Van Valin and LaPolla 1997: 40–52; inter alia). In particular, moving from widest scope to narrowest scope, verbal operators are usually ordered as follows: illocutionary force > evidentials > status and tense > (external) negation > mood and directionals > directionals and (internal) negation > aspect. For example, if a language has distinct forms marking aspect and tense, and if both of these forms appear on the same side of the predicate they modify, the one marking aspect will usually be closer to the predicate than the one marking tense; and so on, for other combinations. (The conjunction *and* indicates that the two operators cannot be ordered relative to each other.)

In short, operators with wider semantic scope are morphologically expressed further from the predicate they modify than operators with narrower semantic scope: relatively speaking, aspect only has scope over the predicate; tense has scope over the predicate and its arguments; illocutionary force has scope over the entire clause; and so forth.

With this last point in mind, it is worthwhile mapping the relative scope of verbal operators onto the relative tightness of complement-taking predicates, as shown in Figure 3.2. As may be seen, the ordering of verbal operators is diagrammatically iconic to the hierarchy of interclausal relations (Kockelman 2004). For example, just as complement-taking predicates encoding aspectual or psych-action relations are involved in tighter constructions than complement-taking predicates encoding propositional attitudes or speech acts, operators that encode aspect or mood have narrower scope than operators that encode status or illocutionary force. Such a fact should not be surprising, for it is well known that many verbal operators arise historically from the grammaticalization of complement-taking predicates (see Bybee 1985; Willett 1988; inter alia). Frequently used lexical predicates become semantically bleached grammatical operators.

Indeed, many discourse particles may be understood as having functions midway between such lexical predicates and grammatical operators. As is well known (Thompson and Mulac 1991a, 1991b; Heritage and Raymond 2005; inter alia), many so-called mental-state predicates and speech-act verbs (I think, he said, I hope) are frequent enough and semantically bleached enough to be considered discourse particles, usually indexing social and communicative aspects of interaction rather than referring to the mental states of actors.

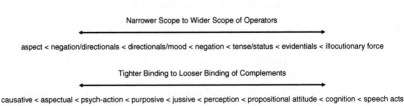

Narrower Scope to Wider Scope of Operators

aspect < negation/directionals < directionals/mood < negation < tense/status < evidentials < illocutionary force

Tighter Binding to Looser Binding of Complements

causative < aspectual < psych-action < purposive < jussive < perception < propositional attitude < cognition < speech acts

Figure 3.2. Operator scope and interclausal tightness compared

These ideas may be related to the discussion of grammaticalization that occurred at the end of section 2. In particular, note that there are two key issues: first, how clausal chaining (qua discourse practice) leads to interclausal relations (qua grammatical structure); and second, how predicate–complement relations (qua tightness) lead to operator–predicate relations (qua scope). (See Figure 3.3.) If tightness is about the relation between two narrated events (one encoding the propositional mode and the other encoding the propositional content), scope is about the relation between a narrated event and certain features of the speech event (the former encoding the propositional content and the latter encoding the propositional mode).

Exactly what features of the speech event are at issue will be the focus of later chapters. In particular, chapter 4 will focus on tense and aspect. Tense will turn on the relation between the speech event and a reference event (encoding features like past and future); and aspect will turn on the relation between a reference event and the narrated event (encoding features like progressive and perfect). Chapter 5 will focus on status and evidentiality. Status will turn on the relation between a commitment event and the speech event (encoding features like factive and optative); and evidentiality will turn on the relation between a source event and the speech event (encoding features like inferred and overheard). And sprinkled throughout this monograph is a focus on mood. Mood turns on a relation between the speech event and a deontic or 'jussive' event (encoding features like permission and obligation). As seen in Figure 3.2, and as discussed later chapters, all of the events indexed by such grammatical operators – reference events, commitment events, source events, and deontic events – have counterparts among complement-taking predicates. Indeed, as will be seen in the conclusion of this chapter, *it is precisely by reference to the eventive construal of mental states by means of complement-taking predicates that we are justified in calling them 'events', even though we will later find it*

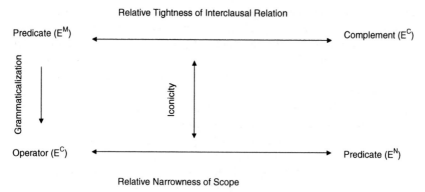

Figure 3.3. Predicate–complement and operator–predicate relations compared

more productive to think of them as participant roles. This approach thereby illuminates the relations between lexical predicates, discourse particles, and grammatical operators.

5.   Semantics and grammar of possessed-heart predicates: locating psyche

In chapter 2, when possessed-heart constructions were introduced, we noted that such constructions mark seemingly abstract mental entities in terms of relatively concrete physical processes. Such a phenomenon is well known, and goes by the term *psycholocation* (McVeigh 1996: 30; and see Jaynes 1976, inter alia). As may now be seen, such possessed-heart constructions are themselves a type of complement-taking predicate, distinguished by the fact that one of their arguments or adjuncts is a possessed heart rather than a person (as the possessor of the heart). Table 2.5 listed the most frequently used possessed-heart constructions in Q'eqchi'. And these constructions may now take their rightful place within class (2d) of Table 3.1, class (5c) of Table 3.2, and class (8b) of Table 3.3.

As may be seen by the column and row headings in Table 2.5, there are a number of interrelated grammatical features that may be used both to characterize these constructions semantically and to order them cross-linguistically. Column (1) lists four classes of possessed-heart constructions, as a function of the argument position of the possessed heart relative to the predicate (be the predicate a verb or an adjective). It also lists various subclasses of each of these classes, as a function of both the inherent aspect of the predicate (activity, state, state-change) and the semantic role of the possessed heart (agent, location, patient).

In this way, through the grammatical constructions they take part in, possessed hearts are semantically construed as undertaking actions, undergoing changes in state, and taking up positions. Depending on the construction in question, a possessed heart is either equatable with its possessor (such that the possessor rather than the heart holds the semantic role in question); or it is differentiated from its possessor (such that it is marked as the holder of a semantic role in its own right). The relationship of possession thereby allows for both identity and difference: one's heart or one's self may be the argument of the predicate in question. For these syntactic and semantic reasons, hearts often seem to constitute smaller-than-individual persons. Linguistically, they are construed as homunculi, with many of the characteristics of individual people. Hearts may also be jointly possessed – thereby constituting larger-than-individual persons. For example, as discussed in chapter 2, a heart need not belong to an individual person alone, but may instead be metaphorically held in common by a couple, family, or community. In short, through possessed-heart constructions, seemingly 'subjective' mental states may be attributed to a part of a person or to several people.

Before describing these patterns in detail, it is worth reviewing *psychologization*, or the modern, western understanding of representational processes in terms of 'mental states', and the range of ontological commitments that go with it. For example, experiments with American and European middle- and upper-class children seem to offer a fairly consistent model of 'western folk psychology'. There are systematic taxonomic and partonomic interrelations among various mental states (D'Andrade 1995; Rips and Conrad 1989; Wellman 1990). There is a notion of the mind as distinct from the body, yet held in the brain and equivalent to the self (Johnson 1987). There is a notion of the privateness of mental states, and their representational capacity (D'Andrade 1995; Wellman 1990). There is a notion of real entities able to be distinguished from mental entities on the basis of sensory evidence, public existence, and temporal consistency (Wellman and Estes 1986). Some of these studies show that there is a tendency to personify the mind, such that children move towards a conception of the mind as an independent entity (Wellman and Hickling 1994). And some studies show that subjects think that people can and should know the mental states of others. These studies accord with the number of mental-state terms in English – some have claimed that there are over 200 words devoted to the emotions alone (Wallace and Carson 1973) – and with the propensity to use such terms in describing the behaviour of others (Friestad and Wright 1995).

More generally, mental states are often taken to have a number of interrelated properties. They are localized (taken to be located in a particular part of a person – say, the mind). They are privatized (taken to be hidden or invisible in a way that other phenomena are not). They are interiorized (taken to be internal rather than external to a person). They are subjectified (taken to be more easily in error, or more person specific, than 'objective' phenomena). They are dichotomized (understood in terms of a set of oppositions: subjective versus objective, interior versus exterior, private versus public). They are individualized (taken to be held by individuals, rather than larger-than-individual or less-than-individual entities). They are moralized (caught up in legal and religious judgments regarding whether one should be responsible for a behaviour or not, and whether such behaviour is 'good' or 'bad'). They are universalized (treated as something all human groups have). They are humanized (treated as something only human groups have). And they are homunculized (treated as having agency, or human-like drives, themselves). In short, the psychologization of mental states tends to see them as little things and events in a domain that is different from common-sense understandings of 'real' things and events – a point we will return to in section 7. It is thus worthwhile comparing these putative properties of mental states with the properties mental states seem to have as a function of their linguistic mediation.

Class (1) consists of those constructions in which the possessed heart is the subject of an intransitive verb. It has three subclasses: (a) those constructions in which the verb is an activity (for example: to do), and the possessed heart is an agent or effector causing the activity; (b) those constructions in which the verb is a state (for example: to exist), and the possessed heart is a patient or theme being in such a state; and (c) those constructions in which the verb is a state-change (for example: to become small), and the possessed heart is a patient undergoing such a change in state. As may be seen in Table 3.2, most of these predicates may take non-finite and nominalized complements.

Class (2) consists of those constructions in which the possessed heart is the argument of the preposition *sa'* (inside), which itself is the adjunct of an intransitive verb. It has two subclasses: (a) those constructions in which the verb is a state (for example: to exist); and (b) those constructions in which the verb is a state-change (for example: to be born). In both of these subclasses the possessed heart is a locale in which such a state or state-change occurs. As may be seen in Table 3.1, these predicates may take full-clause complements, non-finite complements, and nominalized complements.

Class (3) consists of those constructions in which the possessed heart is the argument of the preposition *sa'* (inside), which itself is the adposition of a transitive verb. Most of the verbs in this set are activities (for example: to think). In all of these constructions, the possessed heart is a locale in which such activities occur. As may be seen in Table 3.3, these predicates also take full-clause complements.

And class (4) consists of those constructions in which the possessed heart is the argument of an adjective. It has four sub classes: (a) those constructions in which the adjective is a non-derived state, which may be derived into a state-change (for example: to be(come) painful); (b) those constructions in which the adjective is a non-derived state, which may not be derived into a state-change predicate (for example: to be fast); (c) those constructions in which the adjective is morphologically formed through derivation or compounding (for example: to be two-sided); and (d) those constructions in which the adjective is morphologically composed of a reduplicated positional root (for example: to be seated). I call the first two subtypes 'states' and 'traits', insofar as the former are relatively fluid (be and become, state and state-change) and the latter are relatively fixed (be, state). Only *sa* and *ra* constructions were used with full-clause complements. Even though the others are not examples of complement-taking predicates, they are mentioned here for the sake of completeness in describing the range of possessed-heart constructions as a semantic field.

In column (2), I have listed the Q'eqchi' predicate that is used in each construction, along with a brief English gloss. As may be seen, most of these predicates have relatively concrete meanings, are morphologically simple and frequently used, and can be readily translated. For example, many are arguably cross-linguistic semantic primitives: saying, thinking, feeling, doing, being, and having (Wierzbicka 1988). Many others turn on simple verbs of movement or changes of state: coming, staying, dropping, breaking, and doubling. And many adjectival predicates turn on relatively concrete qualities: colour, taste, position, number, and size.

In column (3), I have given an English gloss for each of the possessed-heart constructions, where each construction consists of a predicate (as per column 2) and a possessed-heart argument (as per column 1). It should be said that, insofar as most of these glosses turn on the English mental lexicon without reference to English grammar, they should be understood as a quick-and-dirty solution to meaning. In addition to the morphosyntactic and semantic account of meaning offered in this section, examples of actual usage, as well as speakers' reflections on the meanings of these predicates, and speakers' use of these predicates to reflect on the meaning of other signs, will be discussed in the next section, and subsequent chapters.

Such caveats about meaning aside, these constructions evince an important set of semantic trends. First, in the case of construction class (1a), to displace the agent of one's thoughts to one's heart is to worry about problems (without chance of their resolution). And to displace the agent of one's actions to one's heart is to desire states of affairs (without chance of their consummation).

In the case of construction class (1b), to possess a heart is to desire to do something. And not to possess a heart is to lose desire (in general).

In construction class (1c), to have one's heart become small is to change one's desire. To have one's heart become two is to gain a conflicting desire. And to have one's heart become broken is to lose one's desire.

In construction class (2), for something to drop into one's heart is to remember it. For something to be lost inside one's heart is to forget it. For something to be born inside one's heart is to decide to do it. And for something to come inside one's heart is to agree to do it.

In construction class (3), to displace the locale of saying to one's heart is to think. To displace the locale of a state of affairs to one's heart is to think incorrectly. And to displace the locale of thinking to one's heart is to plan or intend.

Lastly, in construction class (4), to have a pleasureful or painful heart is to be happy or sad. To have a red, malicious, or foreign heart is to be jealous, malicious, or estranged. To have a tame, fast, straight, malleable, strong, or small heart is to be meek, smart, loyal, humble, brave, or timid. To have a two-sided heart is to be insincere. For several people to have unitary heart is to be concerted (or to undertake an activity in a concerted fashion). And to have a seated, levelled, or standing heart is to be content, satisfied, or animated.

Notice that the meaning of possessed-heart constructions ranges from what western ethnopsychology would construe as belief and knowledge, desire and intention, feeling and emotion, personal traits and cultural values. The heart, then, is not just an 'instrument for thinking' or a 'locus of emotion' or an 'organ of desire', but is rather an all-purpose index of one's relation to the world. Knowing how a man relates to others, we may know something about the state of his heart; knowing the state of a man's heart, we may know something about how he relates to others. As argued in chapter 2, they are a key semiotic resource for disclosing the value-directed reflexive capabilities of persons – almost a bellwether of the self's relation to others and the mind's relation to the world.

Moreover, notice that there are at least four *modalities of displacement* underlying the meaning of possessed-heart constructions, whereby a construction explicitly indicates a marked shift away from an implicit and unmarked situation. Class (1) constructions arise, for example, when the possessed heart rather than the possessor is the effector of an action, and when the action is progressive or ongoing rather than of unmarked aspect. Class (2) constructions arise when a person is explicitly said to possess or not to possess what is normally possessed by any person. Class (3) constructions arise when a heart explicitly becomes two, instead of being implicitly one; when a heart explicitly breaks down, instead of implicitly functioning; and when a heart explicitly becomes small, instead of implicitly being large. Class (4) constructions arise when something is explicitly said inside one's heart, instead of implicitly being said in public; and when something is explicitly thought inside one's heart, which couldn't be thought anywhere else.

Simply stated, many possessed-heart constructions derive their meaning by indicating a shift away from an unmarked state of affairs. That is to say, while possessed-heart constructions most explicitly and efficiently disclose deviations from normal ways of feeling, thinking, believing, and wanting, they also carry with them assumptions about everyday unmarked (or 'normal') modes of intentionality. Loosely speaking, unmarked intentionality consists of having beliefs that are true, intentions that are achievable, worries that are quellable, fears that are founded, desires that are unconflicted, words that are publicly expressed, and thoughts that are controllable. That is to say, what is shown rather than said in such constructions, what is implicated rather than asserted, illuminates local assumptions about everyday unmarked modes of intentionality: *the mapping between mind and world is satiable.* Or, phrased another way, mental states are usually logically coherent with each other and causally coherent with the world. What gets made relatively public and unambiguous with possessed-heart constructions is violations of the norm, or exceptions to the rule: we talk a lot about marked mental states, while unmarked mental states go unmentioned.

6.   Usage of possessed-heart constructions

Alaak sa' ch'oolej and *chalk sa' ch'oolej (Class 2d)*

The intransitive predicate *alaak* may be glossed as 'to be born'. It is the passive form of *alank* (to bear). Both predicates are derived from the word *al* (child). When this predicate occurs with the preposition *sa'* (inside), whose argument is a possessed heart, the construction may be glossed as 'to decide to'. In this way, there is a double sense of initiative: birth (derived from the inalienable possession child), and location in one's own heart (rather than somewhere else). The intransitive verb *chalk* means 'to come'. When it occurs with the preposition *sa'* (inside), whose argument is a possessed heart, the construction may be glossed as 'to agree to'. Notice the relationship between the ingressive deictic 'come' and the meaning of 'agree' – for example, in the English construction, 'he'll come around eventually'. Both of these constructions, then, foreground the personal origins of a desire or intention, stressing that the urge to undertake the action in question arose voluntarily, and thus was not externally imposed by an outside source.

In paraphrasing the meaning of these constructions, speakers do not easily distinguish them from each other. And each is often given as a paraphrase for the other. In general, both are glossed as doing something intentionally (*k'a'uxlank*), 'with all one's heart' (*anchal laa ch'ool*), and without being ordered by another (*maa ani xtaqlan aawe*).[1] They are different, however, in that *chalk sa' ch'oolej* is usually in response to another's request (hence, the glosses given above: one is agreeing to do something asked of one). *Alaak sa' ch'oolej* was explained in terms of gift-giving, in the sense of a purely altruistic gift. For example, one speaker noted: 'whatever I want to give to you, well then it is born inside my heart that I will give it to you' (*qayehaq k'a raj li ru tinwaj xsib'al aawe pues, entons x'alaa sin ch'ool naq tink'e aawe*). In contrast, *chalk sa' ch'oolej* frequently came up in the context of labour-pooling, to indicate that one is working voluntarily – not because one owed another work (as part of a labour-debt), but because one agreed when asked to help out (Kockelman 2007d). In some sense, then, these constructions are used not so much to indicate personal volition, or desire, but to indicate lack of social obligation, or the absence of external compulsion. Personal desire (qua marked mental state) is constituted as the absence of interpersonal obligation (qua unmarked state of affairs).

---

[1] One reason for this ideological synonymy is that speakers only gloss the entailment of these achievements: they use the resultant state to gloss the entire achievement. That is, while this predicate is perhaps best translated as 'to decide to', speakers gloss it as 'to intend' (a gloss for which they have a ready-to-hand predicate, *k'a'uxlank* + *infinitive*, or 'to think about doing').

Naqk sa' ch'oolej, etc. (Class 2d)

There are several different modalities of remembering, all of which turn on a possessed heart as the argument of the preposition *sa'*. First, to have something be inside one's heart (*wank sa' ch'oolej*) is to remember it as a state (and thus not to have just remembered it, but never to have forgotten it). In such a construction, the focus is on what is remembered rather than the act of remembering, and the grounding of the event in personal experience more generally. For example, *wan sin ch'ool naq sa' ink'achinal laa'in xink'ul jun li maatan*, or 'I remember receiving a present when I was young'. Second, to have something stay in one's heart (*kanaak sa' ch'oolej*) is to remember it as a fact, usually in the context of schooling, and the kinds of facts taught there. Third, to have something drop into one's heart (*naqk sa' ch'oolej*) is to remember it, where the focus is on the achievement of remembering in the context of needing to remember. (The intransitive verb *naqk* means 'to drop'. It is often said of fruit, rain, and sickness – where in the last two cases it may alternatively be glossed as 'to begin'.) For example: *xnaq sin ch'ool chi xik*, or 'I remembered to go'. Often this is used in contexts such as: I just remembered that (I need to do something) or I must remember to (do something). And lastly, to have something be lost in one's heart (*sachk sa' ch'oolej*) is to have forgotten it.

Insofar as all of these verbs are intransitive states and state-changes, where the event or object remembered is the grammatical subject, they cannot usually be given as commands to others. Only the construction *sachk sa' ch'oolej* has a transitive version, *sachok sa' ch'oolej*, in which the event or object remembered is the grammatical object, and the possessor of the heart is coreferential with the grammatical subject. Such a construction is very frequent. It can be used negatively: *maasach sa' aach'ool* (don't lose it inside your heart), or 'don't forget it'. And it may be used positively: *chaasach sa' aach'ool* (would that you lose it inside your heart), or 'forgive it'. In this way, the most frequent uses of memory are not in the context of reminiscing about past events, or remembering classroom facts, but rather in the context of a social imperative not to forget to undertake a present command, or a religious imperative to forgive another's slight. That is to say, the lexicalization of memory among the Q'eqchi' is inherently bound up in social obligations: what one must forgive or must not forget to do, as a function of work imperatives or moral values. As with deciding and agreeing, notice the fine line between mental states and social statuses, as the roots and fruits of speech acts.

Yook ch'oolej (Class 5c)

The intransitive activity predicate *yook* is most frequently used as an auxiliary verb to indicate progressive aspect. In such a construction, *yook* occurs with a non-finite verb marked by the complementizer *chi*. Thus, if *wa'ak* is a non-finite verb meaning 'to eat', and *li winq* is a noun phrase meaning 'the man', *yoo chi wa'ak li winq* is a progressive construction meaning 'the man is eating'. When the grammatical subject of *yook* (i.e. the argument that is effecting the progressive activity in question) is a possessed heart instead of a person, the construction may literally be glossed as 'one's heart is doing (something)'. However, by saying that one's heart, rather than oneself, is doing something, the speaker is indicating that 'one's heart is doing what one would like to do but cannot'. In other words, one shifts from describing an action that was actually done, or will actually be done, to an action that is desired but impossible to do. In this way, such constructions mark counterfactual intentions or insatiable desires. For example, in discussing why her family couldn't leave their house even though the roof was leaking, a woman used the construction *yoo inch'ool chi elk, ab'aan maak'a' intumin*, which literally means 'my heart is leaving, but I have no money', but which is perhaps best glossed as 'I would leave, but I have no money'. In other words, she marks a desire for improving her home for her family as frustrated by a constraint of money. What English speakers may do with a modal auxiliary verb inflected for past tense (*would*), Q'eqchi' speakers may do with a shift in aspect from unmarked to progressive, and a shift in actor from inalienable possessor to inalienable possession. Counterfactual constructions will be treated in detail in chapter 5.

Kiib'ank ch'oolej (Class 5c)

The adjective *kiib'* refers to the number two. *Kiib'ank* is a derived intransitive achievement predicate that means to split (divide, cut, smash) something into two pieces: literally, to cause to become two. It is often used to speak of slicing open fruit or vegetables with a machete. When the predicate is used intransitively, and the grammatical subject is a possessed heart, this construction may be glossed as 'to become conflicted', or to have two irreconcilable desires. When used with a non-finite complement, marked by the complementizer *chi*, it may be glossed as 'to no longer feel good about doing something' (insofar as new information has given you a conflicting desire). In cases where the complement is factive, or presupposed as true, it may be glossed as 'to regret (having done something)'.

For example, a woman was speaking to her step-mother about her brother, who had recently foregone marrying his sweetheart, because he saw her talking with another man. She said that his heart doubled, and he didn't marry her, even though he loved her. Notice, then, that this event led to the man 'changing his mind' – just like in the case of *ch'inank ch'oolej* (discussed in chapter 2), but it was due to having a conflicting desire that won out (presumably not to have his proposal rejected in the short term, or be cuckolded in the long run).

In the case of *ch'inank ch'oolej*, one actually changes one's mind, and has no lingering desire left to do what was not done. For this reason, these two constructions may be usefully contrasted: *kiib'ank ch'oolej*, to no longer feel good about doing something, insofar as one now wants to do something else (and one cannot do both); and *ch'inank ch'oolej*, to no longer feel good about doing (having done) something, insofar as one now knows this something would be (was) bad to do.

Po'k ch'oolej (Class 5c)

Unlike other members of this class, the intransitive achievement predicate *po'k* (to break down, become undone) does not seem to be derived from an adjective. Rather, it is related to a transitive accomplishment predicate *po'ok*, which may be glossed as 'to cause to break apart, or undo'. For example, after a boy slams the door, a mother may say to him: *maapo' li pweert*, or 'don't break the door'. One may also 'undo' the stitching on a pair of pants (*xinpo' lix b'ojb'al lin wex*). Or, when speaking of the second-hand gas-powered generator that they bought to power lights to the church, members of this community said *xpo'*, or 'it broke down'. When used transitively, with the grammatical subject being a person, and the grammatical object being a possessed heart, such a construction is best glossed as 'to dissuade' (subject different from possessor) or 'to become dissuaded' (subject equal to possessor).[2] In other words, to break down another's heart is to change their desire (usually by informing them of the potential consequences of acting on such a desire).

Indeed, a key means of dissuasion in such cases is to mention the possibility of fright, of the kind discussed in chapter 2. For example, a young boy wanted to go to the market with his older cousin. His father told him he couldn't go, but he kept insisting. Finally, the father explained to him that he might fall, be left behind by his friends, or get robbed by thieves. The boy ultimately relented. And when discussing the incident with his wife that night, the man said *xinpo' lix ch'ool chi xik sa' k'ayil*, or 'I broke down his heart about going to the market'. In this way, to dissuade someone is to make them change their desire by telling them the entailments, or causal and logical implications, of their previous desire. Note, then, that the complement of such a construction is necessarily counterfactive: if one was dissuaded from doing something, one didn't do it. Such a construction may also appear with the explicit counterfactive clitic *raj*. In such a case, it means that you tried to dissuade another, but they didn't believe your reasoning. So, for example, a woman explained to her brother that he couldn't collect wood from a particular spot in the forest because it

---

[2] This construction may also take a possessed head as a grammatical object, and be glossed as 'to confuse, drive wild, or anger'. In this way, just as one may undo another's heart (thereby dissuading them), one may also undo another's head (thereby confusing them).

belonged to someone else. Her brother didn't believe her (indeed, he assumed she was telling him this so that her own husband could go collect it). When she later told her father that she had tried to dissuade him, she said: *xinpo' raj lix ch'ool chirisinkil li si'*, *ab'an ink'a xpaab'*, or 'I tried (counterfactual) to break down his heart, but he didn't believe (what I said)'.

Yehok sa' ch'oolej, k'a'uxlank sa' ch'oolej (Class 8b)

The transitive activity predicates *yehok* (to say) and *k'a'uxlank* (to think) often appear with the preposition *sa'* (inside), whose argument is a possessed heart. In such cases, the possessor of the heart is necessarily the grammatical subject of the predicate (that is, the one who is saying or thinking). With *yehok*, such a construction may be glossed as 'to say in one's heart', or 'to say to oneself', or even 'to think'. In the case of *k'a'uxlank*, the construction further specifies the locale of thinking. Some younger, more educated speakers will substitute *k'a'uxl* (thoughts) for *ch'oolej* (heart), or even use both together: *sa' lix ch'ool o malaj sa' lix k'a'uxl* (in his heart or his thoughts). In such constructions, the direct argument of the predicates is usually directly reported speech. In this way, besides being a locus of desire, hearts are the locales of internal mono- logues, or private thoughts.

Such a construction (*sa' ch'oolej*) can even be used without a verb of speak- ing or thinking. That is, to make an assertion followed by *sa' inch'ool* (inside my heart) is to mark the assertion as counterfactual. For example, after having discovered that the hat she washed was not her husband's but his brother's, a man's wife said to him: *sin ch'ool laa'in, aawe*, or 'in my heart, it was yours' or 'I thought (erroneously) that it was yours'.

Lastly, there is a very common expression, *maak'a' sa' ch'oolej*, or 'there was nothing in one's heart'. This construction may be glossed as 'unintentionally' or 'by chance' depending on the context. For example, in discussing the raid on his village by soldiers during the civil war, the mayor said: 'when the soldiers came, there was nothing in our hearts', meaning 'we weren't expecting it'. But it is often said of accidents, or chance encounters, to mean 'unprepared'. In legal scenarios it may be used to mean 'unintentional' or 'not premeditated'. And in all of these contexts it invites the implicature that what happened was not deserved, and those that it happened to were not responsible. In short, just as *sa' ch'oolej* is used to reframe public speaking as private thinking, and true knowledge as false beliefs, its negation is used to change intentional actions to unintentional actions, and putatively guilty parties to victims of circumstance.

The next several examples of possessed-heart constructions involve an adjectival predicate rather than a verbal predicate. Thus, while not always good examples of the interclausal relations hierarchy, they are frequently used mental-state predicates, and so are taken up here.

Sa/ra ch'oolej (Class 4a; see Table 2.5)

The adjectives *sa* and *ra* are frequently used to mean 'delicious' and 'bitter', respectively. When predicated of a body part, such as a limb, they indicate that the body part in question is 'pleasureful' (or rather unharmed or fine) and 'painful', respectively. When predicated of a possessed heart, they indicate that the possessor of the heart feels good or feels bad (or is 'happy' or 'sad'). Indeed, the most frequent greeting among speakers of Q'eqchi' is *ma sa (sa') laa ch'ool*, which literally means 'is (inside) your heart pleasureful?' It may be glossed as 'how are you?' Such an invitation to personal disclosure occurs at the beginning of each encounter with another familiar person. Nonetheless, as in the case of the English 'how are you?', the standard answer (or preferred second pair-part) is the relatively unilluminating *sa* or 'fine'.

Either of these adjectives may be derived into a state-change predicate or achievement: *saho'k ch'oolej* (to become happy) and *raho'k ch'oolej* (to become sad). As either adjectives or achievement predicates they may take full-clause complements, marked by the complementizer *xb'aan naq* (because). And they often appear with full clauses marked by the complementizer *naq* in its 'when' sense, rather than in its 'that' sense. Prototypical examples of situations in which one feels bad are those in which a close relative dies, usually a parent. For example, *xraho' inch'ool xb'aan naq xkam inna'* (I was sad because of my mother's death). Similarly, examples of happy situations are those in which one comes across a relative, or hears a relative is well. For example: *xsaho' inch'ool naq xwil ru inna'* (my heart grew pleasureful when I saw my mother's face).

Let me offer some examples of its usage. After hearing that her elderly father hiked the long trail into the village mistakenly (thinking there were eco-tourists to guide), a woman said: 'my heart is bitter that my father went out early without eating breakfast' (*ra inch'ool naq inyuwa xko'o eq'ela ut maak'a' xwa'ak*). Or when hearing that her son had cut himself with a machete while working with his father, a woman said: 'my heart is very bitter because Humberto cut himself' (*mas ra inch'ool xb'aan naq laj Humberto xset' rib'*). Another man was said to be sad because his father had planted where he had wanted to plant (*ra xch'ool xb'aan naq lix yuwa' x'awk b'ar wi' wan lin k'al*). Or, for example, a man talking about a cow he purchased said: 'I am unhappy that I bought it because it died on me, it was difficult to spend money on it, and I threw it away' (*ra sa' inch'ool naq xinloq' (jun li wakax) xb'aan naq kikam chiwu, li tumin xinkab'resi chira chi sa ut xintz'eq*).

Notice, then, that such a construction is frequently used to mark empathetic states: feeling bad because something bad happened to someone who is familiar (in these cases, immediate family: father or son). As discussed in chapter 2, feeling good and feeling bad, 'happiness' and 'sadness', turn on the waxing and waning of one's inalienable possessions, such as the fortunes and misfortunes of one's family and friends, field and home, body and reputation.

Ab'l ch'oolej (Class 4a)

The adjective *ab'l* means 'foreign' or 'strange'. The derived noun *ab'le e* may be glossed as 'foreign property'. And the derived intransitive achieve-ment predicate *ab'lo'k* may be glossed as 'to become foreign or estranged [to someone]'. When the grammatical subject of such a predicate is a possessed heart, the construction may be glossed as 'to be(come) alienated (by/from someone)'. In such constructions, the 'someone' is marked by the relational noun *sa' xb'een* (or 'on top of'). Usually the person from whom one becomes alienated is family, but *ab'l* may also be predicated of dogs (for example, when they bark at their owners). In general, estrangement is caused by an imbalance of possessions or the feelings that such an imbalance gives rise to – in particu-lar, envy of someone (*kaq ch'oolej*), malice towards someone (*lab' ch'oolej*), or anger at someone (*josq'*). That is to say, there is an important reflexivity with this construction: property that belongs to another (i.e. 'foreign property') causes one to become estranged from that person (i.e. 'foreign to that per-son'). And it causes people to treat familiars as non-familiars – by mistreating them, avoiding them, ignoring them, and so forth. That is, it is a bad feeling, caused by a differential in possessions, that causes a rift between possessors – causes deviations from the base-line motivation of care, when the possessors are themselves inalienable possessions of each other.

As an example of these dynamics, one person described the appropriate use of the predicate as follows: 'Suppose one's neighbour (*echkab'al*) resents what I own (*xiik' nareek'a li k'aru we*). He or she is jealous of it (*nixkaqali*). In such a situation, they may become distant to me, or estranged from me (*entons a'an na'ab'lo' chaq xch'ool sa' inb'een*). They will treat me as if I am not familiar to them (*chanchan naq moko laa'in xkomun*), as if I am not their neighbour (*moko laa'in ta rechkab'al*).'

Or, in explaining to her sister-in-law why she no longer lived on the land her father had given her, a woman said that her father resented her (*xiik' ninril*, that is, 'looks at me with anger') because the homestead (*xna'aj lix ch'och' a'in*) where her house was located belonged to him. In this case, because her father disliked her for using the land he had given her, her heart became estranged about remaining there (*x'ab'lo' inch'ool chi wank aran*). And because of this estrangement, she and her husband took their children and their house and moved to a different location.

Tuqtu ch'oolej (Class 4d)

The positional root *tuqtu* may be glossed as 'levelled', or 'flat'. Such a state is typically predicated of the foundation or place (*xna'aj*) of a house: it must be level (*tuqtu*) before one can build there. Indeed, that a housing site is level is said to be a requirement (literally, 'desire') of house building: *tuqtu naraj li kab'lak*.

Levelling is itself the first activity undertaken when building a house, and is the most difficult to achieve – requiring many men shovelling and sweating. The derived noun *tuqtuukilal* literally means 'levelledness', but may be loosely glossed as 'tranquility', 'contentment', 'peace', or 'happiness'. For example, speakers define this term as 'being within goodness' or 'being within friendship' (*li wank sa' chaab'ilal, sa' amigil*). Indeed, there is a common blessing that involves it: 'let there be tranquility (*tuqtuuqilal*) within the home of each family' (*ha'an taxaq li tuqtuukilal chi wanq sa' rochoch li junjunq*). And it is usually predicated of a group of people rather than of an individual: *wanko sa' tuqtuukilal*, or 'we are within tranquility', or 'we are content'. In this way, it necessarily involves several people, usually family members, but also neighbours or members of the same village. Glossed negatively, it is understood as a situation in which people don't fight, mistreat each other, or argue (*ink'a' naqache' qib', ink'a' naqahob' qib', ink'a' naqapleetin qib'*). In this way, not only is levelledness understood as a requirement of the foundations of houses, it is also understood as a goal or value for their inhabitants. It is at once both an instrumental and an existential value.[3]

The positional root *tuqtu* may also be predicated of one's heart. Again, speakers' glosses are often negatively characterized. When one's heart is level, one doesn't worry about things (*ink'a' nakaak'a'uxla chirix*). One's heart isn't always going (*yoo lix ch'ool*), or thinking, about what one has to do: one isn't worrying or planning. But if one's heart isn't level, one wants to move one's house, search for a job, or have money arrive. When one's heart is level, one has no more worries or thoughts (*maak'a' chik junaq laa k'a'uxl*). As with *tuqtuuqilal*, the condition of having a levelled heart is often glossed negatively: in terms of what one does when one doesn't have a levelled heart. As a group value, there is no fighting; as an individual state, there is no worrying. In short, *tuqtu ch'oolej* is like the personal internalization of a collective state – involving security, contentment, peacefulness, and tranquility. It is almost a concrete instance of Aristotle's *eudemonia*; a local instantiation of the *summum bonum*; that end which is not itself a means to another end.

7.   The ontology and epistemology of intentionality

As introduced in chapter 1, mental states are usually understood as having both a propositional mode (belief, intention, perception) and a propositional content (what is believed, intended, or perceived). In this chapter, we have

---

[3] *Usilal*, a nominalization of the adjective *us* (good) is used in a similar fashion. For example, *wanko sa' usilal*, or 'we are within goodness', means that we do not fight with each other or mistreat each other, that we share our food with each other, we lend each other money, we help each other build houses, we do favours for each other.

been focused on linguistic constructions in which both propositional mode and content are made explicit, or relatively public and unambiguous. Understood another way, we have been focused on linguistic processes whereby the propositional modes and contents of mental states are represented by speech acts, functioning as relatively emblematic roles, or stances.

To do this, we have engaged in several pursuits: 1) examining the words that refer to mental states (e.g. *believe, intend, fear*); 2) examining the utterances that predicate mental states of people (e.g. *John is angry*); and 3) examining the utterances that predicate properties of mental states (e.g. *anger is an emotion*). Such words – and the utterances in which they are implicated – introduce a new order of mediation into intentionality: representations of representations. To conclude this chapter, a number of overarching consequences of this lexical mediation should be reviewed. As will be seen, what is fundamental to such processes is the way that mental states are simultaneously construed as quasi-objective (qua real things or concrete events that can be analysed and localized) and quasi-subjective (qua putative psychological processes that have relatively non-sensuous and ephemeral properties that make them different from other kinds of things and events).

With lexicalization, mental states are subject to a number of interrelated processes that construe them as *object-like*. They are conceptualized, caught up in the dynamics of reference and predication. For example, just as we can enquire into the conceptual contents and extensional domains of words like *dog* and *run*, we may enquire into the conceptual contents and extensional domains of words like *desire* and *think*. They constitute a semantic field: such lexemes are comparable via relations of synonymy, antonymy, partonomy, and taxonomy. For example, just as there are different kinds of fruit, and different kinds of food more generally, there are different kinds of emotions, and different kinds of mental states more generally. They are subject to language-internal glossing: speakers may interpret their own usage of such words using other such words. For example, 'belief is a kind of knowledge' and 'fear is an emotion'. They may be derived through metaphorical elaboration: the features of a relatively abstract domain may be conceptualized by mapping them onto the features of a relatively concrete domain. For example, for one's heart to shrink is to become afraid. And, caught up in all these processes, there is projection: features of signs (or speech acts) are taken to be features of objects (or mental states). For example, philosophers and psychologists may project properties of complement-taking predicates (e.g. complementation) onto properties of mental states (e.g. aboutness, or object-directedness). In all of these ways, mental states acquire a kind of objectivity: just as concepts demand referents, relatively vague or implicit relations are defined and explicated, abstract domains are understood in terms of concrete domains, and private representations are understood in terms of public representations.

With lexicalization, mental states are also subject to a number of interrelated processes that construe them as *event-like*. There is displacement: the mode event may be construed as more or less distant from the sign event along dimensions such as time, space, person, and possibility. For example, the verbal operators that act on lexical predicates allow one to ascribe mental states to oneself and others (I believe versus you believe), in the past and present (he believed versus he believes), in actual and possible worlds (he did believe versus he would have believed). In tandem with displacement is tightness: the mode event may be construed as more or less distant from the content event. For example, an event of wanting is more causal of the event wanted than an event of believing is causal of the event believed. There is ascription: the ability to attribute one mental state to another while simultaneously providing evidence of one's own mental state. For example, in saying 'John believes it will rain', I am simultaneously making explicit John's belief (about the rain) and my belief (about John's belief). Here the phenomenon of intensionality arises: representations of others' representations, such that one may construe another's mental states as more or less coherent with each other, more or less adequate to the world, or more or less conforming with one's own. And they are subject to assertability: to make a claim about another's mental state is to subject oneself to evidentiary requirements (for example, why one believes what one asserts: is one justified in believing it? and, if it is true, what other beliefs does it justify?). In short, mental states may achieve a kind of event-like nature: they are localizable in time and space; linked to other events as causes and effects; and caught up in truth claims and evidentiary requirements.

In sum, as a function of the properties of the signs that stand for them, mental states take on properties that make them seem at once object-like and event-like. Such semiotic processes, then, project an ontology: they seem to delimit a set of things in the world, with properties that allow them to be contrasted with other things and compared with each other. With the set of signs we use to disclose mental states, we simultaneously enclose them: giving intelligibility, form, and permanence to things that are otherwise distant, murky, and fleeting (Bakhtin 1990; Kockelman 2007a).

Following Peirce (1955), signs are said to be iconic if they have properties in common with their objects. A question arises, then, as to whether iconicity exists because the sign has accommodated to the object or because the object has been assimilated to the sign. That is, does the sign have such features because the object has them, or does the object have such features because the sign has them? In the first case, iconicity is a species of realism; in the second case, iconicity is a species of nominalism. On the one hand, language adequately mirrors mind; on the other hand, we are only minding language when we talk about mind.

While such questions might be easily resolved in certain domains (e.g. ono-matopoeia), in cases where our access to the objects in question is so exten-sively mediated by signs no obvious answer is forthcoming. So rather than ask what properties mental states have, ask why we believe mental states have such properties. In other words, an understanding of what kinds of things there are in the world (or mind) demands an understanding of how we acquire knowl-edge about such things. An ontology demands an epistemology.

In particular, during the course of acquiring propositional content through words that refer to them or predicate qualities about them, mental states may become the object of empirical investigations, theoretical representations, and practical interventions. This involves two interrelated processes. First, as described above, in addition to predicating mental states of people, mental states have properties predicated of them. And second, via both these kinds of predication, propositional modes (*as* propositional contents) are them-selves inferentially and indexically grounded. Thus, the following kinds of questions arise: what observations or assertions would entitle or commit one to predicate property X of mental state Y, or predicate mental state W of person Z; and if one predicates property X of mental state Y, or predicates mental state W of person Z, what assertions or actions does this entitle or commit one to?

In short, *theoretical representations* of mental states might be understood as assertions which either represent people as having certain mental states, or represent mental states as having certain properties. Such theoretical represen-tations can stand as reasons and in need of reasons. *Empirical investigations* of mental states might be understood as observations of the mental states of people or the properties of mental states. These can stand as reasons for theor-etical representations; and these are indexically caused by states of affairs. And *practical interventions* of mental states might be understood as actions which are directed towards affecting the mental states of people or the properties of mental states. These can stand in need of reasons; and these are indexically causal of states of affairs. In short, this is a way of moving from a theory of mind to a theory of the 'truth' of a theory of mind, or from an account of inten-tionality to an account of the epistemology of intentionality.

Such questions might be asked of any scientific discipline, or institution of enquiry, that has mind, psyche, or mental states as its object of study: from psychoanalysis and behaviouralism to evolutionary psychology and cognitive science. Indeed, the research undertaken in this book is precisely such a mode of enquiry, or epistemology. But they may also be asked of *epistemologies of the everyday* – how members of a given speech community ascribe intentional-ity to each other, the kinds of evidence they use, the kinds of reasons they give, the kinds of ontologies they have, the kinds of analogies they offer, the kinds of actions they license (Kockelman 1999b, 2007c). Indeed, just as yesterday's knowledge is often today's ideology, today's theory of mind will be tomorrow's ethnopsychology.

Thus, while we have finished describing the large-scale morphosyntactic and semantic properties of complement-taking predicates, the following chapters will keep returning to their pragmatics: how speakers use such signs to make sense of mind; how everyday epistemologies reveal implicit ontologies.

4   Myths about time and theories of mind: why the moon married the sun

1.   Introduction

This Q'eqchi'-Mayan myth describes the difficulties suffered by B'alamq'e (the sun) in his attempt to elope with Po (the moon), as they try to outwit and outrun her father Tzuultaq'a (or 'mountain-valley', the telluridian god of the Q'eqchi'). In broad terms, the text may be thought of as a cosmogony of the Q'eqchi' world – narrating events that take place in time, as undertaken by actors who are time, to explain the nature of time. But more prosaically, it provides an ontogeny for, and taxonomy of, all poisonous creatures. It discusses the origins of the heavens, and the populating of the earth. It describes how women put signs of their daily experience into the cloth they are weaving. It explains why men lead women. And it accounts for the origins of coughing.

A key goal of this chapter is to use this myth about time as an entry into local understandings of mind. In particular, by carefully analysing the linguistic and cultural mediation of time, we will gain access to intentional horizons implicit in genres of speaking: the conditions for, and consequences of, differential overlaps in who knows what about others' beliefs, feelings, and intentions. As will be seen, the master trope of this myth is the difference between appearance and essence, deceitfulness and honesty, or character and performer, as elaborated in the local idiom of containers and contents. In short, temporality is used as a means to understand intersubjectivity – the relative symmetry (or asymmetry) of participants' knowledge of each other's subjective experience.

The text itself was narrated in 1909 by Juan Caal, a speaker of Q'eqchi'. Paul Wirsing, a German immigrant, heard Mr Caal recount it during a festival held at his coffee-finca in Alta Verapaz, Guatemala, and later asked him to repeat it so that he could write it down in a Roman script. Wirsing gave this document to Dr Herbert Quirín Dieseldorff, who later gave it to Estrada Monroy, a priest and amateur anthropologist, to analyse. Estrada Monroy then worked with some village elders – Domingo Cuc Xol, Petrona Tení, and Juanita Tení – to translate it (and add some phrases that the original lacked – though where, exactly, is not said). A copy of the original transcription, along with a serviceable Spanish translation and some more details of the text's origins, may be found in Estrada Monroy's book, entitled *Vida esotérica Maya-K'ekchí* (1990: 108–41). In short, as with any text, this one has had a complicated and intriguing history, one worth a study in itself.

Shorter versions of this myth have been collected and discussed by other anthropologists much more recently (e.g. Wilson 1995: 327–8). The version analysed here, however, is by far both the longest and oldest we have. It is a singular instance of grammatical categories unfolding in narrative discourse, as it was spoken 100 years ago. Moreover, as will be seen, the original transcription is very robust: glottal stops, vowel-length distinctions, and other usually overlooked phonological details are consistently marked. Finally, it might even be argued that this text is for the Q'eqchi' what the Popol Vuh is for the Quiche, or Genesis is for Judeo-Christians – an ur-text – and so warrants not only careful analysis, but multiple analyses. In short, while the linguistic focus of this chapter is time and mind, as marked by grammatical categories and discourse patterns, the text is ripe for an analysis of the colonial encounter, gender relations, historical phonology, morphosyntax, intertextuality, and so on. The transcription, interlinear translation, and English glossing offered here should thereby provide tools for other scholars to undertake other kinds of investigations.

The text itself may be found in *Appendix B*. And a summary of the transcription conventions used in my translation of it may be found in *Appendix A*.

To give the reader some familiarity with the whole narrative, it is worthwhile offering a one-sentence-per-scene overview of the entire text. The first scene establishes the topic: this is the story of the sun's theft of the moon, and the suffering undergone by them. Long ago, there lived Tzuultaq'a and his daughter, the moon. She spends her days caring for her father, and weaving in front of the house. One day, the sun sees her as he passes by, and decides to make her his wife. The moon never notices his passing. Nor does she notice that he carries a stuffed goat-hide (making it appear as if he is a skilled hunter). When she finally does notice him, she tells her father about him; but her father doubts the hunter's authenticity, and so together they set a trap. The next day, the sun slips on the cooked corn they have laid in his path – his deception is revealed (the goat-skin bursts), and he runs home.

But in the stuffing of the goat-skin was a seed of tobacco, which germinates along the river by the house of Tzuultaq'a and his daughter. Meanwhile, back home, the sun plots a way to get back to the moon. After three days have passed, he calls a hummingbird, and gives it the bark of a tree in exchange for its feathers. Disguised as such, he flies back to the flowers of the tobacco plant. The moon sees what she takes to be a hummingbird, asks her father to shoot it with his blow-gun, and then collects its limp body. Still in the guise of a bird, the sun is restless in the gourd where the moon keeps him; and so she puts him beneath her blouse and goes back to weaving. At night, she goes to sleep with the bird on her chest.

In the darkness, the sun reveals himself to the moon as a man, and asks her to leave with him; but the moon tells him that they cannot go, explaining that her father has a mirror which he can use to spy on them; so the sun enlists her help in sabotaging the mirror (by clouding its face with smoke). But the moon says that they still cannot go, explaining that her father has a blow-gun; so they sabotage that, by stuffing it with chilli; and then they finally set off from the house.

The next day, Tzuultaq'a discovers his daughter's absence and infers that the hummingbird must have been the sun in disguise; but, in attempting to first see them (in the mirror) and then shoot them (with his blow-gun), he succumbs to the traps they laid for him. When he awakes from a coughing fit (caused by the chilli), he is very angry, and enlists the help of his brother, Thunder. Thunder goes after them, in the guise of stormy weather. By the time Thunder catches up with the fugitives, they have arrived at the edge of the sea; and, having no place to run, they hide themselves in the shells of a friendly turtle and armadillo. Thunder showers them with lightning. The moon cannot swim, is hit, and rendered into many pieces. But the sun escapes by rolling into the sea (thereby causing night to fall).

The next day, the sun discovers the moon's bloody remains, has them collected by dragonflies into thirteen jars, and then gives these to a woman to look after. While he is away for thirteen days, something begins to move inside those jars. This frightens the old lady, and so when the sun returns she tells him to take away the jars. He opens them, one after another, and finds different kinds of poisonous animals in each: snakes, spiders, bees, and so forth. But he does not find the moon until he opens the thirteenth jar, in which she was hiding – now, in a much larger, purified, and beautiful form. The sun asks a passing woodcutter to remove the other jars, telling him not to look inside; but the man gets curious, looks inside, and thereby lets all the dangerous animals loose, so that they escape to infest the world.

The moon, however, is not yet perfected: so the sun enlists the help of a goat to open up a hole between her legs. But this too is not enough, so he gets a deer to open it more; but it still smells good, so he gets a rat to pee there. Finally satisfied with the state of the moon, the sun takes her hand, and brings her up into the sky. Like the first scene, the last scene is again meta-topical: since then, we are told, just as the sun leads the moon in the sky, so too do men lead women on earth.

In the analysis that follows, as dictated by key features of the text, four themes will come up again and again. First, there is the encoding of temporal relations. As seen, the sun and the moon are not only narrated figures (actors in the discourse), their movements also establish the temporal ground relative to which all the narrated events are figured. In some sense, there is a very large-scale parallelism between narrated figures and temporal grounds: time of day and movement of sun, phase of month and state of moon. Also, a key tension is that between containers and contents or, understood another way, between intentional horizons: what some participants (in both the speech event and the narrated event) are privy and not privy to concerning the identities and intentions of other participants. That is, much of the narrative turns on modes of deception whereby an entity's surface appearance contradicts its underlying nature; and how other characters act erroneously because of this, or manage to find out what its true nature is. Third, there is an ontology being developed – a classification of kinds of people and things, and social relations more generally: how they are related to each other, and how they came into existence. Finally, much turns on the nature of motivation and causality: what drives characters to do what they do (and what values are implicit in this); and what are the repercussions of such actions (and how are such effects manifested in the present world).

Note, then, that while it is tempting to reify theories of mind, or even ethnopsychologies, as relatively isolated and self-contained domains, we see here that theories of mind are impossible to separate from religious beliefs, taxonomic reasoning, social hierarchies, and 'culture' more generally.

The next section describes what is meant by temporality for the purposes of this chapter. The following three sections analyse the grammatical encoding of temporal relations, describing the form, function, and frequency of the relevant constructions that occur in the text: from inflectional affixes to discourse particles. Moving from analysis to synthesis, the last four sections interpret several important scenes in the narrative, demonstrating how the key themes (temporality, intentionality, ontology, and causality) work together.

2.   Temporality as a notional domain

For the purposes of this chapter, it is worth characterizing temporality as a notional domain, such that we can analyse the formal means (grammatical categories and discourse patterns) by which features of this domain are encoded and implicated. To be sure, time is multifaceted and highly nebulous – so, in no way is this meant to be a definition of time. Rather, in this section I want to sketch four modes of temporality on which the analysis in this chapter turns.

The winter evening settles down
With smell of steaks in passageways.
Six o'clock.

Take these opening lines of Preludes, by T. S. Elliot. To perceive the poetic function of language, in the sense of Jakobson (1990b), we need merely check the metre: the first two lines have four feet apiece (each foot having two syllables), and these feet have the form unstressed-stressed. In short, not only is each line a token of the type tetrameter, but each foot of each line is also a token of the type iamb. The third line, then, breaks both these types: it has an odd number of syllables (rather than an even number); there are three of these (rather than eight); and the stress pattern of the first foot is stressed-unstressed, or a trochee (rather than an iamb). The first two lines, then, establish a ground relative to which the last line is figured. That is, it is precisely the replicas (qua tokens of a common type) which highlight the singularities (qua unique and surprising tokens).

There is tense and aspect: the winter evening settles down. But it might have been otherwise: the winter evening settled down (past tense); the winter evening will settle down (future tense); the winter evening has settled down (perfect aspect); the winter evening is settling down (progressive aspect). This is another kind of linguistic temporality, turning on the ordering of a reference event relative to a speech event in the case of tense (past, unmarked, future), and the ordering of a narrated event relative to a reference event in the case of aspect (progressive, unmarked, perfect). In this way, the speech event (and, indeed, any narrated event) can be the singularity relative to which the ordering of other events (referenced, narrated, or spoken) is measured. If the first mode of temporality focuses on signs (or objects) in and of themselves, this mode turns on sign–object relations: how the time of some narrated event is determined by reference to the signs that stand for it, themselves related to speech events and other narrated events. This mode of temporality will be the topic of sections 3 and 4.

There are roots and fruits, significant causes and effects of any event – in particular, the sign event. The poem itself may be understood as the interpretant of all the signs that made up one poet's experience (why did Elliot say this?); and this section may itself be understood as an interpretant of such a sign event (what does this stanza mean?). In this way, the poem establishes a local present, whose interpretive roots and significant fruits constitute its past and future. Moreover, not only may any event be simultaneously framable as an interpretant of a prior event and a sign to be subsequently interpreted, but so too may the event it narrates. Indeed, narratives are so often tales of local modes of signification and interpretation: what caused a hero to do what she did, and what became of her for having done it; what are the inferential and indexical roots and fruits of her actions. This mode of temporality, then, turns on sign–object–interpretant relations. Kockelman (2007b) takes up this mode of temporality in detail.

Finally, there is a fourth mode of temporality here: a contrast between natural solar-centric periods, turning on season of year (*winter*) and phase of day (*evening*), and the modern, seemingly empty clock-time of a putative capitalist modernity (*six o'clock*, qua end of workday). As with the metre in which each mode is wrought, clock-time is a singularity that irrevocably disturbs the natural rhythms that went before it. Or, at the very least, this is a widespread cultural understanding, or *Weltanschauung*, about what has happened to time. In some sense, the three modes of temporality just discussed only count as temporal when seen from inside such a frame. This Q'eqchi' myth is itself such a theory of time, and so this entire chapter is such an exegesis of one local understanding of the nature of temporality. Bakhtin's (1981) notion of the chronotope is perhaps most germane here.

3.   Introduction to the system used for describing temporal relations

To analyse tense and aspect, and temporal categories more generally, the three-event system pioneered by Reichenbach (1947), and extended by Bull (1960) and Klein (1994), will be used. In particular, adapting the nomenclature of Jakobson (1990a), there are three events (or intervals) of interest: the speech event (E^s), the narrated event (E^n), and the reference event (E^r). To use an example from Klein, in an answer to a question like *what did you notice when you entered the room?* the speech event is the time at which the answer is given (presumably soon after the question was asked), the narrated event is the time of the situation described by the answer (say, *a man was lying on the floor*), and the reference event, or 'topic time', is the time set by the adverbial clause within the question (*when you entered the room*).

In such an utterance, the grammatical category of *tense* encodes the relation between the reference event and the speech event (E^r/E^s), here realized with the past-tense form of the auxiliary verb (*was*). And the grammatical category of *aspect* encodes the relation between the narrated event and the reference event (E^n/E^r), here realized with the progressive-aspect form of the verb (*be VERB-ing*). To diagram the relevant relations, we may modify the system used by Klein: the star symbol (*) indicates the time of the speech event; the bracket symbol ([]) indicates the time of the reference event; and the wavyline symbol (~~~) indicates the time of the narrated event (here a one-state situation). (See Table 4.1.) If past tense indicates that the reference event is *before* the speech event, progressive aspect indicates that the narrated event *contains* the reference event. (More exactly, the temporal span covered by the narrated event contains the temporal span covered by the reference event.)

To give the reader some more familiarity with this system, it is worthwhile elaborating the prototypic functions of the English tense-aspect system. Using just three tenses (past, unmarked, future), and three aspects (perfect, unmarked, progressive), there are nine possibilities.[1] (See Table 4.2.)

---

[1] Constructions involving both perfect and progressive aspect are not shown: *has been sleeping*, and so forth. While one can read off from the diagram both the relation between the speech event

Table 4.1. *Relation between narrated event, reference event, and speech event* E^n (~~~), E^r ([]), and E^s (*)

'A man was lying on the floor (when you entered the room)'.

~[~]~

*

Table 4.2. *Some prototypic functions of tense and aspect in English*

			Tense: E^r/E^s		
*	E^s				
[]	E^r				
~~	E^n		$E^r < E^s$	$E^r \equiv E^s$	$E^r > E^s$
$\subseteq$	Contained In				
		$E^n < E^r$	had slept	has slept	will have slept
			~~ []	~~~~~ []	~~~~~ []
			*	*	*
Aspect: E^n/E^r		$E^n \equiv E^r$	slept	sleeps	will sleep
			[~~~~~]	[~~~~~]	[~~~~~]
			*	*	*
		$E^n \subseteq E^r$	was sleeping	is sleeping	will be sleeping
			~~[~]~~	~~[~]~~	~~[~]~~
			*	*	*

Several points are in order. First, the *Aktionsart* class of the predicate matters. Different kinds of predicates have different kinds of temporal profiles: there are zero-state, or 'timeless', narrated events (*two plus two equals four*); there are one-state narrated events (*a man lay on the floor*); and there are two-state narrated events (*he died*). As emphasized by Bull and Klein, the inherent aspect of the predicate at issue frames the narrated event, and this in turn frames what interval the reference event is in relation to.

Second, while we speak of events (inheriting Jakobson's terminology), it might be best to speak of intervals or spans: each of the three 'events' might best be understood as an interval, with not only a position (when it occurs per se), but also a beginning, an end, and a duration. As stressed by Bull and Klein, intervals may not only be before, after, or simultaneous with each other, but they may also fully contain, be contained in, or partially overlap with one another. Indeed, many adverbs not only encode E^n/E^r and E^r/E^s relations but, in doing so, also highlight the beginning or end of a state. Table 4.3, for example, diagrams the prototypic functions of four common adverbs in English.

(*) and the reference event ([]), and the relation between the speech event (*) and the narrated event (~~~), one should not read off the relation between the speech event and the narrated event – except relatively.

Table 4.3. *Four common adverbs in English*

Adverb	Diagram	Gloss
already	<~[~]~	onset of E^n before E^r
still	~[~]~>	offset of E^n after E^r
not yet	[] <~~~	onset of E^n before E^r
no longer	~~~> []	offset of E^n after E^r

And finally, exactly what determines the time (or time-span) of the reference event (or interval) is quite varied. In Table 4.1, we had a narrated reference event: *when you entered the room*. In Table 4.2, it was left unsaid. And in the text at issue, such reference events are often previously occurring narrated events. In short, such reference events are often only recoverable through context and co-occurring text, and relatively elliptically at best. Indeed, a common situation, discussed at length by Bull (1960), is that the reference event *is* the speech event, and so the grammatical category of aspect often functions like the grammatical category of tense.

In the textual analysis that follows, then, a number of questions need to be answered for each of the constructions at issue. What is the aspectual profile of the narrated event (e.g. zero-state, one-state, two-state)? How is the narrated event related to the reference event (e.g. before, simultaneous, after; contained, containing, overlapping)? How is the reference event set (e.g. relative to another narrated event, relative to the speech event, relative to a calendrical event)? How is the reference event related to the speech event (e.g. before, simultaneous, after; contained, containing, overlapping)? How is the speech event set (e.g. deictically, relative to another narrated event via reported speech, etc.)? What kinds of formal categories are used to encode such relations (e.g. inflections, derivations, adverbs, complementizers)? What semantic features do such categories encode and implicate (e.g. relations, intervals, orderings, and so forth)? And finally, what pragmatic and discursive functions do such features serve (foregrounding, sequencing, etc.)?

4.   Predicates: inherent aspect and verbal inflection

Table 4.4 summarizes the semantic features encoded by stative and non-stative predicates as they interact with inflectional affixes encoding tense and aspect. It also shows the number of tokens of each type that occurred in the text (where the italicized number indicates that those tokens occurred in reported speech). The work of Stewart on Q'eqchi' morphology is very important for the present analysis; however, my conclusions about the semantic features encoded by such forms are quite different.[2]

---

[2] Compare Stewart (1980a, 1980b).

Table 4.4. *Verbal encoding (inflectional and periphrastic) of temporal features*

	Form	Semantic features (typical function)	Profile	Tokens
Stative predicates (inherently imperfective)	*-Ø/k*	unmarked (present tense)	~[~]~	55
	-(a)q	future tense (optative mood)	~[~]~ *	0
Non-stative predicates (umarked)	*na(k)-*	unmarked (present tense, habitual aspect)	[~~~]	63, 7
	x-	perfect(ive) aspect (past tense)	~~~ []	20, 7
	ki-	perfect(ive) aspect, unexperienced evidential (past tense)	~~~ []	113, 2
	ta-	prospective aspect (future tense)	[] ~~~	3, *21*
	Ø-	imperative mood	NA	0, *17*
	chi-	optative mood	NA	0, *5*
	mi-	optative mood, negative status	NA	0, *2*
Non-finite constructions	*yoo-k INF*	progressive aspect only with non-statives, qua activities	~[~]~	12, *1*
	yoo-q INF	progressive aspect, future tense (optative mood) only with non-statives, qua activities	~[~]~ *	0
	INF -e	E^r at onset of target state of E^n only with two-state non-statives	NA	4

At a very basic level, we may describe the inherent aspect of the predicate itself. In Q'eqchi', there are two main classes of predicates: *statives* and *non-statives*. The former is the marked class: it is smaller in size, and more constrained in distribution. All predicates within the stative class are intransitive; and both their person-number and their tense-aspect-mood marking is suffixed. For example, *chunchu-k-eb'* (be_seated-Pres-A(3p), or 'they are seated'). Many involve reduplicated roots, derived from non-stative predicates: *chapok* (to grab) → *chapcho* (to be grabbed). Included within this class are three of the most frequently occurring predicates in the language: the existential predicate *wank* (to exist, to have, to be located); the progressive auxiliary predicate *yook* (to do); and the speaking predicate *chank* (to say).[3]

In contrast, the class of non-stative predicates is larger in size, and less constrained in distribution. Their *Aktionsart* classes run the gamut of possibility: activities, achievements, accomplishments, and so on. Predicates within this class may be transitive as well as intransitive; their person-number marking is prefixed; and their tense-aspect-mood marking (itself turning on a much larger

---

[3] It should be emphasized that *chank* is the only stative predicate that is semantically more like a perfective action. In some Mayan languages, the verb of reported speech is highly defective as a verb (Lucy 1993b), and is almost a particle (undergoing little if any inflection or derivation). And so it may be that *chank* is just a defective verb, and only looks like a member of the stative class. Also included here is the class of *copulas*. This is the unmarked predicate, having no lexical content at all. Copula constructions are often zero-state events (*John is a man*); but they may also be one-state events (*John is happy*). In such cases, a tense-aspect suffix may occur on the predicating noun or adjective in question, as with any stative predicate, either *-Ø/k* or *-(a)q*.

paradigm) is prefixed. For example, *t-at-in-ch'oolani* (Fut-A(2s)-E(1s)-care), or 'I will care for you'. Finally, perhaps the most obvious temporal distinction between stative and non-stative predicates is that the former are inherently imperfective (the narrated event is construed as unbounded, and the reference event is usually contained within it: ~[~]~); whereas the latter are unmarked in this regard.

There are two inflectional forms that may occur with stative predicates: *-Ø/k* and *-(a)q*. In this text, only the first occurred; and it may be considered the unmarked form (even occurring on non-finite, or citation, forms). While the stative predicate is itself inherently imperfective, this form says nothing about the relation between the reference event and the speech event. See, for example, scene 7, in which it is used in reported speech to mark a present state (*wan*: there is), and scene 14, inter alia, in which it is used to talk about a prior state (*kanko*: is tied). And, indeed, such constructions are used to represent future events, present events, and past events. The second inflectional form *-(a)q* is often said to indicate 'future tense' (as an E^n/E^s relation, as per Jakobson's framework). We might say, rather, that while the stative predicate is itself inherently imperfective, the reference event is itself after the speech event. In short, while both *-Ø/k* and *-(a)q* occur with inherently imperfective stative predicates, *-Ø/k* is unmarked with respect to tense, and *-(a)q* is marked for future tense. Because members of this paradigm do not have any explicitly marked modal operators to contrast with, I suspect that future tense may also function as prospective aspect, optative mood, and irrealis status as it does in many present-day speech communities. However, given the fact that this text contains no tokens of stative predicates inflected with *-(a)q*, I do not want to speculate further.[4]

Non-stative predicates come in a wide variety of *Aktionsart* classes. There are activities, states, and state-changes (punctual and durative); and any one of these might be caused or not. In certain cases, the derivational morphology of the predicate reveals its class; but usually Vendler-Dowty test frames (of a modified sort, as adapted to Q'eqchi') would be the only way to know for sure; and, as is well known, the same predicate may test differently depending on small shifts in meaning. For most situations, only the activity, state, and state-change properties will be at issue. In general, just as statives are inherently imperfective, non-statives are often perfective: the beginning, end, or entirety of a state is being profiled.

The inflectional prefix *na(k)-* is often glossed as 'present habitual'. It usually marks habitual aspect; but it is unmarked for tense. Habitual aspect may itself be understood as quantifying over reference events: that is, it indicates that there is a set of reference events, usually periodically arranged, such that

---

[4] The suffix *-(a)q* also occurs with optative mood, and *-q* might function to mark not so much that the reference event is after the speech event, but rather that the reference event is in a different (non-real) world from the speech event.

the narrated event occurred at each one of them ([~~~] ... [~~~] ... [~~~]). The reference events themselves may be indicated by adverbs like 'every day' (*rajlal kutan*); or, more often, they are inferable via context. For example, it may be widely known that the action described is undertaken daily (such as cooking), or undertaken yearly (such as planting). In scene 3, for example, the switch from *ki-* inflected forms to *na(k)-* inflected forms resonates with the daily activities of the moon, as correlated with the day-to-day movements of the sun (as narrated in scenes 4–6). This inflectional form is, of course, the unmarked form of the paradigm, and so can also function as simple present (no habitualness implied), as well as nomic present (true for all time, or timeless); indeed, it may also refer to events that occur in the past, in the future, or in a possible world.

The inflectional prefixes *x-* and *ki-* belong together insofar as both are marked for perfect(ive) aspect. That is, they indicate that at least part of the reference interval occurs after the relevant state of the narrated event. Exactly how far after the narrated event is not specified. And nothing is said about the relation between the reference event and the speech event. As mentioned, the reference event is often taken to be the speech event, and so they may function like past tense. Indeed, linguists have called them 'recent past' and 'remote past', respectively. The difference between them, rather, is that *ki-* is also marked for unexperienced evidentiality – that is, it indicates that the narrated event was not experienced by the speaker, and is rather known through another source: inference, second-hand speech, or, as is most often the case in this narrative, mythic speech.[5] Recall the discussion in section 4 of chapter 3, in which such source events were compared to reference events, commitment events, and deontic events. To best see the evidential function of *ki-*, first note that the majority of utterances in this mythic retelling are inflected with *ki-* (except in cases of directly reported speech); moreover, the two cases of directly reported speech in which *ki-* occurs (scenes 17a and 20b) involve a character who has just seen some effect and inferred its cause. In the first, the moon is missing, so her father infers that the sun must have taken her (*kielq'an*). In the second, the moon sees storm clouds, and infers that her father must have sent her uncle, Thunder, to kill them (*kixtaqla*). We will return to evidentiality at the end of chapter 5.

The inflectional prefix *ta-* is usually understood as 'future tense'. As will be shown here, it is best understood as prospective aspect: the reference event occurs before the narrated event. In particular, it occurs in non-future-tense

---

[5] In present-day Q'eqchi', as it was spoken in my fieldsite, this is complicated by the fact that women and old people seemed more conservative in their usage (using this form to mark inference), whereas some men tended to use it only for narrating mythic and remote events. In this way, for some speakers, it is beginning to function more like remote past tense. And this should make sense: perfective aspect plus unexperienced evidential easily functions as past tense.

locales, and so is inherently non-deictic. Again, as with perfect aspect, the reference event may be taken to be the speech event, and so this form frequently functions as future tense. While predicates inflected with *ta-* usually occur in directly reported speech, it is useful to examine the tokens in which it occurs in normal speech (scenes 5, 15, and 29b). In scene 5, it occurs in a dependent clause (*tanume'q*), where the independent clause is inflected with *nak-*. In scene 15, it occurs in a dependent clause (*tixkanab'*), where the independent clause is inflected with *ki-*. And in scene 29b, it occurs in a counterfactive construction (*tixnaw*). These contexts most clearly show that it is not marked for future tense, but rather prospective aspect.

Finally, there are three inflectional forms that are not marked for tense or aspect, but rather for mood and polarity: *Ø-*, *chi-*, and *mi-*. The first of these is just a standard imperative. Its function may be seen in scenes 7, 12a, 12b, 15, 16, and 26. The second is an optative, functioning in scenes 4 and 10. And the third usually functions as a negative imperative, but may also function as a negative optative. Tokens may be found in scenes 12a and 15. In the text at issue, all these tokens are confined to reported speech. And not much will be said about them in this chapter, except insofar as they relate to aspect-encoding adverbs.

Any non-stative, inherently perfective predicate may function like an imperfective predicate via a progressive construction, which itself involves the stative predicate *yook* (to do), the particle *chi*, and the non-finite form of the non-stative predicate. Even though both constructions are diagrammed as ~[~]~, the predicate is construed as an activity not a state. Nevertheless, the narrated activity contains the reference interval. (This difference between activities and states is not captured by the diagrams.) For example, if *nak-Ø-aatinak* (Pres-A(3s)-speak) means 'he speaks' ([~~~]), *yoo-Ø-Ø chi aatinak* (do-Pres-A(3s) Comp speak) means 'he is speaking' (~[~]~). In other words, the narrated event is 'ongoing' – its beginning was before the reference interval and its end will be after the reference interval (if, indeed, it is even construed as having a beginning or end). Examples of the progressive construction may be found in scenes 8, 11, 12a, 12c,13a, 20a, 24a, 24b, 25, 28, 30a, and 31.[6]

In addition to the progressive, there is one other kind of non-finite construction that is used with non-stative predicates. It involves a non-finite predicate followed by a relational noun which usually marks dative case (i.e. the recipient of a gift, the addressee of an utterance, etc.). For example, *xik w-e* (go E(1s)-RN) means 'I'm off'. (This is often translated with the Spanish construction *me voy*, which is sometimes said to foreground that one is leaving the

---

[6] While the auxiliary predicate *yoo* of such progressive-aspect constructions can be inflected either with *-k* or *-q*, there are no tokens of the latter. This would presumably mark future tense and progressive aspect.

current place, rather than the subsequent destination: i.e. one is going *away*.) In this construction, one indicates that one is 'already going' or that one's going is already under way – the preparations are made, one has set down the path, and so on. Often, these involve predicates of movement, and achievement predicates more generally: *elk* (to leave), *ewuk* (to become night). There is only one scene (20a) in which they occur in the text. (Though scene 18 may also have a token.) Several occur there, at once, in parallel; and two of these tokens occur with the adverb *ak* (already). This is a crucial scene in which the sun and moon have run as far as they can (to the edge of the sea), night has fallen, and the moon's uncle, Thunder, has finally caught up with them in order to kill them. The adverb *ak* (discussed below) indicates that the onset of the narrated event is before the reference event, further highlighting the sense of 'it's too late' – there is nowhere left to run, and their fate is sealed.

5.   Temporal adverbs and adpositions

Table 4.5 lists all the inherently temporal arguments, adverbs, adpositions, negations, and complementizers that occurred in the text. From left to right, it lists the morphological form of the construction, an English gloss, and then the scene numbers in which tokens of such constructions occur. In this way, the relative frequency of each construction is shown, as well as the context in which it occurs (reported speech tokens are in italics). Most of the constructions mark aspectual relations (E^n/E^r), but a few mark tense-like relations (E^r/E^s). Many are inherently interclausal, and are thus similar in function to the constructions described in chapter 3: they specify how one narrated event relates to another narrated event (as a reference event). As will be seen, the underlying meanings turn on speed (how fast), duration (how long), frequency (how often), and position (when). From top to bottom, the constructions have been loosely ordered as a function of scope: from relatively narrow-scope constructions at the top (arguments and adverbs), to relatively wide-scope constructions at the bottom (negations and complementizers). As may be seen, only a handful of such constructions are used with any frequency in the text.

As shown in Table 4.5, there are only two tokens of an argument encoding a temporal relation. These, then, are instances where temporality – here as a privileged period (e.g. *kutan*, or 'day') – is explicitly referred to, and some property is predicated of it (e.g. *nume'k*, or 'passing'). To be sure, insofar as the movements of B'alamq'e parallel the movements of the sun, every narrated event in which he is a topic is potentially construable as temporal, or referring to time. Indeed, the same predicate (*nume'k*) is also used several times to describe the movements of B'alamq'e (in the guise of a hunter) as he passes before Po's house each day (scenes 4, 5, 7). So, as will be further explored in later sections, the parallelism is quite strong between implicit and explicit

Table 4.5. *Temporal features encoded by arguments, adverbs, adpositions, negations, and complementizers*

Form-class	Semantic type	Morphology	English gloss	Tokens (by scene number; italic if reported speech)
Arguments	**subject of verb**	*xnume' kutan*	'(as the) day passed'	12c
		kinume' oxlajuj kutan	'(when) thirteen days passed'	26
Adverbs	**onset or offset of E^n**	*ak*	'already'	18, 20a, 20a, 20a, 24a
		ink'a' chik	'no longer'	8, 15, 17b, 18, 26
		ink'a' ajwi'	'still not', 'not yet'	10, *16*
	solar-centric	*eq'la*	'early'	17a
		q'ojyin	'(in the) darkness/night'	15
		ewu	'(in the) afternoon/dusk'	14
		(toj) hulaj	'(in the) morning', 'tomorrow' 'the next day'	24a
	deictic	*anaqwan*	'now'	*15, 16, 16,* 20b, *30d*
		ho'on … iho'on	'now'	*17a, 29b*
	speed	*tikto*	'immediately'	*15,* 17c, 27
		yal jun	'at once'	*16,* 17a, 17c
		junpaat	'quickly', 'soon'	8, 16, 17a, 20b, 24b
		timil	'slowly'	*12a,* 25, 29b
	frequency	*wi' chik* or *b'i' chik*	'again'	8, 10, 12c, 15, *16,* 18, 27, 30a
		hulaj hulaj	'each day'	25
		junelik	'always'	13c, 15
		rajlal kutan	'every day'	6, 6
		jun wa ka' wa	'one time, two times'	17a
	duration	*najt*	'for a long time' 'lengthily'	18
Adpositions	**meta- narrative**	*sa' mayer kutan*	'in olden days'	2
		chalen a'an	'since then'	31
	solar-centric	*chiru oxib' kutan*	'after three days'	10
		sa' oxlaju kutan	'in thirteen days'	*24c*
		chi kutan	'during the day'	6, 31

Table 4.5. (*cont.*)

Form-class	Semantic type	Morphology	English gloss	Tokens (by scene number; italic if reported speech)
		chiru q'ojyin	'during the night'	6, 31
		chiru k'iila kutan ...	'during the many days and nights'	26
	speed	*sa' aanil*	'quickly' ('running')	8, *16*, 20b, 30a
		sa' junpaat	'quickly' ('soon')	*15, 26*
		chi junpaat seeb'	'quickly' ('soon', 'hurrying')	27
	establish E^r	*sa' ROOT-ik*	'at the time of E^n'	4, 17c, 18, 19, 24a, 25, 29c
Negations	frequency	*chi maa-wa*	'not once'	*29a*
		maa-jun (wa)	'not once'	*12a*, 17a
		maa-jaruj	'never'	*15*
		maa-jaruj tana chik	'never again, perhaps'	28
		maa-min (tana)	'in no way'	5, *10, 16*, 30c
Comple-mentizers	establish E^r	*toj, toja'*	'when' (establishes narrated E^r), 'still'	2, 3, 9, *10*, 15, *16*, 17b, 18, 18, 24a, *24c*, 25, 26, 28, 30c
		jo'q'e	'when'	3, 5, *7*
		naq	'when'	4

solar-centric phases. In the two constructions tabulated here, however, it is done explicitly rather than by proxy.

The class of adverbs encoding temporal relations is the largest. Such adverbs are usually non-inflected particles, or combinations of such particles, which occur before a finite predicate. Several such adverbs, however, occur after the finite predicate (e.g. *wi' chik*). And one such adverb is circumflexed around a finite predicate (e.g. *ho'on ... iho'on*). As may be seen in Table 4.5, the first three adverbs (*ak, ink'a' chik, ink'a' ajwi'*) turn on the beginning or end of a narrated event. The next four (*eq'la, q'ojyin, ewu, hulaj*) establish solar-centric reference events. The next two (*anaqwan, ho'on ... iho'on*) are deictic, turning on the relation between the reference event and the speech event. The next four (*tikto, yal jun, junpaat, timil*) turn on speed, or how quickly the narrated event occurs after the reference event, itself usually the preceding narrated event. The next five (*wi' chik, hulaj hulaj, junelik, rajlal kutan, jun wa ka' wa*) turn on frequency, quantifying over reference events. And the last one (*najt*) turns on duration, establishing how long a narrated event lasted.

The first three adverbial constructions are similar in function to the English adverbials 'already', 'no longer' and 'not yet', which were diagrammed in Table 4.3. The adverb *ak* (already) indicates that the beginning (of the relevant state) of the narrated event occurred before the reference event (<~[~]~). The adverb *ink'a' chik* (no longer) is similar in function to *ak*: it indicates that, by the time of the reference event, the narrated event has ended (~~~> []). The adverb *ink'a' ajwi'* (not yet) is also similar: it indicates that, at the time of the reference event, the narrated event has not yet begun ([] <~~~). Each of these adverbs, then, highlights the beginning or end of a narrated event, and relates this onset or offset to a reference event. Not only do we have a similar set of constructions in English, but we also have *still*, an adverb which indicates that, at the time of the reference event, the end of the narrated event has not yet occurred (~[~]~>). As will be discussed below, the particle *toj* often has a function similar to 'still'. Finally, note that two of these adverbs include *ink'a'*, the marker of wide-scope negation. The other marker of negation used in adverbs (*maa-*) has narrower scope, and its presence establishes a subclass all to itself in Table 4.5.

The next four adverbs indicate when a narrated event occurs relative to a reference event, which itself turns on a phase of the day: early in a day, or morning/dawn (*eq'la*); late in a day, or afternoon/dusk (*ewu*); at night (*q'ojyin*); and the next morning (*hulaj*). Here, then, a day (*kutan*), or solar period, is not homogeneous, but rather has phases; and each of these phases may be used to establish a reference event, or interval, relative to which the time of a narrated event may be established. As mentioned in the introduction, such solar-centric phases are themselves often correlated with the movements of the main character, B'alamq'e, who is himself the sun in disguise. One key incident (scene 23), discussed at length in section 8, involves the passing of one day into the next, which itself is paralleled by the sun's rolling himself into the water one evening and emerging the next morning. The construction *hulaj* ('the next day', or 'in the morning') often functions as the deictic 'tomorrow', and this is how it is usually translated. But this gloss is really only appropriate when the reference event is treated as the speech event. It is part of larger, somewhat productive paradigm which turns on two orders and several magnitudes. (See Table 4.6.) This construction often means the (morning of the) day after the reference event, and thereby functions as a kind of aspect: E^n/E^r.

The adverbs *anaqwan* (now) and *ho'on ... iho'on* (now) are the only obviously deictic temporal constructions in the text: they relate the reference event to the speech event. As may be seen, they only occurred in reported speech. The adverb *anaqwan* occurs twice after a command (including a hortative construction: *now let's go*), in scenes 15 and 16; and twice in a copula construction (*now*

Table 4.6. *Solar-centric constructions*

Root meaning	E^n/E^r (before)	E^r/E^s (after)
hulajik (its arrival), *ewu* (dusk)	*hulaj* (in one day)	*ewer* (one day ago, yesterday)
kab' (two)	*kab'ej* (in two days)	*kab'ejer* (two days ago)
ox (three)	*oxej* (in three days)	*oxejer* (three days ago)
kaa'ib' (four)	*kwehej, kohej* (in four days)	*kwehejer, kohejer* (four days ago)
hoob' (five)	*ob'ix, hob'ej* (in five days)	*hob'ejer* (five days ago)
hab' (year, rain)	–	*jun hab'er* (one year ago)
may (old)	–	*mayer* (long ago)
najt (far)	–	*najter* (long ago)
rub'el (beneath)	*rub'elaj* (before)	–

it is good), in scenes 16 and 30d. Its use in scene 20b is the most interesting, as it occurs with a predicate that is inflected for perfect aspect: *anaqwan x-oo'-oso'* (now Perf-A(1p)-be_finished). This utterance is spoken by the moon, just after she has inferred that her father sent her uncle to kill them. It may be glossed as 'now we are finished' or 'now we are done for'. This is more evidence that the inflectional prefix *x-* is doing the work of perfect aspect and not past tense (for which such a construction would be contradictory). In particular, perfect aspect (of the inflection) functions fine with present tense (of the adverb): *anaqwan* indicates that the reference event contains, or is simultaneous with, the speech event; and *x-* indicates that the relevant state of the narrated event (i.e. the state of being finished) is before the reference event. Impressionistically, the construction says: 'it's too late' or 'we're already dead'. Finally, the adverb *ho'on … iho'on* is usually circumflexed around a predicate. Like *anaqwan*, it is glossed as 'now': the reference event occurs at the same time as, or contains, the speech event. In scene 17a, it occurs with *ta-*, providing more evidence that *ta-* is a marker of prospective aspect and not future tense.

The next four adverbs (*tikto, yal jun, junpaat, timil*) might be understood to mark *speed*, or 'how fast', in a very loose sense. Indeed, speed itself, while on the boundary of what might be considered temporal, is usually understood as the change in distance divided by the change in time – and it is not clear that any of these constructions are encoding speed in such a strict sense. Rather, most of these constructions might be better characterized as marking 'soonness' or 'quickness'. The adverbs *tikto* and *yal jun* indicate that the narrated event occurred immediately after the reference event, where the reference event is itself usually the last narrated event. In effect, they say that the current narrated event occurred 'on the heels of' the last narrated event. In this way, they mark interclausal relations. They are often best glossed with an English adverb like 'immediately' or 'at once'. In scenes 17a and 17c, for example, Tzuultaq'a has two key actions (grabbing his mirror and grabbing his blow-gun) qualified by such adverbs, in both cases indicating that the actions followed immediately after a decision he made, or a conclusion he came to. The adverb *junpaat*, itself probably a contraction of the prepositional phrase *sa' junpaat* (in an instant) involves the morpheme *jun* (one) and *paat* (bit). This latter unit is non-gradable. And such a construction is often used with achievement predicates, indicating the state was achieved quickly. For example, in scene 8, we are told that the sun quickly gathered himself up (after slipping on the cooked corn that the moon laid on his path). And in scene 17a it is used to qualify Tzuultaq'a's getting up from bed when his daughter does not respond to his calls. Finally, the adverb *timil* is best glossed as 'slowly'. It describes the manner in which an action was undertaken (rather than the speed at which an event occurred), and often indexes a human concern like carefulness or anxiety. In scene 12a, for example, the moon uses it when she tells her father to slowly aim his blow-gun at the sun (who is disguised as a bird, and who she would like to protect from harm).

The next five adverbs mark iterations or frequency: *wi' chik, hulaj hulaj, junelik, rajlal kutan, jun wa ka' wa*. In some sense, they quantify over reference events. Some constructions indicate that a narrated event occurred at all reference events: *junelik* (always). In other words, no matter what reference event is chosen, the narrated event contains it (*John was always happy*), or it contains the narrated event (*John was always sneezing*). That is, at any point in time the narrated event holds. Sometimes the reference events are periodically occurring intervals: *hulaj hulaj* (day after day) and *rajlal kutan* (every day). Like the set of adverbs just discussed, these iterations are solar-centric. The construction *wi' chik* (again) means that, just as the narrated event happened during a previous reference interval, it also happened during the current reference interval. It does for predicates what *jun chik* (another) does for nouns: compare 'he did it again' and 'I'll have another'. Finally, the frequency with which a narrated event occurs may be precisely specified and counted out: *jun wa ka' wa* (once, twice). The word *wa* is a noun meaning 'time' (as in 'two times' or 'twice'). It is also the word for tortilla, a round and flat object. It functions like a classifier, and should be compared with a similar construction used in Nahuatl calendars (Kockelman 1998), an areally related language with a similar time-reckoning system.

And the last adverb marks duration, or 'how long'. Usually, the adverb *najt* functions as a distance marker (*far*). In scene 18, however, it is used to describe how long a certain state lasted (*for a long time Tzuultaq'a remained fallen like this*). Sometimes this same root shows up with the suffix *-er*, which is best glossed as 'ago'. It indicates that the reference event occurred a long time before the speech event, and so is inherently deictic. (Recall Table 4.6.)

The set of adpositions all involve a preposition (*chi, sa', chalen*), or a preposition with a relational noun (*chiru*), where the dependent argument of such a head is a temporal construction. Most of these constructions occur before the predicate but, in certain imperative and hortative constructions, they can occur after the predicate.

The first two constructions (*sa' mayer kutan*, *chalen a'an*) are meta-textual, the first occurring at the beginning of the text (scene 2), and the second occurring at the end of the text (scene 31). They locate the entire narrative, as a collection of individual narrated events (E^{n1}, E^{n2}, ...), relative to the speech event (and worldly, geocentric events more generally). The first, *sa' mayer kutan* (in olden days), establishes a large-scale reference event (or rather, reference interval) which is to contain all the narrated events (by virtue of locating the initial scene-setting narrated events (scene 2) which all later narrated events are implicitly related to), and which is established relative to the speech event. In particular, *mayer* (olden) is made of two morphemes: *may* (old) and *-er*. The second morpheme is also used on numbers (and some seasons) to indicate how many such periods ago a reference event occurred relative to the speech event: *jun hab'-er* (one rain/year ago), *oxej-er* (three days ago), *kab'aj-er* (two days ago), and so forth. (Recall Table 4.6.) As may be seen by the glosses, its function is similar to the English postposition 'ago'.[7] The second construction, *chalen a'an*, occurs at the end of the text, and is used to establish an interval (E^r) relative to the set of narrated events ('ever since the events just recounted') – in particular, relative to the last event recounted (when the sun takes the moon's hand, and leads her up into the sky). The final construction, then, narrates what occurs in that interval, and implicitly up until at least the *now* of the speech event: the leading of women by men. Besides person and evidentiality, both of which are established relative to the participants in the speech event (and leaving aside constructions used in reported speech, such as the adverbs *anaqwan* and *ho'on ... iho'on*), these are the only inherently deictic temporal constructions used in the narrative – i.e. the only constructions that relate the narrated events (or reference events) to the speech event that was taking place over one hundred years ago.

The next five constructions locate a narrated event by reference to a solar-centric interval (turning on some phase of the day, or period of a day). As with adverbs, the only unit ever used in this text is 'day' (*kutan*) and, to some degree, its marked complement 'night' or 'darkness' (*q'ojyin*). In Q'eqchi', as in English, the word *kutan* (day) is unmarked relative to *q'ojyin* (night or darkness), and can either mean an entire twenty-four-hour period, or just the relatively sunny part of such a period. No other relatively periodic temporal intervals are used – such as hour, week, month, or year. (Though certain phases of the moon may be inferred, as discussed below. And the Q'eqchi' have an

---

[7] My sense is that the suffix *-er* is deictic (E^r/E^s), and the suffix *-Vl* is non-deictic (E^n/E^r). The latter does get a deictic reading as 'future' via its contrast with *-er*. But, as partly revealed by the fact that *-er* is suffixed onto *-Vl*, it is not that the latter marks future and the former marks past, but rather that the latter is aspectual and the former tensed.

extensive lunar-centric reckoning system that is not used here.) The first two constructions locate a narrated event by quantifying the distance to a reference event by means of such a construction: *chiru oxib' kutan* (after three days); *sa' oxlaju kutan* (in thirteen days). The next two constructions establish the time of a narrated event by reference to a given phase of the day: *chi kutan* (during the day); *chiru q'ojyin* (during the night). And the last, somewhat mixed, construction turns on both the phase of day (and night) and the number of days (and nights): *chiru k'iila kutan jo' wi' q'ojyin* (during the many days and nights). It is used in reported speech, in scene 26, when a woman complains to the sun about how long she had to guard the jars containing the moon's remains.

There are three adpositional constructions which might be said to mark 'speed': *sa' aanil, sa' junpaat, chi junpaat seeb'*. The adposition *sa' aanil* turns on the root 'to run', and might best be glossed in terms of manner: 'running'. And the two constructions involving *jun-paat* (an instant) really indicate how soon after a reference event the narrated event occurs: 'soon after'. The root *seeb'*, which occurs with the last construction, is usually found in a reflexive transitive construction: *seeb'a aawib'*, or 'hurry!' (See, for example, scenes 16 and 26.) Again, it is best understood as manner, rather than speed: 'hurrying'. Such constructions, then, are at the border of what might be called 'temporality'. Almost all tokens of each of these constructions occur immediately pre-predicate (and usually sentence initial). But there are two exceptions: *sa' aanil* is used once at the end of a hortative construction (in reported speech, scene 16); and *sa' junpaat* is used once at the end of a prospective-aspect construction (again in reported speech, scene 26). Taking into account adverbial constructions marking speed as well, it should be noted that there are six constructions marking high speed, and only one construction marking low speed. Indeed, as tokens rather than types, there are twenty-one constructions marking high speed, and only three constructions marking low speed. So note the relative salience of such different types of manner.

There is one derivational suffix that is directly relevant to temporality: *-ik*. It derives a possessed noun (which specifies the time of an event) from a predicate (which denotes such an event); and may thereby transform a narrated event into a reference event. For example, if *kamk* means 'to die', *x-kam-ik* (E(3s)-die-Nom) means 'his time of dying' or 'his death'. Such derived nouns often occur as the argument of the preposition *sa'* (at). (See, for example, scenes 4, 24a, and 29c.) And such an adposition, when occurring as the adjunct of a predicate, indicates that the narrated event (denoted by the predicate) occurred at the same time as the reference event (encoded by the derived possessed NP). This construction should be compared with spatial constructions involving two verb phrases (VPs), one of which is dependent on the other (and marked by the enclitic *wi'*). (See, for example, scenes 4, 6, 7, 11, and 16, inter alia.) Such constructions indicate that the event denoted by the predicate in the independent clause occurred in the same place as the event denoted by the predicate in the dependent clause. Such a *wi'*-marked construction may usually be glossed as 'at the place of', and so is similar in its relational function to *-ik*.

The next four constructions all involve the negative prefix *maa-* (not). They serve two functions: first, they establish a kind of reference event; and second, they indicate that the narrated event did not occur at such a reference event. Strictly speaking, the first construction (*chi maa-wa*) is an adposition, headed by the preposition *chi*. It indicates that there is not a single reference event (or reference interval) at which the narrated event occurs. It may be glossed as 'not once', or 'at no instance'. The second construction *maa-jun wa* ('not one time' or 'not once') is similar. The construction *maa-jaruj* indicates that, for all time (any reference event you choose), the narrated event does not obtain. In contrast to the construction *maa-jaruj*, the construction *maa-jaruj tana chik* (not ever again perhaps) indicates that, while the narrated event has occurred before the reference event, it will no longer occur at any possible reference event after that reference event. Compare the construction *ink'a' chik* (no longer), which was discussed above. The *tana* in this construction marks afactive status (perhaps, possibly), indicating that the speaker is not fully committed to the proposition. In general, status (*tana*) has scope over polarity (*maa-*), which has scope over aspect. Finally, the construction *maa-min* ('no way' or 'in no manner') is on the boundary of this category. It seems to indicate that there was no means or manner by which the narrated event could obtain, but may also be glossed as 'never' in certain contexts – it seems to do for possibility (in no world) what *maa-jaruj* does for temporality (at no time).

The last three constructions (*toj, jo'q'e, naq*) are clause-initial particles which indicate that the narrated event denoted by the clause in question is a reference event to which another more focal narrated event is related. They usually function as the first clause in the following kind of construction: 'when X was happening, Y happened', where X is the relatively backgrounded event headed by the particle, and Y is the relatively foregrounded event. In particular, the particles *jo'q'e* and *naq* function as relatively standard 'when' constructions. *Jo'q'e* also functions as a wh-word. And *naq* also functions as a full-clause complementizer (that) and, following the dative construction *r-e*, a purposive (in order that). (These other functions of *naq* are not counted among the tokens in Table 4.5.) In short, the main function of all three of these constructions is interclausal: the relatively backgrounded clause, headed by the particle in question, is a reference event at which time, or during which time, the relatively foregrounded clause is said to occur.

As may be seen in Table 4.5, *toj* is by far the most frequently used of these constructions. Its meaning is likewise the most complex and variable; and so it deserves a more detailed discussion. It may head a background clause (E^r) which *precedes* a foregrounded clause (E^n), indicating that the second event occurred at the same time as the first event (or within an interval established by the first event). In this usage, it is most similar to *jo'q'e* and *naq*, and is glossed as 'when'. (See, for example, scenes 2, 3, 24a, 25, and 26.)

It may also head a backgrounded clause (E^r) which *succeeds* a foregrounded clause (E^n). In this usage, it may be glossed as 'but' or 'still', so far as the backgrounded clause explains why the event denoted by the foregrounded clause did not occur. (See, for example, scenes 15, 17b, and 18.) Recall the discussion above about the adverbs *ak* (already), *ink'a' chik* (no longer), and *ink'a' ajwi'* (not yet). In some sense, it is saying that the previous narrated event occurred while the *toj*-headed narrated event was still happening – and thus could not happen: *he asked her to go, but (at that time of asking) she was (still) scared* (scene 15).

It may head a clause which is not syntactically related to another clause, but to a presupposed reference event (usually the narrated event denoted by the previous utterance). In such a function, it is often best glossed as 'but', 'still', 'but still', or 'however'. In scene 16, for example, it has scope over the adverb *anaqwan* (now), which encodes the relation between the reference event and the speech event (indicating they are simultaneous, or that the reference event contains the speech event), and the *toj* uses the reference event established by *anaqwan* to set the time of the narrated event established by the hortative: *so now (finally, after all that) let's go!*

Finally, *toj* may establish a reference world, or commitment event, relative to which a narrated world could occur: and hence interacts with the grammatical category of status in counterfactual conditionals. In such a usage, it is glossed as 'unless' or 'not if'. In scene 10, for example, it specifies what world would have to be the case for the consequent not to occur: *I would die from the cold, unless I were wrapped in the threads of the ceiba tree*. In other words, rather than establishing the time at which something occurs, it establishes the world in which something occurs. Compare the contrast, discussed above, between *maa-min* and *maa-jaruj*.[8] Here, again, we see the underlying similarity between the three-event nature of tense and aspect and the three-event nature of mood and status (Kockelman 2005a), a connection that will be further explored in chapter 5.

6.   Temporality: from linguistic encoding to cultural framing

If the last three sections were analytic in nature, focusing on individual categories from the standpoint of grammatical structure, the next three sections are synthetic in nature, focusing on co-occurring categories within an ongoing

---

[8] All the constructions just discussed are morphosyntactic in nature, and it is not terribly difficult to argue that they encode features which turn on temporal relations: either E^n/E^r or E^r/E^s. One more construction should be mentioned, so far as it is used in the text and might plausibly be considered temporal: interclausal relations of the kind discussed in chapter 3.

narrative. The point is not to interpret exhaustively each sentence or scene in the text, but rather to take several relatively interesting examples and walk the reader through their nexus of forms, features, and functions. Some of these examples are important because they are replicas, occurring again and again throughout the narrative; and some of these examples are important because they are singularities, occurring only once in the narrative to special effect. All have been chosen for their relevance to the four themes mentioned in the introduction: temporality, intentionality, ontology, and causality.

More specifically, the next three sections discuss the transformations that Po (the moon) undergoes in moving from being the daughter of her father (Tzuultaq'a) to the wife of B'alamq'e (the sun). This is, in some sense, both a transformation in social status that drives the entire narrative, and a transformation in physical state (from human entity to celestial divinity) that creates the cosmos. To support this claim, I argue for and analyse the following set of parallelisms. First, the spatial movements of B'alamq'e will parallel the narrative's day-to-day and twenty-day-long temporal development. Less overtly, the transformations that Po undergoes will parallel the changing phases of the moon. In other words, the temporal background relative to which all narrated events unfold is itself grounded in the movements and transformations of two narrated figures. Second, solar-centric temporal phases such as day and night, and dawn and dusk, will parallel types of actions undertaken: at night, activities which attempt to deceive; during the day, activities which attempt to remedy such dawn-discovered deceptions. And third, hierarchies of intentional horizons (such as those relating narrator, addressees, and non-participants) will parallel techniques of reference (such as the use of proper names, identifying descriptions, and status designators). This is not a very complicated point: certain events only the speaker is privy to (but not the addressees); and certain events only one actor is privy to (but not the others). Po will be shown to transform relative to such a temporal background, because of such deceitful or deceit-remedying actions, and as figured by such referential techniques.

In the next three sections, I analyse three parts of this text in detail: Po being seen by B'alamq'e; Po being killed by her uncle; and Po being reborn as the moon and taken up into the sky by B'alamq'e.

7.   Inalienable possessions and the tension between containers and contents

Scenes 2–6 describe the initial sighting of the moon by the sun. And it is especially at the end of this section (scene 6) that the movements of B'alamq'e first seem to parallel the position of the sun: both their daily habitualness, and their diurnal and nocturnal phasing. He passes by Po's house each day ostentatiously carrying what seems to be a real goat; and he moves into the darkness of the forest each night to hide what is actually a goat-skin.

The daily actions of Po resonate with the daily movements of B'alamq'e: his watchful passing by the house where she sits weaving during the day, and his hiding the fake goat inside the darkness of the forest at night (scenes 3–6). Predicates in both of these sequences are inflectionally marked, using the prefix *nak-* (i.e. unmarked and typically habitual). This is in accordance with the day-to-day habitualness of these activities, the backgrounding of these scenes relative to the punctuated events that follow, and the fact that the twenty days of narrative development have not yet begun. And this is in contrast to most other events (such as the initial sighting of Po by B'alamq'e, in scene 4), which are inflectionally marked, using the prefix *ki-*, as perfect aspect and indirectly known experience (usually characterized as 'remote past'). It is only when Po sees B'alamq'e, tells her father how much he pleases her, and together suspicious father and trusting daughter lay a trap to show that what seems to be a goat is merely a goat-hide, that the temporal unfolding of the narrative begins. Until then, there is just undifferentiated passing of days, parallel to B'alamq'e's passing by Po's house, parallel to the sun's daily journey.

Besides carrying a stuffed goat-skin, B'alamq'e is also disguised as a hunter (scene 4). This is his first attempt to deceive other characters, either by means of personal disguises or altered equipment. Later, he will wrap himself in the feathers of a hummingbird, and then reveal himself to be a man to Po. And still later, he will enlist Po's help in sabotaging both her father's blow-gun (by stuffing chilli inside it) and her father's mirror (by covering its face with smoke). We have been introduced, then, to a key trope, itself grounded in solar-centric phases: the distinction between inside and outside, light and dark, appearance and essence, day and night. Or, to phrase this distinction in less metaphysical terms, *the tension between containers and contents*. Such a distinction maps directly onto the three main characters: B'alamq'e is essentially deceitful (by altering appearances, and shifting between dark and light); Po is essentially gullible (by believing appearances, and seeing only the light); and her father is essentially suspicious (by distrusting appearances, and peering into the dark).

Indeed, looking at the narrative as a whole, there are at least ten such incidents. In scenes 5 and 6, there is the goat-skin and the hunter-disguise. In scene 10, B'alamq'e borrows the feathers of a bird so he can disguise himself. In scene 15, the surface of a mirror is smoked so that it can no longer be used to see. In scene 16, a blow-gun is stuffed with chilli so that the user will inhale it upon use. In scene 20, the shells of a turtle and armadillo are borrowed to hide in (as well as for protection). In scene 19, Thunder wraps himself in clouds, disguising himself as the weather. In scene 25, the bloody remains of the moon, which have been put into jars, come alive, and nobody knows what is causing the sounds that emanate from them. In scene 28, the moon is found to be hiding in the remaining jar. And in scene 27, a woodcutter gets curious about the jars and opens them up, thereby allowing the poisonous animals that are hiding inside to escape.

Many of these essence/appearance or content/container incidents turn on inalienable possessions: clothing (*aq'ej*), skin, shells, feathers, and hides (*ixej*), names (*k'a'b'aej*), bodies (*tz'ejwalej*), and even kinship relations. As discussed in chapter 2, inalienable possessions are a class of nouns, consisting of some body parts, most kinship terms, and words like name, shadow, clothing, and place. Such words have an extra morpheme (*-b'ej* or *-ej*) when not possessed, and are typically possessed by humans. In some sense, then, the treachery or trickery is even more insidious: for characters are donning the inalienable possessions of other creatures, and thereby making their disguises even harder to penetrate. Indeed, there are also more canonical markers of inside and outside, or contents and containers, that turn on inalienable possessions. For example, at different points in the narrative B'alamq'e (scene 4), Tzuultaq'a (scene 17a), and a woodcutter (scene 29b) do not just speak (*chank*), but speak to themselves, or 'think'. The actual construction used is 'say inside one's heart' (*chank sa' ch'oolej*). Recall the discussion of possessed-heart predicates in chapter 3. This is another place where an inalienable possession (heart, *ch'oolej*) is used to mark information that some characters are privy to, and others are not.

The word for name (*k'a'b'a'ej*) is also an inalienable possession in Q'eqchi', and the names of the main characters in this text are particularly telling. For example, when topicalized for the first time in scene 4, B'alamq'e is immediately referred to by his proper name and a status designator (*qaawa'*, translated here as 'sir', but perhaps rendered best by the Spanish *don*, or even the English *lord*). Loosely speaking, his proper name is composed of two morphemes: *b'alam* is usually glossed as the 'state of being partially hidden', and may be demonstrated by hiding one's body – except for a limb or two – behind a tree; and *q'e* is a relatively polysemous noun, meaning 'riddle', 'prediction', 'day', or 'time'. Indeed, there is a web of semantic associations for each of these morphemes. For example, there are other words like *b'aalam* (cacao, jaguar), *b'alak* (dirty), *b'alb'a* (hell), and *b'alb'o* (hidden, behind something else). And there are other words like *q'eel* (old), *q'ehink* (for the time of something to arrive), *q'eq* (black), and *jo'q'e* (when). Perhaps most tellingly, B'alamq'e is phonetically similar to *b'alaq'*, which means 'lie' or 'deception' and, when preceded by the status designator *aj*, means 'deceiver'. And this is what Po's father later calls B'alamq'e (scene 17c) when he realizes his daughter has run off and infers that B'alamq'e – whom he suspected all along – is her accomplice. Indeed, his actual words are: 'now I will see you, deceiver!' That is, the deceiver will finally be seen. Lastly, B'alamq'e is always referred to by his proper name, and never explicitly referred to as the 'sun' (*saq'e*) until the last scene of this text. And it is therefore tempting to think of him as a 'hidden sun' (*b'alam(sa)q'e*), as much as the trickster figure that he is traditionally taken for. The Q'eqchi', then, have a deeply entrenched dichotomy between containers and contents, or appearance and essence, or light and dark – one which undergirds both the personalities of actors and the logic of events.

Tzuultaq'a, the father of the moon, also has a telling name: it consists of two morphemes: *tzuul* (mountain) and *taq'a* (valley). Such complementary geological formations are appropriately combined for such a telluridian deity: 'mountain' plus 'valley' implying 'landscape' or 'earth'. This is a classic example of Mesoamerican parallelism (see Hanks 1989 and Norman 1980 for more details). For example, in Nahuatl there is the famous *aaltepeetl*, from *aatl* (water) and *tepeetl* (mountain), together meaning a 'town (and its people)'. His brother is Kaaq, or Thunder. And together they are the guardians of earth and sky. In some sense, the activities of the sun and moon are designed to escape this orbit – to get out of their reach. They have run as far as they can – to the edge of the sea, or the end of land – when Kaaq catches up with them (in scene 20). And it is precisely their failure to cleanly escape that effects the transformations that help constitute the heavens.

Of the many characters in this text, Po is the only one introduced and explicitly named – i.e. the one whose name is asserted rather than assumed (in scene 2). And in contrast to B'alamq'e, her proper name is explicitly the same lexeme that is usually used to refer to the moon. In other words, she is immediately referred to as what she is not yet; whereas B'alamq'e is never referred to as what he already is. (Except insofar as his proper name – deceiver, or hidden sun – tells us that he is not what he seems.)

Po is also the only character whose physical and social characteristics are extensively described. This is usually done by way of identifying descriptions. She is alternately referred to as a daughter (scene 2), an unmarried girl (scenes 3, 8, inter alia), and a virgin or maiden (scene 5). Such descriptions foreground her age, gender, civil status, and humanness. In later scenes, when she is the discursive theme, she will be referred to as *ix Po*, a combination of status designator (used with girls or young women) and proper name (scene 7). When she is not the discursive theme, she is often referred to by way of her kinship relation to whomever currently is – for example, 'his daughter' (scene 17a) or 'my wife' (scene 4). In still later scenes, when she has begun to physically transform, she will be referred to simply as *a'po* (that moon), with a demonstrative and no status designator (scene 30a). She is also referred to as *rahom* (his desired one), both when B'alamq'e is plotting to get back to her (after his goat-skin ruse has been outed), and when B'alamq'e sees her blood on the water after she has been killed by Thunder (scenes 10 and 24a, respectively). And, at the end of the narrative, when she has completed her transformations and is taken up into the sky to be B'alamq'e's wife (the celestial version of consummation), she will be referred to as *qana' po*, a combination of new status designator (used with married or older women, literally 'our mother') and old proper name. This transformation accords with her being first introduced by the narrator as her father's daughter (scene 2), and soon referred to as 'my woman' or 'my wife' in the reported speech and optative-mood construction of B'alamq'e (scene 4). In short, she is caught up in both the demands of her father (to care for him) and the desires of B'alamq'e (to marry her). From the very first scene, then, Po's future transformations from daughter to wife, and from earth-bound human to celestial entity, have been explicitly figured.

It is worthwhile describing this set of kinship relations in more detail. As elaborated in scenes 1 and 2, Po is the daughter of Tzuultaq'a and about to become the wife of B'alamq'e. Moreover, in the opening meta-topical scene, Tzuultaq'a is also referred to as 'our grandfather' (*qamama'*), and Po is referred to as 'our mother' (*qana'*). To be sure, these terms are just as often used as status designators ('our lord' and 'our lady') as kinship determiners. But it is not difficult to thereby relate the main characters in the narrated event to the participants in the speech event: the latter have as their mother Po (and, we assume, as their father B'alamq'e), and as their grandfather Tzuultaq'a. Kaaq, or thunder, is the brother of Tzuultaq'a, and so the uncle of Po (and hence the great-uncle of the participants in the speech event). In short, the union described here not only brings into being the heavens (through bringing into being their most salient denizens, the sun and moon), it also brings into being the speaker's and addressees' parents. These relations are shown in Figure 4.1. If, as we are told in scene 2, all these narrated events occurred 'when not a

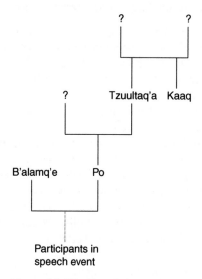

Figure 4.1. Kinship relations referred to in text

single man was yet born on earth', they also serve to explain where men and women would eventually come from. In short, with the separation of earth and sky comes the condition of possibility for people. This text, then, describes the events that inaugurate a new age, or mode of temporality – the time of men.

Finally, as for the mapping of motivation onto kinship relations, these early scenes are fundamental. In scene 3, for example, we learn that the moon spends her day caring for (*ch'oolanink*) her father. And that only when she finishes the work associated with this, does she take out her weaving equipment and sit in front of the house, where B'alamq'e can see her. As mentioned in chapter 2, this predicate is derived from the inalienable possession *ch'oolej*, or heart, and is used to describe the caring of children by parents, the caring of domestic animals by people, and the caring of patients by nurses. Clearly, Tzuultaq'a has good reasons for not wanting Po, whom we have learnt is 'his only companion' (scene 2), to go. Reciprocally, in scene 4, once B'alamq'e has seen Po, he says to himself, 'she's nice' and then, 'would that I could take her as my wife'. And B'alamq'e's thoughts about taking Po as his wife are precisely that: words he says inside his heart, or thoughts he has about what constitutes his object of desire (*r-aj-om* (E(3s)-desire-Nom), literally 'his desired one'). Such motivations provide reasons for the events that are about to take place: a father's need for his daughter's care, a husband's desire for a wife. It is the tension between the most basic consanguineal and affinal kinship relations, each itself an inalienable possession, that constitutes the cosmos.

8.   Sun and moon as both narrated figures and temporal grounds

From here the text proceeds in a similar fashion, counting off some twenty days of actions and events. Table 4.7 shows the temporal outline of the entire text. As may be seen, it consists of twenty days of narrated events, book-ended by relatively periodic events that came before (Po caring for her father) or after (the moon following the sun in the sky). These are referred to as pre-days and post-days, respectively. The twenty days between these book-ends constitute the majority of narrated events in the text. There are some days that receive very little description: the third and fourth days (when B'alamq'e is at home planning); and the eighth through nineteenth days (when B'alamq'e has left the scene and something is coming alive inside the jars that once held Po's remains). Finally, two major events take place at night rather than during the day: B'alamq'e and Po escaping from her house, and sabotaging her father's instruments; and Thunder catching up with them and killing Po for what they did to her father. Both crime and retribution, cause and effect of cosmological proportion, occur at night.

This table was constructed using the relevant temporal constructions from the text. Recall Table 4.5. For example, the pre- and post-time was established

Table 4.7. *Day-by-day breakdown of narrated events*

Days	Narrated events	Scenes
Pre-Days	Pre-narrative days of Po caring for father, being watched by B'alamq'e	Scenes 2–6
1st Day	Po notices B'alamq'e, and thinks he's a hunter	Scene 7
2nd Day	B'alamq'e slips on corn laid out by Po and her father, runs home to hide	Scene 8
3rd Day	B'alamq'e at home, planning his return; tobacco plant growing	Scenes 9–10
4th Day		
5th Day	B'alamq'e borrows feathers from bird, flies back to tobacco plant	Scenes 10–14
(5th Night)	B'alamq'e shows himself to moon, they sabotage mirror and blow-gun	Scenes 15–16
6th Day	Tzuultaq'a discovers daughter's absence, sends his brother after them	Scenes 17–21
(6th Night)	Po killed by her uncle, B'alamq'e rolls self into sea	Scenes 22–23
7th Day	B'alamq'e discovers Po's remains, has them put in jars, gives these to woman	Scene 24
8th Day	Stuff moving in jars, B'alamq'e away, Moon transforms, woman scared	Scene 25
9th Day		
10th Day		
11th Day		
12th Day		
13th Day		
14th Day		
15th Day		
16th Day		
17th Day		
18th Day		
19th Day		
20th Day	B'alamq'e returns, finds animals, finalizes Po's changes, goes up to sky	Scenes 26–30
Post-Days	Ever since then, post-narrative days of Sun and Moon in orbit	Scene 31

with the two meta-textual constructions: *in olden days ...* and *since then ...* As well, there were important shifts between relatively descriptive, periodic events and relatively narrative, sequential events – with corresponding shifts from *nak-* (present-habitual, or unmarked) to *ki-* (perfect aspect and unexperienced evidential). The numbers of days – especially the three days that B'alamq'e schemed and brooded at home, and the thirteen days that Po was dead – were established by adpositions like *after three days* and relative clauses like *when thirteen days had passed*. Solar-centric phases were established by adverbs and adpositions like *during the day* and *at night*. The passing of one day (the first day after the pre-time) was not marked explicitly, but rather inferred by scenes 3–8: with

Po having finally noticed the sun, and informing her father of her interest in him, Tzuultaq'a has the moon set a trap for the next time the sun passes – which should be the next day, given what we have been told of his daily travels.

There is certainly some story to be told about the nature of the two key numbers – 13 and 20 – and the Mayan calendar. The 'sacred almanac of 260 days', as Sharer (1994: 560) calls it, involved a succession of 260 days, each of which was uniquely assigned one of thirteen numbers and one of twenty day names. Some have noted that this period corresponds, more or less, to human gestation (e.g. Sharer (1994)). Thirteen is certainly a number that plays a role in this text, as the thirteen days (*kutan*) in which B'alamq'e goes away, Po is dead, and something comes alive in the jars; it also corresponds with the number of jars and taxa of deadly creatures that emerge from them. And gestation is certainly a key trope: at the end of these thirteen days (scene 30a), we are told that the moon was 'born again' (a construction that will be further discussed in the next section). There are many interesting questions that arise, then, when these narrated events are related to what we know about Mesoamerican calendars. But here I can only raise them.

While the focus of Table 4.7 is solar-centric phases as they relate to narrated events, there are also some lunar-centric phases. In particular, just as the sun passed by her house each day and disappeared into the forest at night, the moon does disappear for thirteen days. (Interestingly, those thirteen days constitute the greatest single, cohesive interval of time in the text, yet contain the smallest number of narrated events. In effect, it is the one time-span in the text during which each of the two main characters completely disappear from the scene.) And when she does finally show up again (scene 30a), she is referred to as a 'new moon' (*ak'po*), which is a standard construction for referring to a moon just beginning to wax. Finally, after this reappearance, the activities of B'alamq'e involve making her large and whole again – not just purified, but full. Indeed, it is only then that he pronounces her good, and takes her up into the sky (scene 30).

Moreover, earlier in the text (scenes 22 and 24c), when he disappears into the sea and she is killed by Thunder, her blood is seen on the surface of the sea. For example, the construction used at the end of scene 22 is *kaq kaq kub'e ix kik'el sa'xb'een ha'palaw*, or 'red red flowed her blood on top of the sea'. One might think of sunsets and sunrises, and the colour of the water at those times – which is when she was killed (right before B'alamq'e rolls into the sea), and when B'alamq'e leaves the sea and discovers her remains. It is these bloody remains that B'alamq'e has collected into jars; and it is from these remains that all the poisonous species of creatures are born. Thus, it is not a large conceptual leap to relate these events to menstruation. In this way, somewhat more tenuously, just as the man's curiosity causes all the poisonous animals to populate the earth (themselves born of the moon's remains), Po's no longer caring for her father (and eloping with B'alamq'e) led to her bloody death and eventual purified resurrection. In short, the repercussions of B'alamq'e's trickery and Po's assistance are vast indeed: sunsets and sunrises, menstrual cycles and lunar phases, are all explained.

But back to solar-centric events – in particular, the sixth day, which describes the death of the moon. As discussed above, it is late afternoon. Po has fled from her father's house with B'alamq'e, and they have come to the edge of the earth where the sea begins. (I assume it is the western edge, for in what other direction could the sun flee?) Seeing the approaching storm clouds, they infer her father has sent his brother to kill them (scene 20), and hide themselves in the shells of a turtle and an armadillo. Po's uncle, Thunder, begins to throw his axes down on them in the form of lightning bolts. Po is not a swimmer, alas, and she is killed by her uncle's axe. This is described in scenes 20–22.

Immediately after we learn of her death, scene 23 begins, now told from the standpoint of B'alamq'e rather than Po. Unaware of the death of his beloved, B'alamq'e rolls himself into the sea to escape the axes of Thunder. After these first two lines, which have B'alamq'e as their topic, we learn that 'the sun was extinguished and darkness was lowered on the earth'. This is the first time the word 'sun' (*saq'e*) is used, and the relation between these two lines is a brilliant albeit non-canonical example of Mayan parallelism. In canonical Mayan parallelism, as Norman has described for K'iche', two adjacent lines are identical in all but one respect, and the non-identical parts form a pair of terms which are said to act as a single lexical unit with a single metaphorical interpretation (1980; and see Hanks 1989). Recall the Nahuatl construction *aaltepeetl*, and compare the relation between the second and third lines of scene 31. Here, in contrast, the two utterances describe relatively sequential, topically chained events, the first from the standpoint of B'alamq'e (as narrated participant), and the second from the standpoint of solar-centric events (as temporal background).

This particular parallelism should be discussed in detail (and see Hofling 1993, who analyses a similar trope in Itzaj Maya narratives). First, notice that this sequence (the second and third lines of scene 23) is told using the inflectional form *ki-*, which is marked for perfect aspect. The narrated events stand in a relationship of temporal sequencing, not simultaneity, nor foreground to background. Second, the first time a new discursive theme is explicitly topicalized (marked in Q'eqchi' by clause-initial positioning) is the initial sentence of scene 23. To be thematically cohesive, the first four lines of this scene should therefore share the same discursive theme, even though the noun phrases used to refer to this theme change from *B'alamq'e* (the human being) to *saq'e* (the stellar object).

Notice that there is no syntactic parallelism at work here: the second line consists of a derived transitive predicate used reflexively along with a prepositional phrase and a dependent clause (functioning as a purposive: *in order to*); and the third line consists of a passivized predicate with no adjuncts. Notice as well that there is no semantic parallelism: the events referred to are temporally consecutive. There is only thematic cohesion and, if B'alamq'e is indeed the sun, logical ordering. It is as if there are two parallel worlds: a narrated one of B'alamq'e and his movements, and an indexed one of the sun and its position. Here, near the middle of this text, just when Po's death begins the process that will transform her into the moon, the indexed world is for a brief moment referentially figured, only to fade to temporal background again.

9.   People and things in relation to identifying descriptions and intentional horizons

After the moon has died, her father and uncle, and thus only consanguineal and lineal kin, are never mentioned again. Nor is she ever referred to using the identifying descriptions used in the first section, which themselves presume a human referent. Nor is she referred to using her proper name and a status designator. She has lost her social identity, to the extent that it had been expressed by such referential techniques. From now on she will be referred to as merely 'the moon' (*po*), and the qualities predicated of her – round, white, large, and pure – will slowly come into accordance with her new identifying descriptions. In short, until the last scene of the text, when she has finally been perfected by the actions of B'alamq'e, her name no longer functions as a proper noun, but is reduced to functioning as a common noun – a true movement from person to thing, one which correlates with her reduced topicality (she is much less frequently mentioned) and semantic role (when she is referred to, it is usually as patient rather than agent).

So back to the narrated events, taking up where we left off in the last section. It is the morning of the seventh day, and B'alamq'e has just discovered what has happened to Moon (scene 24a). With the aid of some dragonflies, he has her blood and guts gathered and put into thirteen jars (scene 24b). These he places under the eaves of a woman's house at the edge of the sea. He tells this woman to watch over the jars, and that he will return in thirteen days (scene 24c).

While B'alamq'e is away, we are told that 'something was born' inside those jars (scene 25). Here, a set of containers fills up with new contents, but contents which are unknown (something: *k'a'aq ru*) to both the participants in the narrated event and the participants in the speech event. This is one of three places in the text where the phrase 'to be born' (*yoolak*) is used. The first occurred in scene 2, when the entire narrative was set in 'olden times, when not a single man was yet born on earth' (a claim belied, it should be said, by the existence of the old woman and the travelling woodcutter). And, as mentioned above in the discussion of gestation, the third token occurs in scene 30a. In particular, right after the poisonous animals – which were born in the jars – escape to populate the earth, the moon is 'born again'. In short, in a time before men were born, poisonous animals are born from the remains of a dead moon, and this moon is reborn when these animals are let loose. Finally, it is a woman who oversees the jars during the birth of the animals, and whose key emotion is fear as to their unknown contents (*xuwak*). And it is a man who lets them loose, thereby leading to the moon's rebirth, and whose key emotion is at first curiosity (*tixnaw raj*) as to the jars' unknown contents, and later fear (*xiw*) of their known contents.

So back to the progression of events. When he returns on the twentieth day, B'alamq'e opens up the jars one-by-one. The first twelve contain relatively dangerous and disgusting creatures (snakes, spiders, scorpions, wasps, lizards, and so forth). These animals, then, are what were making the noises. The constructions used to refer to them provide some of the most difficult words in this text to gloss so far as they essentially constitute a list, or enumeration, of poisonous creatures of relatively far-flung taxonomic origin (scene 27). In this way, physical space (jars), gestation period (days), and taxa (species) are numerically linked. Space, time, and ontology are not only treated as isomorphic to each other, they are also represented in terms of contents and containers.

Having opened the first twelve jars, none of them baring any trace of the moon's remains, B'alamq'e finally gets to the thirteenth jar. After we learn that the moon has been hiding herself, because 'it is not pleasing to her that the sun could be her husband' (scene 28), and after hearing the lamentations of B'alamq'e, that 'never again perhaps will I see the face of my loved one', he opens the thirteenth jar. There, at last, is the moon; and two inalienable possessions are involved in her description: her covering (*ixej*) is brilliant; her body (*tz'ejwalej*) is white. Everything about her, we are told, is beautiful and good. The state of the moon, then, is in stark contrast to the nature of the dangerous and disgusting animals just discussed. Indeed, we are told that she is the true or complete one (*tz'aqal*). And she is even referred to as 'our mother moon' (*qana' po*), just as she was in the opening scene, and just as she will be in the closing scene.

But the moon must not yet be absolutely perfect, for the focus shifts from her to the woodcutter throughout scene 29. As mentioned, B'alamq'e calls the woodcutter to throw away the jars into the sea. While the man is doing this, he gets curious about what is inside, thinks he will not be seen (again, saying these words 'inside his heart'), and uses his finger to look inside and see what is moving. A snake slides out across his arm, he screams, drops the jars, and they burst open, letting all the species of dangerous and disgusting animals escape over the surface of the earth. Finally, we are told this was the fault (*x-maak*) of the man, because he did not believe the words, or obey the command, of

B'alamq'e. Again, a key trope arises: the man is curious about contents that he cannot see (due to an inference he has made about something he can hear), and in attempting to find out what is inside the containers, the contents are let loose. A human motivation, grounded in a container/content distinction, itself located in mythic time, leads to lasting consequences for the present time.

Only after this escape of the creatures are we told that 'the new moon was born again' (scene 30a). Now we learn that she no longer has the small body she used to have. Her physical transformation, then, is still under way: not only is she white and pure, she is also larger – as if moving from new moon to full moon, a process caused by all the little events we have been discussing. But her transformations are not yet finished. In a somewhat opaque series of events (scenes 30b–30d), B'alamq'e enlists the help of a goat and a deer in order to open the hole between her legs with their hooves and horns. After some effort, they are successful. Sweet-smelling froth shoots forth, but B'alamq'e is not yet pleased. So he has a rat urinate there, and only then does it improve. Her transformations finally complete, he pronounces her good, and takes her by the hand, leading her up into the sky to be his wife.

In scene 31, the last scene of the text, itself meta-topical, B'alamq'e is referred to with a status designator in conjunction with the word for sun (saq'e), here being used as his proper name. He has finally explicitly become what he has always implicitly been. In a syntactically parallel fashion, Po takes on the new status designator of a mature woman, and her old proper name. As is their new nature, he is to watch over the earth during the day, and she is to watch over the earth at night, such that their extraterrestrial movements will forever parallel the movements of earth-bound men and women: as B'alamq'e has led Po, the sun is to lead the moon, men are to lead women – and perhaps even production (agriculture) is to lead reproduction (child-rearing).

To conclude, notice that at least three intentional horizons have been set up due to B'alamq'e's various identities: one, B'alamq'e's disguises (hunter, hummingbird, human) as seen by other narrated characters; two, B'alamq'e within his disguises (proper name) as seen by addressees (including us); and three, B'alamq'e in his role as a calendrical index (solar entity) as seen by the speaker. Each of these intentional horizons – character, performer, and calendar – encompasses the ones before it. (See Table 4.8.)

In the case of Po, the situation is slightly different. She is the only character actually named in the narrative, and the name she is given explicitly, and horizon-independently (i.e. in all worlds), prefigures what she is going to be. In other words, while B'alamq'e is already physically the sun, but not explicitly, Po is explicitly the moon, but not physically. As we have seen, Po's physical transformation requires each of B'alamq'e's many identities – as either the disguised figure intentionally deceiving her, the named and agentive figure actively transforming her, or the solar-centric temporal ground in which her

Table 4.8. *Techniques of reference and horizons of intentionality*

Techniques of reference	Identity	Experiential horizons		
Narrative-event-internal index	Saq'e (sun)			Narrator (Mr Caal)
Proper name	B'alamq'e (hidden-sun)		Addressee (Us)	
Description of disguise	Hummingbird, Hunter, etc.	Non-Partic. (Po)		

death, thirteen-day gestation, and rebirth occur. All of B'alamq'e's identities are therefore the condition for Po to become what she is prefigured to be. Finally, this occurs only when the horizons set up by B'alamq'e's identities become identical. Just as in the middle of the text (scene 23) Po's death is the condition for his indexical identity to emerge for an instant, here at the end of the text (scene 31) her rebirth is the condition for all of his identities to merge forever.

What we have seen, then, is a complex, relatively covert, and mutually implicated set of parallelisms: first, the movements of a narrated figure and a solar-centric temporal background; second, the intentional actions of narrated characters (deception versus discovery) and solar-centric phases; and third, a hierarchy of intentional horizons (narrator, addressee, and non-participants) and techniques of reference (proper names, identifying descriptions, and status designators). Finally, we have also seen a set of transformations that occurs relative to, and as a function of, such parallelisms: the moon's movement from daughter to wife, from girl to woman, from human being to lunar entity, and from loquacious subject to muted object. From such a set of parallelisms, and Our Mother Moon's attendant transformations, we catch a glimpse of both cultural tensions and narrative techniques, legends about time and theories of mind.

5   Other minds and possible worlds: when psychological depth is dialogical breadth

1.   Grammatical categories and participant roles

Kant offered a classic definition of the principles of modality: they 'add to the concept of a thing, of which otherwise they say nothing, the cognitive faculty from which it springs and in which it has its seat' (1964 [1781]: 252). In some sense, Kant was making a distinction between signs that stand for objects and signs that stand for the signer's relation to those objects. If signs of the first type refer to and predicate qualities about a given state of affairs (e.g. *my dog died*), signs of the second type refer to and predicate qualities about the speaker's relation to a given state of affairs (e.g. *I was sad that …*). Indeed, the two kinds of signs (signs of mode events and signs of content events) are also true of noun phrases, as expressed in the idiom of primary and secondary properties: *a beautiful green book*. In this example, one kind of sign is relatively descriptive (focusing on the object: *green*) and the other kind of sign is relatively evaluative (focusing on the signer's relation to the object: *beautiful*). In certain constructions (such as those involving complement-taking predicates), where description ends (the complement) and evaluation begins (the predicate) is relatively easy to specify. But in other constructions (such as those involving interjections), description and evaluation are difficult to disentangle. For these reasons, besides tacking between the cross-linguistic and the language specific, or typology and description (as a means to circumvent the tacit assumptions of the analyst), we also need to tack between linguistic and meta-linguistic practices. *In particular, while we initially defined stances as relatively emblematic roles of mental statuses, we should also consider them as signs speakers take to be relatively evaluative rather than descriptive, or ways of construing an event that are maximally caught up in the personhood, or subjectivity, of the speaker.*

Recall the opening scene of chapter 1, in which we analysed the brief interaction between a Q'eqchi'-speaking boy and his mother. This chapter continues where we left off, providing a detailed account of the morphosyntax, semantics, and pragmatics of modal clitics in Q'eqchi'-Maya. It argues that status, or epistemic modality, is a shifter that marks the speaker's commitment to a narrated event relative to the speech event; and that commitment should

120

be understood as a kind of participant role. It details the complicated types of commitment events that are semantically encoded and pragmatically implicated in various contexts. It shows the ways in which multiple commitment events – inhabited by the speaker, addressee, and actor – combine in various contexts to serve complex functions, ranging from satiatives and dubitives to bluffatives and surprisitives. And it shows the ways in which these complicated, overlapping commitment events may be understood in terms of mental states – from desire and worry to belief and hope. In this way, it grounds the 'possible worlds' of logicians and the 'intentional worlds' of psychologists in terms of participant roles; and it thereby interprets logical and psychological presumptions in terms of social and semiotic practices.

The first three sections discuss the grammatical forms, semantic features, and pragmatic functions of the modal clitics. The next four sections take up each clitic in turn, detailing its usage in context. Section 9 generalizes the framework to include that other dimension of epistemic modality – evidentiality. And the conclusion returns to the issue of subjectivity in language.

2.   Morphosyntactic properties of the modal clitics

The modal clitics may be thought of as operators that take clauses as their operands. In Q'eqchi', a clause usually consists of a predicate (for example, an intransitive verb), the obligatory arguments of this predicate (for example, a grammatical subject), the obligatory grammatical categories that occur with this predicate (for example, tense, aspect, or mood), and any non-obligatory arguments that may occur (for example, adjuncts such as prepositional phrases, adverbs, or relational nouns). If a modal clitic occurs in an utterance, it usually occurs after the predicate and before any arguments or adjuncts. However, if some constituent (such as an argument or adjunct) has been preposed into the verb-initial focus position (for the purposes of emphasis, relativization, or questioning), the modal clitic occurs after the preposed constituent. Similarly, in cases of clausal, or 'broad-scope', negation, marked by the nonfactive particle *ink'a'*, the modal clitics are also preposed, occurring immediately after this particle. In other words, while modal clitics have grammatical scope over clauses, they only have informational scope over the foci of utterances – that part of an utterance which is being asserted or questioned. Let me illustrate these points.

1) **x-Ø-hulak chaq ewer**
Perf-A(3s)-arrive hither yesterday
he arrived yesterday

2) **t-at-x-k'am chaq sa' li w-ochoch**
Fut-A(2s)-E(3s)-take hither Prep Dm E(1s)-house
he will bring you inside my house

3) **x-Ø-hulak pe' chaq ewer**
    Perf-A(3s)-arrive F hither yesterday
    he did arrive yesterday (addressee-focused) or *he arrived yesterday!* (speaker-focused)

4) **t-at-x-k'am tana chaq sa' li w-ochoch**
    Fut-A(2s)-E(3s)-take AF hither Prep Dm E(1s)-house
    perhaps he will bring you inside my house

5) **moko laa'in ta x-in-hulak ewer**
    NF A(1s) NF Perf-A(1s)-arrive yesterday
    it was not I who arrived yesterday

6) **joq'e raj t-at-x-k'am chaq sa' li w-ochoch**
    when CF Fut-A(2s)-E(3s)-take hither Prep Dm E(1s)-house
    when would he bring you inside my house

7) **moko laa'at taxaq t-at-x-k'am chaq sa' li w-ochoch**
    NF A(2s) Opt Fut-A(2s)-E(3s)-take hither Prep Dm E(1s)-house
    if only it will not be you that he brings inside my house

Example (1) shows a clause consisting of the intransitive predicate *hulak* (to arrive), its obligatory argument (marked on the predicate with the third-person-singular absolutive affix -Ø-), its obligatory operator (marked on the predicate with the perfect-aspect prefix *x*-), the directional particle *chaq* (hither), and the temporal adverb *ewer* (yesterday). Example (2) shows a clause consisting of the transitive predicate *k'amok* (to take), its obligatory arguments (marked on the predicate with the second-person-singular absolutive affix -*at*- and the third-person-singular ergative affix -*x*-), its obligatory operator (marked on the predicate with the future-tense prefix *t*-), the directional particle *chaq* (hither), and the prepositional phrase *sa' li w-ochoch* (in my house). Example (3) shows the clause from example (1) being operated on by the factive clitic *pe'*. And example (4) shows the clause from example (2) being operated on by the afactive clitic *tana*. As may be seen from these last two examples, the modal clitics occur after the predicate and before any adjuncts. In example (5), the nonfactive clitic *moko … ta* occurs circumfixed around the first-person-singular pronoun *laa'in*, which is cross-referenced on the predicate by the first-person-singular absolutive affix -*in*-. In example (6), the counterfactive clitic *raj* occurs after the wh-word *joq'e* (when). As may be seen from these last two examples, the pronoun and the wh-word are in the verb-initial focus position. Their glosses reflect the fact that the modal clitics have scope over the foci of utterances. Lastly, in example (7), the optative clitic *taxaq* occurs after the nonfactive clitic *moko … ta*, which occurs circumfixed around the second-person-singular pronoun *laa'at* (which is cross-referenced on the predicate by the second-person-singular absolutive affix -*at*-). Here, then, two modal clitics occur together (with morphophonemic fusing: *moko*

Table 5.1. *Grammatical distribution and operator scope of the modal clitics*

Distribution and scope	Modal clitics				
	pe'	*tana*	*taxaq*	*raj*	*moko … ta*
Verbal or stative enclitic (unmarked)	+	+	+	+	+
Preposed with focusing	+	+	+	+	+
Preposed with relativization	+	+	+	+	+
Preposed with Wh-movement	+	+	+	+	NA
Preposed with clausal negation	+	+	+	+	NA
Scope over core operators (MATEs)	+	+	+	+	+
Scope over focus	+	+	+	+	+
Scope over clausal negation	+	+	+	+	NA
Scope within illocutionary force	+/-	+/-	+/-	+	+

… *ta taxaq* becomes *moko … taxaq*), indicating that the modal clitics do not form a paradigm, but rather a set.

As may be seen from Table 5.1, the modal clitics constitute a cohesive form class insofar as they have distributional patterns and logical scopes in common.[1] As may also be seen, the nonfactive clitic *moko … ta* is the only clitic whose distribution is slightly different – which accords with its semantics (it marks polarity rather than status) and its morphology (it is the only circumfixed form). This table also shows that the modal clitics *pe'*, *tana*, and *taxaq* interact with illocutionary force in much more complicated ways than *raj* and *moko … ta*, insofar as only these last two clitics return utterances with unmarked illocutionary force. As will be seen, this interaction with illocutionary force correlates with the fact that *raj* and *moko … ta* can be operated on by the other modal clitics, but not vice versa. Let me now turn to the semantics of the modal clitics in order to justify the glosses I have been providing.

3.   Semantic properties of the modal clitics

When occurring with declarative illocutionary force, the clauses in examples (1) and (2) may function as assertions, and thereby express a proposition (*p*) which may be true or false depending on whether the state of affairs it represents corresponds with the world or not. Or, to phrase this in terms of communication rather than logic, such an assertion indicates the speaker's commitment to the truth, or at least the unchallengeability, of *p* at the time of

---

[1] There are several other forms that bear a family resemblance (in semantics and morphology), some of which were discussed in chapter 4: *aj wi'* (also, only), *wi' chik* (again), *wi'* (locative, instrumental), *chik* (else, more). As may be seen, several are aspectual in nature.

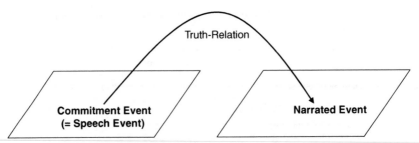

Figure 5.1. Unmarked status. Figure showing the relationship of truth between narrated event and commitment event when commitment event is identical to speech event (i.e. principal = animator)

the utterance. Notice, then, that unmarked assertions – that is, utterances with declarative illocutionary force and no modal clitics – indicate that the world in which one is committed to the truth of a proposition is identical to the world in which one expresses that proposition. Or, to phrase this in terms of participant roles: unmarked assertions indicate that the one who is committed to the truth of a proposition is identical to the one who expresses that proposition.

In order to formulate this claim more carefully, let me recap three terms. Following Jakobson (1990a), I use the term *narrated event* to refer to the state of affairs represented by an utterance, and the term *speech event* to refer to the context in which an utterance is made. I use the expression *commitment event* to refer to the world in which the speaker is committed to the truth of the proposition expressed by his or her utterance. In this idiom, the foregoing claim may be stated as follows: in an unmarked assertion, the *status* of the commitment event is left unspecified, and is thereby usually indistinguishable from the speech event. In other words, an unmarked assertion indicates that the event (or 'world') in which one is committed to the truth of a narrated event is identical to the speech event. (See Figure 5.1.)

My reason for using such an elaborate terminology to make such a simple claim is that the modal clitics, when operating on a clause that is uttered with declarative illocutionary force, specify the status of the commitment event, and thereby serve to distinguish it from the speech event. That is to say, in assertions with marked status – indicated by the presence of modal clitics – the locale of a commitment event is specified, and is thereby usually differentiated from the speech event. Phrased in terms of Goffman's well-known decomposition of the speaker into animator, author, and principal (1981a: 144), status disambiguates animators from principals (or speech event from commitment event), just as person disambiguates speakers from actors (or speech event from narrated event), and reported speech disambiguates animators from authors (or speech event from reported speech event). (See Figure 5.2.)

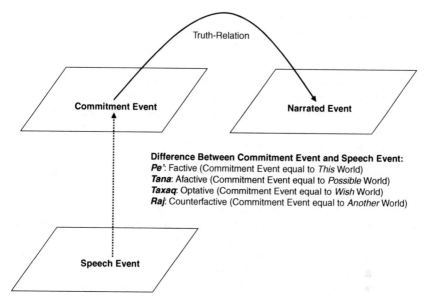

Figure 5.2. Marked status. Figure showing the relationship of truth between narrated event and commitment event when commitment event is different from speech event (i.e. principal ≠ animator)

In Q'eqchi', there are four modal clitics that encode the status of the speaker's commitment event.[2] The factive clitic *pe'* signals that the commitment event is in *this world* (i.e. the world of the speech event), and therefore markedly encodes what is usually assumed. This is expressed in the glosses of example (3) by either the presence of the verb *do* (addressee-directed function: insistive or contradictive) or the presence of the exclamation mark (speaker-directed function: surprisitive or dubitive). The afactive clitic *tana* signals that the commitment event

---

[2] There are three related forms which I discuss elsewhere at length (Kockelman 2005b): *tab'i'* marks a question as rhetorical (the speaker already knows the answer, and may be contradicting something the addressee said); *tawi'* marks a question as posed (the speaker presumes the addressee doesn't know the answer, and is expressing their own wonder); and *ta* (which is the second half of the nonfactive clitic *moko … ta*, but which also shows up alone in irrealis contexts, especially in older texts). There are a number of complement-taking predicates that license the use of the positive clitic *tawi'* in their complements. The most frequent predicate is 'not knowing …' (*ink'a' ninnaw ani tawi'* or *moko ninnaw ta ani tawi'* or 'I don't know who it could be'). Other forms are 'who knows' (*saber*, the Spanish non-finite form of 'to know'), 'not seeing' (*moko xaawil ta ani tawi' lix k'ab'a'* or 'you didn't see who it was'), 'no longer knowing' (*maaji' nakaanaw ani tawi' raj* or 'you no longer know who could have done it'), and questions regarding 'truth' (*ma yaal naq jo'kan tawi'* or 'is it true that it could be like this?'). Notice, then, that (lack of) knowledge, (lack of) perception, and (uncertain) truth constitute a covert class of predicates whose reactance is their conditioning of the occurrence of the positive clitic *tawi'* in a relative clause.

is in a *possible world*. This is expressed in the gloss of example (4) by the presence of the modal adverb *perhaps*. The optative clitic *taxaq* signals that the commitment event is in a *wish world*. This is expressed in the gloss of example (7) by the sentence-initial phrase *if only*. And the counterfactive clitic *raj* signals that the commitment world is in *another world* (i.e. a world other than the speech event). This is expressed in the gloss of example (6) by the modal auxiliary verb *would*. Notice, then, the *shifter*-like nature of the clitics: the status of the commitment event is specified relative to the speech event. Lastly, notice that while the nonfactive clitic *moko ... ta* belongs to this set by way of its grammatical distribution, semantically it marks constituent-scope negation and thereby specifies the logical valence, or polarity, of the narrated event rather than the status of the commitment event. This is expressed in the glosses of examples (5) and (7) by the word *not*. As mentioned, such a semantic distinction is mirrored by its form and distribution: not only is the nonfactive clitic the only circumfixed form, but, as revealed by example (7), all the other modal clitics have scope over it.[3] Lastly, these modal clitics should all be contrasted with unmarked status and unmarked polarity (signalled by the absence of a modal clitic), which leaves the status of a commitment event and the polarity of a narrated event unspecified. Table 5.2 summarizes this information.[4]

4.   Pragmatic properties of the modal clitics

Perhaps the most peculiar feature of the modal clitics is that they often say two things at once: in semantically encoding the status of the speaker's commitment to a narrated event, they pragmatically implicate the status of *another's* commitment to an *inverted* narrated event. This 'other' may be the addressee, the speaker, or the actor (i.e. the one being spoken about). Their commitment to an inverted narrated event may be temporalized, internalized, or dialogized. And the existence of this implicated commitment event may be the equivalent of old information or new information to participants.

More specifically, certain commitment events must exist for the use of modal clitics to be appropriate. In the case of pragmatically *presupposed*

---

[3] *Moko ... ta* should be contrasted with the nonfactive particle *ink'a'*, in that it has narrow focus (usually negating core constituents, such as the predicate or one of its arguments), whereas *ink'a'* has broad focus (usually negating predicate phrases or entire clauses). *Ink'a'* has fewer constraints on its interaction with modal clitics than *moko ... ta*, and can be part of a clause that is operated on by two modal clitics. In addition, *ink'a'* can serve as the negative answer to a yes/no question. And, in accordance with its unmarked focus-structure, *ink'a'* occurs much more frequently than *moko ... ta* in conversation.

[4] For reasons of space, two key semantic properties of the modal clitics are not addressed: their co-occurrence relations with each other; and their interaction with obligatory grammatical categories (like tense, aspect, and evidentiality). A detailed account of these properties is offered in Kockelman (2005b).

Table 5.2. *Semantic meaning of modal clitics when contrasted with unmarked status and polarity*

Form	Name	Grammatically Signals
Ø	Unmarked	in a non-specified world, speaker is committed to the truth of p
pe'	Factive	in **this** world, speaker is committed to the truth of p
tana	Afactive	in a **possible** world, speaker is committed to the truth of p
taxaq	Optative	in a **wish** world, speaker is committed to the truth of p
raj	Counterfactive	in **another** world, speaker is committed to the truth of p
moko … ta	Nonfactive	in a non-specified world, speaker is committed to the truth of **not** p

commitment events, the commitment in question is also revealed by some-thing already existing in context (other than the utterance containing the modal clitic itself); and, in the case of pragmatically *created* commitment events, the commitment in question is revealed only through the utterance containing the modal clitic. Recall, from chapter 1, Durkheim's distinction between emblems that clarify (already existing) group sentiment and emblems that create (newly existing) group sentiment. And see especially Silverstein's distinction between indexical presupposition and creation (1995 [1976]), itself inspired by Austin's distinction between pragmatic presupposition and entailment. In the terms of Sperber and Wilson (1986), the key issue is whether another's commitment to an inverted narrated event is 'mutually manifest' (or intersubjectively known) to the participants before the utterance (akin to the topic of an assertion), or comes to be 'mutually manifest' to them because of the utterance (akin to the focus of an assertion).

In short, there are two distinct loci of commitments: one encoded by the modal clitics; and the other implicated by the occurrence of these modal clitics in context. It is important, then, to understand the ontological status of these others' commitments to inverted narrated events – where they reside, and what they give rise to, both as indexed in actual discourse and as represented in speakers' interpretations of such discourse.

Consider, for example, an utterance containing the factive clitic *pe'*. To emphasize that one is committed to p in *this* world, is to invite the implicature that someone is not committed to p in *another* world. Such an utterance would be appropriate in the pragmatically presupposed context of the *addressee*'s commitment to not p. This commitment may have been revealed any number of ways: by the addressee's previous assertion not p, by her assuming not p in a question, by her overtly stating 'I believe not p', etc. In such cases, the meaning of the utterance containing the factive clitic *pe'* is best captured by an addressee-focused gloss, as in example (3). Such an utterance would also be appropriate in the pragmatically created context of the *speaker*'s commitment to not *p*. This commitment need not have been revealed prior to this utterance. (But it may be reinforced after the utterance: by the addressee's response, by the speaker's co-occurring comments, etc.) In such contexts, the meaning of the utterance containing the factive clitic *pe'* is best captured by a speaker-focused gloss, as in example (3).

Notice that, relatively speaking, in the addressee-focused function, the other's commitment is *dialogized* (belonging to the addressee); and in the speaker-focused function, the other's commitment is *internalized* (belonging to the speaker herself). This is a pervasive dichotomy underlying various functions of the modal clitics. The process of *internalization*, whereby addressee-focused functions iconically relate to speaker-focused functions – and hence whereby the participant format of private interiority maps onto the participant format of public conversation – was introduced in chapter 3. Loosely speaking, it may be phrased as follows: *psychological depth is the internalization of dialogical breadth*.

Given that modal clitics often simultaneously semantically encode one commitment event and pragmatically implicate another (inverted) commitment event, the *disjunctures* between such encoded and implicated commitment events may index other kinds of mental states. For example, to use the factive clitic *pe'* to semantically encode that one is committed to *p* in this world, and thereby implicate that one was committed to not *p* in another world, may index 'surprise' (if the other world or event is construed as prior to this one, and belonging to oneself), or 'doubt' (if the other world or event is construed as simultaneous with this one, and belonging to another). In this way, the disjunctures between semantically encoded and pragmatically implicated commitment events often index mental states more complicated than the simple beliefs underlying the commitment events themselves.

The modal clitics not only index mental states, they also index social statuses. For example, using the optative clitic *taxaq* to indicate that one wishes for an event often indexes a shared perspective between the speaker and the addressee: that both have a similar commitment to the narrated event in question by way of having shared social roles or relations (a husband and wife discussing the price of corn; a man and his work assistants discussing the possibility of rain).

Finally, the modal clitics are subject to interpretations by speakers themselves. Such interpretations are often construed in a temporal or psychological idiom. For example, the factive clitic *pe'* is often interpreted by speakers as meaning 'you just learnt'. In this way, they gloss the meaning of a modal clitic using a mental-state verb (to know) and a temporal adverb (just). Similarly, the afactive clitic *tana* is interpreted by some speakers as meaning 'you don't want to say'. In this way, epistemic possibility is glossed not in terms of logic or certainty, but in terms of not wanting to have to commit oneself to the narrated event in question, given the responsibilities of commitment. In short, when characterizing the meaning of these forms, speakers use many of the constructions described in chapter 3 (complement-taking predicates) and chapter 4 (tense-aspect inflections and temporal adverbs).

Each of these kinds of meaning will be at issue in the examples that follow.

5.   Afactive status: *tana*

The afactive clitic *tana* encodes the speaker's commitment to *p* in a *possible* world. And it may implicate that the speaker or addressee is committed to not *p* in a possible world. It may usually be glossed as 'perhaps'. For example, arriving at the home of her sister, a woman notices the door is locked. She asks:

8a) **S1: b'ar wan-Ø-Ø**
     where exist-Pres-A(3s)
     where is she?

And her husband answers:

8b) **S2: xko'o'-Ø tana sa' k'ayil, maa ani**
     go(Perf)-A(3s) AF Prep market Neg who
     perhaps she's gone to the market, she's not around

Example (8) shows a very frequent use of *tana*: providing uncertain information in the context of an addressee's question. While providing uncertain information outside of the context of an addressee's previous question is relatively marked, it does occur in the context of attributing negative motivations to others. For example, in recounting to her friend how her first child's godfather refused to be the godfather of her second child (after he had heard that the child's parents were unsure about asking him again), a woman described his refusal:

9a) **S1: ut yal x-Ø-x-ye chaq w-e naq sik' li w-eeqaj**
     and only Perf-A(3s)-E(3s)-say hither E(1s)-RN Comp seek(Imp) Dm E(1s)-substitute
     and he said to me 'find my substitute'

9b) **x-b'aan tana li-x josq'il**
     E(3s)-RN AF Dm-E(3s) anger
     because of his anger perhaps

9c) **sa' junpaat tana x-Ø-chal li-x josq'il**
     Prep quickly AF Perf-A(3s)-come Dm-E(3s) anger
     quickly perhaps came his anger

9d) **naq ki-Ø-r-ab'i li aatin a'an**
     Comp Inf-A(3s)-E(3s)-hear Dm word Dm
     when he heard that word (i.e. when he heard the parents were unsure about asking him again)

9e) **naq sik' jun-aq w-eeqaj chan-k-Ø**
Comp seek(Imp) one-NS E(1s)-substitute say-Pres-A(3s)
that he said 'seek a substitute for me'

9f) **S2: aah**
Interj
aah

9g) **S1: ab'an laa'in x-Ø-in-sik'**
but A(1s) Perf-A(3s)-E(1s)-seek
so I sought one

The afactive clitic *tana* is used in lines (9b) and (9c). In both instances, the speaker is discussing the anger (*josq'il*) of her son's godfather. In line (9b), what is being modalized as possible is not the existence of the man's anger, but its causal relation to what the man said. And in line (9c), what is being modalized is the suddenness of the man's anger upon hearing that the woman was unsure about asking him again (9d). In both cases, however, the existence of the man's anger is presumed. Indeed, in lines (9a–b), the anger is taken to be the cause of an utterance. And in lines (9c–d), the anger is taken to be caused by another utterance. In this way, what is being modalized is not the existence of a negative emotion (nor its attribution to an actor), but the causal relation between a negative emotion and an utterance: in the first instance, emotion causing utterance; and in the second instance, utterance causing emotion.

Another frequent use of *tana* is speaker-initiated repair. In particular, after having assumed information the speaker later realizes the addressee may not know, the speaker may ask the addressee whether they do indeed know the information, followed by *ink'a' tana*, or 'perhaps not'. For example, in telling her sister-in-law about two children who had suffered the same illness, a woman said the following:

10a) **S1: kama'an x-Ø-x-xok r-e lix Laur r-e laj Manu**
like.this Perf-A(3s)-E(3s)-gather E(3s)-RN SD Laura E(3s)-RN SD Manuel
in this manner was lost a child belonging to Laura, and another belonging to Manuel

10b) **S1: ma aaw-il-om jun-aq x-k'ula'al laj Manuel, ink'a' tana**
Int E(3s)-see-Nom one-NS E(3s)-child SD Manuel Neg AF
did you see Manuel's child? perhaps not

10c) **S2: ink'a'**
Neg
no

10d) **S1: jun x-k'ula'al naq wan-Ø-Ø ki-Ø-kam**
one E(3s)-child Comp exist-Pres-A(3s) Inf-A(3s)-die
one of his children died

In line (10a), the speaker presumes information (the existence of a child belonging to Manuel). In line (10b), the speaker checks to see whether it was okay to presume this information, followed by the phrase *ink'a' tana*, or 'perhaps not'. When the addressee responds in line (10c) that she did not know about the child, the speaker then asserts in line (10d) what she previously presumed in line (10a). In this way, *ink'a' tana* indexes the markedness of a question asking what was just presumed – giving, in effect, a reason for such a question. In other words, one may tentatively answer one's own question negatively (that is, with the afactive clitic *tana*), in the context of one's having just implicitly answered it affirmatively.

As was seen in example (8), the low certainty that is indexed by *tana* may be due to the inferential nature of the speaker's knowledge. In example (11), a man uses *tana* in the context of a second-person, future-tense predication, along with an explanation for his modalization:

11a) **S1: ma t-at-chalq**
Int Fut-A(2s)-come
will you come (tomorrow)?

11b) **S2: aah, saber, ink'a' n-Ø-in-naw ma t-in-chalq tawi'**
Interj who.knows Neg Pres-A(3s)-E(1s)-know Int Fut-A(1s)-come Pos
aah, saber, I don't know whether I'll come

11c) **S1: t-at-chalq tana, porke ralal kutanq nak-at-k'ulun**
Fut-A(2s)-come AF because every day Pres-A(2s)-come
you'll probably come, because you come every day

In line (11c), *tana* seems to be marking uncertainty in the context of the speaker's description of the future actions of his addressee. Indeed, the speaker in line (11c) is weakly contradicting his addressee, who was the speaker in line (11b). Here, then, the second clause of line (11c) gives the rationale for the speaker's commitment to *p* in a possible world. In this way, *tana* functions as a weak contradiction of a co-present participant in the context of inference through attention to habit.

There are many utterances in which the afactive clitic *tana* occurs with the afactive particle *mare* (maybe).[5] All of my tokens of such utterances are answers to questions which are posed (using the positive clitic *tawi'*) rather than asked, and thereby function to express a speaker's wonder or puzzlement rather than to secure an addressee's answer. In this way, just as being asked a question to which one doesn't know the answer can license a single afactive

---

[5] Like *tana*, *mare* marks epistemic modality, signalling that there is a possible world in which the speaker is committed to some proposition. *Mare* differs from *tana* in that it has unmarked (or broad) focus, rather than narrow focus. One might compare *mare* and *tana* to 'maybe' (as an adverb, having scope over a sentence) and 'may' (as a modal auxiliary verb, used in its epistemic sense, having scope over a clause).

clitic (recall example 8), being in the context of a posed question to which one doesn't know the answer can license both an afactive particle and an afactive clitic. For example, in discussing the direction in which a new house had been built, a man said to his friend:

12a) **S1: b'ar tawi' li-x jayalil, ma arin o ma arin**
      where Pos Dm-E(3s) direction Int here or Int here
      where could it be facing? here or here? (along with two gestures)

And his friend answers:

12b) **S2: aah, mare arin tana**
      Interj, maybe here AF
      aah, maybe here perhaps (along with one gesture)

With wh-words, *tana* marks indefinite assertions. For example, in discussing his plans to travel to the United States to find work, a man said:

13a) **joq'e tana t-in-xik aran**
      when AF Fut-A(1s)-go there
      someday I will go there

13b) **ab'an toj maak'a' in-tumin, toj maak'a' in-hu**
      but still not.exist E(1s)-money still not.exist E(1s)-paper
      but I still don't have money, I still don't have papers

In line (13a), the wh-word *joq'e* (when) occurs in conjunction with the afactive clitic *tana*, and I gloss the construction as 'someday'. That such an utterance acts as an indefinite assertion (rather than a question) is corroborated by the speaker's second utterance (13b), in which he qualifies his previous utterance – giving, in effect, the conditions under which a possible world would correspond with the actual world. Indeed, such indefinite assertions can be remodalized using the afactive particle *mare*, showing they are truly not questions. For example, in telling her husband that the door to their house was unlocked when she returned home from church, a woman said:

14)   **mare ani tana x-Ø-ok sa' li q-ochoch**
      maybe who AF Perf-A(3s)-enter Prep Dm E(1p)-house
      perhaps someone entered our home

In example (14), the sentence-initial particle *mare* signals epistemic possibility, and the wh-word *ani* (who), in conjunction with the afactive clitic *tana*, may be glossed as 'someone'. Notice that the presence of the afactive particle *mare* shows that the utterance does not have interrogatory illocutionary force (and that *mare* has scope over *tana*). And notice that indefinite NPs, signalled by the presence of a wh-word in conjunction with the afactive clitic *tana*, are always in focus position (insofar as wh-words are always in focus position). In this way, indefinite NPs are focused NPs.

In glossing the meaning of such indefinite assertions, speakers often use the exact same construction with the positive clitic *tawi'* in place of the afactive clitic *tana*. As mentioned above, this clitic serves to pose questions without actually asking them. Thus, in line (13a), if *tana* were replaced with *tawi'*, the utterance would be glossed as 'when could I (ever) go there?' One reason such constructions might be said to be equivalent is that the utterances with *tawi'* have as their presupposition the utterances with *tana*: to ask 'who could have done something' is to presuppose that 'someone did something'. A second reason is that utterances with *tawi'* also lose their interrogative illocutionary force: they function not as questions, but as assertions or exclamations. And lastly, speakers' interpretations of both constructions often turned on a milpa that had been broken (or trampled) or a house that had been entered (or robbed). In other words, uncertainty (indexed by *tana*) and wonder (indexed by *tawi'*) map onto prototypical fears of villagers: damage by unknowns, or nonspecifics, to one's most vulnerable inalienable possessions (field and home, livelihood and hearth).

Speakers gloss *tana* as 'you don't know, you only think' (*ink'a' nakaanaw, yal nakaak'a'uxla*). Similarly, they say that it marks 'just a thought' (*yal ta jun lix k'a'uxlankil*). In addition, speakers may add to these constructions the prepositional phrases *sa' aach'ool* (inside your heart) or *sa' aak'a'uxl* (inside your thoughts), thereby glossing *tana* as 'you only think inside your heart, you don't know'. Such decontextualized interpretations resonate with more contextualized interpretations. In particular, *tana* may occur in relative clauses headed by the predicate *k'a'uxlank* (to think): *yookin chixk'a'uxlankil naq tchalq tana, pero maaji' ninnaq joq'e*, or 'I am thinking that he will possibly come, but I still don't know when'. And *tana* may also occur in relative clauses headed by the prepositional phrase *sa' ch'oolej* (inside one's heart): *sin ch'ool laa'in tchalq tana*, or 'inside my heart he will perhaps come'. Notice, then, that the relation between possibility and actuality maps onto the relation between thinking and knowing, inside and outside, and within one's own heart versus within the hearts of others. In this way, the commitment event semantically encoded by *tana* (in contrast to the commitment event of an unmarked utterance) is interpreted as intentionalized (thought), localized (inside the heart or thoughts), and personalized (the heart or thoughts are inalienable possessions of the speaker).

Future-tense, first-person predications are often glossed with two disjunctive clauses. For example, one speaker said that to say *tinchalq tana*, or 'perhaps I will come', is to say *mare tinchalq, mare ink'a' tinchalq*, or 'perhaps I will come, perhaps I will not come'. In this way, speakers may explicitly characterize (with the afactive particle *mare*) what is pragmatically implicated (with the afactive clitic *tana*). Moreover, some speakers gloss the use of *tana* in such constructions as *ink'a' raj taawaj xyeb'al*, or 'you wouldn't want to say (but you have to)'. Thus, they interpret such utterances as indicating the speaker's lack of desire to commit herself to the actions represented by the utterance. Resonating with this presumption, they note that *tana* often occurs in answers to questions (*lix sumenkil*). In this way, when occurring in utterances which are the second part of a pair-part structure (question–answer), *tana* indexes socio-pragmatic compulsion: the obligation to respond when addressed (even when one doesn't know the answer).

Such an understanding of *tana* also arises in cases where people try to explain why *tana* is awkward with first-person, non-future predications. For example, in asking an informant whether one could say *ninchal tana*, or 'perhaps I come (from over there)', she said: *ink'a' tana, chanchan ink'a' nakaanaw b'ar tawi' nakatchal*, or 'maybe not, it's like you don't know where you could be coming from'. Notice, then, that this explanation presumes that people should have certain knowledge of their own habitual or recently undertaken actions. The speaker then suggested that such a construction could be used in a situation in which one was using a compass to find the cardinal direction (north-south-east-west) from which one came.

Lastly, unlike the other modal clitics, *tana* serves as an easily articulated marker of village identity. In particular, speakers agree that while *tana* is used in their village (and in all of the villages surrounding the *municipio* of San Juan Chamelco), the afactive clitic *na* is used in the villages surrounding the *municipios* of San Pedro Carchá and Coban. (And this accords with my experience.) Thus, one villager said: *laa'o naqaye jo'kan tana chanko*, or 'we all say *jo'kan tana'*, whereas *eb' li Coban neke'xye jo'kan na*, or 'those from Coban say *jo'kan na*'. In this way, a grammatical form marking epistemic possibility provides the most easily thematized linguistic locale for speakers' accounts of village-based identity.

6.   Optative status: *taxaq*

The optative clitic *taxaq* signals the speaker's commitment to *p* in a *wish* world. I say that the commitment world is a wish world for two reasons. First, as used here, a wish is different from a desire in that the speaker has little or no control over the state of affairs in question – and thus has no means to effect such an end. In this way, a wish cannot usually serve as the cause of its own fulfilment. And second, a wish indexes epistemic uncertainty: a wished-for event is unlikely to happen (though not impossible). In this way, by semantically encoding the speaker's commitment to *p* in a wish world, *taxaq* pragmatically implicates the speaker's commitment to not *p* in a *possible* world. In accordance with these features of wishes, most of my tokens of *taxaq* occur with narrated events involving the weather, national politics, and eco-tourism – all desirable events outside of the speaker's control. Most of the remaining tokens occur with narrated events involving the actions of one's addressee in the context of polite suggestions or prayers. In most cases, the addressee shares the speaker's commitment to the narrated event in question. That is to say, *taxaq* is said in the context of addressees whose commitments are similar to those of the speaker. Loosely speaking, while only the speaker is in the role of animator, all the participants in the speech event are in the role of principal: *several hearts are spoken for with a single mouth*. In this way, merely being in the presence of another's wish is enough to be interpolated as similarly wishful. Let me offer some examples.

15) **ink'a' taxaq yoo-Ø-Ø li hab'**
     Neg Opt do-Pres-A(3s) Dm rain
     if only it doesn't rain

Example (15) shows an utterance that was preceded and followed by silence. The speaker had just looked out the window of his house: the sky was dark and cloudy. He said, 'if only it doesn't rain', and then turned back to his breakfast. The men who would be helping him clear his field that day glanced out the window, but remained silent. Notice, then, that such an utterance – like an interjection – can punctuate silence. Notice also that here the event in question is out of the control of both the speaker and his addressees. Indeed, the state of affairs represented by his utterance will prove to be counter to the facts: it will indeed rain, as intimated by the clouds. Such an event affects each of these people equally as members of a group that is about to be engaged in a coordinated activity in shared environs. In this way, the man's utterance publicizes (and potentially topicalizes) a sentiment as a shared sentiment, thereby indexing the coordination of commitment worlds. In sum, the wishes signalled by the optative *taxaq* are often shared and relevant wishes – perhaps even the wishes of a single social person. Indeed, if one does respond to another's wish, one often just repeats the wish itself (suitably truncated): you share my commitment world; I share your commitment world; we share a commitment world. For example:

16a) **S1: yamyoo-Ø-Ø li kutan**
      clear-Pres-A(3s) Dm day
      the sky is clear

16b) **S2: jo'kan-aq taxaq li kutan hulaj, x-b'aan naq toj wan-Ø-Ø in-trabaj**
      like.this-NS Opt Dm day tomorrow E(3s)-RN Comp still exist-Pres-A(3s) E(1s)-work
      if only it's like this tomorrow, for I still have much work

16c) **S1: jo'kan taxaq**
      like.this Opt
      if only it is like this

In example (16), a woman has just returned from feeding her chickens. She tells her husband the sky is clear (16a). He replies by indicating his wish that it will be similar the next day (16b). And she responds by seconding his wish (16c). Notice that the man's upcoming work, while not directly affecting his wife, does affect her in that they share in the return of the domestic mode of production. Indeed, his well-being is her well-being, insofar as they maximally share inalienable possessions – children, home, field. In other words, their shared commitment world is a function of their shared personhood. Lastly, notice that the certainty of the narrated event in question is greater in this example than it was in example (15). That is, the strength of the speaker's commitment to not p in a possible world may be relatively weak or strong as a function of context. Let me offer an example of an exchange that occurred between a husband and wife regarding eco-tourists:

17a) **S1: t-e'-chalq len li qa-turista**
Fut-A(3p)-come they.say Dm E(1p)-tourist
they say our tourists are coming

17b) **S2: ma yaal tawi'**
Int true Pos
could it be true?

17c) **S1: mare yaal nek-Ø-e'x-ye, mare maak'a'-eb'**
maybe true Pres-A(3s)-E(3p)-say maybe not.exist-A(3p)
perhaps it's true what they say, (but) maybe there aren't any (tourists)

17d) **S2: yaal taxaq**
true Opt
if only it's true!

In this example, a man has just heard from his neighbour that the eco-tourism project has radioed to say that there will be eco-tourists arriving the next day. When the man tells this to his wife (17a), he uses the reportative particle *len*, saying 'they say our tourists are coming'. His wife replies using the positive clitic *tawi'* (17b), saying 'could it be true?' And the man answers without commitment (17c), saying 'perhaps it is true, or perhaps there aren't any (tourists)'. Lastly, his wife responds using the optative clitic *taxaq* (17d), saying 'if only it's true!'. Notice that the woman says *yaal taxaq*, or 'if only it's true!', in the presupposed context – line (17c) – that, perhaps it's not true (i.e. there are no tourists). Here the arrival of the tourists is uncertain, not so much because news of their arrival comes from a disreputable source (neither the neighbour, nor the project), but because the arrival of tourists is known to involve much contingency (they can get lost, arrive late, decide not to come at the last minute, etc.). Again, such a wish is a mutual wish for this couple: each will take part in the care of tourists when they arrive (the

husband guiding and the wife hosting), and each will benefit from the money
the tourists spend.

Let me offer an example in which the optative clitic occurs with a first-
person, optative-mood predication:

18)   **ink'a' taxaq chi-Ø-n-k'ul li rahilal**
        Neg Opt A(3s)-E(1s)-receive Dm suffering
        let me not receive the suffering!

A woman uttered line (18) one morning after having just told her husband
about a dream she had in which she fell ill. In the afternoon, she told her
mother the same story, ending with the same utterance. And that night she told
the story to her older sister, again ending with the same utterance. Notice, then,
that this utterance is serving as the resolution of the narrative itself. First-person
utterances involving *taxaq* are appropriate when the speaker has no control
over the event in question (in this utterance, the woman is in the semantic role
of experiencer, or recipient). Notice as well that while such a narrated world is
truly relevant to only one person (the speaker herself), she uses the utterance
in the context of interlocutors who are her closest relatives: husband, mother,
and older sister. In such cases, inalienable possessors who are also inalienable
possessions are the closest and most similar people to the speaker, and thus
my point about shared perspectives still holds: what is at stake for oneself is
at stake for one's closest kin. In this way, *taxaq* indexes social relations with
those from whom one expects empathy and compassion.

Lastly, let me point out that this woman's utterance is highly stylized, in that
wishes not to receive suffering are included in most prayers. In such contexts,
they are often followed by the phrase *laa'at qawa'*, or 'you are our father'. In
other words, in prayers, the optative clitic *taxaq* occurs in constructions that
are addressed to an interlocutor who *does* have some control over the events
in question. In this way, wishes become requests in the context of a powerful
enough interlocutor – and effecting this shift (from wish to request) is one
of the functions of prayer. Thus, while this woman is not ostensibly address-
ing god in her utterance, her utterance invokes such a context. In this way,
taxaq not only indexes shared commitment worlds, but also shared religious
commitments.

Second-person, future-tense or optative-mood predications often occur
with *taxaq*, but usually in the context of making polite suggestions or giving thanks – that is, wishing that one's interlocutor be reciprocated for some
favour that he or she has just done. For example, in directing her father-in-law
to a table, a woman says: *chunchuuqat taxaq re naq ink'a' tatlub'q*, or 'if only
you would be seated in order that you don't grow tired'. Here a suggestion to
sit is framed as a wish, and the speaker wishes for a narrated event in which

her addressee's comfort is at issue. Similarly, after receiving a small loan in
the market from a friend, a woman blesses her friend, and is then thanked for
this blessing:

19a) **S1: t-Ø-aa-k'ul taxaq li r-eeqaj l-aa usilal x-b'aan li qaawa'**
      Fut-A(3s)-E(2s)-receive Opt Dm E(3s)-substitute Dm-E(2s) favour E(3s)-RN
      Dm god
      if only you will receive a substitute for your favour from god

19b) **S2: b'aantiox**
      thank you (from *x-b'aan tiox* (E(3s)-RN god), or 'because of god')

Notice that in both of these examples a shared commitment world is being
indexed. Indeed, in the first example, what one might call 'politeness' or
'deference' is due in part to the speaker indicating that her wishes are her
interlocutor's wishes, and in part to the fact that a wish world entails weak
possibility: one's suggestion, as a suggestion, is left entirely in one's interlocutor's hands. As with utterances involving *tana*, the speaker is not fully committed to the truth of the utterance, because the truth of the utterance is in the
addressee's hands. And, in the second example, god is explicitly marked as the
potential agent of the favour (the relational noun *-b'aan* (because) is usually
used to mark demoted agents in passive constructions). In sum, sharedness of
a commitment world, weakness of certainty, lack of control, and petitioning
of a shared god for another's care are all features indexed by *taxaq* that can be
enlisted for expressing deferential social relations.

Taxaq can occur with interrogatory illocutionary force, but interacts with it
in a way that is similar to *tana*. Thus, in the case of wh-questions, the wh-word
is usually interpretable as 'someone' (or 'sometime', 'somewhere', etc.), such
that the utterance serves as an indefinite wish, rather than a question. Let me
offer an example in which a woman used such a construction after a church
meeting in which villagers had discussed where to find money to fix the roof
of their church:

20)   **ani taxaq ta-Ø-to'oninq r-e li tumin**
      who Opt Fut-A(3s)-lend E(3s)-RN Dm money
      if only someone would lend (us) the money!

In example (20), the wh-word *ani* (who) occurs in conjunction with *taxaq*,
and I gloss the entire construction as an indefinite wish. This utterance was said
by the woman to her mother as they were walking out of church. Essentially,
it is an echo of a claim made by participants in the preceding church service
to the effect that money was necessary to repair the roof of the church (which
was developing a leak). That is to say, the sharedness of the commitment world
is maximally presumed, being explicitly characterized in a previous, shared
context. What is initially phrased as a village-wide need, and what is initially

addressed to a congregation of villagers, is subsequently converted into the wish of a single villager, and said in the context of immediate family.

Wishing is itself not directly lexicalized in Q'eqchi' – which is similar to 'surprise' in relation to the factive clitic *pe'*. But some speakers' interpretations of the afactive clitic *taxaq* turned on the verb of desire (*ajok*), in conjunction with the counterfactive clitic *raj*. For example, these speakers suggested that *a'an taxaq* (Dm Opt), or 'if only that', may be glossed as *t-Ø-inw-aj raj a'an* (Fut-A(3s)-E(1s)-want CF Dm), or 'I would like that'. In this way, a desire predicate, inflected for future tense and first person, and followed by a coun-terfactive clitic, serves as a paraphrase for *taxaq*. Notice, then, how the shared-ness of the commitment world is not at issue in these speakers' interpretations of *taxaq*. Many speakers also paraphrased the use of *taxaq* using *taxaq*, as *us taxaq wi yaal naq Full-Clause* (good Opt if true Comp Full-Clause), or 'it would be good if it were true that ...'. Here the optative clitic follows the adjective *us* (good), and is itself followed by a full-clause complement (repre-senting the narrated event in question) introduced by the expression *wi yaal*, or 'if it's true'. In such a seemingly circular glossing (i.e. the use of *taxaq* to gloss *taxaq*), speakers lexicalize both an epistemic judgement (*yaal*) and an evaluative judgement (*us*), as the antecedent and consequent clauses of a con-ditional. In this way, speakers' interpretations of *taxaq* may frame wish worlds in terms of public values as much as personal desires.

However, many speakers offered examples of contexts in which *taxaq* would be used, rather than attempt to gloss its meaning at all. In such examples, speakers often turned to political arrangements. One man offered the follow-ing example of usage: 'Let's say perhaps that you are talking about a job. A really big job. Let's say a job done by a politician, someone who is going to be president. They will build roads. They will construct water tanks. They will construct electricity lines. They will construct everything. But they are only talking about the beginning of such tasks. And, after that, it is usually said (to them), "it would be good if you would do your tasks" (*us taxaq naq taab'aanu aak'anjel*).' I don't think such an utterance would actually be said to a pol-itician (and I have no such tokens), for clearly it is ironic: 'while I too want what you want to do, I am doubtful that you will do it'. Notice, then, that in such contexts, *taxaq* indexes doubt (or weakness of probability) as much as it indexes desire. And, in tokens of reported speech, it marks the speaker's and addressee's shared pessimism (or 'wishfulness') in the context of the promises of the reported speaker. Notice, then, the mood indexed by this modal clitic (and compare anxiety and *tana*): pessimism towards politicians' promises of progress. In this way, the most easily thematized, and perhaps prototypic, function of *taxaq* expresses ironic pessimism rather than hope. In some sense, then, *taxaq* can index memory as much as desire – frequent experiences over-taking common dreams, and thereby contributing to the split in subjectivity presupposed in the genre of irony. What is semantically encoded gives way to what is pragmatically implicated.

7.   Factive status: *pe'*

The factive clitic *pe'* signals the speaker's commitment to *p* in *this* world, thereby markedly specifying what is usually assumed. With unmarked illocutionary force, it has three general functions. First, it may be used to assert *p* in the context of either the addressee's non-commitment to *p* or the addressee's commitment to not *p*, thereby serving as either an *insistive* or a *contradictive*. Second, it may be used to exclaim *p* in the context of the speaker's recent learning of *p*, creating the context of the speaker's prior or current non-commitment to *p*, thereby serving as a *surprisitive* or *dubitive*. And third, it may be used to exclaim *p* in the context of the speaker's recent learning of *p*, in the context of the speaker's learning of *p* being in question, thereby serving as a *satiative*. I will exemplify these functions in turn.

Functioning as an insistive or a contradictive, *pe'* often follows an explicit assertion contradicting what the addressee has just said. It may also occur with first- and second-person, future-tense predications, in which the speaker informs their addressee what will happen to them, or what the speaker is planning to do. In such contexts, *pe'* can have a function similar to deontic necessity, or obligation. (Compare *tana* as epistemic possibility functioning as deontic possibility, or permission.) With third-person predications, it is often used for emphasis. For example:

21)   **moko li winq ta, ha' pe' li ixq x-Ø-b'aanun r-e**
NF the man NF Focus F Dm woman Perf-A(3s)-do E(3s)-RN
it was the woman who did it, not the man

22)   **ha' pe' laa'at t-at-kamq**
Focus F A(2s) Fut-A(2s)-die
you will die! (From Berinstein 1985)

23a)   **ani tawi' ta-Ø-xik**
who Pos Fut-A(3s)-go
who could go?

23b)   **m-at-k'a'uxlaak, ha' pe' laa'in t-in-xik**
NImp-A(2s)-worry Focus F A(1s) Fut-A(1s)-go
don't you worry, I will go

Example (21) shows the factive clitic *pe'* in the context of contradicting what the addressee has just said: in the first clause, their assertion is denied; and in the second clause, the narrated event to which the speaker is committed is asserted against this ground using *pe'* with the focus particle *ha'*. Example (22) shows a relatively rare second-person, future-tense predication.

It was taken from a story in which one character informs the other about their impending fate. Example (23) shows *pe'* in the context of answering a speaker's posed question, marked by the positive clitic *tawi'* in line (23a). Line (23b) also shows the speaker's lexicalization of the addressee's emotional state ('to worry', the antipassive form of *k'a'uxlank*, 'to think'), presumably indexed by their usage of the positive clitic *tawi'* in line (23a).

Let me offer some examples of speaker-directed uses, serving as satiatives, surprisitives, and dubitives. It is early in the morning, a woman is fixing breakfast, and her husband is warming himself by the hearth fire. She asks:

24a)   **S1: jarub' hoor tawi'**
       how.many hour Pos
       what time could it be?

He answers:

24b)   **S2: saber, toj maaji' a las syete**
       who.knows still not at the seven (Spanish construction)
       who knows, it's not yet seven

They listen to the radio until the announcer says it is seven-fifteen. The man then says:

24c)   **S2: ak x-Ø-nume' pe' a las syete**
       already Perf-A(3s)-pass F at the seven
       it's already past seven!

In line (24c), the factive clitic *pe'* signals that the speaker is now committed to this proposition, against the ground of his previous enunciated weak commitment to 'not yet seven' (24b). It should be emphasized that the woman was listening to the radio as well, and thus heard the announcement when her husband did. That is to say, the man is neither informing his wife of the time, nor correcting her belief about the time. He is rather correcting his own previous assessment (however weak it was, as indexed by *saber*, or 'who knows'), in addition to expressing something akin to 'surprise'.

As seen in this last example, the factive clitic *pe'* often follows constructions involving the positive clitic *tawi'*. There is often an intervening period in which the speaker or addressee engages in some activity designed to discover the answer to their original question (for example, listening to the radio, searching for something, or asking someone). Interestingly, against the ground of 'wonder' or 'worry' indexed by the positive clitic *tawi'*, as in lines (23a) and (24a), the factive clitic *pe'* can be used outside the context of the speaker's prior commitment to the contrary. In such *satiative* contexts, the factive clitic *pe'* is used against the ground of the speaker just learning – and often through difficulty – what they were previously wondering about. For example, in learning how to use an A-frame with a plumb line to terrace his field, a man placed the instrument in a number of positions, trying to figure out how it worked. When he realized the plumb line was supposed to fall down the middle of the A-frame whenever its feet rested on a contour line, he said: *jo'ka'in pe'* (like. this F), or 'like this (it's supposed to work)!'

I have one token of *pe'* occurring with the ostensive evidential deictic *wili'*, or 'look there'. This token occurred in a man's reporting of his own speech, in the context of giving an example of the meaning of the factive clitic *pe'*. Here he had been discussing how, after he found that someone had smashed his corn field (*li xyok'ok li wawimj*), he lay in wait for them (*sa'muqmu*) to return again. When they did return, and he finally saw who they were, he said (to himself), *aah, wili' pe' li nab'aanun re li wawimj*, or 'aah look (factive) at who is doing this to my field!' Here, then, the difference between the speaker-directed and addressee-directed functions of *pe'* is blurred. Indeed, the ostensive evidential *wili'* is essentially functioning as an imperative to look, such that the man reports himself telling himself to look at evidence for a narrated event he is committed to in *this* world of the reported speech event. And here, once again, local anxieties regarding the violation of home and field come to the fore in speakers' interpretations of various commitment worlds indexed by the modal clitics.

Such a use in reporting one's own speech, and thereby describing one's own reaction, is quite common. *Pe'* also frequently occurs in the reported speech of others, even as their internal speech. Recall from chapter 1 the example taken from the legend of the sun and the moon: after discovering that his daughter (the moon) is not in bed, the moon's father realizes that the hummingbird she had brought to bed with her the night before was not a real hummingbird (but actually the sun):

25a) **ma ink'a' x-Ø-w-eek'a moko tz'aqal tz'unun ta**
      Int Neg Perf-A(3s)-E(1s)-sense NF real hummingbird NF
      'did I not sense it (was) not a real hummingbird?'

25b) **a'an pe' ki-Ø-elq'an r-e in-rab'in**
      Dm F Inf-A(3s)-steal E(3s)-RN E(1s)-daughter
      'he must be the one who stole my daughter!'

25c) **chan-Ø-Ø r-aatinank-il r-ib' li-x junes**
      say-Pres-A(3s) E(3s)-speak-Nom E(3s)-Rflx Dm-E(3s) alone
      he says, speaking to himself alone

Notice that contradictives and insistives are relatively addressee directed, whereas exclamatives and dubitives are relatively speaker directed. In the first case, the addressee's commitment is already known (or presupposed); in the second case, the speaker's commitment is newly known (or created). In other words, in shifting from addressee focus to speaker focus (person), we shift from present to past (time), assertion to exclamation (illocutionary force), and old to new (information). In this way, the commitment world being *this* world can be contrasted internally (with the speaker's previous commitment world) or dialogically (with the addressee's current commitment world). That is to say, there are symmetries between speaker-focused and addressee-focused usages – such that each may be understood as a mirror image of the other: surprise is the mirror image of insistence; and doubt the mirror image of contradiction. (Though, from a developmental perspective, speaker-directed functions may be the *internalization* of addressee-directed functions.)

The factive clitic *pe'* is judged to be marginally appropriate with first-person predications. Given that the factive clitic signals that the speaker is committed to the truth of the narrated event in *this* world, this makes intuitive sense: people should have knowledge of their own actions. And, indeed, the relatively few tokens I have of such constructions occur with future-tense predications. In line (23b), for example, a speaker makes a promise. And in example (26), a man was describing his attempt to use a pay-phone in the city of Coban. Never having used one before, and not understanding Spanish, he had tried several times without success. Finally, he got discouraged and sat down to watch someone else use it. A Ladino woman came over, put her money in, and made a call. In describing himself watching this, this man reported his own internal speech:

26)   **jo'kan pe' t-Ø-in-k'e chan-k-in s-in ch'ool**
       like.that F Fut-A(3s)-E(1s)-give say-Pres-A(1s) Prep-E(1s) heart
       'like that I'll do it!' I said inside my heart

One informant told me there were certain situations in which the factive clitic could be used with present-tense predications. And he offered the example of using a compass to figure out where one has just come from. In setting up this example, he says that one is 'wondering' where one came from – literally 'thinking inside one's head where it could be'. And as soon as one finds out where one is (using the compass), one may say *aah, ninchal pe' arin*, or 'aah, I came (F) from here!' In such cases, then, it is not so much 'surprise' that one is indexing, but release from puzzlement or wonder. Thus, such a first-person predication, in conjunction with *pe'*, is appropriate when functioning as a satiative.

The factive clitic *pe'* is also judged to be marginally appropriate with second-person predications. Again, such constructions usually involve future-tense predications. In example (22), there exists the rather ghastly – and one imagines rare – case of a speaker informing an addressee about his impending death. Given the semantics of this clitic, the general inappropriateness of such constructions makes intuitive sense: people should not be asserting information about others to those others insofar as those others should already have knowledge of their own actions. (Notice that in this example the narrated event (dying) is a state-change, and the subject is in the semantic role of theme or patient rather than effector or agent.) Accordingly, my only tokens of this clitic with future-tense predications are speaker directed (rather than addressee directed). For example, a man's brother comes to dinner and is talking to the man's wife about his work on a distant plantation in lowland Guatemala. The man says:

27a)   **S1: laa'in x-in-nume' chaq Corozal**
        A(1s) Perf-A(1s)-pass hither Corozal
        I passed by Corozal

And the woman says:

27b)   **S2: aah, x-at-nume' chaq le', n-Ø-in-naw li k'aleb'aal a'an**
        Interj Perf-A(2s)-pass hither there Pres-A(3s)-E(1s)-know Dm village Dm
        aah, you passed by there, I know that village

And then she continues:

27c)   **S2: aah x-at-chal pe' le'**
        Interj Perf-A(2s)-come F there
        aah, so you came from over there!

Notice that the use of *pe'* in line (27c) does not immediately follow the speaker's learning of the information in question. Rather, she has already indexed her commitment to the truth of the speaker's assertion in the first clause of line (27b); and she has already lexicalized the relevance of his assertion to her – a hitherto unknown degree of connection – in the second clause of line (27b). In this way, *pe'* need not immediately follow the presentation of new information, so much as the processing of that information.

When asked to offer interpretations of the meaning of *pe'*, speakers say that it means 'you just discovered now' (*toje' xaataw anaqwan*), or that 'you just now know' (*toja' naq xaanaw laa'at*). In this way, speakers interpret *pe'* in terms of recently perfected aspect (*toje'*, or 'just', along with the MATE *x-*) and either the predicate *na'ok* (to know) or the predicate *ta'ok* (to discover). More contextualized interpretations of *pe'* occur mid-utterance, and often turn on what was 'inside one's heart' rather than what one has just learnt. For example, in discussing his day at the market, a man described himself asking a vendor where he could buy apples (presuming that the vendor didn't have any to sell). When the vendor replied that she had apples left, the man reported his own speech as *wan pe' manzaan, sin ch'ool laa'in maak'a' chik*, or 'there are still apples!' (said to vendor in reported speech event); 'inside my heart there were no more left' (said to actual addressees in current speech event). Here the man explicitly described to his current addressees ('inside my heart …') what he pragmatically implicated with his previous utterance to his reported speech addressee ('there are still apples!'). In some sense, then, to speakers of Q'eqchi' the factive clitic *pe'* prototypically indexes new and correct knowledge against the ground of old and erroneous belief. And this disjuncture between erroneous and actual worlds is easily interpreted in terms of the localization of facts: explicitly inside one's heart (erroneous) versus implicitly outside in the world (actual). Recall how the speaker's possible commitment world, indexed by *tana*, was localized in the speaker's heart, and said to be mere 'thought' rather than 'knowledge'. In this way, both error and uncertainty are located in the heart, one's deepest and most hidden inalienable possession: with *pe'*, what *was* in the heart as 'belief'; and with *tana*, what *is* in the heart as 'thought'.

Lastly, notice that the factive clitic *pe'* was never glossed as 'surprise'. Indeed, there is no obvious word for surprise in the Q'eqchi' language (though there are several for 'fright', as discussed in chapter 2). This is not because 'surprise' (or satiation) is a rare phenomenon, but perhaps rather it is salient enough to have been grammaticalized in a clitic. A similar fact seems to exist for the positive clitic *tawi'*, which often indexes 'wonder'; the optative clitic *taxaq*, which often indexes 'wishing'; and the counterfactive clitic *raj*, which often indexes 'intention'. In each of these cases, then, a highly salient, but nonetheless non-lexicalized, intentional state is prototypically expressed by a grammatical operator. Indeed, as discussed in section 4, it is really expressed by the disjuncture between the semantically encoded commitment and the pragmatically implicated commitment. Through the highly motivated relation between encoding and implication, it is as if these clitics are iconic indices of mental states as much as conventional symbols.

The factive clitic *pe'* may be used with interrogatory illocutionary force in three general contexts. First, it may be used to question *p* in the context of the addressee presuming the speaker's commitment to *p*, creating the context of the speaker's non-commitment to *p*, thereby serving as a *repairative*. Second, it may be used to question *p* in the context of the speaker's commitment to *p*, and in the context of the addressee's commitment to *p* being in question, thereby serving as a *quizzative* or *bluffative*. And third, it may be used to question *p* in the context of the speaker's commitment to *p* being in question, in the context of the addressee's commitment to *p*, thereby serving as a *confirmative*. If the usage of interrogative illocutionary force usually presumes that the speaker doesn't know the answer and the addressee does, the various functions of *pe'* turn on violations of this assumption. Let me offer some examples.

The most frequent use of *pe'* with interrogatory illocutionary force is in the context of asking an addressee a question whose answer should already be known to the speaker. For example, if one has previously learnt the name of another person, but then forgotten it, one may ask the person's name again, but this time with the factive clitic: *ani pe' aa-k'ab'a'* (who F E(2s)-name), or 'what's your name again?' Similarly, if one comes into a story late, and cannot figure out who or what the current topic is (for example, the antecedents of anaphoric expressions such as pronouns), one may use *pe'* to learn the presumed identity of the referent. For example, in recounting a story about some vandals who had stolen a statue from the church in a nearby town, a man was interrupted by his father, who had just joined the conversation:

28a) **S1: xko'o'-eb' tana, ab'an b'ar tawi', ink'a' n-Ø-in-naw**
go(Perf)-A(3p) AF but where Pos Neg Pres-A(3s)-E(1s)-know
they probably took off, but where (they could have gone) I do not know

28b) **S2: ani pe' xko'o'-Ø**
who F go(Perf)-A(3s)
who took off?

28c) **S1: eb' li kristyan li x-e'-muxuk r-e li iglesya**
A(3p) Dm people Dm Perf-A(3p)-profane E(3s)-RN Dm church
the people who profaned the church

In line (28a), the speaker assumes that his addressee can identify the topic (those people who 'took off' after they stole the statue). In line (28b), the speaker questions that assumption – against the ground of his recently entering the conversation, not against the ground of the previous speaker's erroneous assumption. And in line (28c), the first speaker makes explicit the presumption.

For the ethnographer, the most frequently used repairative occurs with the wh-word *chanru* (how), and occurs in the context of being asked a question, thereby indicating that the speaker did not understand the question. Here the expression *chan pe' ru* functions as 'how's that?', or perhaps even 'come again?'. Let me offer an example in which I mispronounced a word upon introducing it as a topic:

29a) **S1: ma us t-o-aatinaq chi-r-ix li eeqa**
Int good Fut-A(1p)-speak Comp-E(3s)-RN Dm substitution
is it okay that we speak about substitution (mispronounced)?

29b) **S2: cham-pe'-r-u**
how-F-E(3s)-face
how's that?

29c) **S1: li eeqa**
Dm substitution
substitution (mispronounced)

29d) **S2: eeqaj**
substitution (stressed)

29e) **S1: eeqaj**
substitution

29f) **S2: hehe'**
yes

Cham- pe'-ru is also used in the context of message distortion because of poor channels or distant addressees: a woman in her house calling to a child outside; a man in his field talking to a distant passer-by. Indeed, my room was between the main house (where a mother worked) and the yard (where her children played), so I heard such exchanges yelled back and forth all day. For these reasons, perhaps, speakers tend to gloss such repairative constructions (*champe'ru*) as 'I didn't hear very well what you said' (*ink'a' xwab'i chi us li k'aru xaaye*). And they will often interpret such constructions as commands to 'say it to me again' (*ye we wi'chik*).

In confirmative utterances, *pe'* may be used to question *p* in the context of the speaker's commitment to *p* being in question, in the context of the addressee's commitment to *p*. In such contexts, it occurs with the word 'truth' (*yaal*), and serves as a tag question following an otherwise unmarked assertion: 'p *pe' yaal?*' For example, after offering a Spanish gloss for a Q'eqchi' word to his wife, a man turned to me and said: *pe' yaal*, or 'it's true, isn't it?' And I answered: *yaal, kama'an*, or 'it's true, that is how it is'. Such constructions thereby also index local assumptions about hierarchies of expertise. (Such a construction is often used to gain the addressee's assent to an assertion before using that assertion as a reason in an argument or inference.) As a confirmative, it can also be used to express one's surprise, and thereby serve as a positive minimal response. Thus, after the speaker has been informed of some assertion *p*, he or she can say *pe' yaal*, 'in truth (F)'. And the addressee can respond *yaal*, or 'in truth', and keep talking. For example, in an aside about the meaning of the word *ajom* (desire) in the context of an ethnographic interview, a man said the following:

30a)   **l-aaw-aj-om w-ik'in a'an jun tzolok, pe' yaal**
       Dm-E(2s)-desire-Nom E(1s)-RN Dm one study F true
       your desire with me is a study (i.e. dissertation), isn't it?

The anthropologist nodded his head, and the man continued:

30b)   **pues si, a'an na-Ø-r-aj na-Ø-x-ye li aatin, li r-aj-om**
       well yes Dm Pres-A(3s)-E(3s)-want Pres-A(3s)-E(3s)-say Dm word Dm E(3s)-desire-Nom
       indeed, that what the word 'its desire' means

30c)   **a'an li ajel li r-u r-e, r-e li mas t-at-aatinaq, pe' yaal**
       Dm Dm importance Dm E(3s)-RN E(3s)-RN E(3s)-RN Dm most Fut-A(2s)-talk F true
       that's the most important for, for us to talk the most about, isn't it?

In example (30), the speaker seems to be trying to get away from talking about his role in the church (the current interview topic) by turning my questions back to grammar. To do this, he tries to show that his reluctance to talk about his role is due to his sense that my real desire, or purpose, had to do with language rather than religion. His use of the tag question *pe'yaal*, then, served to get my confirmation to his own claims about what my real desire was, such that he could shift the discussion back to less personal matters. (Notice the implicit avoidance of directly asserting what one's addressee's desire is.) Here, then, the confirmative function of *pe'* is in the service of relatively polite (if somewhat condescending) thematic evasion.

The factive clitic *pe'* is also used either to quiz people about what they should know or, in more marked cases, to call someone's bluff about what they purport to know. The first case is by far the most frequent, and occurs in catechism (questions designed to elicit the recital of doctrinal knowledge) or, less frequently, a parent asking a child about some fact they learnt in school. Such a question can also be used to ask someone whether they did something they were supposed to do, such as something they were ordered to do. For example, after having left a task for his son to do while he was away, a man said to the son upon his return: *k'a pe' ru xaab'aanu* (what F Perf-A(3s)-E(2s)-do), or 'what (F) did you do?' (i.e. 'you did it, didn't you?). Notice, then, that quizzative uses of *pe'* may be functionally similar to confirmative uses.

Finally, *pe'* is used as a bluffative (or 'callyourbluffative') in contexts where an addressee has presumed to know *p*, and the speaker is trying to expose their conceit. For example, returning to my host's house, I asked his son if he knew where his father had put my sleeping bag. I said this in front of the host himself, partly in jest: for he would always reassure me that his children didn't know where he put my stuff while I was away (so they couldn't mess around with it). When the child said yes, the man mocked chagrin to me, and then asked his son: *b'ar pe' x-Ø-in-k'e* (where F Perf-A(3s)-E(1s)-give), or 'where (F) did I put it then?' The child hesitated, shook his head, and said: *ink'a' nin-naw*, or 'I don't know'. And the man smiled and said to me: *ab'i*, or 'listen!' (as in 'didn't I tell you so').

8.   Counterfactive status: *raj*

The counterfactive clitic *raj* signals the speaker's commitment to *p* in *another* world. By signalling this commitment, it invites the implicature that the speaker is committed to not *p* in *this* world. Its morphology links it to the verb *ajok* (to want), which, in its nominalized and possessed form, is *r-aj-b'al* (E(3s)-desire-Nom), or 'its desiring'. Broadly speaking, this clitic has three interrelated functions. In dependent clauses, it may mark hypothetical or intentional worlds. With future-tense predications, it may mark deference or contingency. And, as seen in the opening example of this monograph, with past-tense or perfective-aspect predications, it may mark attempting without success, intending without action, or 'almosting' without consequence.

To signal a hypothetical world, speakers often use the predicate *yehok* (to say), in the first-person-plural, imperative mood: *qayehaq*, or 'let's say'. In this way, hypotheticalness is signalled by explicitly localizing the speaker's commitment in a shared and implored speech event – a hortative world of speaking. In Q'eqchi', the noun *na'leb*, which is an instrumentalization of the verb *na'ok* (to know), is used to refer to 'examples' (as well as to 'habit', 'reason', 'custom', 'thought', and 'advice'). In particular, when offering such hypothetical examples, speakers of Q'eqchi' will often qualify what they are saying using this word, explaining of the state of affairs in question that 'it's only an example' or 'instrument for knowing' (*ka'ajwi' jun na'leb'*). Once a hypothetical frame has been signalled in such a way (often in conjunction with the afactive particle *mare*), the first utterance representing a narrated event within it may be marked by the counterfactive clitic *raj*. In other words, *another world* (in which the speaker is committed to some narrated event) is explicitly localized in a hortative speech event. Subsequent utterances, characterizing other narrated events in the hypothetical frame, need not be marked by *raj*: the assumption of counterfactuality is carried throughout the frame. Let me offer two examples:

31) **qa-ye-haq mare t-Ø-in-ket raj tzekeemj**
   E(1p)-say-NS perhaps Fut-A(3s)-E(1s)-eat CF food
   let's say perhaps I was going to eat some food

32a) **qa-ye-haq, eeh, mare wan-Ø-Ø jun-aq aa, eeh, k'aru jun-aq li w-amigo**
   E(1p)-say-NS Interj perhaps exist-Pres-A(3s) one-NS Interj Interj what one-NS Dm E(1s)-friend
   let's say, um, perhaps you have a, um, I have a friend

32b) **li w-amigo ak x-Ø-in-b'oq chaq**
   Dm E(1s)-friend already Perf-A(3s)-E(1s)-call hither
   the friend I just called over

32c) **eeh, ak x-Ø-in-b'oq chaq, mare ewer-aq**
   Interj already Perf-A(3s)-E(1s)-call hither perhaps yesterday-NS
   um, I just called over, perhaps yesterday

32d) **entonses, eeh, t-Ø-k'ulunq chik jun-aq li**
   then Interj Fut-A(3s)-come again one-NS Dm
   then, um, someone else will come

32e) **qa-ye-haq mare in-yuwa' raj ki-Ø-k'ulun w-ik'in**
   E(1p)-say-NS perhaps E(1s)-father CF Inf-A(3s)-come E(1s)-RN
   let's say perhaps my father came to me

32f) **entons t-Ø-in-ye raj r-e t-Ø-chalq raj li winq a'an**
   then Fut-A(3s)-E(1s)-say CF E(3s)-RN Fut-A(3s)-come CF Dm man Dm
   then I would say to him, 'that man was going to come'

Example (31) shows a hypothetical event marked by *qayehaq* (let's say) and *mare* (perhaps). As may be seen, the narrated event in question is described using the counterfactive clitic *raj*. Example (32) shows a much more extended hypothetical event. In line (32a), *qayehaq* and *mare* are used to introduce a topic, but the existence of this topic is not itself marked by *raj*. In line (32e), the speaker again uses *qayehaq* and *mare* to introduce a second, related event. Here, however, the topic itself (the existence of the speaker's father) is presumed, and it is only the action of the father that is at issue: it is counterfactually indicated by *raj*. And line (32f) brings both events together: the speaker tells his father that he expected another man to come (but instead the father did). Notice that there is a double embedding of counterfacticity in this line: the first *raj* locates the event of reported speaking in the hypothetical world signalled by *qayehaq* and *mare*; the second *raj* locates the event of coming in the reported speaker's commitment world (which is a world *other* than the reported-speech world).

The counterfactive clitic seems to be obligatory in the consequent clauses of counterfactive conditionals (and it often occurs in the antecedent clauses as well). Let me offer an example in which a woman is describing to her friend how her step-mother told the godfather of her first child that she was having misgivings about having him be the godfather of her second child (causing him to become angry with her – the repercussions of which were discussed in example (9)):

33a) **S1: a'an li r-ixaqil l-in yuwa'**
Dm Dm E(3s)-wife Dm-E(1s) father
she is the wife of my father

33b) **S2: us**
good
okay

33c) **S1: li li qana' Rosario, ma nak-Ø-aa-naw b'i' r-u**
Dm Dm SD Rosario Int Pres-A(3s)-E(2s)-know then E(3s)-face
Doña Rosario, do you know her then?

33d) **S2: hehe'**
yes
okay

33e) **S1: a'an, x-b'aan naq a'an x-kab' in-na'**
Dm E(3s)-RN Comp Dm E(3s)-second E(1s)-mother
her, because she's my step-mother

33f) **S1: moko tz'aqal in-na' ta chik**
NF real E(1s)-mother NF again
she's not my real mother

33g) **S2: hehe'**
yes
okay

33h) **S1: ... mas yik'ti' x-Ø-x-numsi r-e li r-iitz'in**
much lie Perf-A(3s)-E(3s)-pass E(3s)-RN Dm E(3s)-younger.brother
she has passed on lots of lies to her younger brother

33i) **S1: r-iitz'in a'an li-x wa', x-wa'chin laj Humb'erto**
E(3s)-younger.brother Dm Dm-E(3s)-? E(3s)-godfather SD Humberto
her younger brother is the godfather of Humberto

33j) **S2: aah**
Interj
aah

33k) **S1: x-b'aan yik'ti' a'an na-Ø-x-numsi r-e**
E(3s)-RN lie Dm Pres-A(3s)-E(3s)-pass E(3s)-RN
because of the lies she passes on to him

33l) **S2: aah**
Interj
aah

33m) **S1: naq wi raj tz'aqal in-na', moko x-Ø-x-numsi ta raj li aatin a'an**
Comp if CF real E(1s)-mother NF Perf-A(3s)-E(3s)-pass NF CF Dm word Dm
if she were my real mother, she would not have passed on those words

In example (33), a counterfactive conditional does not appear until line
(33m). There, both the antecedent (or 'if-clause') and the consequent (or 'then-
clause') are marked by the counterfactive clitic *raj*. Notice that the propositions
expressed by each of these clauses were explicitly contradicted in previous
lines: for the antecedent, line (33f); and for the consequent, lines (33h) and
(33k). Example (34) shows a counterfactive conditional in which only the consequent is marked by the counterfactive clitic *raj*. The antecedent, which is
known to be false only by its own uttering (that is, while the clause presumes
that the speaker did indeed gather up all the clothing, this was the first time this
action was mentioned in the speech event). In both examples, the antecedents
of counterfactual conditionals lexically characterize, or make explicit, the conditions that would have to hold for the speaker to be committed to the consequent: they represent the relevant features of *another* world.

34) **wi ta ink'a' x-Ø-qa-xok li t'ikr, x-Ø-taq'aak raj**
if IR Neg Perf-A(3s)-E(1p)-gather Dm clothing Perf-A(3s)-become.wet CF
if we hadn't gathered up the clothing it all would have become wet

The counterfactive clitic *raj* also occurs in the dependent clauses of certain complement-taking predicates. Let me offer an example, with the verb
k'a'uxlank (think, intend):

35a) **x-Ø-in-k'a'uxla wib' sut, malaj oxib' sut, naq n-in-xik raj**
Perf-A(3s)-E(1s)-think two time or three time Comp Pres-A(1s)-go CF
I thought two times or three times that I was going to go

35b) **pero ink'a' wi'chik n-in-xik**
      but Neg again Pres-A(1s)-go
      but again I didn't go

Line (35a) shows the predicate *k'a'uxlank* (to think) followed by a full-clause complement, marked by the counterfactive clitic *raj*. It is as if another world (in which the speaker is committed to the state of affairs represented by the complement) is being located in a thought world (represented by the complement-taking predicates). The *raj* in this construction is not obligatory: it seems that the pragmatic implication of *raj* (that the speaker is not committed to the truth of the narrated event in this world) is the real information. In other words, such constructions indicate that one's thoughts or expectations did not correspond with the world. Line (35b) shows that this pragmatically implicated context may be lexically reinforced: it is not redundant to subsequently assert the implication.

The second major function of the counterfactive clitic *raj* is to mark contingency of actions and thus deference towards actors. Such constructions usually involve future-tense predications, and signal that an event is contingent upon the addressee's desires and decisions, thereby serving as polite requests. For example, when leaving a work group one day, a man says goodbye to his father-in-law, and then says:

36a) **S1: ma wan-q-at sa' aaw-ochoch hulaj**
      Int be-Fut-A(2s) Prep E(2s)-home tomorrow
      will you be home tomorrow?

The father-in-law replies:

36b) **S2: hehe'**
      yes

And the man says:

36c) **S1: aah pues t-in-chalq raj aaw-ik'in hulaj**
      Interj well Fut-A(1s)-come CF E(2s)-RN tomorrow
      aah, well I was going to come to your house tomorrow

And the father-in-law replies:

36d) **S2: us b'i'**
      good then

In line (36a), a man asks his father-in-law whether he will be home the next day. When his father-in-law says yes, the man states his plan using a future-tense predication and the counterfactive clitic *raj*. That is, rather than saying he will come the next day, he says there is *another* world in which he will come, and pragmatically implicates that in *this* world he will not come. Here the counterfactive clitic *raj* serves to mark one's contingent intentions – contingent because they depend on the actions or desires of one's addressee. In effect, line (36c) provides a reason for the question in line (36a): 'if you were going to be home (and otherwise available), I was going to come (but if not, then I won't)'. Such an utterance, then, allows one's addressee to decide whether *this world* or *another world* will be the actual world the following day. In this way, politeness is achieved by signalling that one's own actions are contingent on one's addressee's actions. Notice, then, that with future-tense predications, insofar as the narrated event has not yet come to pass, the difference between the speech event and the commitment event is interpretable as a choice between two options rather than as an intention versus an action, or a hypothetical world versus an actual world. Indeed, speakers characterize such future-tense counterfactive constructions as *sa' wib' li ru naxye* or 'it says two things (at once)', *qayehaq mare wan aahonal, ut mare ink'a'*, or 'perhaps you (the addressee) have time, and perhaps you don't'.

Similarly, with second-person, future-tense predications, the counterfactive clitic *raj* may be used to make suggestions. For example, in setting up an ethnographic interview, a man said: *t-in-aaw-aatina raj chaq kab'ej* (Fut-A(1s)-E(2s)-speak CF hither two.days.hence) or 'you would come to speak to me in two days'. Here, his utterance says, in effect, 'in another world we will speak in two days', and leaves the pragmatically implicated context (in this world we will not speak in two days) to be reinforced or defeased by the addressee's decision to go, or not to go. Again, it is left in the addressee's hands whether another world or this world, the semantically encoded world or the pragmatically implicated world, will be the actual world.

Such future-tense, counterfactive constructions often occur with the adjective *us* (good) to signal polite suggestions (second-person predications) or uncertain desires (first-person predications). Such constructions function as conditionals in which the second clause (qua antecedent) specifies the relevant properties of *another* world (which would be the good world). Because *another* world is a future world, it is still in the speaker's or addressee's hands as to whether the future world will be a good world. Let me offer some examples:

37a) **us raj t-o-xik toj eq'ela, malaj sa' kaa'ib' hoor**
good CF Fut-A(1p)-go still early or Prep four hour
it would be good if we left early, (perhaps) at four o'clock

37b) **x-b'aan naq t-Ø-qa-seeb' q-ib' sa' qa-trabaj**
E(3s)-RN Comp Fut-A(3s)-E(1p)-hurry E(1p)-Rflx Prep E(1p)-job
because we can speed up our task

38) **us raj t-Ø-aa-seeb' aaw-ib' chi-x-tzol-b'al l-aa k'anjel**
good CF Fut-A(3s)-E(2s)-hurry E(2s)-Rflx Comp-E(3s)-study-Nom Dm-E(2s)
job
it would be good if you hurry learning your job

39)   **us raj t-in-xik, ab'an toj maji' n-Ø-in-naw**
good CF Fut-A(1s)-go but still not.yet Pres-A(3s)-E(1s)-know
it would be good if I go, but I still don't know (whether I will)

In example (37), a group of men have just finished clearing a section of the speaker's land. In line (37a), the speaker uses the construction *us raj* to suggest that they begin work again early the next day; and, in line (37b), he then gives a reason for this suggestion. In example (38), a man tells his younger brother to hurry up learning his job. And in example (39), a man is discussing the possibility that he will go to work on a plantation in the lowlands, where he hears there is a relatively high-paying job.

In glossing constructions likes those shown in examples (37–39), speakers' interpretations turn on trying to convince another person to do something which they do not want to do: literally, 'they do not think (intend, desire) to do it'. In this way, such suggestions arise in the context of trying to change another's desire – such that they will act on their own accord in a way that is aligned with the speaker's desire. But rather than frame the speaker's desire as a desire (what you want versus what I want), it is framed as an impersonal value (what is good). For example, one speaker's interpretation was as follows:

40a)   **qa-ye-haq mare mas wan-Ø-Ø jun ajb'al li r-u qa-trabaj**
E(1p)-say-NS perhaps much exist-Pres-A(3s) one important Dm E(3s)-face E(1p)-task
let's say perhaps we have an important task

40b)   **pero laa'at maak'a' mas aa-k'a'uxl chi xik**
but A(2s) not.exist much E(3s)-thought Comp go
but you don't have much desire to go

40c)   **eeh chi-x-b'aanunk-il li qa-trabaj a'an**
Interj Comp-E(3s)-do-Nom Dm E(1p)-task Dm
eeh, to do this task of ours

40d)   **entonses t-Ø-in-ye raj aaw-e, us raj t-o-xik hulaj**
so Fut-A(3s)-E(1s)-say CF E(2s)-RN good CF Fut-A(1p)-go tomorrow
so I would say to you, 'it would be good if we go tomorrow'

40e)   **mas naab'al chik qa-trab'aj kab'ej**
(because) more much again E(1p)-task two.days.from.now
because we will have more work in two days

Deferential relations are also signalled by the use of the counterfactive clitic *raj* in conjunction with the nonfactive particle *ink'a'*, and a yes/no question. For example:

41)   **ma ink'a' raj t-Ø-aa-b'aanu us-il-al, eeh, t-in-aaw-aatina raj**
Int Neg CF Fut-A(3s)-E(2s)-do good-SF-SF Interj Fut-A(1s)-E(2s)-speak CF
would you not do me a favour, eeh, you would speak to me

The first clause in example (41) has five separate factors contributing to its status as highly deferential. First, there is the predicate itself, which characterizes the addressee's action as the doing of a favour, or 'goodness' (*usilal*). Second, this predicate is inflected for future tense, so the narrated event is still open, and thereby contingent upon the addressee's actions. Third, as signalled by the non-factive particle *ink'a'*, the polarity of the narrated event is negative. Fourth, with the counterfactive clitic *raj*, the speaker marks his commitment to the narrated event (itself already inverted and future tensed) as holding in *another* world, pragmatically implicating that he is committed to the addressee doing a favour in *this* world. And fifth, with the question particle *ma*, the speaker signals that the truth of the proposition is known by the speaker – and thus it is within the speaker's control (given that the predicate is an activity inflected for second person). In this way, the second clause represents an event that the speaker will be committed to in *another* world – one in which the addressee's answer to the first clause is yes. In sum, interrogative illocutionary force, negative polarity, future tense, and counterfactive status (plus a construal of the action as a favour) is a highly deferential – if somewhat wheedling and obsequious – form of suggestion.

The last function of the counterfactive clitic *raj* is the least marked and perhaps the most frequent: it may be used with perfect-aspect predications (usually functioning as past tense) to mark the speaker's commitment to *p* in *another* world, pragmatically implicating the speaker's commitment to not *p* in *this* world. Notice that, like future-tense predications, there are two possible worlds being signalled; however, unlike future tense (where which world is the actual world is yet to be determined), one world is actual and the other is counterfactual. In such constructions, *another* world may be intentionalized, ethicalized, or almost-ized. And, when intentionalized, the intentional world in question may belong to the speaker or narrated actor, depending on the animacy of the narrated actor, their relation of control to the event in question, and whether the narrated actor is a participant in the speech event or not. Let me offer some examples:

42) **x-in-k'ulun raj ewer, pero ink'a' x-in-e'x-toj**
Perf-A(1s)-come CF yesterday but Neg Perf-A(1s)-E(3p)-pay
I would have arrived yesterday, but they didn't pay me

43) **ink'a' raj x-Ø-x-loq' li lamina**
Neg CF Perf-A(3s)-E(3s)-buy Dm lamina
he shouldn't have bought the roofing

44) **x-Ø-in-sik' raj ab'anan ink'a' x-Ø-in-taw**
Perf-A(3s)-E(1s)-search CF but Neg Perf-A(3s)-E(1s)-find
I searched for it but I did not find it

45) **ak x-Ø-jor-e' raj li joom**
already Perf-A(3s)-break-Psv CF Dm cup
the cup almost broke

46)   **na-Ø-chal raj in-xa'ow, chalk raj na-Ø-r-aj in-yajel**
        Pres-A(3s)-come CF E(1s)-vomit come CF Pres-A(3s)-E(3s)-want E(1s)-illness
        my vomit was going to come, my sickness wanted to come

Example (42) shows a canonical use of *raj*: to mark one's intention, desire, or plan against the ground of one's actual actions (first clause) – and to provide an excuse for the frustrated action in question (second clause). Such an intentionalization of *another* world is often lexicalized with the prepositional phrase *sa' inch'ool*, or 'in my heart'. Thus, one may say *xko'o raj sin ch'ool*, or 'in my heart he was going to go'. Again, however, one may use the expression 'inside my heart' without a modal clitic. My sense is that such an overt indication of the locale of another world usually emphasizes the implicature (that he didn't go), and characterizes more specifically the other world in question. (So there is no ambiguity in deciding whether it was what he said he'd do, or what he thought he'd do, or what he tried to do.)

Example (43) shows *raj* being used to mark an ethical ground: an action undertaken when it shouldn't have been. Here *another* world is not a private intentional world, but a shared moral world. Example (44) shows the use of *raj* to mark not the counterfacticity of an event, but the counterfacticity of the achievement of the action. That is to say, the speaker did indeed search for the object (a source of water), but did not actually find it. Such counterfactual results of action usually occur with activity predicates or progressive-aspect constructions. Example (45) shows the use of *raj* with a third-person predicate describing the trajectory of a cup that fell off the table. I have glossed the construction using 'almost'. Such a gloss is appropriate in the context of non-animate subjects or uncontrolled actions. (And such constructions can be subsequently intentionalized in terms of the speaker's expectations against the ground of the outcome: 'I thought it would break'.) And example (46) shows a construction involving a man's vomit. Here, in the second clause, the sickness is intentionalized: in *another* world, my sickness wanted to come; but in *this* world, it didn't. The opening scene of this monograph already discussed the potentially high stakes of such assertions.

Finally, negative polarity and counterfactive status often occur with the predicate *ajok* (to want), to mark polite refusals or grudging acceptances. For example, a mother tells her son to get out of bed and feed the chickens:

47a)   **S1: ayu, ayu, k'e r-e li kaxlan**
        go(Imp) go(Imp) give(Imp) E(3s)-RN Dm chicken
        go! go! give (this) to the chickens!

The son, quite sleepily, replies:

47b)   **S2: ink'a' raj na-Ø-w-aj**
        Neg CF Pres-A(3s)-E(1s)-want
        I wouldn't want to

And his mother replies:

47c)   **S1: ma ink'a' tab'i' x-Ø-aaw-ab'i, ayu ayu**
       Int Neg Contradictive Perf-A(3s)-E(2s)-hear go(Imp) go(Imp)
       did you not hear?! go! go!

48)   **ink'a' raj na-Ø-w-aj, mas x-in-wa'ak**
       Neg CF Pres-A(3s)-E(1s)-want much Perf-A(1s)-eat
       I wouldn't want to, I have eaten much

Examples (47) and (48) both involve the same utterance: 'I wouldn't want to' (*ink'a' raj nawaj*). In line (47b), this utterance is between grudging acceptance and defiant refusal. And example (48), said by a man when he was offered food at his brother's house, functions as a polite refusal. In these utterances, the counterfactive clitic *raj* locates the absence-of-desire in *another* world, and pragmatically implicates the presence-of-desire in *this* world. In both of these utterances, another world is mapped onto the speaker as an individual (with personal preferences) and this world is mapped onto the current world of speaker and addressee (with interpersonal obligations). In other words, while the speaker does not want to feed the chickens (or to eat the food), they index that they will engage in such activities in the context of their addressee's desires (indexed by a prior imperative or offer).

Let me offer an example of a speaker's gloss of a construction similar to line (47b):

49a)   **qa-ye-haq mare t-Ø-in-taqla laj Efraín sa' eswela**
       E(1p)-say-NS perhaps Fut-A(3s)-E(1s)-order SD Efraín Prep school
       let's say perhaps I send Efraín to school

49b)   **ink'a' raj na-Ø-w-aj xik chan-Ø-Ø**
       Neg CF Pres-A(3s)-E(1s)-want go say-Pres-A(3s)
       'I don't want to go', he says

49c)   **t-Ø-in-taqla s-in fuerz**
       Fut-A(3s)-E(1s)-send Prep-E(1s) force
       I will order him with force

49d)   **ab'an a'an ink'a', ink'a' na-Ø-chal sa' x-ch'ool naq t-Ø-xik a'an**
       but Dm Neg Neg Pres-A(3s)-come Prep E(3s)-heart Comp Fut-A(3s)-go Dm
       but it doesn't enter into his heart (he doesn't agree) to go

Notice a few features of the interaction described in example (49). First, the child's response is highly marked: rather than undertake a given command, a child expresses his feelings about the command. (Compare the interjection (stressed) *eh*, which will be discussed in chapter 6.) Second, there is a question of two wills: the adult's desire, indexed by his ordering the child to go to school; and the child's lack of desire, characterized as 'non-agreement' (going to school 'did not enter the boy's heart'). Third, the child's utterance has four components: the nonfactive particle *ink'a'*; the counterfactive clitic *raj* (preposed to encliticize with the nonfactive particle); the predicate *ajok* (to want); and the non-finite predicate *xik* (to go). Here, then, the child locates his not wanting to go in another world, and pragmatically implicates that he wants to go in this world. Now, without too much interpretation, one can see how these worlds are localized in the son and father, respectively. In other words, with this utterance, the child is localizing two distinct wills, and saying which one will be acted on in this world. In short, with commands, *raj* serves to mark grudging acceptance. And with offers, *raj* serves to mark polite refusals. In both cases, the *this* world and *another* world aspect of the clitic, what is pragmatically implicated versus what is semantically encoded, serve to mark a disjuncture, or conflict, between an interpersonal expectation or obligation, and a personal preference or desire. Personal desire gets construed as that which exists in a world other than the interpersonal obligations of this world. As we saw in chapter 3 with possessed-heart constructions, it is as if subjectivity is a marked reaction to intersubjectivity as an unmarked state of affairs.

9.   From status to evidentiality: commitment events and source events

In this chapter, we examined a set of modal clitics: *tana* (afactive), *taxaq* (optative), *pe'* (factive), *raj* (counterfactive), and *moko ... ta* (nonfactive). We detailed their morphosyntactic properties, the features they encode, the contexts they implicate, the functions they serve, and the interpretations they receive. We focused on the disjunctures created by encoded and implicated meanings, as well as the ways speakers interpret these disjunctures using mental-state predicates. We framed the features and functions of these grammatical categories in terms of the roles of the participants. And we thereby understood how these attributions and undertakings of putative mental states map into social relations among the participants: speaker–addressee, speaker–actor, and even speaker–speaker. While such complicated stances are not as explicit as those marked by complement-taking predicates, they are salient enough and frequent enough to have been grammaticalized. In some sense, we understood them as diagrams of mental states, weaving together the relations between several participant roles at once, such that psychological depth was often framed as the internalization of dialogical breadth.

More generally, one of the goals in the foregoing chapters has been to link participant roles and morphosyntax to subjectivity in a way that tacks between language-specific and cross-linguistic categories. Although subjectivity can be construed in any number of ways, the emphasis has been on stances – those semiotically indicated modes of evaluative and intentional orientation that speakers take toward states of affairs: from epistemic possibility and necessity to deontic permission and obligation; from fear and desire to memory and disgust. In this way, the focus has been on what seemingly moral, epistemic, and psychological modes of subjectivity have in common, insofar as they are expressed in grammar and the lexicon. In this section, I want to widen the scope of the foregoing analysis by using it to frame an understanding of evidentiality.

Just as status turns on the disambiguation of a commitment event from a speech event (or a principal from an animator), evidentials may be understood as turning on the disambiguation of what we may call a 'source event' from a speech event (or an author from an animator). For example, Jakobson (1990a) famously characterized them as E^nE^{rs}/E^s: the relation between a narrated event and a reported speech event is figured relative to the speech event. (Recall the discussion, in the conclusion of chapter 3, of the ways in which such participant roles get construed as objective or eventive via various modes of projection.) In this way, although evidentials are often lumped together with status under the broad category of epistemic modality, they encode very different features. I briefly consider why this happens, how to distinguish the two phenomena, and what predictions are warranted given the relationship between grammatical categories and complement-taking predicates that was discussed in section 4 of chapter 3.

Recall our discussion of the inflectional affix ki- (unexperienced evidential) in section 4 of chapter 4, and our discussion of the complement-taking predicates chank (to go) and yehok (to say) in chapter 3. As will be seen in section 4 of chapter 6, chank may also be used to gloss the meaning of a gesture or facial expression in first-person terms: when a small boy puts old food in front of the anthropologist, and the anthropologist frowns and turns away, the boy's older brother can say to him: 'I don't want it, he says' (ink'a' nawaj chan). In addition to these three highly frequent forms, there is also the particle len, which is usually best translated as 'it is said', thereby eliding reference to the participants of the reported speech event (so far as they are unknown or unimportant). It occurs after the verb, but may be preposed to encliticize with elements in the focus position. For example, a man sent his son to his brother's house, to ask his other son to return home. Stopping at the door to the house, the boy enquired whether his brother was there, and said his father wanted him to come home. The girl at the door then reported this to the boy's brother inside. When she returned, she said, ink'a' nawaj xik chan, or "I don't want to go", he says'. When the boy reported what transpired to his father, he said: ink'a' len xraj chalk, or 'it was said (len) that he doesn't want to come'. Notice, then, that while the original message was probably just 'I don't want to go', in its first reporting it became '"I don't want to go", he says', and in its second reporting it became 'it was said he didn't want to come'. Following a pattern typical of shifters, the message was changed from first person, present tense and going, to third person, past tense and coming.

And the marker of reported speech was changed from *chank* (directly reported speech), to *len* (indirectly reported speech). Other messages reported in this way include news from the radio or information about eco-tourists garnered via walkie-talkies (recall example 17, above). In this way, *len* indexes indirectly reported speech from a source that was unexperienced (second-hand, third-hand, etc.), or impersonal (radios, rumours, etc.).[6]

By encoding a disjunction between the commitment event and the speech event, markers of status imply a disjunction between the source event and the speech event. That is, to say I am weakly committed to a proposition invites the defeasible implicature that my source of evidence is not very strong. Similarly, by encoding a disjunction between the source event and the speech event, evidential markers imply a disjuncture between the commitment event and the speech event.[7] That is, to say that my source of evidence is weak is to invite the defeasible implicature that I am not strongly committed to a proposition. To differentiate, then, one must enquire into the kinds of scalar implicatures that evidentials and status allow for: if an evidential encodes a weak source event it implies a not-strong source event (to say I heard something implies I did not see it); and if a status marker encodes a weak commitment event it implies a not-strong commitment event (to say it may happen implies it is not the case that it must happen). If it is true that we should understand source events by analogy to commitment events, and if we assume that markers of evidentiality may arise historically from the grammaticalization of complement-taking predicates (section 4, chapter 3), we can predict that evidential markers whose source events are perceptual (seen, heard, sensed) should have narrower scope than evidential markers whose source events are cognitive (inferred, reasoned, remembered), which should have narrower scope than evidential markers whose source events are reportative (hearsay, second-hand account, third-hand account, myth, etc.). This is predicted by the fact that perceptual predicates have narrower scope than cognitive predicates, which have narrower scope than speech predicates. In short, one should probably distinguish between source-based stance taking (which turns on the disjuncture between source event and speech event) and commitment-based stance taking (which turns on the disjuncture between commitment event and speech event). Although

---

[6] Speakers emphasize that the use of *len* does not affect the truth value of an utterance – that they are just as likely to believe an utterance which involves *len* as any other. (And this makes sense, for although the speaker is unknown, the message usually comes from the radio.) However, they do emphasize that the use of *len* indicates that one doesn't know an event well (*ink'a' nakaanaw chi us, moko chaab'il ta naq nakaanaw*). In addition, speakers characterize the use of this particle as involving incidents which one didn't see or hear (*len porke moko xwil ta, ut moko xwab'i ta*). This presumes that the events denoted by utterances unmarked by *len* are known to their speakers by direct sensory expression.

[7] Loosely building on the general ideas of Grice (1989b, 1989c); and see Hanks (1991), Horn (1984), and Levinson (2000).

commitment-based stance taking has been the focus of this chapter, source-based stance taking deserves an analogous but analytically distinct treatment.

10.   Meta-stances and subjectivity

In this chapter, I have been focused on what might be termed stances – that is, the seemingly moral, epistemic, and psychological orientations we take toward states of affairs. However, as an inherent part of this analysis, I have also been focused on meta-stances – that is, the orientations we take toward our own and others' orientations. In particular, I have examined the interaction of grammatical categories encoding stances (status and evidentiality) with lexical forms denoting stances (complement-taking predicates), the potentially infinite embeddings that such interactions are a condition for, as well as speakers' understandings and evaluations of stances themselves. Such commitments to commitments are crucial to understanding various modes of reflexive subjectivity, or selfhood: choice (desiring particular desires); empathy (feeling others' feelings); conscience (evaluating one's own motivations); and ethnopsychology (local understanding of stances and stance taking).

Such meta-stances should not, however, be seen as the next step in analysis; rather, they should be understood as part and parcel of the first step. In particular, as summarized in Kockelman (2004), scholars often use the term stance (marker) to refer to any linguistic form that seems to imply an evaluation – without, however, specifying the criteria for determining where description (the state of affairs) ends and evaluation (the speaker's stance toward the state of affairs) begins. This allows the analyst's untheorized notions of intentionality and value – with, perhaps, some reference to a Cartesian subject (through Benveniste and Lyons) or a Kantian person (through Jespersen and Jakobson) – to play a determinate role in analysis. In short, scholars' own (meta-) stances are maximally implicated in their analysis of others' stances.

This monograph has attempted to minimize such analyst-based effects by accounting for stance in terms of cross-linguistic categories, whose properties (e.g. expression, grouping, scaling) are characterized by social and semiotic features (e.g. participant roles and morphosyntax) rather than psychological or metaphysical ones (e.g. evaluation or subjectivity). However, in addition to minimizing analyst-based effects, we must also maximize speaker-based effects by employing local understandings of what it means to be a person. In particular, any robust account of personhood must ground itself not only in the intentional and evaluative aspects of being human, but also in the self-reflexive aspects: the fact that our understanding of who we are (as intentional and evaluative beings) is partially constitutive of who we are (cf. Lucy 1993a; Taylor 1989). Recall our discussion in chapter 2 of the irreducibly reflexive nature of inalienable possessions and personhood. Ironically, although reflexivity is one of the defining characteristics of human subjectivity, or personhood, it drops out of analysts' accounts of stance even though stance is understood to be the exemplary locus of the linguistic encoding of subjectivity.

The question is how to bring reflexivity, as a defining characteristic of personhood, into our account of stance. One way is to supplement the cross-linguistic account of stance provided by typology with a community-specific account provided by ethnography. In particular, if by event construal we mean the way in which the event of signing contributes to the sign of an event, then we should examine speaker-based understandings of stance markers as any sign that members of a community associate with a speaker's personal contribution to event construal (where stances are possible kinds of personal contributions).

In this light, perhaps the defining characteristic of stance markers (from a community-specific perspective) is that while they are intersubjectively or interpersonally constituted (like any other sign involved in communication), they are understood by speakers to be subjective or personal. Indeed, one might hypothesize that it is precisely the discrepancy between these two levels that enables many of the most important functions of these signs. In this way, emphasis by linguists on the study of 'subjectivity in language' should be reformulated to focus on the relationship between the language of subjectivity and the subjectivity of language: that is, the relation between formal structures and discursive practices that seem to mark modes of subjectivity, and speakers' understandings of and strategies with these structures and practices. Stances – as relatively emblematic roles of mental states – stand at the intersection of a cross-linguistic account of mode events and a community-specific understanding of a speaker's contribution to event construal. To frame stance in any other way risks projecting the psychological and metaphysical presumptions of the analyst onto the social and semiotic practices of the actor.

6 Interjections: why the centre of emotion is at the edge of language

1. Introduction

Suppose that human beings are those entities whose agency is both enabled and constrained by the fact that their practices and their representations of their practices are never commensurate. Were this the case, the relevant locale for cross-culturally comparing what is distinctly human would not be a set of grammatical categories, a lexical field, a class of mental states, a range of ritual practices, or an ensemble of social relations. Nor would it be a philosophy, a linguistic ideology, an ethnopsychology, a system of religious beliefs, or a *Weltanschauung*. Rather, it would be a relationship between two sets of practices, where one set relates to the other set as sign to object, or interpretant to sign. That is, what is shared between any two human populations may be sought by *inter*-culturally comparing the *intra*-cultural relationships between two sets of practices, in which one set functions as a representation of the other.

In this chapter, I use ethnographic and linguistic data to relate two sets of practices among speakers of Q'eqchi'-Maya: first, the usage of interjections (such as the particles *oof*, *ouch*, and *yikes*); and second, the representation of the meaning of those interjections through the meta-linguistic usage of complement-taking predicates (such as the verbs *desire, fear, see, say*, and *know*). This relationship is compared to interpretations of interjections offered by western philosophers and linguists. In particular, I show that the interpretations of interjections offered by both these groups not only elide similar pragmatic functions, but also project similar semantic features.

More generally, I develop a methodology for comparing the semiotic mediation of mental states across speech communities: the language-internal relation between cross-linguistic form–functional domains. Although I focus on interjections in this chapter, other domains that this method could be applied to include: facial responses; prosodic structures; grammatical categories such as mood and status; lexical fields encoding semantic domains such as colour or kinship, space or time; topic–focus constructions; and hierarchies of intentional horizons presupposed in genres of speaking (for example, how observers narrate the dynamics of false-belief tests).

This methodology allows one to analyse, in local ethnographic and linguistic terms, stereotypic mental states, while minimizing – or rather purposely eliciting and systematically generalizing – observer effects. For example, by choosing cross-linguistic form–functional domains, no particular language is privileged. By allowing language to turn back on itself, the pragmatics of a relatively expressive domain is interpreted in terms of the semantics of a relatively referential domain. (Recall the questions, concerns, and conundrums raised in the introduction of this monograph: *here the domain being encoded is itself a process of encoding; the extensional background to which we point is itself a set of practices of pointing.*) And by focusing on both what people do with language and what people say they do with language, usage and interpretations of usage, language and meta-language are granted equal weight. While this technique was implicitly undertaken in previous chapters, in this chapter it is made explicit.

The first half of this chapter argues against interpretations of interjections that focus on mental states – in particular, emotion – by providing an account of their meaning in terms of situational, discursive, and cultural context. Section 2 discusses the grammatical form of interjections as signs. Section 3 characterizes the objects and interpretants of interjections in Q'eqchi' relative to a semiotic and conversational analytic framework that may be generalized for other languages. Section 4 ethnographically details the various social and discursive functions that interjections serve. And section 5 discusses the relative frequency with which interjections actually serve such functions.

The second half of this chapter focuses on speakers' interpretations of their own usage, and compares these interpretations to those offered by western linguists and philosophers. Section 6 reviews the linguistic and philosophical literature. Section 7 describes various conditions of possibility for interjections to be so readily understood in terms of emotion. Section 8 describes the relation between meta-language and ethnopsychology among the Q'eqchi'. Section 9 describes the semantic features of predicates used to describe interjections, drawing on details of the interclausal relations hierarchy from chapter 3. And the conclusion introduces the idea of relations between relations, focusing on the interplay between natural constructions and social kinds.

2.   Grammatical form of interjections

The twelve most frequently used interjections are shown across the top of Table 6.1 From left to right, they are as follows: *sht, ih, ah, eh, eh* (stressed), *ay, ay dios, ay dios atinyuwa', uy, uyaluy, t'*, and *chix*. Before discussing their meaning, as schematized in the rest of this table, I want to discuss their grammatical form. In a tradition that goes back to Bloomfield (1984 [1933]), there are four prototypic criteria by which interjections may be differentiated from

Table 6.1. Situational and discursive objects of interjections

Interjections	Sht	Ih	Ah	Eh	Eh (stressed)	Ay	Ay dios	Ay dios atinyuwa'	Uy	Uyaluy	T'	Chix
Situational context												
Object or event (Sign-based decentring) (Addressee-based decentring)					Mistake	Quantity (sign-based) Pain (sign-based) Mistake	Quantity (sign-based) Mischief/Mishap (sign-based)	Quantity (sign-based)	Transition (sign-based)	Danger (sign-based) (Adrs-based)	Glitch	Loathsomeness (sign-based) (Adrs-based)
Discursive context												
Preferred solicited response		Register-ative	Answer expected									
Non-preferred solicited response			Answer unexpected	Answer unexpected	Command ignored Request denied Dubitive (of speaker)	Answer unexpected Offer refused Dubitive (of source)	Answer unexpected Offer refused					
Non-solicited response												
Addressed non-response	Remonstrative Channel-Opener											
Non-addressed non-response				Floor-holder Self-repair			Floor-taker Topicalizer					

other linguistic forms within a particular language, and generalized as a form class across languages.[1]

All are conventional lexical forms, or words, that can constitute an utterance on their own. In other words, the sign component is a relatively standardized and arbitrary phonological form that may be segmented into phonemes. Contrast, for example, 'ouch' with a grunt. And they enter into no syntactic relations with other linguistic forms, except parataxis – in which two forms are 'united by the use of only one sentence pitch' (Bloomfield 1984 [1933]: 171). For example, 'ouch, that hurts!'. In this way, they can stand alone as a perfectly sensible stretch of talk, before and after which there is silence. This is the key criterion for characterizing these forms.

With few exceptions, none of the interjections are simultaneously members of another word class. That is, such forms are used only as interjections, and do not have another grammatical role as, say, a noun or verb. In this way, almost all of these interjections are what Bloomfield (1984 [1933]: 121) calls *primary interjections*. Compare the English primary interjections 'oops' and 'ouch', which may only be used as interjections. In Q'eqchi', the main exceptions are those interjections built, through lexical extension, from the primary interjection *ay*. In the case of *ay dios*, the additional element, *dios*, is a loan-noun from Spanish, meaning 'god'. In the case of *ay dios atinyuwa'*, besides the Spanish loan-word, there is an additional Q'eqchi' expression, *at-in-yuwa'*, or 'you (are) my father'. This latter class of interjections, which are or involve forms that belong to other word classes, will be called *secondary interjections*, following Bloomfield. Compare the English secondary interjections 'damn' and 'heavens', which may be used as both interjections and verbs or nouns.

With few exceptions, all of the interjections are composed of a single morpheme, and undergo neither inflectional nor derivational processes (Wilkins 1992). That is, they cannot be inflectionally marked for grammatical categories, such as tense or number; and they cannot be further derived into another form class, such as a noun or verb. In this way, such forms are often classified as a subclass of 'particles' or discourse markers (Jespersen 1965; Schiffrin 1987; Zwicky 1985). There are three exceptions to this characterization. First, *uyaluy* is what I will call a *reduplicative interjection*, being composed, through syllabic reduplication, from the interjection *uy*. Second, as mentioned, *ay dios* and *ay dios atinyuwa'* are what I will call *extended interjections*, being composed, through lexical extension, from the interjection *ay*. And lastly, the interjection *ay* may undergo further derivation into a delocutionary verb (becoming *ayaynak*, which means 'to cry or yell continually', often said of dogs howling),

---

[1] As should be clear from the number of qualifications, interjections, like most linguistic forms, are difficult to characterize with necessary and sufficient conditions (Haviland 2003: 480–1; Taylor 1995; Zwicky 1985).

which may then undergo some limited verbal inflection for grammatical categories such as tense, aspect, person, and number.

Lastly, although not a criterial feature, it should be said that some of these forms are phonologically or morphologically anomalous, having features which mark them as odd or unique relative to the standard lexical forms of the language. For example, unlike most Q'eqchi' words, in which stress falls on the last syllable (Stewart 1980a), the interjection *uyaluy* has syllable-initial stress. Similarly, while reduplication is a common morphological process in Q'eqchi', the reduplicative interjection *uyaluy* is derived through a non-standard morphological form. While many Q'eqchi' words involve a glottalized, alveolar stop, the interjection *t'* is also implosive. While the Spanish loanword *dios* is usually phonetically assimilated in Q'eqchi' as *tiox* when used as a noun, in the interjection *ay dios* there is no de-voicing of the initial consonant of this noun (i.e. /d/ does not become /t/) nor palatalization of its final consonant (i.e. /s/ does not become /x/). And the interjection *sht* differs from ordinary Q'eqchi' words in using /sh/, rather than a vowel, as a syllabic (cf. Bloomfield 1933: 121).[2]

3.   The meaning of interjections

Although interjections are relatively easy to characterize from the standpoint of grammatical form, there is no framework relative to which one may organize and compare their *meanings* – that is, the types of objects they stand for, and the types of interpretants they give rise to. This section provides such a framework as a means to move past previous understandings of interjections as emotive, and reframe their use in terms of situational, discursive, and cultural context. I will begin with an extended example, through which the more general framework will become clear.

As may be seen at the far right of Table 6.1, the interjection *chix* indexes loathsome things in the situational context. For example, when picking up his bowl of food from the ground, a man notices he has set it in chicken faeces. *Chix*, he says, scraping the bowl on the dirt to wipe off the faeces. His wife, herself responsible for the chickens, then takes his bowl for herself and gives him a new one. Similarly, when opening the door to her house early one morning, a woman notices that the dog has vomited right outside the doorway. *Chix*, she says, and her five-year-old son comes over to look. She tells him to scrape it away with a machete. In short, this interjection indexes loathsome things such as faeces and vomit. Like most interjections that have objects in the situational

---

[2] There are three types of signs that should be considered interjections by these criteria which I leave out of this account: animal calls (Kockelman 2002: chapter 5); the entire register of cussing in Spanish that young men may participate in during soccer matches, drinking bouts, and so forth; and several high-frequency words like 'yes' (*hehe'*) and 'no' (*ink'a'*).

context, it serves to call another's attention to the thing – thereby constituting a joint-attentional frame. And as a function of responsibility assessment (husband > wife > child), it directs another's attention to what must be cleaned up, fixed, or avoided.

The interjection *chix* may also be decentred to index a sign that refers to, or predicates a quality of, such a loathsome thing. That is, in such cases of *sign-based decentring*, the interjection is in a relationship of contiguity with a sign that stands for the thing or event in question (rather than being in contiguity with the actual thing or event, as in the *centred* usage of *chix* just discussed). In other words, it is as if the speaker is inhabiting the frame of the narrated event (Bühler 1990; Hanks 1991). In this way, the interjection *chix* does not just index loathsome things, but also signs of loathsome things. Insofar as the object of such a sign has the same qualities as the thing itself, the modality of contiguity (being able to taste, touch, see, or smell the object in question) is suspended, while the ontological class of the object (loathsomeness itself) is maintained. Interjections, then, may achieve displacement (creating distance between the speech event and the narrated event, or between the sign and the object) through replacement (the substitution of a sign of an object for the object itself).

For example, in telling a story to a group of men about a friend who was bitten by a poisonous spider while working on a plantation in the lowland area of Guatemala, the speaker describes the pus-blisters that rose up on his friend's arm. *Chix*, says one of the men listening. The other men laugh, and the speaker adds that the pus-blisters took two weeks to heal, before continuing his story. Like most interjections that undergo sign-based decentring, such usage often serves as a back-channel cue, thereby indicating that the speaker is listening, but cannot or does not want to contribute to the topic at hand (Brown and Yule 1983: 90–4; Duncan 1973). Compare the usage of 'mmm' or 'jeez' in English.

Lastly, the interjection *chix* may be decentred to index an addressee's relation of contiguity with a loathsome object. That is, in such cases of *addressee-based decentring*, the situational object is decentred to a person other than the speaker. In such cases, the speaker's sign is audible (a relation of contiguity) to the addressee who is in a relationship of contiguity with the object. In other words, it is as if the speaker is inhabiting the addressee's current corporal field (Bühler 1990; Hanks 1991). And, again, the modality of contiguity is suspended, while the ontological class is maintained. (See Figure 6.1.)

For example, a mother watching her three-year-old son approach a dog who is defecating calls out to him, *chix*. The child stops his advance and watches from a distance. In this most addressee-focused way, the sign is used by a parent to indicate that a child is within reach (typically tactile) of a loathsome object, and serves as an imperative not to touch the object. At the end of section 4,

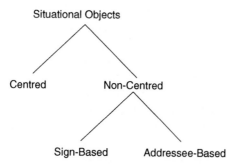

Figure 6.1. Situational objects of interjections

we will return to this interjection. For the moment, note that it may be the case that speaker-focused usages are, developmentally speaking, *centrings* of addressee-focused usages: one's expressive, or speaker-focused usage, is the outcome of a parent's directive, or addressee-focused usage.

Interjections, then, are primarily *indexical* (Peirce 1955), in that they stand for their objects by a relationship of contiguity, rather than by a relationship of convention (in the case of symbols), or similarity (in the case of icons). Although the indexical relation of interjections to their objects is emphasized in this chapter, the conventional properties of interjections are always present in at least two interrelated ways. First, as mentioned in the previous section, the interjection itself has a standardized but relatively arbitrary phonological form that is regularly used by members of a given speech community. Second, interjections conventionally stand in a relation of contiguity with particular classes of objects. For example, just as *chix* typically occurs in proximity to something belonging to the class of loathsome things, the interjection *t'* typically occurs after a *glitch*, that is, a minor setback in the midst of a task-orientated activity (e.g. a nail bends while hammering it).

These conventional classes of objects are present in two ways. First, across interjections, one may characterize what *semiotic class* of objects is being indexed. In Table 6.1, these are shown in the left-most column (for example, 'sign-based decentring' or 'non-preferred solicited response'). And second, in the case of any particular interjection, one may characterize what *ontological class* of objects is being indexed. These are shown in each particular entry (for example, 'loathsomeness' or 'unexpected answer'). Notice, then, interjections not only direct another's attention to an object, they also provide information about the object. This is similar to, but not the same as, reference and predication in some truth-conditional sense. Compare, for example, 'yuck' and 'that is disgusting'.

Besides standing for objects in the immediate context, interjections give rise to interpretants. Addressees and overhearers adjust their behaviour upon hearing them: they may turn to look; they may run for help; they may continue talking; and so forth. In many cases, an interjection serves as an attentative – securing mutual awareness of the presence of some kind of object. And, as a function of this joint-attentional frame (addressee attends to what speaker is attending to, with each being aware of the other's attention), an inference is made regarding what to do next. In other words, the process is very often like this: an interjection, as a relatively direct sign, calls another's attention to an object; and that object, in the context of having had attention called to it, serves as a relatively indirect sign of what to do next (depending on the social relations between the participants, the type of activities being undertaken, and so forth). In the example above, a husband calls his wife's attention to the chicken faeces; and then she gives him a clean bowl. In this way, interjections are caught up in sign–interpretant chains: the first interpretant is often a change in attention which brings new signs to light which lead to new interpretants.[3]

As a function of being caught up in such sign–interpretant chains, or means–ends hierarchies, interjections may have multiple functions. For example, *chix* variously serves as an attentative (when centred), a back-channel cue (when undergoing sign-based decentring), and an imperative (when undergoing addressee-based decentring). In Jakobson's terms (1990b), they may have a variety of non-referential functions: directive, expressive, phatic, and so forth. In Austin's terms (2003 [1955]), they may have a variety of illocutionary forces.

And lastly, interjections may stand for more than one kind of object at once. In particular, they may index things and events in the immediate context (what I will call situational objects). These are listed in the top half of Table 6.1. They may index other linguistic signs in an ongoing speech event (discursive objects).[4] These are listed in the bottom half of Table 6.1. They may index social relations between participants (social objects), turning on roles like gender, ethnicity, and age, or grounded in relations like power and solidarity. And, most stereotypically, they may index the mental states of the speaker (expressive objects), such as feelings of pain or fear. Social and expressive objects will be treated in later sections, and are not shown in Table 6.1.

As an example of these four broad types of objects that interjections may simultaneously index, note that *chix* may index not only a loathsome object in the situational context, but as well a social relation (parent–child, husband–wife, sounder–overhearer) and, in many cases, an internal state ('disgust').

---

[3] Indeed, from another semiotic frame, interjections are themselves interpretants; and the objects they stand for are themselves signs: to utter an interjection is to construe the immediate context in a particular way – as painful, fearsome, loathsome, etc.

[4] While it is tempting to put sign-based decentrings into the discursive context for the purposes of schematizing the data, I don't do this because sign-based decentrings make sense only in terms of the qualities of the objects referred to by the sign indexed by the interjection, not by the role of the sign itself in terms of ongoing discourse.

Similarly, as will be discussed in section 3, an interjection like *ay* not only indexes a painful object in the situational context or an unexpected answer in the discursive context, but it may also index an internal state in the expressive context (i.e. 'pain'), and a status in the social context (in particular, female gender). In this way, the very same sign may index all of these objects simultaneously – it may give rise to interpretants which turn on, or orient to, the features of different kinds of objects.

Discursive objects deserve a more detailed discussion. As may be seen in the left-hand column of the bottom half of Table 6.1, interjections may co-occur with, or constitute, the following kinds of conversational moves: responses and non-response; within responses, solicited and non-solicited responses; within solicited responses, preferred and non-preferred solicited responses; and within non-responses, addressed and non-addressed responses. (See Figure 6.2.)

In the case of a response, the use of an interjection occurs after, and only makes sense relative to, the addressee's previous utterance. For example, the interjection *ih* indexes an addressee's previous statement, and serves as a registerative: indicating that the speaker heard and understood the statement. In the case of a non-response, the interjection may elicit an addressee's utterance (and thereby occur before it), or it may occur in the midst of the speaker's own utterances (and thereby bear little or no relation to an addressee's previous or subsequent utterances). For example, the interjection *ay dios* is often used to take the floor or initiate a new topic. Notice, then, that interjections are not just signs that lead to subsequent interpretants; they are also interpretants of prior signs. And while they may constitute a response or non-response by themselves, they are also incorporated into larger utterances that serve similar functions.

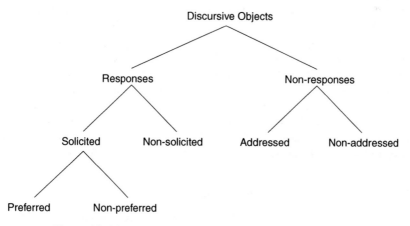

Figure 6.2. Discursive objects of interjections

Some responses are solicited, and some are non-solicited. That is, in the tradition of conversational analysis (Goffman 1981b; Sacks *et al.* 1974; and see Levinson 1983), some of the addressee's previous utterances may be the first part of a 'pair-part' structure (e.g. questions, commands, or offers), and thereby solicit overt responses (e.g. answers, undertakings, or acceptances). For example, the interjection *ah* often prefaces an answer to a question, thereby co-occurring with (and hence indexing) a solicited response. In contrast, some of the addressee's previous utterances, such as simple assertions, may not solicit overt responses. For example, the interjection (stressed) *eh* is often used as a dubitive in relation to the addressee's previous assertion, thereby constituting a non-solicited response.

Some solicited responses are preferred, and some are non-preferred. By 'preferred' is meant the expected or unmarked form (Sacks *et al.* 1974). For example, questions are unmarkedly followed by answers, requests by acceptances, orders by undertakings, and so forth. Thus, the use of the interjection *ah* in an answer to another's question is an example of an interjection indexing a preferred solicited response. A non-preferred answer to a question may arise when the answer is unknown, the request is not accepted, the command is not undertaken, and so forth. For example, the interjection *ay dios* may precede either an unexpected answer to another's question, or a refusal to another's offer. As is well known, non-preferred responses often co-occur with a temporal delay, a prefacing comment, etc.

And lastly, non-responses may be addressed or non-addressed. Addressed non-responses are designed to elicit an interpretant: they are purposefully expressed for the sake of another's interpretant. They typically have phatic or directive functions, serving to direct the addressee's attention to the presence of the speaker, or acting as an imperative. For example, the interjection *sht* often serves to get an addressee's attention. In contrast, non-addressed non-responses are not in an indexical relation with another's signs, but rather with the speaker's own co-occurring signs. Typical non-responses are discourse markers that have turn-taking functions (floor holders, floor-returners, turn-enders); or they contribute to topic organization; or they serve as various means of self-repair (see Levinson 1983; Sacks *et al.* 1974; Schiffrin 1987). For example, the interjection (unstressed) *eh* is often used as a floor holder, similar to 'um' in English. Clearly, non-responses are at the boundary of what may be called interjections, insofar as they cannot stand alone as an utterance. They are included here as a limit case, insofar as some of the interjections discussed may sometimes function as such.

4.   Extended ethnographic examples

Any account of the objects and interpretants of interjections requires devoted attention to ethnographic detail. As will be seen in this section, the various ontological classes of situational, discursive, and social objects turn on all things cultural: epistemic values involving sources of evidence and speaker sincerity; social relations implicated in gifts accepted and answers offered; deference hierarchies turning on politeness, gender, and age; cultural norms of quantity and quality; local construals of what counts as loathsome, dangerous, painful, and so forth.

Sht: The interjection *sht* is an attention-getting device or channel-opener and, when strongly accented, a disapproval signal or remonstrative. In this way, it serves as an addressed non-response. That is, it serves to secure the attention of an addressee and, in so doing, allows the speaker to communicate subsequent information to them. Its primary usage is therefore phatic (Jakobson 1990b; Malinowski 1936): it opens up the possibility for further communication by establishing eye contact or mutual recognition of the speaker's presence. In some sense, it establishes a joint-attentional frame, thereby pointing to the possibility of pointing. It may be followed by a question, statement, or command. For example, while silently overtaking a friend on the trail to the village, a man says *sht*. When the friend turns, the speaker smiles, catches up, and asks where he's going. A conversation ensues and the men walk together. Or, a young man seeing his friend one pew ahead in church says *sht, Pedro*, and Pedro turns. They shake hands and smile, and then turn back to the mass. Or, as the fight between two boys over a toy escalates, the father says *sht*, loudly – that is, with more force and greater palatalization than with the phatic function of *sht*. They turn, sheepish, to look at him, and stop their fighting. This last usage is often followed by an imperative (to pipe down, stop fighting, go to sleep, etc.). As such examples demonstrate, *sht* indexes a relationship of familiarity between the speaker and addressee. The speaker is friends with, or an older social relation of, the addressee. It is considered impolite to use it otherwise, as indicated by parents' disapproval of their children's usage of *sht* with strangers or elders.

Ih: The interjection *i(i)h* is used to index the speaker's registering of the addressee's previous comment. In this way, it serves as a preferred solicited response to another's utterance. For example, as a man walks by a house on his way to his field he says *hulaj chik*, or 'until tomorrow'. The woman inside the house replies *ih*, presumably recognizing the man by his voice or habits. Or, thanking a host for his dinner, a man says *xik we laa'in*, or 'I'm off now'. His host replies *ih*. Or, leaving his brother-in-law's house, a man addresses his step-father *inpapa'*, or 'my father', and the step-father says *ih*. Such usages serve, then, as relatively non-committal registeratives. That is, walking past a house, advising that one is leaving, or taking leave of an acquaintance are actions that require no subsequent action on the part of the addressee.

This particular function of *ih* is illuminated by contrasting it with the word *us*, an adjective meaning 'good', which is also used as a registerative, and often functions as a secondary interjection. In particular, *us* is often used as a relatively committed registerative. That is, it is used in situations where the speaker's actions are directly implicated in the actions of the addressee. For example, after thanking a host for food with the words *b'antiox inwa'* or 'because of god my food', the host says *us*. Or, while walking past a group of women coming from the market, one may say *cheeril eerib'*, or 'that you would watch yourselves', and the women will chime in unison *us*. Or, the anthropologist, while leaving from breakfast, informs his host that he's off to go get his coffee mug, and the host says *us*. When he returns with his mug, she is adding sugar to the coffee pot in anticipation. In this way, *us* registers utterances that have some illocutionary force other than a simple statement, and thereby implicate both speaker and addressee in a more complicated social relation: thanking, blessing, aiding, or informing. In contrast, *ih* is used to register utterances that are informing the addressee of an individual's unrelated actions. Compare two key functions of so-called future-tense constructions in English: 'I'll get coffee (for us)' and 'I'm gonna get coffee (for myself)'.

Ah: The interjection *ah* has two discursive objects. It indexes preferred and non-preferred solicited responses, in particular, answers to questions. In such cases, it occurs after a restatement of the topic of the question, before the answer to the question, or before an admission that the speaker does not know the answer. Such usage is particularly frequent among women, and men can cut in on their responses at precisely these junctures. Such usage is also prevalent in directly reported speech, again prefacing answers to questions – and thus serves as a means to indicate a change in speaker. It often occurs with *us* or *bueno* (good), in its registerative function, after another's explanation of some fact. If I may be impressionistic, it seems to mark 'information processing' (Gardner *et al.* 1988): that is, learning new information (that one must use to make a decision), or being asked to provide information (that one must think about as an answer to a question). Example (1) shows the use of *ah* as a preferred solicited response. Example (2) shows a man cutting in on his wife's response to the ethnographer's question. And example (3) shows the use of *ah* as a nonpreferred solicited response, again in response to an ethnographer's question:

1) **S1: jarub' libra wan chi sa' li saak**
   how many pounds are in the sack?
   S2: ah, jun kintal
   ah, a hundred pounds

2) **S1: ut ani li xb'een kristyan arin**
   and who were the first people here? (anthropologist speaking)
   S2: ah
   ah (wife speaking)
   S3: saber wankeb' tana
   who knows who they were (husband speaking)

3) **S1: ut jo' nimal xtz'aq li jun siir li k'iche'**
    and how much does a parcel of forest cost?
    S2: ah, ink'a' ninnaw, mare oxib' mil
    ah, I don't know, perhaps three thousand (quetzals)

Second, the interjection *ah* indexes denials to requests, as non-preferred solicited responses. For example, when one does not know whether one can comply with a request to assist someone, one may preface one's refusal and subsequent explanation with *ah*. For example, a man asks his brother-in-law if he can join a labour-pool to construct a house the next day. The brother-in-law replies *ah, ink'a' ninnaw, wan naab'al ink'anjel*, or '*ah*, I'm not sure, I have much work to do'. Example (4) shows a speaker using *ah* first as a non-preferred response to a question (non-preferred because it asks another question, rather than giving an answer), and later as a non-preferred response to the original request (non-preferred because it doesn't accept the request, but rather explains why the speaker cannot yet accept it, not knowing if he'll be free).

4) **S1: b'aanusilal, ok chi awk wik'in**
    please do me a favour and come to plant with me
    S2: ah, joq'e raj
    ah, when would it be?
    S1: hulaj
    tomorrow
    S2: ah, ink'a' ninnaw ma tinruuq tawi'
    ah, I don't know whether I'll be free

Eh: Unstressed, the interjection *eh* has two distinct discursive objects. First, *eh* indexes non-responses, serving as a floor holder and self-repair initiator. It occurs directly after the full-clause complementizer *naq*, or 'that', *qayehaq*, or 'let's say that', and *pues*, or 'well/then', and after constituents in the pre-posed topic position. As well, it occurs between inflectional prefixes and the verb stems they modify. And women use *eh* in this way less frequently than men, perhaps because they are less likely to floor-hold. In this usage, it is comparable to 'um' in English. In example (5), *eh* occurs in between a repetition of the complementizer *naq*. And in example (6), *eh* occurs after *qayehaq* and after *pues*.

5) **qayehaq wan jun lix na'leb' naq eh naq laa'in xinhulak chaq chi b'eek ...**
    let's say there's a story that, um, that I arrived in order to walk ...

6) **qayehaq eh, kama'eb' lin kok'al pues eh tintaqla chi si'ik ...**
    let's say that, um, like my children, for example, um, I send them to cut wood ...

And second, *eh* indexes non-preferred solicited responses, in particular, marked answers to questions. In such cases, it appears at the beginning of the utterance, or after a restatement of the topic of the question. For example, if a question presupposed information that the addressee does not agree with, or that does not make sense, their response may be prefaced with *eh*. Or, if a question cannot be answered favourably, the addressee may preface their response with *eh*. Again, this function is used more frequently by women, than by men. Compare the interjection *ay (dios)*, which indexes an unanswerable question or an unfavourable answer, versus this use of *eh*, which indexes that the question is poorly posed. In example (7), the second speaker takes issue with the presumption of the first speaker's question (i.e. that what they received was a gift). And example (8), taken from an ethnographic interview, shows *eh* occurring after a restatement of the topic, and in response to a poorly posed question.

7) **S1: ut joq'e xaak'ul laa maatan**
    and when did you receive your gift?
    S2: eh, mare moko maatan ta
    um, perhaps it's not (really) a gift

8) **S1: chankiru lix na'leb' li kaxlan**
    what's a chicken's sense (or 'reason') like?
    S2: li kaxlan, eh, maak'a' mas lix na'leb'
    chickens, um, they don't have much sense

Eh (stressed): The interjection stressed *eh*[5] has three objects. In the situational context, with lowered pitch and descending intonation, *eh* indexes a *mistake*: that is, a frustrated or poorly performed action, which may be partially blamed on the actor. For example, in attempting to throw a fruit pit out the window of his younger brother's house, a man's aim is off, and the pit whacks the edge of the window, falling back into the house. The man says *eh*, but makes no movement to retrieve it. Or, as two men are levelling the site for a house using a plough-like instrument, the instrument skips over the dirt instead of digging in. The man whose house is being built, and who was in charge of the activity, says *eh* and the two men reposition to try again. Lastly, while a man is standing on a rooftop in order to hammer in tin-roofing, the nails he has stored in his back pocket fall out onto the ground. *Eh*, he says, as another man moves to sweep them up and hand them back. In contrast to *t'*, which indexes glitches, such mistakes are directly caused by the speaker's actions. In particular, they seem to occur through inadvertent actions due to lack of attention, and one may be held responsible for them. Similarly, such mistakes are typically larger in magnitude than those indexed by *t'*, and require more effort to be fixed.

Second, as discursive objects, stressed *eh* indexes non-preferred solicited responses to another's request or command, and is often uttered by children. In particular, it indexes grudging compliance with commands and grudging

---

[5] Also, it is often said with an uvular fricative at the end, as in /ej/.

acceptance of requests. For example, in the midst of playing with his friends, a five-year-old boy is called into the house by his mother, who says *kim arin*, or 'come here'. *Eh*, says the boy, still playing with his friends before slowly going home to his mother. Or, after being asked to climb back up a hill to retrieve his father's jacket (after both had just returned home), a boy says *eh*, before trudging back up the hill.

And third, stressed *eh* indexes non-solicited responses to another's utterance, serving as a dubitive. Such usage often co-occurs with eye and head movement, in particular, with turning one's head slightly off to the side while continuing to look one's interlocutor in the eye (a movement which is also enacted in the reported speech of such dubitives). My only tokens of such usage are from contexts in which young men are speaking with each other. Clearly, such usage may be construed as impolite. However, most usages occur in seemingly joking situations. That is, speakers use stressed *eh* when their interlocutor is clearly exaggerating or pulling their leg.

The interjections *ay*, *ay dios*, and *ay dios atinyuwa'* are related insofar as they all are constructed out of the form *ay*, either through reduplication or extension. The interjections *ay* and *ay dios* are probably loanwords from Spanish. In her examination of the use of interjections by a young speaker of Mexican Spanish, Montes (1999) characterizes *ay* as 'subjective', insofar as it '[focuses] on the internal reaction of affectedness of the speaker with respect to the referent' (1289). She notes that it is one of the most frequently used interjections in her corpus, and is traditionally thought to mark pain. She finds that although it is sometimes used to mark pain, it is usually used 'to express a negative reaction in general and in a number of cases to express pleasure or an explicitly approving attitude' (1307). Indeed, she notes that '[i]f "pain" were taken as the basic meaning for *ay* there would be no way to associate this meaning with positive expressions like *ay, qué lindo!* "ay, how nice!"' She concludes that '[i]f being affected (feeling) is taken as basic, then the various uses are explainable'. As will be seen, the functions of the Q'eqchi' interjection *ay* resemble those of the Spanish interjection, especially in its stereotypic (though infrequent) usage to indicate painful events, and in its highly frequent usage to indicate marked quantities (whether positively or negatively valued). However, *ay* also serves a range of functions not mentioned by Montes.

Ay: As may be seen from Table 6.1, this interjection has several situational objects. First, *ay* indexes painful, or potentially painful, objects and events. For example, a woman quickly retracts her hand after attempting to pick up a coffee pot that had been standing too close to the fire. *Ay*, she says, and then reaches for a rag by which to hold it. Such usage may also be decentred to index a sign of a painful event. For example, while listening to a story about a boy who burnt his hand by straying too close to the hearth fire, an elderly woman who was listening says *ay*, clenching her fist.

Second, it may be used to index a marked amount of a recently revealed object (present before the speaker) or its sign-based decentring to a recently mentioned object (such as a noun phrase whose referent has similar qualities). This marked amount may be size, weight, length, width, duration, number, price, and even goodness. Functionally, its use ranges from a back-channel cue to an offer refusal. For example, a five-year-old boy asks for a tortilla to soak up the rest of his broth. His mother hands him a whole tortilla, and he says *ay, mas nim*, or '*ay*, that's really big!' She retracts her hand, tears off half of the tortilla for herself, and gives him the remainder. While indexing the marked size of the tortilla, this usage also functions as an offer refusal. As another example, a woman, upon hearing the price of potatoes in the market that morning, says *ay, mas terto*, or '*ay*, they're expensive!' and her interlocutor nods and continues speaking. Again, while indexing the marked price of the corn, this usage also functions as a back-channel cue. Such usages relate, then, to a whole metaphysics of quantity (what qualities can be quantified, and what is considered a marked amount of a quality – relative to body size, norms of distance, etc.). Indeed, *ay* may even be used in place of *chix* and *uyaluy* in the expressions *ay, mas chu*, or '*ay*, that's very gross', and *ay, mas xiw*, or '*ay*, that's very scary'. Notice, then, that an adjectival phrase is typically added to this interjection, thereby further specifying the quality being quantified. Compare 'this' and 'this piece of fruit'. In this way, the marked-quantity usage of *ay* is the most versatile and frequently occurring function.

And third, *ay* indexes mistakes, or activities frustrated through the actions of one of the people involved in the activity. For example, several boys are kicking a ball about, and one inadvertently kicks it into the underbrush. *Ay*, he says, before making off to retrieve it. This usage should be compared with *t'*, which indexes a minor setback, usually involving a tool, that occurs in the midst of task-orientated activity. And, as discussed above, it should be compared with stressed *eh*, which is usually said by men to index a mistake that is larger in magnitude, and usually the fault of the speaker rather than a tool.

In the discursive context, the interjection *ay* may be used to index non-preferred solicited responses – in particular, refused offers. For example, while on his way to church a young man stops by his brother-in-law's house to enquire whether they too are going. His brother-in-law's family is eating breakfast, and so his sister hands him the tortilla-basket and a bowl of beans. *Ay, ink'a' ninnaw*, he says, not taking them, or '*ay*, I don't know'. And he explains that he just ate, and is very full. She continues holding them out with her hand. He finally takes the tortillas, saying that he will eat them later.

Second, and again as a non-preferred solicited response, *ay* may be used to index unexpected answers to questions. For example, when a woman is asked by her neighbour whether she has any peppers left to sell, she says *ay, maak'a'*, or '*ay*, there are none left'. She then suggests to the neighbour that another nearby-living woman may have some, and so he should check there. Notice, then, that these last two uses of *ay* index the violation of an expected pair-part structure: in the first case, offer–acceptance; in the second case, question–answer.

Lastly, *ay* may index a non-solicited response, which itself is serving as a dubitive. Importantly, such a dubitive function is source directed, and *ay* is usually followed by the expression *ma yaal tawi'*, or 'could it be true?' That is, it casts doubt on the source of the information on which the dubious utterance is based, and does this explicitly. For example, while listening to a friend report that he had heard that a bus flipped over, killing all the people inside, a man says *ay, ma yaal tawi'*, or '*ay*, could it be true?!' This should be contrasted with the dubitive use of the interjection stressed *eh*, which is speaker directed. That is, it casts doubt on the truthfulness of the speaker (which is why it is considered highly impolite, and is used primarily among young men, or in joking situations).

Ay dios: The interjection *ay dios* may be used to index a marked amount of a recently revealed object (present before the speaker) or its sign-based decentring to a recently mentioned object (a noun phrase whose referent has similar qualities). In this way, it is similar to the interjection *ay* discussed above. A relevant characteristic of this use of *ay dios* is that it exists as the mid-range form of an intensity cline, such that one can say *ay, ay dios*, or, as discussed below, even *ay dios atinyuwa'*. Here the length of the utterance is iconically related to the extent of quantity, and is perhaps iconically related to the intensity of one's reaction. This is a form of diagrammatic iconicity that is pervasive throughout language (Friedrich 1979; Peirce 1955): it is not that a sign has a quality in common with its object; it is that the relation between signs has a quality in common with the relation between objects. As will be discussed below, unfavourable answers and refused offers will be marked by *ay dios*, or merely *ay*, but not *ay dios atinyuwa'*, so the intensity cline seems to be truncated for these functions.

Like the interjection *ay*, *ay dios* is also used to markedly respond to another's question or offer as a non-preferred solicited response.

The third use of *ay dios* is to index a child's accident or misbehaviour in context. So if a woman's three-year-old son stumbles as he walks by the fire, or whacks his five-year-old brother as he passes by, the mother says *ay dios* and stands him upright or admonishes him. Similarly, if a five-year-old boy sees his three-year-old brother misbehave – say, he kicks his food over – he can say *ay dios* to call his mother's attention to the act. Recall the opening scene of chapter 1. Very simply, then, when one stands in a relationship of care or responsibility to someone – such as a mother or older brother to a child – the mistakes and misbehaviours of the cared-fors elicit *ay dios* from their caretakers. Of course, these responses shade into each other: a child falling is initially comforted; but, if unscathed, is then rebuked for horsing around. Such usage can also undergo sign-based decentring, such that hearing about a child's mistake can elicit such a response. Notice that this is similar to, but not the same as, the use of the interjection *ay* to index one's own mistake. In some sense, the actions of one's inalienable possessions affect one no less than one's own actions.

The last use of *ay dios* is as a topicalizer or floor taker, indexing the speaker's turn to talk (usually out of turn) or the introduction of a new topic for discussion (often far afield from present concerns). For example, during a ceremonial meal, the host, leaning back from the table after he has finished eating, says *ay dios* and waits for the other men to come to attention before he begins to speak. Here, the interjection marks a break between two phases of a ritual, and enables the speaker to take the floor to initiate prayer. As another example, a woman, cooking while her husband talks with his brother about the price of corn, says *ay dios*, and then mentions what she just remembered she forgot to do. A conversation then ensues, which includes her and is about this topic, before the men return to their conversation about corn. This use often piggybacks with the marked-amount usage discussed above: one may jump into a conversation by indexing with an interjection a just-referred-to marked quantity, and then explaining why it struck one as marked, etc.

Ay dios atinyuwa': As mentioned above, the interjection *ay dios atinyuwa'* is used to index highly marked amounts, and exists at the far end of an intensity cline with *ay* and *ay dios*. For example, after speculating about how heavy a man's sack is, one of the discussants goes to pick it up. Visibly struggling with it, he says *ay dios atinyuwa'*, while the others laugh. He then estimates its weight for them, *wan tana jun kintal*, or 'there's about 100 pounds (inside)'. Or, when two boys drag a small tree into the house and over to the hearth, after being asked to collect branches for firewood, their mother says *ay dios atinyuwa'* (expecting, it seems, a much smaller amount), and moves to prepare a space for it.

The interjections *uy* and *uyaluy* are related insofar as the latter is a reduplicated version of the former. Again, *uy* is probably a loan-interjection from Spanish; whereas the reduplicated form is particular to Q'eqchi'. In her examination of the use of interjections by a young speaker of Mexican Spanish, Montes (1999) characterizes *uy* as 'subjective', insofar as it '[focuses] on the internal reaction of affectedness of the speaker with respect to the referent' (1289). Although she found very few tokens of *uy* in her sample (1309), she suggests that most of the cases were 'used in the context of something unexpected, sudden or urgent, often negative'. As will be seen below, this usage faintly resembles the usage of *uy* and *uyaluy* among speakers of Q'eqchi'.

Uy: The interjection *uy* is not frequently used, but it seems to index what one may term *transitions* or, somewhat metaphorically, 'close calls'. Compare Goffman's discussion of the transition display (1981c). That is, it indexes dangerous events that almost proved harmful, taxing activities that have just ended, and even distasteful practices that are not practised 'now' or 'here'. For example, upon sawing through a particularly thick board while building a house, a man says *uy*, and pauses to wipe the sweat out of his eyes. Or, as a man unloads himself of a heavy burden, he says *uy* as he exhales. This interjection is often decentred to index signs of such events and practices, serving as a back-channel cue. For example, when the anthropologist mentions that in another Q'eqchi' community he had eaten gophers, his interlocutor says *uy*. Or, as a man recounts how he was almost bitten by a dog, his interlocutor says *uy*. If I may be impressionistic, what is common to all of these usages is the distinction between two possible worlds (what happened versus what could have happened; what we do here versus what they do there) or a transition between activity phases (being in the midst of an activity versus being at its completion). In addition, one of the possible worlds or activity phases is more favourable than the other. In particular, the one we have just left or mentioned is more dangerous, stressful, or unappealing than the one we are now in.

Uyaluy: The reduplicative interjection *uyaluy* indexes dangerous objects, events, or situations. For example, while building a house, a thirty-five-year-old man traverses a relatively unstable board, about ten feet off the ground: hammer in one hand, board bending, and nothing to hold onto. Halfway through this traverse he stops and says *uyaluy*, eyes flicking up to his assistant. They laugh together, and then he continues his traverse, arriving safely at the other side.

This interjection may also be decentred to index a sign referring to such a dangerous situation. For example, having just returned from working on a plantation in the northern lowland area of Guatemala, a young man is describing what he saw in the way of flora and fauna to his family members. When he mentions that he saw a snake (*k'anti'*), his sister-in-law says *uyaluy*. Again, when he describes this snake as very large (*mas nim*), she says *uyaluy*. In both cases, her utterance of this interjection functions as a back-channel cue, and the man continues talking.

And lastly, this interjection may undergo addressee-based decentring to index an addressee's relation to a dangerous object, event, or situation. For example, after filtering spring water into a plastic bottle, the anthropologist takes a long drink. His host, a twenty-eight-year-old woman, who is watching from her home, says *uyaluy*. He stops drinking to look at her, and she says *mas ninxiwak xb'aan naq mas ke li ha'*, or 'I get very frightened because the water is so cold'. She then offers to boil it for him.

T': The interjection *t'* is an implosive, glottalized, alveolar stop, often called a 'dental click'. It indexes minor equipmental malfunctions and unplanned outcomes. That is, it indexes what one may call a *glitch*: a minor setback, usually involving a tool, that occurs in the midst of a task-orientated activity.

For example, a nail bends while a man is hammering it. He sounds *t'*, stops hammering to inspect the nail, and then proceeds to tap the nail gently from the side in order to straighten it, before pounding it in. Or, while sawing a piece of wood, a man notices that his cut is not going exactly straight, and says *t'*. He pulls out his saw, switches places so he can saw in from the other side, and begins sawing in order to meet his old cut halfway – thereby using his old cut while minimizing its effect. Such minor disturbances are usually fixable with equipment on hand. One merely redirects one's old efforts; and thus one does not need to begin again, throw out what has just been done, retrieve another tool, call for help, etc. Compare stressed *eh*, discussed above, which is used to index a mistake, or botched action, that seems to be larger in magnitude and the fault of the speaker.

The only tokens I have of this interjection were sounded by men engaged in house-building activities. Women do not seem to use it in the midst of every-day household activities, and men do not seem to use it much in the midst of agricultural activities. This may be due, in part, to the fact that such agricultural activities, although done collectively, require the repetition of a single machete-mediated action again and again by each individually working man. Similarly, the goal of such agricultural activities is relatively macroscopic – to clear, seed, weed the field; whereas in house building there are many discrete, co-articulated activities. For example, if in tossing a corn-seed into a hole when planting one missed, I usually heard *eh* (stressed), not *t'*; whereas in house building, tasks usually require two men – one as lead (pounding, sawing, meas-uring) and the other as assistant (holding, steadying, weighting). The man who is leading usually says *t'*, and the man who is assistant merely adjusts to the figure's new, fixing, actions. In this way, *t'* may not only index the speaker's gender, it may also index the type of activity in which he is engaged.

Chix: Although this interjection was discussed in section 3, I want to discuss its addressee-based decentrings. Importantly, whereas centred usages of this interjection involve any modality of contiguity (smell, taste, touch, or sight), addressee-based decentrings usually occur when the addressee is within tactile proximity. Indeed, in such decentred usages, parents often describe the object as disgusting (*mas chu a'an*, or 'that's disgusting') and order the child not to touch it (*maach'e' a'an*, or 'don't touch it'). Thus, although such addressee-based decentrings serve as a warning or imperative, one may add an explicit imperative without redundancy. Parents may also say *moko us ta xch'e'b'al a'an*, meaning 'it is not good to touch that', or *ink'a' naru xch'e'b'al a'an*, meaning 'one is not allowed to touch that'. Notice, then, the set of relations in which a child is simultaneously implicated: one is in proximity to an object; one hears an interjection; one learns of the object's salient qualities; one is ordered not to touch the object; and one is taught what one may and may not touch. Not to privilege this as an *ur-moment* of development, but just as a child is about to close in on some loathsome object, a whole schema of quality, modality, authority, and sensibility unfolds which links this immediate world to all possible worlds, thereby radically generalizing the experience.

As a function of such an addressee-based decentring, *chix* may also be used as an adjective or noun, but only in a limited number of cases involving parents speaking with children (and is thus on the border between primary and secondary interjections). For example, a three-year-old holds up a slimy chicken-foot to the anthropologist, who is still eating. The anthropologist turns his head away and grimaces while the child's mother watches. She says to her child '"that's really gross", he says' (*mas chix li ru chan*). Through faux direct reporting, she thereby attributes to the anthropologist a description of the chicken-bone as 'gross', using the sign *chix* as the adjective in question. Such usage as an adjective is defective in the following senses: unlike most other adjectives, *chix* can neither be inflected for person (**chix-in* and **chix-at*, or 'I am gross' and 'you are gross' are both ungrammatical), nor further derived into a state-change predicate (**chix-o'k* or 'to become gross' is ungrammatical). This interjection can also be used as a noun, when talking to a child, to refer to snot. For example, after a child sneezes his mother looks at him and says *maak'a' chix*, or 'there's no snot (so no need to wipe your face)', instead of the usual *ayu chi aatink*, or 'go off to wash (your face)'. Again, such usage occurs only in the relatively circumscribed register of parents speaking to young children.

Of interest is that this usage implies that the focal and first-learnt loathsome object is not produced by an other, or discovered outside, or dangerous to touch. Rather, the prototype of a loathsome thing (snot) is not *that* loathsome (one can swallow it without getting sick – compare faeces), and is produced by, and publicly displayed on, the self. Also note that insofar as one first hears this interjection as a parent's warning, and only subsequently uses it oneself as an interjection, it may be the case that one's expressive, or speaker-focused usage, is a *recentring* into oneself of a parent's directive, or addressee-focused usage. Warning then becomes exclamation, and social imperative becomes individual emotion. In short, if loathsome objects in the situational context co-occur with 'disgust' as an expressive object, objects of 'disgust' are originally self-created (snot); and 'disgust' itself, as a private emotion, is an internalization of a parent's imperative, as a public value.

5.   Relative frequency of various functions

Before turning to speakers' reflections on their own usage, let me discuss the relative frequency with which interjections were used in their various functions. Given that I engaged in two different modes of token collection (one via participant observation, and the other via conversational analysis), and given that I was not equally attentive to usage during all of my fieldwork, or across all social contexts, I will focus on their relative frequency during one month of my research.

During this month, I recorded about ten hours of dinner-time conversation, and I wrote down every usage of interjections I noticed during the course of each day. From these two sources, I noted two uses of *chix* indexing loathsomeness (both addressee-based decentred). I noted two uses of *uyaluy* indexing danger (one centred and one sign-based decentred). I noted three uses of *uy* indexing transitions (one addressee-based decentred and the others centred). I noted six and seven uses of stressed *eh* and *t'* indexing mistakes and glitches, respectively. I noted six uses of stressed *eh* serving as a dubitive. And I noted ten uses of stressed *eh* indexing non-preferred solicited responses. Of the thirty-five tokens I noted of *ay*, only two indexed a painful event (both of which were sign-based decentrings). Fifteen tokens indexed marked quantities, ten of which were sign-based decentrings (and functioning as back-channel cues). One indexed a non-solicited response, serving as a dubitive. Nine indexed non-preferred solicited responses (offer refusals and unexpected answers). And seven indexed mistakes. I also noted ten uses of *ay dios* to index a child's misbehaviour or mistake, ten uses of *ay dios* indexing marked quantities (nine of which involved sign-based decentring), and five uses involving non-addressed non-responses (functioning as floor takers or topicalizers). And I heard three uses of *ay dios atinyuwa'* indexing marked quantities, two of which were sign-based decentrings. During this same time, I noted uses of *ih* and *sht* as least once a day. And I could not count the number of times I heard unstressed *eh* indexing a non-addressed non-response (functioning as a floor holder or self-repair), or *ah* indexing a preferred solicited response (with answers to questions), because they occur in nearly every utterance of every conversation.

As may be seen from these numbers, interjections vary greatly in the frequency with which they are used. In particular, interjections that index situational objects such as transitions (*uy*), danger (*uyaluy*), loathsomeness (*chix*), and painful events (*ay*), and which would usually be characterized as indexing internal states such as 'relief', 'fear', 'disgust', and 'pain' – i.e. those which seem the most traditionally interjectional – are the least frequently used. Slightly more frequent are interjections indexing mistakes (*ay* and stressed *eh*) and glitches (*t'*), or functioning as source- and speaker-directed dubitives (*ay* and stressed *eh*). Interjections indexing marked quantities (*ay, ay dios,* and *ay dios atinyuwa'*) were relatively frequent, especially in cases of sign-based decentring, as were interjections indexing non-preferred solicited responses (*ah, eh,* stressed *eh, ay,* and *ay dios*). More frequent still were interjections indexing preferred solicited responses, functioning as registeratives (*ih*), and interjections indexing addressed non-responses, functioning as remonstratives or channel openers (*sht*). Lastly, by far the most frequently used interjections indexed preferred solicited responses (*ay*) and non-addressed non-responses (*eh*).

By and large, then, interjections with discursive objects (or sign-based decentrings of interjections with situational objects) are far more frequent than centred interjections with situational objects. And interjections with many different kinds of objects and functions are far more frequent than interjections with fewer kinds of objects and functions.

Lastly, regarding social objects, interjections are intimately related to gender roles and relations. As mentioned in the preceding section, the interjection *eh* as a non-addressed non-response (floor holder) or non-preferred solicited response is used mainly by men; whereas *ah*, as a preferred solicited response, is used mainly by women. (I did not count either of these uses, because they were too frequent.) Stressed *eh* is used mainly by men to index mistakes or to serve as a dubitive. In particular, during this month, all uses of stressed *eh* were said by men; but I have observed women using them at other times. *Ay* (and *ay dios* and *ay dios atinyuwa'*) are used mainly by women in all of their functions. In particular, during this month, both uses of *ay* indexing painful events were said by women. Ten of the fifteen uses of *ay* indexing marked quantities were said by women (and four of the remaining five were said by boys). The single dubitive usage was said by a woman. Five of the nine uses of *ay* to index non-preferred solicited responses were said by women. And three of the seven uses of *ay* to index mistakes were said by women (the rest were said by boys or girls). I have no tokens of *uy* being used by women during any part of my fieldwork. And I have no tokens of *t'* being used by women during any part of my fieldwork. Clearly, these numbers are not meant to have statistical significance; but they should provide a sense of the gendered distribution of tokens.

Regarding women's frequent use of the interjections *ay*, *ay dios*, and *ay dios atinyuwa'* to index marked quantities, it is important to note that speakers' explanations of this usage often make reference to women being physically smaller than men, and more likely to be impressed by the size of something, or the painfulness of something. This accords with widespread ideas about women's inability to measure up to men, their tendency to be more easily affected by the world, and their inability to substitute for men in labour-pools (Kockelman 2002, 2007d). Missing from such explanations is the fact that women are more likely to concede the floor in conversations – precisely by using this interjection with its back-channel function. In other words, while women do indeed use *ay (dios atinyuwa')* more than men, I think this is because of its discursive function (serving as a back-channel cue such that women can concede the floor), rather than because of its stereotypical situational objects (painful events or marked quantities). In short, women's relatively frequent use of *ay (dios)* is probably based in a sociolinguistic inequality (i.e. who can control the floor in a conversation to introduce new topics) which is naturalized as a bio-physical inequality (i.e. who is smaller in size or weaker in constitution).

To conclude the first half of this chapter, interjections have an extremely rich and well-structured indexical relationship to context – be it situational, discursive, or social. Indeed, so far I have made only minimal reference to mental states such as emotion, yet I have managed to characterize the objects and interpretants of interjections in a framework that is easily generalized to other languages and cultures. Notice, then, that interjections exist as a cross-linguistic form–functional domain, whose particular signs, objects, and interpretants, although variable, are comparable. Notice as well that by focusing on mental states (or, rather, expressive objects), the actual richness of interjections – their situational, discursive, and social regularities – is all too easily elided. What we gain in succinctness by ascribing mental states, we lose in understanding by eliding context.

In the rest of this chapter, I examine the common understanding among philosophers, linguists, and lay-folk that interjections have mental states as their meaning, in particular *emotion*. Simultaneously, I show what a rigorous account of their expressive objects would actually entail.

6.   Relation to mind and emotion in linguistic theory

In western philosophy and linguistic theory, interjections have been traditionally thought to be both at the periphery of language and primordially related to emotion. For example, the Latin grammarian Priscian defined interjections as 'a part of speech signifying an emotion by means of an unformed word' (Padley 1976: 266). Müller (1862) thought they were at the limit of what may be called language. Sapir (1921) said that interjections are 'the nearest of all language sounds to instinctive utterance' (6–7). Bloomfield (1933) said they 'occur under a violent stimulus' (177). Jakobson (1990b) thought they were an exemplar of the 'purely emotive stratum of language'. And Jackendoff (2003) has said that he 'would like to think of such words ... as "fossils" of the one-word stage of language-evolution – single-word utterances that for some reason are not integrated into the larger combinatorial system ... Their semantic and pragmatic diversity suggests that they are island remnants of a larger system, superseded by true grammar' (240).

While interjections are no longer considered peripheral to linguistics, and while they are now carefully defined with respect to their grammatical form, their meaning still remains vague and elusive. In particular, although interjections are no longer characterized purely in terms of emotion, they are still characterized in terms of 'mental states'. For example, Wierzbicka (1992) characterizes interjections as '[referring] to the speaker's current mental state or mental act' (164). And, as mentioned above, Montes (1999) notes that many interjections '[focus] on the internal reaction of affectedness of the speaker with respect to the referent' (1289).

Philosophers have offered similar interpretations. For example, Herder thought that interjections were the human equivalent of animal sounds, being both a 'language of feeling' and a 'law of nature' (1966: 88). And Rousseau, in his quest for the origins of language, theorized that proto-language was 'entirely interjectional' (1966: 71). Indeed, such philosophers posit a historical transition from interjections to language, where the latter, in contrast to the former, allows us not only to index pain and express passion, but also to denote values and exercise reason (see D'Atri 1995). In this way, interjections have been understood as a semiotic artefact of our natural origins, and the most transparent index of our emotions.

Such an understanding of interjections is deeply rooted in western thought. Aristotle, for example, posited a contrastive relationship between *voice*, proper only to humans as instantiated in language, and *sound*, shared by humans and animals as instantiated in cries (2001). This contrastive relation was then compared with other analogous contrastive relations, in particular, value and pleasure/pain, polis and household, and *bios* (the good life, or political life proper to humans) and *zoe* (pure life, shared by all living things). In short, the folk distinction made between interjections and language proper maps onto a larger set of distinctions in western thought: emotion and cognition, animality and humanity, nature and convention, female and male, passion and reason, bare life and political life, pain and value, private and public, id and superego, motivated and arbitrary, and so on (compare Lutz 1988; Strathern 1988; inter alia).

The foregoing claims notwithstanding, it should be said that some linguists thought differently. Jakobson and Sapir, for example, qualified their descriptions of interjections. And two of the best accounts of interjection-like things – 'response cries' in Goffman (1981c) and 'emblematic gestures' in Sherzer (1993) – explicitly take into account social interaction and ethnographic description. And there exist many good accounts of interjections functioning as discourse particles (Ehlich 1986; Meng and Schrabback 1999; inter alia). Indeed, as usual, Erving Goffman had something insightful to say, providing us with a useful segue:

[I]nterjections … comport neatly with our doctrine of human nature. We see such 'expression' as a natural overflowing, a flooding up of previously uncontained feeling, a bursting of normal restraints, a case of being caught off-guard. That is what would be learned by asking the man on the street if he uses these forms – and, if so, what he means by them (1981c: 99).

7. Why are interjections so easily analysed in terms of emotion?

There are several reasons why interjections are so easily analysed in terms of emotion. For example, if cognition and emotion are understood as two complementary psychological phenomena, and if language (with its ability to refer to, and predicate qualities about, the world) is taken to be emblematic of cognition, then interjections (insofar as they seem to stand on the borders of language) are easily framed as emotive.

Relatedly, if emotions are understood in their own right (and thus not in contrast to cognition) as natural, irruptive, uncontrollable, feeling-mediated reactions to the immediate context, then interjections in their own right (and thus not in contrast to language) seem to have similar properties.

Insofar as interjections are particularly difficult to characterize semantically and socially, they are amenable to characterization in terms of a relatively non-linguistic and non-social idiom, such as folk psychology – with its toolbox of invisible mediating forces.

Interjections constitute a very salient class of words (both in their formal properties and in their peculiarities of usage), so linguists and lay-folk should find them relatively easy to thematize, and thus be more likely to have theories about them in the first place.

Finally, as discussed in chapter 3, complement-taking predicates (and words referring to mental states more generally – such as *fear*, *anger*, and *disgust*) have certain formal and functional properties that provide a rich language-internal resource for reasoning about both the motivations of others and the meaning of utterances. In this way, linguists, philosophers, and lay-folk never have to leave language in order to engage in psychology. In Goffman's terms, each 'man on the street' already has his own elaborate meta-language which he may use to undertake ethnopsychology.

Let me begin with the first three conditions. As shown in sections 2 and 3, interjections have many features which suggest that they are simultaneously distinct from what is commonly understood as 'language', similar to what is commonly understood as 'emotion', and difficult to characterize semantically and socially. For example, interjections are often phonologically and morphologically anomalous. That is, they may be distinct from more stereotypic linguistic forms, and often seem more natural, motivated, or iconic.

Interjections are able to stand alone as an utterance, so that their meaning does not seem to be dependent on their relation to other signs. That is, one cannot specify their meaning in terms of their grammatical distribution. As a function of this, interjections cannot easily be said to 'refer' or 'predicate' like other more stereotypic linguistic units (e.g. nouns and verbs, which are caught up in rich paradigms and constructions); and they do not seem to have truth-conditioned meanings like other signs which express propositional contents.

Interjections may be uttered in non-communicative and seemingly non-social encounters, and seem to be speaker focused rather than addressee focused. In this way, it is difficult to say what their communicative intention, or 'message to another', would be. Relatedly, interjections do not seem to have a *dictum*, or 'I say' component, and are often difficult to report as direct speech. For example, one does not so much *say* 'ouch!' as *exclaim* it.

Speakers seem to have less agency over interjections than other kinds of linguistic utterances: they have less control over the expression of the sign, less composition of the sign–object relation, and less commitment to another's interpretant of this relation (Kockelman 2007c). In Goffman's terms (1981a), it is as if one is in the role of 'sounder' rather than 'speaker', and thus more of a patient than an agent.

Finally, interjections seem hopelessly bound to the immediate context of sensually present facts, insofar as they are unable to indicate temporally, spatially, or modally distant objects or events. That is, there seems to be minimal spatial-temporal buffering between the object and the sign that stands for it, and between the sign and the interpretant it gives rise to. Not only is there minimal displacement, but there also seems to be minimal distance (Goffman 1981a; Kockelman 2005a): the onion-skin layering – where actors perform characters who are themselves actors performing characters, ad infinitum – does not seem to be as present with interjections.

But, as seen by how interjections are used in this Q'eqchi' community, each of these claims has a host of caveats. For example, interjections can be displaced via various types of decentring. Interjections are highly conventional. Interjections do enter into relations of parataxis with other linguistic constructions. Interjections are said in social situations, and do secure others' responses. Many interjections are manifestly addressed – or purposefully expressed for the sake of another's interpretant. And so forth. More generally, as argued most presciently by Austin (2003) and Jakobson (1990b), the referential and conventional properties of language have been overstated anyway: there are many other uses of language than reporting facts to uninformed others by means of arbitrary signs. So the distance between interjections and 'language' is already much smaller than it would first appear.

Regarding the fourth condition, that interjections are relatively salient linguistic forms, we need only make reference to the Boasian tradition of postulating various conditions for speakers to become aware of their own linguistic patterns (Boas 1989a [1889], 1989b [1910]; Sapir 1985 [1927]; Silverstein 1981; Whorf 1956a, 1956b; and see various summaries and syntheses of this tradition, such as Hill and Mannheim 1992; Lucy 1992b; Kockelman 2007c). For example, interjections are *formally isolatable*, insofar as they do not simultaneously occur with other linguistic signs. Contrast, for example, intonation, which necessarily co-occurs with another sign. Second, they are *segmentable* (Silverstein 1981), insofar as they are amenable to phonemic description in terms of distinctive features, and may be transcribed using the conventional orthography of a language. Contrast, for example, non-segmentable forms, be they prosodic (e.g. stress, length, intonation) or non-prosodic (e.g. laughter, screaming, sighing). Third, they are *continuous* (Silverstein 1981), insofar as they are not broken up (temporal-linearly) by intervening signs. Contrast, for example, circumfixed forms (e.g. clitics of negation in French or Q'eqchi': *ne ... pas, moko ... ta*). For all of these reasons, one may predict that speakers can easily *become aware* of interjections.

Or, so as not to privilege the internal state of 'awareness', let me just say that speakers can discursively thematize interjections. That is, they can take them up as a theme, or topic of discourse, in order to comment on their meaning and usage. And, having thematized interjections, they may go on to characterize their forms and functions, as well as reason about their relation to other forms and functions (Kockelman 2007c). In short, insofar as interjections are formally and functionally salient signs, they are more likely to be thematized, characterized, and reasoned about by speakers.

Interjections, then, seem distinct from language (and cognition), similar to emotion, difficult to semantically or socially characterize, and easy to discursively represent. Notice that such conditions involve not only common-sense understandings of language and mind, but also relatively concrete facts about the grammatical form and pragmatic function of interjections. But rather than take this to mean that one may use common-sense or expert understandings of emotion (or intentionality) to understand interjections, let me use interjections – not just their structure and function, but also speakers' representations of them – to understand local understandings of emotion.

The large-scale problem, then, is three-fold. First, we want to avoid eliding the non-expressive meaning of interjections. Thus, the previous sections, by focusing exclusively on the situational, social, and discursive objects of interjections, tried to account for everything but their expressive meaning. Second, we want to account for why it is so easy to elide their non-expressive meaning. Thus, this section has tried to show a number of conditions involved in this elision. And third, we want to account for the expressive meaning of interjections in more than western ethnopsychological terms.

Returning, then, to the fifth and last condition, constructions referring to mental states (such as complement-taking predicates, as discussed in chapter 3, or 'mentalese' more generally) provide a rich, language-internal resource for characterizing the meaning of interjections. Let me discuss not only why such constructions are so useful, but also why using them in this way is so risky.

Such mental-state predicates are relatively *subsuming*. That is, to say that an interjection indexes 'fear' (as an expressive object) solves the problem of characterizing situational and discursive objects: they are merely all events and objects that are *fearsome*. In other words, one may easily use any intentional mode (fear, disgust, desire, etc.) to characterize any intentional content (frightening things, disgusting things, desired things, etc.). In this way, by specifying expressive objects first, situational and discursive objects come for free. As shown in previous sections, however, situational and discursive objects have a rich structure all of their own. If we elide such richness, then we miss not only the pragmatic class of objects (decentrings, non-solicited responses, etc.), but also the ontological class of objects (the local construal of what counts as a glitch, a transition, an unexpected answer, a marked quantity, etc.). Indeed, as was shown in section 4, it is precisely by ethnographically attending to situational, discursive, and social objects that one sees how kinship relations, communicative functions, ethical values, parenting philosophies, politeness norms, and ceremonial rites are enacted. And thus to subsume all these objects by focusing on expressive objects is to miss most of what constitutes their meaning – and thus much of what it means to be a person in local terms.

As shown in chapter 3, the semantic and morphosyntactic properties of complement-taking predicates allow one to cross-linguistically compare, and language-internally classify, the lexical expression of mental states and speech acts. As was argued there, a key means of classifying, scaling, and ultimately translating the lexical expression of mental states is the degree to which the mode event and content event are mutually implicated – be it grammatically (morphologically and syntactically) or semantically (logically and causally). In other words, such constructions project causal properties onto the events they describe – such as the usage of interjections: what causes one to utter an interjection; and what the uttering of an interjection causes another to do.

In regard to speech acts, Austin (2003 [1955]; and see Silverstein (1981) on transparency) made the important claim that certain verbs are explicit: one may not only perform a speech act by using them (*I promise to ...*), one may also describe the performance of a speech act with them (*he promised to ...*). In terms of mental-state predicates, we may say that complement-taking predicates are important because speakers may use them not only to express their own mental states (*I fear that ...*), but also to ascribe mental states to others (*John feared that ...*), as well as predicate properties of mental states (*fear is ...*). In short, such mental-state predicates allow speakers to interpret the meaning of interjections by means of their representations of them, rather than in terms of their reactions to them.

Finally, some mental-state predicates are arguably semantic primitives, insofar as other predicates (pertaining to mind, speech acts, and so forth) seem to depend on them as a component of their meaning. For example, one necessarily makes reference to 'wanting' when defining 'wishing', one necessarily makes reference to 'saying' when one describes 'promising', and one necessarily makes reference to 'feeling' when defining 'anger' (Van Valin and Wilkins 1993; and Wierzbicka 1988; and see the rich tradition in analytic philosophy). In short, such mental-state predicates may constitute essential building blocks in the definition of more complicated predicates.

For all of these reasons – subsumption, classification, explicitness, displacement, and primitiveness – speakers may readily and conveniently use mental-state predicates to interpret other signs of mental states – thematizing them, characterizing them, and reasoning about them. In this way, speakers and analysts alike never have to leave language to engage in psychology.

There are, however, several problems with such an approach. First, such an extensive mental lexicon may indicate a particular community's preoccupation with one domain of phenomena, rather than anything salient about the world. For example, it has been claimed that English has over 200 words referring to the emotions alone (Wallace and Carson 1973); whereas in Q'eqchi', there are only twenty or so words one would be tempted to classify as referring to emotions and, as will be seen in the next section, no obvious superordinate term for emotion in the first place. In this way, there is no reason to assume emotion (feeling or affect) is a valid category in the local context.

Second, there is no reason to believe that in all languages (or in any language) mental-state predicates cover interjections. For example, one may easily imagine a case where a community's interjectional repertoire (vis-à-vis the emotions) was larger, or more elaborated, than their lexical one. (See Silverstein 1995 [1976], for an analogous critique of the literature on speech acts.)

And finally, there is no consensus about what any of these words mean (e.g. *belief, desire, fear*, etc.), or indeed what emotions are in the first place (Griffiths 1997), so that to define interjections in terms of words referring to emotions may merely shift the problem to knowing what these words mean (conceptually), or what their referents are (biologically, psychologically, or socially). In other words, in attempting to ground a linguistic fact in a psychological one, we end up calling on another no less problematic linguistic fact.

Indeed, most generally, the danger of lexeme-based semantic decomposition is *radical decontextualization*. In particular, individual responses are analysed at the expense of social encounters; semantics is analysed at the expense of pragmatics; mental states are analysed at the expense of situational, discursive, and social context; and relatively occurrent, thematic, or reflective meanings are characterized at the expense of tacit, habitual, or embodied ones. In other words, non-expressive and expressive objects, semantics and pragmatics, usage and reflections on usage, habitual comportment and self-conscious action, the categories of analysts and the categories of actors are all conflated.

This does not mean that one must relinquish mental-state predicates as a linguistic resource. As argued in chapter 3, a particular subset of such words (complement-taking predicates) constitutes both a cross-linguistic form–functional domain and a cross-cultural index of intentionality. In this way, with a host of caveats, such lexemes provide a powerful language-internal tool for understanding interjections. In particular, complement-taking predicates may be used as key interpretants of interjections, such that the latter may be translated into the former, so long as we avoid radical decontextualization. In this way, returning to the concerns and conundrums raised in section 2 of chapter 1, language usage itself becomes the extensional background or standard of comparison for analysing the meaning of mental-state predicates. The following sections, which describe the way speakers of Q'eqchi' use complement-taking predicates to interpret their usage of interjections, are meant to complement, rather than replace, sections 3 and 4, which described the range of non-expressive objects and non-representational interpretants of interjections. The issue, then, is not just to offer an account of all the various objects and interpretants of interjections, but to account for why representational interpretants of interjections focus on expressive objects – be these interpretations offered by speakers of Q'eqchi' or western philosophers and linguists.

## 8.	Meta-language and ethnopsychology among speakers of Q'eqchi'

This section shows how, in their reporting of interjections, speakers use the quotative verb *chank* (to go) rather than *yehok* (to say), thereby implying that interjections are 'sounded' rather than 'said'. It shows how those interjections which are most easily thematized by speakers are also the least frequently used. In particular, speakers most elaborately characterized the interjection *chix*, which indexes foulsome things, the interjection *uyaluy*, which indexes dangerous things, and the interjection *ay*, when it indexes painful events. It shows how speakers, in their characterizations of these interjections, routinely use members of a covert class of verbs, which may be loosely glossed as 'feelings'. And it shows how the scripts offered by speakers about sign events involving interjections turn on the following kind of causal chaining: an event in the world causes a feeling in a person, which in turn causes the person to sound the interjection.

Before I go into these points at length, let me briefly motivate why one should worry about speakers' reflections in the first place. First, such an account is data in its own right which may be compared with linguists' reflections, and which has a bearing on the 'structure-practice-ideology' literature first theorized by Bourdieu (1977 [1972]), as attributed to Marx, and taken up and transformed by linguistic anthropologists (Silverstein 1979, 1981; Hanks 1991; Schieffelin *et al.* 1998). Second, speakers often have quite sophisticated understandings of their own practices and, in the case of mental states, one may use this understanding to access what otherwise must be inferred (Hanks 1993; Talmy 2000). Third, such reflections may be implicated in the beliefs and values of speakers, and thus affect language use – for example, by guiding the strategies of actors. Fourth, much descriptive and theoretical work in linguistics proper depends on such reflections (consider, for example, the central role speakers' judgements play in formal linguistics). In this way, one is merely problematizing and theorizing what was always tacitly practised. Fifth, enabling and constraining reflexivity may be thought to ontologically define us as a species (Peirce 1955; Vygotsky 1978), so that to not account for it explicitly is to miss much of what it means to be human (Lucy 1993a). And lastly, as mentioned in the introduction, one may relate such reflections on usage (what Bourdieu calls 'discourses about practice') to actual usage (or 'practice'), and then compare such relations across languages, in order not so much to minimize observer effects, as to instigate and analyse them.

Let me first discuss some of the ways interjections are uttered in direct and reported speech, and mentioned in meta-linguistic practices. First, just as in actual use (and reported speech), the interjections usually had to be stressed *in mention* in order to be understood as interjections. For example, in first topicalizing the interjection *chix* with a speaker, I uttered an unstressed token, and the speaker kept correcting me, insisting that I meant *tixl*, which refers to the danto, a large and rare animal. Only when I enacted a usage, with stress, did the speaker understand what I meant. Similarly, speakers themselves stress interjections in mention. Hence, interjections are represented as delocutionary, thereby evincing their illocutionary force as exclamation in addition to their linguistic form. This is in agreement with Bloomfield (1933), who thought that interjections were 'the most characteristic intense forms' (156), having their own 'special secondary phoneme [!]'.

Second, both in reported speech and in mention, speakers almost always used the quotative verb *chank* (to go), instead of the otherwise frequently used verb of directly reported speech *yehok* (to say).[6] In other words, it is tacitly understood that speakers do not so much 'say' *chix* as 'go' or 'sound' *chix*. This supports claims by linguists like Goffman (1981c; and see Ameka 1992 and Wierzbicka 1992), who claim that interjections do not involve a *dictum*, or 'I say' component. That is, unlike canonical speech acts, such as imperatives, questions, and assertions, they do not seem to be addressed, or intentionally expressed for the sake of another's interpretant. As will be seen below, this agrees with the amount of control speakers are tacitly accorded in uttering interjections.

Next, those interjections about which speakers can offer the most extensive and textured reflections are overall the least frequently used. In particular, the interjections *chix* (foulness), *ay* (painful events), and *uyaluy* (danger) are easily thematized, and their situational and expressive objects are elaborately characterized and extensively enumerated, even though their token frequency is extremely low relative to other interjections. For example, of the almost two hundred tokens I collected of *ay* within a twelve-month period, only five indexed painful events. The majority involved quantity predications (serving

---

[6] See Lucy (1993b) for a discussion of a similar quotative construction in Yucatec Maya.

as positive minimal responses) and non-preferred solicited responses (serving as offer refusals and unexpected answers). Similarly, in this same period, I collected only nine and six tokens of the interjections *uyaluy* and *chix*, respectively. Contrast interjections which mark mistakes (stressed *eh*, *t'*, and *ay*), of which I had at least one token per week. And contrast interjections which index non-addressed non-responses (unstressed *eh* as a floor holder or marker of self-repair) or preferred solicited responses (*ah* used with question–answers), which occur in most utterances. In sum, those interjections which are most easily thematized and extensively characterized are the least frequently used. Crucially, the issue is not that speakers have nothing to say about the meaning of the other interjections, or about the discursive function of these interjections; it is that when talking about such stereotypically emotive functions they 'go all out' – offering very detailed scripts, with a kind of energy and richness that is otherwise lacking.

Let me now discuss the types of characterizations speakers offered for these interjections. The interjection *uyaluy* is easily topicalized, and speakers can offer detailed accounts of its usage. There is agreement on the following points. First, it is used when you become frightened before something dangerous (*tatxiwaq chiru li xiwajel*) – in particular, when you 'see' (*taawil*) such a dangerous thing. Second, the word used to refer to the class of dangerous things, *xiwajel*, is an abstract noun derived from the noun for 'fear' (*xiw*), which may be glossed as 'fearsome thing'. In this way, an adjective derived from a word denoting an emotional state is used to characterize typical objects. Notice, then, that just like with linguists' accounts of the meaning of interjections, expressive objects subsume situational and discursive ones. Third, stereotypical dangerous things are rather concrete: poisonous or large animals, such as snakes (*k'anti'*), tigers (*hix*), and bulls (*k'ol wakax*). When such creatures are angry (*josq'*) they are thought to be particularly dangerous – recall the discussion of fright (*xiwajenaq*) from chapter 1. More abstract forms of danger are not mentioned. And lastly, the sounding of the utterance itself is caused by one's fear. Let me explain. In characterizing *uyaluy* in this way, speakers use the relational noun *-b'aan*, which may be glossed as 'because of', and which is commonly used to mark the demoted agents in passive constructions (compare *by* in the English passive construction: 'he was killed *by* lightning'). Such a construction implies that the cause of the utterance is not due to the volition of the speaker, but rather the state of fear which the speaker is in. In this way, this construction resonates with speakers' use of the quotative verb *chank*. For example, speakers routinely used utterances such as:

9) **x-b'aan aa-xiw '*uyaluy*' chan-k-at**
    E(3s)-RN E(2s)-fear Interj say-Pres-A(2s)
    *because of your fear, you go '*uyaluy*'*

As mentioned above, the interjection *chix* is difficult to topicalize unless said with stress. But once topicalized, speakers can offer detailed descriptions of its usage. First, it is said when your disgust comes (*naq xchal aayib'yib'al*). Second, this happens when one is close to, typically within reach of, objects such as faeces (*k'ot*), vomit (*xa'aw*), dirt or filth (*tz'aj*), wounds (*xtiq'ilal*), and rotten (eggs). Third, such objects are usually characterized as disgusting (*yib'ru*), gross (*chu*), or dirty (*tz'aj*) – a set of referents which were collectively referred to as 'foulsome' in section 3. Moreover, the adjective 'disgusting' (*yib'ru*), used to describe typical objects that elicit this interjection, may be further derived into the noun for 'disgust' (*yib'yib'al*). Again, then, expressive objects, couched in terms of words referring to emotional states, easily subsume discursive and situational objects. And finally, in characterizing the usage of this interjection, speakers say that one sounds this interjection *because of* one's disgust. Here again the relational noun *-b'aan* is used. For example, one speaker said the following:

10) **x-b'aan naq x-Ø-aa-yib' li x-tiq'ilal li winq '*chix*' chan-k-at**
E(3s)-RN Comp Perf-A(3s)-E(2s)-disgust Dm E(3s)-wound Dm man Interj say-Pres-A(2s)
because the man's wound has disgusted you, you go 'chix'

The interjection *ay* is easily topicalized when it indexes painful events. The stereotypic objects of pain are said to be cuts (*yok'ol*), blows (*tochok*), falls (*t'ane'k*), and burns (*k'atok*). All such objects share the characteristic of being very painful (*mas ra*). The uttering of the interjection itself is said to be caused by the pain (*rahilal*) of the cut, blow, fall, or burn. Importantly, such usage is extended to explain the other usages (when such usages are pointed out to the speaker), thereby subsuming with an expressive object (pain) all the other situational and discursive objects of *ay* discussed in section 4.[7] And lastly, just like with *chix* and *uyaluy*, the sounding of *ay* is caused by the pain of the cut, blow, fall, or burn. Again, the relational noun *-b'aan* is used. For example:

11) **naq x-Ø-aa-yok aa-wib' '*ay*' chan-k-at x-b'aan aa-rahilal**
Comp Perf-A(3s)-E(2s)-cut E(2s)-Rflx Interj say-Pres-A(2s) E(3s)-RN E(2s)-pain
when you have cut yourself, you go 'ay' because of your pain

Notice the bias such stereotypy introduces into speakers', and presumably linguists', accounts of the meaning of interjections: the most manifestly expressive uses of interjections, which are also the least frequently occurring, are the most readily topicalized and the most extensively characterized. And notice the theory of causality that is implicit in these constructions: an internal state, itself

---

[7] Elicitation turned on two commonly used meta-linguistic constructions: 1) 'what does "ay" mean' (*k'aru naraj naxye 'ay'*), where the verb 'to mean' may be glossed as 'to want to say' (*naraj xyeb'al*); 2) 'when do you say/sound "ay"' (*joq'e taaye/cha'qat 'ay'*).

caused by an object or event in the world, causes the sounding of the interjection. That is, as tacitly acknowledged in their use of *chank* instead of *yehok*, and in their use of the relational noun *-b'aan* in conjunction with a possessed feeling state, speakers of Q'eqchi' treat sounders of interjections as having little control over their utterances; and they treat the sounding as the effect of a mental state, itself the effect of a loathsome thing. Compare the causal relation between anger and utterance discussed in example 9 of chapter 5.

9.   Semantic class of predicates used to gloss interjections

Having just summarized how mental-state predicates are used by speakers of Q'eqchi' to characterize interjections, let me now relate such predicates to various cross-linguistic grammatical categories. As discussed in section 3, the point of this is not to rewrite expressive objects in terms of mental states, but rather to use the cross-linguistic categories that organize such mental lexemes as a framework relative to which one may frame interjections in terms of ontological class, relative control, and causal logic.

As seen in the last section, the interjections *ay*, *uyaluy*, and *chix* are characterized in terms of the possessable nouns for 'fear' (*xiw*), 'disgust' (*yib'yib'al*), and 'pain' (*rahilal*). These three mental-state predicates belong to a category of lexemes that are covert (Whorf 1956a), insofar as one cannot tell which words are members of this category by examining their phonological or morphological features alone. Rather, membership in such a category must be determined by grammatical analysis of the kind used in chapter 3: their morphosyntactic distribution relative to other forms in the language. Let me discuss these criteria in detail.

Table 6.2 shows a class of Q'eqchi' verbs (and the nouns with which they are derivationally associated) that are grammatically similar in the following way. All are intransitive. They may all take non-finite complements marked by the complementizer *chi*. For example, if *xinchal* means 'I have come', *xinchal chi aatinak* means 'I have come to talk'. These verbs seem to fall into two classes based on their meaning: movement and feeling. All of the predicates listed under the heading 'feeling' are state-changes (when they occur with complements). In this way, they are semantically similar to the intransitive English verbs 'redden' (to become red) and 'die' (to become dead). And finally, there are at least ten such predicates, and they may be divided into three sub-categories as a function of their semantics. First, there are those having to do with heat and anger: *josq'o'k* (to become angry) and *q'ixno'k* (to become hot/angry). Second, those having to do with fear and shame: *xiwak* (to become afraid) and *xutaanak* (to become ashamed). And third, there are those having to do with generic bodily states: *lub'k* and *tawak* (to become tired), *titz'k* (to become exasperated), *jiq'e'k* (to become choked or breathless), *raho'k* (to

Table 6.2. *Covert predicate classes: movement and feeling*

Verb class	Q'eqchi' verb	English gloss	Q'eqchi' noun	English gloss
Movement	*xik*	'to go'	Not Applicable	
	k'ulunk/hulak	'to arrive'		
	kanak	'to stay'		
	elk	'to leave'		
	nume'k	'to pass by'		
	wank	'to be located'		
	chalk	'to come'		
Feeling	*titz'k*	'to become exasperated'	*titz'ik* (?)	'exasperation'
	lub'k/tawak	'to become tired'	*lub'ik*	'tiredness'
	tawaak	'to tire'	*tawajik*	'tiredness'
	raho'k	'to get hurt'	*rahilal*	'pain'
	yib'o'k (?)	'to become disgusted'	*yib', yib'yib'al*	'disgust'
	jiq'e'k	'to become choked'	*jiq'*	'cough'
	q'ixno'k	'to become angry/hot'	*q'ix(il)* (?)	'heat'
	tiqwo'k	'to become angry/hot'	*tiq*	'heat/fever'
	josq'o'k	'to become angry'	*josq'il*	'anger'
	xutaanak	'to become ashamed'	*xutaan*	'shame'
	xiwak	'to become afraid'	*xiw*	'fear'

get hurt), and *yib'o'k* (to become disgusted). All of these predicates may be ascribed to humans, and most may also be ascribed to animals. These classes of complement-taking predicates were first introduced in chapter 3, under the headings of purposive predicates and intransitive affectuals (recall Table 3.2).

As may be seen from Table 6.2, all of the members of the feeling-class have nominal counterparts.[8] These nouns are either derived from, or derivable into, the verbs themselves. For example, if *ra* is an adjective meaning 'painful', *rahilal* is a derived noun meaning 'pain(fulness)', and *raho'k* is a derived verb meaning 'to become painful' (or, more idiomatically, 'to get or be hurt'). As nouns, they may be possessed. And, once possessed, they may occur with the existential verb *wank*, and be glossed as 'to possess such a state'. Or, they may occur with the verb *chalk*, 'to come', and be glossed as 'to come into possession of such a state'. Notice that both of these verbs, *wank* and *chalk*, belong to the class of movement predicates. Such noun + movement-verb constructions act as state-changes, taking non-finite complements marked by the complementizer *chi*. In this way, they are semantically equivalent to feelings. Compare the following two examples, the first of which is a noun + movement-verb construction, and the second of which is a feeling-verb construction:

---

[8] Constructions marked with a question mark (?) are considered grammatical by speakers of Q'eqchi'. However, I don't have any tokens of their actual usage in my corpus.

12) **x-Ø-chal in-xiw chi r-il-b'al li wakax**
Perf-A(3s)-come E(1s)-fear Comp E(3s)-see-Nom Dm bull
my fear came about (I came into possession of fear) upon seeing the bull

13) **x-in-xiwak chi r-il-b'al li wakax**
Perf-A(1s)-be.afraid Comp E(3s)-see-Nom Dm bull
I got scared upon seeing the bull

Notice that there is no superordinate category or lexeme among the Q'eqchi' that would pick out this set of terms. That is, this is not only a covert grammatical category, but also a covert cultural category. Moreover, while many members of this class seem like stereotypic emotions (e.g. fear, anger, shame, etc.), others do not (e.g. tiredness, breathlessness, etc.). For this reason I call them 'feelings'. What they all seem to have in common semantically, besides being state-changes, is that the grammatical subject of such constructions is more like a *theme* or *patient* than an *agent* or *instigator*. That is, whoever is referred to by a construction having such a semantic role is accorded no more control over the event (of becoming some state) than a window is accorded when it breaks, or wallpaper is accorded when it yellows. Finally, in the case of the noun + movement-verb constructions just discussed, the grammatical subject is the possessed state itself (not the person to whom it belongs). In effect, one is saying: 'I came into possession of my nausea (fear, etc.) because of what I saw (did, discovered, etc.)'. In other words, the person to whom the feeling state belongs is not in control of the state, or causal of the state; rather, the object of the complement is (i.e. *what* one saw, did, discovered, etc.). This accords with speakers' implicit theory of control discussed in the previous section, in which an object or event causes a feeling state, which in turn causes an utterance.

This class of verbs (and their associated nouns) may be compared with the types of mental entities found within the western folk theory of mind. As discussed in chapter 3, D'Andrade (1995; and see Lillard 1998; Rips and Conrad 1989) argued that the European American Social Science Model of Mind has five parts, which are lexicalized in English as *perception, thought, feeling, wish,* and *intention*. These parts are causally interrelated. For example, an event causes a perception, which causes a thought, which causes a feeling, which causes an expressive action. But also a wish can influence a thought, which can cause a feeling, and so on. And a thought or a feeling can cause a wish, which can cause an intention, which can cause an action. Importantly, D'Andrade (1995) notes that 'not all actions in the folk model are intended. There is a category of reflex actions, like sneezing, and a category of expressive actions, like smiling and crying, which are not under voluntary control [but are rather] thought to be caused by a salient feeling or emotion' (162). Notice, then, that the western folk-understanding of 'feeling', as described by D'Andrade, has exactly the same relations of causality and control as the covert grammatical category of 'feeling' in Q'eqchi'.

In short, as seen in the case of complement-taking predicates, one's achievement of a certain feeling state is out of one's control (being caused by what one just did, discovered, encountered, etc.). And, as seen in the case of the relational noun -*b'aan*, and the quotative verb *chank*, one's achieved feeling state is the cause of the utterance of the interjection. Very simply, then, newly learnt knowledge causes a feeling which causes a reflexive action – the utterance of the interjection itself. Just like the western ethnopsychological understanding of feelings and reflexive actions, as discussed above, this is the underlying theory of causality and control for a small number of interjections in Q'eqchi'. In other words, as implicit in speakers' understandings of the least-frequently used, but most-extensively characterized interjections, there is a theory of relative control, causal logic, and ontological class that parallels western ethnopsychology and many linguistic accounts of the primary meaning of interjections. That is, speakers of Q'eqchi' not only *elide* the same set of social and discursive functions (focusing on expressive objects), they also *project* a similar agentive, causal, and ontological understanding of emotion as western linguists and lay-people. In accounting for one form–functional domain (interjections) in terms of another form–functional domain (complement-taking predicates), there is not only a shared projection of semantic features, there is also a shared elision of pragmatic functions. Indeed, it may be precisely this discrepancy that enables a key function of emotional phenomena, in comparison to other modes of intentionality: the mitigation of responsibility (Averill 1980; Kockelman 2006, 2007c).

10.   The relation between imperatives and implements

One may take a cross-linguistic (typological) perspective, and examine the general features of interjections as a form–functional domain. And one may take a language-specific (descriptive) perspective, and examine the particular details of the class of interjections within a given language. In other words, one can examine, in either relatively general or relatively particular terms, the signs that express them, the objects they stand for, and the interpretants they give rise to. This was undertaken in the first half of this chapter. To paraphrase Marshall Sahlins (1976), such cross-linguistic form–functional domains are not the imperatives of culture, but its implements.

Crucially, most interpretants are themselves signs – for example, complement-taking predicates used to gloss the meaning of interjections. And so again one may take a cross-linguistic (typological) perspective, and examine the general features of complement-taking predicates as a form–functional domain. And one may take a language-specific (descriptive) perspective, and examine the particular details of the class of complement-taking predicates within a given language. This was undertaken in chapter 3.

In this way, the meaning of signs from one form–functional domain were established in terms of the meaning of signs from another form–functional domain. The continuities and discrepancies between cross-linguistic and language-specific structures were evinced. And the continuities and discrepancies between two sets of linguistic practices, one which relates to the other as sign to object or interpretant to sign, were evinced. In other words, by moving between typology and description (general and particular), and between signification and interpretation (language and meta-language), the identities and differences between the levels of description and the domains described were evinced.

By cross-linguistically comparing two such language-internal interpretations (how western philosophers and linguists, and how speakers of Q'eqchi'-Maya, understand the usage of interjections), we have found similar mappings of semantic features and similar elisions of pragmatic functions. In some sense, both speech communities interpret and misinterpret the meaning of interjections in similar ways: the relation between the practices and interpretations of those practices was incommensurate, or skewed, in very similar ways.

If human beings are indeed those entities whose agency is both enabled and constrained by the fact that their practices and their representations of practices are never commensurate, then the relevant locus for cross-cultural comparison should not be a set of practices, nor a set of representations (of practices), but rather such relationships between the two.

7 Conclusion: natural constructions and social kinds

1. Methodology as theory

As implicit in the foregoing chapters, a key methodological assumption of this monograph is that analysis must take into account relations between relations. This phrase is borrowed from Evans-Pritchard (1940: 266), who concluded his seminal study of Nuer social structure by reference to it. For present purposes, it means that analysis should not only privilege relations over relata, it should also privilege relations between relata that are themselves relations. While this is a relatively abstract idea, it is central to any comparative project, and has undergirded the analysis undertaken in each chapter. It is best explained by demonstrating the variety of uses to which it has been put, all of which were a means to resolve the questions, concerns, and conundrums introduced in chapter 1.

A key class of grammatical constructions that were examined involves complement-taking predicates, such as *she believes he is rich*, *I want to call him*, and *Dave heard that she had been injured*. Generalizing some concepts and terms from Jakobson (1990a), such constructions may be understood as involving three events: the speech event (e.g. the event of communicating beliefs, desires, and perceptions); the mode event (e.g. the event of believing, desiring, or perceiving); and the content event (e.g. the event believed, desired, or perceived). By using grammatical categories such as person, tense, deixis, status, and evidentiality, the mode event may be displaced from the speech event, and the content event may be displaced from the mode event. That is, these three events may be construed as more or less distal to each other along dimensions such as person (I vs. you), space (here vs. there), time (now vs. then), status (actuality vs. possibility), and evidence (experienced vs. inferred). Displacement enables a host of other functions. For example, not only may such constructions be used to ascribe mental states to people (*John is afraid to fly*), they may also be used to predicate properties of mental states (*anger is an emotion*).

In addition to displacement, these constructions have three other key features that are central to any comparative approach to mind. By lexically encoding the mode event and the content event, they allow one's mental state to be relatively public and unambiguous, and hence constitute relatively emblematic roles. Because of this lexical encoding, a large variety of different kinds of mode events and content events may be expressed: a potentially infinite palette of beliefs and desires, experiences and inferences, moods and emotions. And because of the generative nature of complementation, content events may themselves be mode events, such that mental states may be reflexively embedded, providing a key locale for meta-representations, and the onion-skin layering of subjectivity: *I believe she wants him to think that*... (Goffman 1981a). Crucially, other kinds of linguistic resources – whether in the same language, or across different languages – may be compared as a function of their partaking of these features. In particular, interjections and verbal operators, like status and evidentiality, allow for different degrees of displacement, emblemeticity, construal, and embedding. Such differing degrees of explicitness and flexibility have important consequences for the kinds of functions such linguistic resources serve, and the kinds of meta-representational practices in which they are implicated.

Finally, lexical categories denoting mode events often grammaticalize into, and are used by speakers to interpret, verbal operators that index the other kinds of events – or rather participant roles – that were analysed in this monograph: reference events (tense and aspect); commitment events (status); source events (evidentiality); and deontic events (mood). This shows the important relationship between tightness (the relation between mode event and content event), displacement (the relation between speech event and narrated event), and scope (the relation between such verbal operators and the predicates they modify).

A foundational insight of modern linguistics is this: within a given language, the relation between any particular linguistic form and its meaning (say, a word and a concept) must be analysed in relation to the relations between other linguistic forms and their meanings (say, other words and concepts within a particular construction type or semantic field). More generally, the distributional patterns of any particular linguistic item, the kinds of constructions it may enter into within a particular language, provide a privileged vantage for characterizing both its morphosyntactic form and its semantic content (Bloomfield 1984 [1933]; de Saussure 1983 [1916]). This insight is especially relevant in the case of signs of mental states which, having no obvious extension (qua public, perceivable referent), require careful analysis to reveal their intension (qua conceptual structure). Indeed, as seen, degree of displacement, itself determinable by reference to morphosyntactic patterns, provides a key means to categorize and compare the semantic features encoded by complement-taking predicates. This was a crucial analytic resource for describing the form and function of not just complement-taking predicates, but also verbal operators like status and evidentiality.

Such principled attention to relations between relations is not only the main entry into language-specific structure, it is also the main entry into cross-linguistic structure, and language typology more generally. To start with the most famous example, implicational universals are always couched in terms of relations between relations. For instance, if a language has two kinds of number (say, singular and plural), the form encoding plural will have at least as many morphemes as the form encoding singular (Greenberg 1963). Moreover, this is the key idea behind diagrammatic iconicity. For example, just as the sentence *I want to go to the store* looks like a single clause in relation to the sentence *I believe that she will go to the store* (which looks like two clauses), the state of affairs represented by the first sentence looks like a single event in relation to the state of affairs represented by the second sentence (which looks like two events). While desire and belief constructions will differ in many ways across languages, such diagrammatic iconicity will hold in any language (Givón 1980; Van Valin and LaPolla 1997). That is, the degree of displacement between mode event and content event in the case of desire predicates is always less than or equal to the degree of displacement between mode event and content event in the case of belief predicates. Such results may be generalized for a wide range of mental states so far as they are encoded in lexical and grammatical categories.

Not only is language structure best analysed by reference to relations between relations, but so is language use. In particular, any meaningful process has three components: a sign (or representation) is whatever stands for something else; an object is whatever is stood for by a sign; and an interpretant is whatever a sign gives rise to insofar as it stands for an object (itself often another sign). These three components relate to each other in the following way: a sign stands for its object, on the one hand, and its interpretant, on the other, in such a way as to make the interpretant stand in relation to the object in a way that corresponds with how the sign stands in relation to the object (Peirce 1931–35: passage 8.332; Kockelman 2005a). (See Figure 7.1.) For example, *joint attention* is a meaningful process: a child turning to observe what her father is observing involves an interpretant (the child's change of attention), an object (what the parent is attending to), and a sign (the parent's direction of attention). Similarly, an interjection may serve to call one's attention to an object; and this object, in the context of the newly established intersubjective frame, may itself invite the implicature that one should undertake some action with the object. What is at issue in meaningfulness, then, is not one relation between a sign and an object (qua 'standing for'), but rather a relation between two such relations (qua 'correspondence').

This characterization of language use also provides a method for explicating the objects of signs by reference to their interpretants, or proper effects. This is especially useful when the objects in question are mental states or social

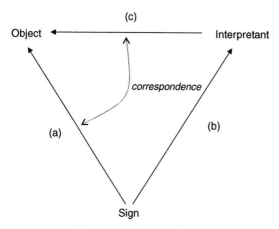

Figure 7.1. Semiosis as correspondence

statuses, and hence maximally imperceptible to an observer. In particular, the object of a sign is really that to which all (appropriate and effective) interpretants of that sign correspondingly relate (Kockelman 2005a). Objects, then, are relatively abstract entities by definition. They should not be confused with 'objects' in the Cartesian sense of *res extensa*. Nor should they be confused with the 'things' that words seem to stand for. Indeed, it is best to think of the object as a correspondence-preserving projection from all interpretants of a sign. They may be more or less objective (in the stereotypic sense). They may be more or less precisely delimited (allowing for narrower or wider leeway of interpretation), as seen by the dotted portion of Figure 7.2. And they may be more or less intersubjectively shared (being more or less normatively spread across a population). For example, if the interjection *ouch* is a sign, the object of that sign – whether construed as a social status or mental state – is a correspondence-preserving projection from the set of behaviours (or interpretants) humans may or must do (normatively speaking, within some particular community) in the context of, and because of, that interjection: turning to look, asking 'are you okay?', saying 'don't be such a baby!', offering a sympathetic pat on the back, and so on. Each of these interpretants is a normatively available outcome of a joint-attentional act, and hence all point to the meaning of that act.

Any meaningful process may be understood as the chaining together of two or more semiotic processes. For example, a mental state, insofar as it represents a state of affairs, may give rise to a speech act; and a speech act, insofar as it represents a state of affairs, may give rise to a mental state. One may examine such enchained semiotic processes from two perspectives: either mental states (and social statuses) may be understood as the roots and fruits of speech acts

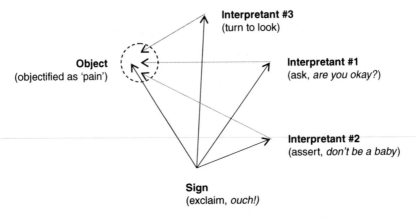

Figure 7.2. Object as correspondence-preserving projection

(and sign events more generally); or speech acts may be understood as the roots and fruits of mental states (and social statuses). The two views are equivalent, like the two faces of a Necker cube. What is at issue, then, is the relation between the context that was in place before the speech act and the context that comes to be in place because of the speech act. Indeed, it has been hypothesized that, from the standpoint of an observer, a key feature of human cognition is the ability to infer roots from fruits or fruits from roots (Tomasello and Call 1997). For example, to infer another's anger from what they have just seen; or, having inferred that another is angry, to predict how they will subsequently act. (See Figure 7.3.) Here, then, particular instances of language structure – qua lexical and grammatical constructions underlying actual utterances – are examined in relatively concrete, culturally specific contexts. This is the best site to study the unfolding of those normatively causal and logical processes which stand at the intersection of language, culture, and mind.

Crucially, when we speak we speak to others and often about others. This means that, just as a meaningful process has three interrelated components (sign, object, interpretant), a meaningful process relates three key actors: the speaker (whoever speaks), the addressee (whomever is spoken to), and the character (whomever is spoken about). Any speech event, then, may express social relations among at least three actors. For example, it is often the case that a speaker may or may not ascribe mental states to actors who relate to the speaker in particular ways (say, to one's neighbour rather than to one's son); moreover, one may or may not report one's own mental states in the context of certain addressees (say, in front of one's spouse rather than in front of a stranger). Finally, key modes of self-reflexivity may be examined from this perspective – for example, when the one speaking is the same as the one spoken about (identity of speaker and character); or when the one spoken about is

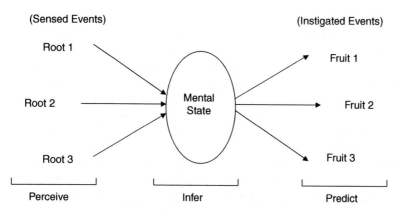

Figure 7.3. Roots and fruits

the same as the one spoken to (identity of character and addressee); or when the one speaking is the same as the one spoken to (identity of speaker and addressee). Such self-reflexive and meta-representational practices provide a privileged site for analysing local modes of selfhood, cultural understandings of what it means to be a person (Lucy 1993a; Taylor 1989).

Finally, we may examine meta-representational practices: mental states or speech acts which represent other mental states or speech acts; or meaningful processes whose objects are themselves meaningful processes (Frege 1997 [1892]; Jakobson 1990b). The classic locus for this is *intensionality* (notice the spelling). Focusing on mental states for a moment, not only may I represent what and how you believe (qua object and sign), I may also represent what your belief will give rise to (qua interpretant of it as a sign), as well as what gave rise to your belief (qua sign of which it is an interpretant). More generally, one can represent the incoherence of another's representation (relative to one's own standard of coherence). For example, not only may I believe that the man over there is a spy, I may also believe that John believes that the man over there is a waiter. Indeed, I may represent why John believes this (given his past perceptions and beliefs); and I may represent what John will say and do (given his future beliefs and intentions). That is, I may represent where exactly his representations went awry, as well as the ramifications of this. Tests turning on intensionality are the classic locus for theory of mind – for example, the ability to pass a false-belief task (cf. Wimmer and Perner 1983); or the ability to track, create and maintain shared and non-shared horizons of intentionality.

Indeed, all the interpretants discussed above are meta-signs. And so any utterance that interprets the meaning of another utterance – for example, by glossing it (within the same language), or by translating it (across different languages) – is a meta-representation in this sense. And not only may speakers interpret the meaning of various grammatical and lexical forms, they may also interpret the meaning of speech acts and discourse patterns more generally: offering local understandings of what mental states and social statuses need to be in place for a discursive move to be appropriate, or come to be in place when a discursive move is effective (Austin 2003 [1955]; Silverstein 1995 [1976]; and see the essays in Lucy 1993b). Indeed, inverting the frame, speakers often describe the 'meaning' of a mental state (or a social status) in terms of the kinds of actions and events that may lead to it (as its roots) and the kinds of actions and events that may follow from it (as its fruits). For example, what events can cause a person to feel fear; and what actions can fear cause a person to do? Such linguistic meta-representations of locally salient and normatively appropriate indexical and inferential scripts are a key analytic resource for comparing culture-specific understandings of mind.

In short, a domain that at first seems to be the most private and invisible (mind) was rendered both empirically tractable and widely comparable by reference to the cultural processes and linguistic practices that mediate it. Stances, then, provide a public face for, and a social perspective on, the inferential and indexical processes that constitute the essence of intentionality, one of the defining characteristics of mind.

Appendix A: Transcription conventions

INTERLINEAR

Abs	Abstract
A(2p)	Absolutive pronoun (second-person, plural-number)
AF	Afactive
CF	Counterfactive
Comp	Complementizer
Dm	Demonstrative
E(1s)	Ergative pronoun (first-person, singular-number)
F	Factive
Fut	Future tense or prospective aspect
Hnr	Honorific
Imp	Imperative (essentially a null-marker at beginning of verbs)
Inf	Unexperienced evidential ('remote past')
Int	Interrogative
Interj	Interjection
IR	Irrealis
Neg	Negation
NF	Nonfactive
NImp	Negative imperative
Nom	Nominalizer
NS	Nonspecific
Opt	Optative
Part	Particle
Perf	Perfective
Plr	Plural marker
PN	Proper Name
Pos	Positive (poses question)
Prep	Preposition
Pres	Unmarked (present) tense-aspect (prefix or suffix)
Prt	Participle
Psv	Passive

Rdp	Reduplication
Rflx	Reflexive
RN	Relational noun
SD	Status designator
SE	Sound effect
SF	Stem formative
(Hor)	Hortative (suppletive)
Ø	Zero-morpheme (usually A(3s) affix)
–	Morpheme boundary

TEXT

()	Phoneme or character added to text
[]	Phoneme or character removed from text
(?)	Unsure of meaning
–	Morpheme boundary (in original text)

ENGLISH GLOSS

| () | Substantial content added to fill out ellipses |

Appendix B: The Marriage between the Sun and the Moon

1. **ix na'-leb' qaawa' b'alam-q'e**
   E(3s) know-Nom SD hidden-divination (=PN)
   (this is) the character of Lord B'alamq'e

   chanru chi elq'an-b'il ki-Ø-x-ta(m)[n] jo' r-ixaqil qana' po (x)-rab'in qa-mama' qaawa' tzuul-taq'a
   how Prep steal-Prt Inf-E(3s)-A(3s)-unite Part E(3s)-wife SD moon (=PN) E(3s)-daughter E(1p)-grandfather SD mountain-valley (=PN)
   how, by theft (of her), he united with his wife Lady Moon, (the) daughter (of) our grandfather Lord Tzuultaq'a ...

   jo' wi' ra-hil-al mach'ach'kil k'ul-b'il-Ø-Ø x-b'aan-eb'
   Part Part pain-Abs-Abs ? receive-Prt-Pres-A(3s) E(3s)-RN-Plr
   ... as well (as how) suffering was received by them

2. **sa' mayer kutan toj maa-jun wi[i]nq ki-Ø-yo'la chi r-u(u) chi ch'och'**
   Prep old day Part Neg-one man Inf-A(3s)-be_born Prep E(3s)-RN Prep earth
   in olden days, (when) not a single man was yet born on earth ...

   sa'-in x-yi(i) nim-la-k'i-che'-b'aal sa' jun chaab'il r-ochoch pek aran ki-Ø-wan qa-mama' qaawa' tzuultaq'a
   Prep-Dm E(3s)-RN large-SF-many-tree-Nom Prep one good E(3s)-house stone there Inf-A(3s)-be E(1p)-grandfather SD PN
   ... here in the centre (of a) large mountain, inside a good cave, there lived our grandfather Lord Tzuultaq'a

   ka'aj wi' ix rab'in r-uchb'een
   Part Part E(3s) daughter E(3s)-RN
   only his daughter (was) his companion

   po ix k'a['ʼ]b'a'
   moon E(3s) name
   Moon (is) her name

3. **a' ixqa'al a'an ki-Ø-ch'o(o)lani[i]nk r-e ix yuwa'**
   Dm girl Dm Inf-A(3s)-care E(3s)-RN E(3s) father Part
   it was this unmarried girl who cared for her father

toj jo'q'e (k)i-Ø-x-raq ix k'anjel na-Ø-x-k'am ix kem-leb' mu-kab'
when Inf-A(3s)-E(3s)-finish E(3s) work Pres-A(3s)-E(3s)-carry E(3s) weave-Nom
shadow-house
when she has finished her work, she carries her weaving-equipment (into the)
house's shadow (corridor)

na-Ø-x-b'ak' ix t'uy-al chi r-ix r-oqechal
Pres-A(3s)-E(3s)-fasten E(3s) cord-Abs Prep E(3s)-RN E(3s)-post
she fastens her cord (for weaving) behind the post (of the house)

na-Ø-chunla chi kemok
Pres-A(3s)-sit Prep weave
(and) she sits down to weave

4. **aran ki-Ø-il-e' x-b'aan qaawa' b'alamq'e sa' ix num-ik wi' naq na-Ø-xik aj**
    yo r-ub'el k'i-che'
    there Inf-A(3s)-see-Psv E(3s)-RN SD PN Prep E(3s) pass-Nom Part Comp Pres-
    A(3s)-go SD hunter E(3s)-RN many-tree
    there she was seen by Lord B'alamq'e in his passing by (there), when, (as a) hunter,
    he goes beneath the forest

    ix ch'in-a-kaq[']-i-tz'i' k'am-ol b'e chi r-u
    E(3s)small-SF-red-SF-dog carry-Nom road Prep E(3s)-RN
    his small red dog (is) a leader before him

    a'an us-Ø-Ø chan-Ø-Ø sa' ix ch'ool
    Dm good-Pres-A(3s) say-Pres-A(3s) Prep E(3s) heart
    'she's nice', he says inside his heart

    a'an ch-Ø-in-k'am-aq ta jo'-(a)q w-ixaqil
    Dm Opt-A(3s)-E(1s)-carry-NS IR Part-NS E(1s)-wife
    'would that I could take her as my wife'

5. **a tuq'-ixq ink'a' ki-Ø-x-taq['] si r-u**
    Dm young-woman Neg Inf-A(3s)-E(3s)-raise E(3s)-face
    that young woman did not look up

    maa-min (n)i-Ø-x-k'e r-eetal jo['] q(')e ta-Ø-num-e'q jun chi yuk iiq'o-Ø-Ø
    x-b'a(a)n sa' ix champa
    Neg-Part Pres-A(3s)-E(3s)-give E(3s)-sign when Fut-A(3s)-pass-Psv one Prep
    goat carry-Pres-A(3s) E(3s)-RN Prep E(3s) bag
    never (in no manner) does she realize when he passes by (that) a goat is carried
    by him inside his bag

    qaawa' b'alamq'e ix maak ink'a' na-Ø-x-taw jun chi xul
    SD PN E(3s) RN Neg Pres-A(3s)-E(3s)-discover one Prep animal
    it is the fault of Lord B'alamq'e (that) she does not discover an animal

6. **rajlal kutan ki-Ø-x-k'am jun r-ix yuk**
    every day Inf-A(3s)-E(3s)-carry one E(3s)-hide goat
    every day he carried a goat's hide

ki-Ø-x-b'ut' chi (x)-sa' k'im chaq-i-xaq chaj cha
Inf-A(3s)-E(3s)-fill Prep E(3s)-RN grass dry-SF-leaf pine ash
he had filled it inside (with) straw, dry leaves, pines, and ashes

ki-Ø-x-b'oj chi chaab'il r-e naq tz'aqal xul na-Ø-k'utun
Inf-A(3s)-E(3s)-sew Prep good E(3s)-RN Comp complete animal Pres-A(3s)-appear
he had sewed it well in order that it look like a real animal

a'an na-Ø-x-muq chi r-u q'ojyi[i]n r-ub'el k'i-che' sa' na-Ø-xik wi' chi kutan a' ut wi(') na-Ø-su[t]q'i
Dm Pres-A(3s)-E(3s)-hide Prep E(3s)-RN darkness E(3s)-RN many-tree Prep Pres-A(3s)-go Part Prep day Dm Part Part Pres-A(3s)-return
(and) this he hides in the darkness beneath the forest inside (of which) he goes during the day and from which he returns

rajlal na-Ø-r-iiqa ix yuk sa' ix champa
each Pres-A(3s)-E(3s)-carry E(3s) goat Prep E(3s) bag
each (day) he carries his goat inside his bag

7. **wa'-chi(i)n chan-k-Ø ix po['] r-e ix yuwa'**
SD-Hnr say-Pres-A(3s) SD moon E(3s)-RN E(3s) father
'sir', says Moon to her father

Ø-il-Ø a' wi[i]nq a'in
Imp-see-A(3s) Dm man Dm
'look at this man'

a'an aj yo
Dm SD hunter
'he is a hunter'

jo' na-Ø-hulak chi w-u jo'q'e na-Ø-num-e(')k
Part Pres-A(3s)-arrive Prep E(1s)-RN when Pres-A(3s)-pass-Psv
'how much he pleases me when he passes!'

wan-Ø-Ø jun chi yuk k'am-k'o-Ø-Ø ix b'a(a)n
be-Pres-A(3s) one Prep goat carry-Prt-Pres-A(3s) E(3s) RN
'is there a goat carried by him?'

ah hmm hmm maa yuk ta an' ki-Ø-chaq'ok qaawa' tzuultaq'a
Interj Interj Interj Neg goat IR Dm Inf-A(3s)-respond SD PN
'mmm, that's not a goat' responded Lord Tzuultaq'a

Ø-k'am-Ø chaq ix ch'aj-b'al l-aa b'uch aran ta
Imp-carry-A(3s) Part E(3s) wash-Nom Dm-E(2s) cooked_corn there IR
'take the washings of your cooked corn there'

Ø-hoy-Ø sa' ix b'e na-Ø-num-e' wi'
Imp-sprinkle-A(3s) Prep E(3s) road Pres-A(3s)-pass-Psv Part
'sprinkle it on the road where he passes'

q-il-aq k'a'ru na-Ø-uxk
E(1p)-see-NS what Pres-A(3s)-happen
'let us see what happens'

8. **qaawa' b'alamq'e maak'a' na-Ø-yo'oni**
SD PN not_exist Pres-A(3s)-expect
Lord B'alamq'e suspects nothing

ki-Ø-chalk wi' chik ix chaq-i-yuk sa' ix champa
Inf-A(3s)-come Part Part E(3s) dry-SF-goat Prep E(3s) bag
he came by again (with) his dried-goat inside his bag

q'es r-u r-ik'in a' ixqa'al x-mu kab'
sharp E(3s)-eye E(3s)-RN Dm girl E(3s)-shadow house
sharp (are) his eyes on the girl (in) the house's shadow

ink'a(') ki-Ø-r-il ix b'e
Neg Inf-A(3s)-E(3s)-see E(3s) road
he did not watch his path

ki-Ø-yolk'ok sa' ix yol-yolk-il ch'aj-b'al b'uch
Inf-A(3s)-slip Prep E(3s) slip-Rdp-Nom wash-Nom nixtamal
he slipped on the slipperyness of cooked-corn washings

ki-Ø-t'an-e'
Inf-A(3s)-fell-Psv
he fell (was knocked over)

bum ki-Ø-puk(')-e' r-ix yuk
SE Inf-A(3s)-break_open-Psv E(3s)-skin goat
boom! the goat-hide burst (open)

na-Ø-(h)[j]irlok cha k'im chaq-i-xaq chaj sa' b'e
Pres-A(3s)-scatter ash grass dry-SF-leaf pine Prep road
ashes, grass, dried leaves, (and) pines scatter onto the road

junpaat ki-Ø-x-xok r-ib'
quickly Inf-A(3s)-E(3s)-gather E(3s)-Rflx
quickly he gathered himself (up)

nim-la-xutaan r-eek'
large-SF-shame E(3s)-feeling
very shameful is his feeling

k'a'-jo(') ki-Ø-se(')e (x)-b'a(a)n ixqa'al
what-Part Inf-A(3s)-be_laughed_at E(3s)-RN girl
so much he was laughed at by the girl

jun ch'in-a-tz'ik sa' r-u'uj k'i-che' yoo-Ø-Ø r-e(e)tz'unk-il
one small-SF-bird Prep E(3s)-top many-tree be-Pres-A(3s) E(3s)-ridicule-Nom
a small bird in the top (fingers) of the forest is making fun of him:

ma x-Ø-aaw-il i yuk
Int Perf-A(3s)-E(2s)-see Dm goat
'did you see the goat?'

ma x-Ø-aaw-il i yuk k'am-k'o-Ø-Ø
Int Perf-A(3s)-E(2s)-see Dm goat carry-Prt-Pres-A(3s)
'did you see the goat (that) was carried?'

sa' a(a)nil x-Ø-hulak sa' r-ochoch x-muq-b'al r-ib'
Prep run Inf-A(3s)-arrive Prep E(3s)-home E(3s)-hide-Nom E(3s)-Rflx
running, he arrived at his house (in order to) hide himself

9.   **toj sa' cha ki-Ø-hir-e' wan-Ø-Ø tana jun r-u saq-il may**
Part Prep ash Inf-A(3s)-scatter-Psv be-Pres-A(3s) AF one E(3s)-RN white-Abs seed
but inside the ashes (that) were scattered there must have been a seed of white tobacco

a'an ki-Ø-moq chi r-e r-oq ha' r-ochoch qaawa' tzuultaq'a
Dm Inf-A(3s)-germinate Prep E(3s)-RN E(3s)-foot water E(3s)-home SD PN
that (seed) germinated along the river (to the) house of Lord Tzuultaq'a

ki-Ø-nimank
Inf-A(3s)-enlarge
it grew

ki-Ø-e[e]l ix xaq
Inf-A(3s)-leave E(3s) leaf
its leaves went out

nim-la-mu[u]l x-Ø-hu[u]lak
large-SF-foliage/trash Perf-A(3s)-arrive
much foliage came out

ki-Ø-ok chi atz'umak
Inf-A(3s)-enter Prep flower
it began to flower

ki-Ø-hir-e' atz'um
Inf-A(3s)-scatter-Psv flower
flowers were scattered

k'i x-Ø-(x)-k'e
many Perf-A(3s)-E(3s)-give
so many it gave

10.   **qaawa' b'alamq'e ink'a' aj wi' x-Ø-Ø-kanab' ix k'a'uxlank-il ix ra-om**
SD PN Neg Part Part Perf-A(3s)-E(3s)-leave E(3s) think-Nom E(3s) love-Nom
Lord B'alamq'e did not stop thinking about his loved-one

ki-Ø-x-sik' ix b'e[e]-lil chanru na-Ø-nach'ok wi' chik r-ik'in
Inf-A(3s)-E(3s)-search E(3s) road-Abs how Pres-A(3s)-near Part Part E(3s)-RN
he looked for a way that he could get near to her again

chi r-u oxib' kutan ki-Ø-x-b'o(q)[b'] jun ch'in-a-tz'unun
Prep E(3s)-RN three day Inf-A(3s)-E(3s)-call one small-SF-hummingbird
after three days he called a small hummingbird

tz'unun tz'unun cha(n)[h]-Ø-Ø r-e
hummingbird hummingbird say-Pres-A(3s) E(3s)-RN
'hummingbird, hummingbird', he says to it

ch-Ø-a(a)-b'a(a)nu ta ka(a)-laju['] uxtaan w-e
Opt-A(3s)-E(2s)-do IR four-ten favour E(1s)-RN
'would that you do a great favour for me'

ch-Ø-a(a)-k'e ta w-e
Opt-A(3s)-E(2s)-give IR E(1s)-RN
'would that you give (them) to me'

ch-in-to'oni aaw-aq(')
Opt-A(1s)-be_loaned E(2s)-clothing
'would that I be loaned your feathers'

t-Ø-in-k'e raj chi w-ix
Fut-A(3s)-E(1s)-give CF Prep E(1s)-RN
'I would (like to) put them on me'

maa-min tana chan naq ki-Ø-chaq'ok a ch'in-a-tz'ik
Neg-Part AF how Comp Inf-A(3s)-respond Dm small-SF-bird
'that would be impossible', responded the small-bird

t-in-ka[a]mq raj (x)-b'a(a)n ke toj t-in-b'at-e'q sa' x-noq'-al inup
Fut-A(1s)-die CF E(3s)-RN cold Part Fut-A(1s)-wrap-Psv Prep E(3s)-thread-Abs
ceiba
'I would die because of cold, unless I were wrapped in the threads of a ceiba-tree'

jo'-ka'in ki-Ø-x-sume[']
Part-Dm Inf-A(3s)-E(3s)-respond
in this manner (the hummingbird) accepted

11.   **qaawa' b'alamq'e ki-Ø-x-yo'ob' r-ib' chi tz'unun**
SD PN Inf-A(3s)-E(3s)-change E(3s)-Rflx Prep hummingbird
Lord B'alamq'e turned himself into a hummingbird

br rum rum x-ko(')o-Ø wan-Ø-Ø wi' li may
SE SE SE Perf-go-A(3s) be-Pres-A(3s) Part Dm tobacco_plant
br-rum-rum he went to where the tobacco-plant was

rum rum ki-Ø-purik chi r-u atz'um
SE SE Inf-A(3s)-fly Prep E(3s)-RN flower
rum-rum he flew before the flowers (of the tobacco plant)

yoo-Ø-Ø r-uk'-b'al ix ya'al chi (x)-sa'
be-Pres-A(3s) E(3s)-drink-Nom E(3s) juice Prep E(3s)-RN
(and) is drinking their juice inside

12a. **Ø-il-Ø in-yuwa' chan-Ø-Ø ix po**
Imp-see-A(3s) E(1s)-father say-Pres-A(3s) SD moon
'look (at it) my father', says Moon

Ø-il-Ø a tz'unun a'an
Imp-see-A(3s) Dm hummingbird Dm
'look at that hummingbird'

yoo-Ø-Ø chi purik chi r-u may
be-Pres-A(3s) Prep fly Prep E(3s)-RN tobacco_plant
'it is flying in front of the tobacco-plant'

**num ch'i[i]n-a['
]-us r-ix**
much small-SF-good E(3s)-RN
'so beautiful is its plumage'

maa-jun wa w-il-om jun-aq chi jo'-ka'in
Neg-one time E(1s)-see-Nom one-NS Part Part-Dm
'not once have I seen one like this'

Ø-puub'a-Ø b'i' w-e r-ik'in l-aa puub'-che'
Imp-shoot-A(3s) Part E(1s)-RN E(3s)-RN Dm-E(2s) gun-tree
'shoot it for me then with your blow-gun'

timil t-Ø-aa-k'e r-eetal
slowly Fut-A(3s)-E(2s)-give E(3s)-sign
'you will aim slowly'

m-Ø-aa-kamsi
NImp-A(3s)-E(2s)-kill
'don't kill it'

12b. **ki-Ø-x-k'am ix puub'-che' a mama'**
Inf-A(3s)-E(3s)-carry E(3s) gun-tree Dm old_one
that old-one (her father) took his blow-gun

ki-Ø-x-ka'ya
Inf-A(3s)-E(3s)-watch
he aimed it (the blow-gun)

ki-Ø-r-apu
Inf-A(3s)-E(3s)-blow
he blew it

ki-Ø-x-rum chi ch'och' a tz'ik
Inf-A(3s)-E(3s)-cast Prep ground Dm bird
he cast that bird onto the ground

Ø-ch'uy-Ø Ø-ch'uy-Ø chan-Ø-Ø
Imp-pinch-A(3s) Imp-pinch-A(3s) say-Pres-A(3s)
'pinch it, pinch it!' he says

12c. ki-Ø-xok-e'k x-b'aan li ixq
Inf-A(3s)-collect-Psv E(3s)-RN Dm woman
(the bird) was collected by the woman

ki-Ø-x-kuj chi (x)-sa' ix seel li na-Ø-x-k'u(u)la wi' r-ela' ix noq'
Inf-A(3s)-E(3s)-place Prep E(3s)-RN E(3s) gourd Dm Pres-A(3s)-E(3s)-keep
Part E(3s)-extra E(3s)-thread
she put him inside her gourd where she keeps her extra thread

ut na-Ø-chunla wi' chik chi kemok
Part Pres-A(3s)-sit Part Part Prep weave
and she sits again weaving

**k'i(i)-la r-u yoo-Ø-Ø chi x-k'e-b'al chi (x)-sa' x-kem-om jo' r-eetal-il chi
jun-il k'a'-aq r-u ki-Ø-uxk x-Ø-num-e' kutan**
many-SF E(3s)-face be-Pres-A(3s) Prep E(3s)-give-Nom Prep E(3s)-RN E(3s)-
weave-Nom Part E(3s)-sign-Abs Prep one-Abs what-NS E(3s)-RN Inf-A(3s)-
happen Perf-A(3s)-pass-Psv day
*many (are the) faces/figures she is putting into what she weaves, as signs of every-
thing that happened (as) the day passed*

13a. a' tz'unun ink'a' na-Ø-h['']ulak chi r-u wa[a]nk sa' se(e)l
Dm hummingbird Neg Pres-A(3s)-arrive Prep E(3s)-RN be Prep gourd
it does not please the hummingbird to be inside the gourd

ink'a' na-Ø-hila[a]nk
Neg Pres-A(3s)-rest
he does not rest

na-Ø-ch'uy-ch'ut
Pres-A(3s)-pinch-Rdp
he nips

na-Ø-jochlok
Pres-A(3s)-scratch
he scratches (constantly)

na-Ø-xujluk
Pres-A(3s)-circle
he circles around (constantly)

yoo-Ø-Ø chi eek'a'[a]nk junelik
be-Pres-A(3s) Prep move always
he is always moving

13b. jo'-ka'in ki-Ø-x-chap
Part-Dm Inf-A(3s)-E(3s)-grab
because of this she grabbed him

ki-Ø-x-kuj r-ub'el ix po'ot
Inf-A(3s)-E(3s)-place E(3s)-RN E(3s) huipil
she put him beneath her huipil (blouse)

aran ki-Ø-ch'ana
there Inf-A(3s)-become_calm
there he was calmed

ut x-Ø-(x)-ye a'an ah arin na-Ø-hulak chi r-u wa[a]nk
Part Perf-A(3s)-E(3s)-say Dm Interj here Pres-A(3s)-arrive Prep E(3s)-
RN be
and she said 'aah, here it pleases him to be'

14. **ewu ki-Ø-x-xok ix kem-leb'**
evening Inf-A(3s)-E(3s)-gather E(3s) weave-Nom
(in the) evening she gathered her weaving utensils

ki-Ø-ok chi wa[a]rk sa' kab'
Inf-A(3s)-enter Prep be Prep house
she went to sleep inside the house

ki-Ø-yokla chi r-u ix ch'aat
Inf-A(3s)-lie_down Prep E(3s)-RN E(3s) bed
she laid down on her bed

kan-k['']o-Ø-Ø li tz'unun chi r-e ix maqab'
tie-Prt-Pres-A(3s)Dm hummingbird Prep E(3s)-RN E(3s) chest
the hummingbird is tied next to her chest

tuq-tu-Ø-Ø
be_tranquil-Prt-Pres-A(3s)
he is tranquil

15. **q'ojyi[i]n qaawa' b'alamq'e ki-Ø-x-k'ut ix wi[i]nq-il-al**
darkness SD PN Inf-A(3s)-E(3s)-display E(3s) man-Abs-Abs
(in the) darkness Lord B'alamq'e displayed his manliness

t-at-in-k'am chan-Ø-Ø r-e ix po
Fut-A(3s)-E(1s)-carry say-Pres-A(3s) E(3s)-RN SD moon
'I will take you', he says to Moon

toj a'an xiw r-eek'
Part Dm fear E(3s)-feeling
but her feeling (was) fear

ink'a(') na-Ø-chaq'ok
Neg Pres-A(3s)-respond
'no', she responds

yo'o
go(Hor)
'let's go!'

t-oo-eelelik anaqwan
Fut-A(1p)-flee now
'we will flee now'

ink'a(') raj na
Neg CF AF
'I don't want to'

m-at-k'a'(ux)[xu]wa[a]nk
NImp-A(2s)-think
'don't worry'

maa-jaruj t-oo-ruuq ix b'a(a)nunk-il
Neg-how_much Fut-A(1p)-be_able E(3s) do-Nom
'never would we be able to do it'

tikto t-oo-il-e'q ix b'aan l-in yuwa' sa' ix lem
immediately Fut-A(1p)-see-Psv E(3s) RN Dm-E(1s) father Prep E(3s) mirror
'we would immediately be seen by my father in his mirror'

chi jun-il n-e(')-k'utun chi (x)-sa'
Prep one-Abs Pres-A(3p)-show Prep E(3s)-RN
'everything shows inside it'

sa' junpaat t-oo-ta'liiq
Prep quickly Fut-A(1p)-be_discovered
'in a moment we would be discovered'

Ø-sib'i-Ø a lem chan-k-Ø r-e ix po
Imp-smoke-A(3s) Dm mirror say-Pres-A(3s) E(3s)-RN SD moon
'smoke the mirror', he says to Moon

a'an ki-Ø-x-paab'
Dm Inf-A(3s)-E(3s)-believe
she obeyed him

ki-Ø-x-k'am chaq
Inf-A(3s)-E(3s)-carry Part
she brought it

ki-Ø-x-q'axtesi sa' r-uq' b'a['a]lamq'e
Inf-A(3s)-E(3s)-give Prep E(3s)-hand PN
she handed it over to B'alamq'e

a'an ki-Ø-k'atok chaj
Dm Inf-A(3s)-burn pine
he burnt pines

ki-Ø-x-sib'tesi a lem sa' ix sib'-el chaj
Inf-A(3s)-E(3s)-smoke Dm mirror Prep E(3s) smoke-Abs pine
he smoked that mirror (using) the smoke of the pines

q'eq q'eq x-Ø-kana
black black Perf-A(3s)-remain
very black it was left

ink'a' chik na[']-Ø-ilok naq lem
Neg Part Pres-A(3s)-see Comp mirror
no longer does it see (as a) mirror

ki-Ø-x-q'ajsi wi' chik sa' r-uq' ix po r-e ti-Ø-x-kanab' b'i' sa' ix na'aj
Inf-A(3s)-E(3s)-return Part Part Prep E(3s)-hand SD moon E(3s)-RN Fut-A(3s)-E(3s)-leave Part Prep E(3s) place
he returned it again to the hands of Moon in order that she (would) put it back in its place

jo'-ka'in ki-Ø-x-baanu
Part-Dm Inf-A(3s)-E(3s)-do
like this she did it

16. **yo'o anaqwan chan-Ø-Ø r-e ix po**
go(Hor) now say-Pres-A(3s) E(3s)-RN SD moon
'let's go now', he says to Moon

ink'a(') aj wi(') sa t-o(o)-eelq
Neg Part Part good Fut-A(1p)-leave
'it's still not good that we go'

wan-Ø-Ø ix puub'-che' in-yuwa'
be-Pres-A(3s) E(3s) gun-tree E(1s)-father
'my father has a blow-gun'

r-ik'in a'an t-o(o)-ix-jiq'
E(3s)-RN Dm Fut-A(1p)-E(3s)-smother
'with it he will shoot (inhale/smother) us'

rek' t-o(o)-ix-tz'ob'
good (?) Fut-A(1p)-E(3s)-suck_via_straw
'he will cause us to wheeze (suffocate)'

t-o(o)-ix-xeeya r-ik'in
Fut-A(1p)-E(3s)-pant E(3s)-RN
'he will cause us to pant with it'

maa-min t-o(o)-kol-e(')q['] chi r-u
Neg-Part Fut-A(1p)-save-Psv Prep E(3s)-RN
'there's no way we'll be saved from him'

yal jun t-o(o)-ix-kamsi chi kab'-i-chal-o
Part one Fut-A(1p)-E(3s)-kill Prep two-SF-root-A(1p)
'at once he will kill the two of us'

Ø-k'am-Ø chaq ut a puub'-che' chi jo'-kan chan-k-Ø b'alamq'e [e] r-e
Imp-carry-A(3s) Part Part Dm gun-tree Prep Part-Dm say-Pres-A(3s) PN E(3s)-RN
'bring the blow-gun like this', says B'alamq'e to her

Ø-seeb'a-Ø aaw-ib' ix k'e-b'al jun moch'-ol chi saq-i-ik
Imp-be_quick-A(3s) E(2s)-Rflx E(3s) give-Nom one handful-Abs Prep white-SF-chile
'be quick giving a handful of white chilli'

junpaat ki-Ø-x-k'e k'aj ik
quickly Inf-A(3s)-E(3s)-give piece chile
quickly she gave pieces (of) chilli (powdered chilli)

b'alamq'e ki-Ø-x-b'u[b']t' chi (x)-sa' pu(u)b'-che'
PN Inf-A(3s)-E(3s)-fill Prep E(3s)-RN gun-tree
B'alamq'e put them inside the blow-gun

anaqwan us chan-Ø-Ø
now good say-Pres-A(3s)
'now (it's) good', he says

Ø-xaqab'-Ø b'i' chik sa' ix na'aj x-Ø-a(a)-taw wi'
Imp-stand-A(3s) Part Part Prep E(3s) place Perf-A(3s)-E(2s)-find Part
'stand it again in the place where you found it'

toj anaqwan yo'o sa' aanil
Part now go(Hor) Prep run
'but now let's go quickly'

jo'-ka'in ut x-e['[eb'-eelelik sa' wi'-b'al
Part-Dm Part Perf-A(3p)-flee Prep Part-Nom
like this (it was done), and so they fled from that place

17a. **eq'la ki-Ø-ajk qaawa' tzuultaq'a**
early Inf-A(3s)-awake SD PN
Lord Tzuultaq'a awoke early

ki-Ø-x-b'oq ix rab'in jun wa ka' wa
Inf-A(3s)-E(3s)-call E(3s) daughter one time two time
he called his daughter once, twice

maa jun na-Ø-chaq'ok chi r-u
Neg one Pres-A(3s)-respond Prep E(3s)-RN
not once does she answer him

junpaat ki-Ø-wakli
quickly Inf-A(3s)-rise
quickly he got up

ki-Ø-r-il sa' ix na'aj
Inf-A(3s)-E(3s)-see Prep E(3s) place
he looked for her in her (usual) place

ki-Ø-r-il chi r-u ix ch'aat
Inf-A(3s)-E(3s)-see Prep E(3s)-RN E(3s) bed
he looked for her on her bed

maa ani wan-Ø-Ø ix rab'in
Neg who be-Pres-A(3s) E(3s) daughter
his daughter was not there

ma ink'a(') ta x-Ø-w-eek'a moko tz'aqal tz'unun ta
Int Neg IR Perf-A(3s)-E(1s)-feel NF real hummingbird IR
'did I not sense it (was) not a real hummingbird?'

a'an pe' ki-Ø-elq'an r-e in-rab'in chan-Ø-Ø r-aatinank-il r-ib' ix junes
Dm F Inf-A(3s)-steal E(3s)-RN E(1s)-daughter say-Pres-A(3s) E(3s)-say-Nom
E(3s)-Rflx E(3s) alone
'he is the one who has stolen my daughter!' he says, speaking to himself alone

ho(o)n t-at-inw-il iho(o)n aj b'alaq(')
now Fut-A(2s)-E(1s)-see now SD deception
'now I will see you, deceiver'

yal jun ki-Ø-x-sa(a)pu ix lem r-e na-Ø-ch'u(u)ki[i]nk raj chi (x)-sa'
Part one Inf-A(3s)-E(3s)-snatch E(3s) mirror E(3s)-RN Pres-A(3s)-spy CF Prep
E(3s)-RN
at once he snatched up his mirror so that he could spy inside of it

17b. **toj a lem ink'a' chik na-Ø-ilok (x)-b'a(a)n ix pim-al ix sib'-el pom pa x-Ø-**
moy wi' r-u
Part Dm mirror Neg Part Pres-A(3s)-see E(3s)-RN E(3s) thick-Abs E(3s) smoke-
Abs copal ? Perf-A(3s)-obscure Part E(3s)-RN
but that mirror could no longer see because the thickness of the copal smoke had
obscured its face

ka'aj wi' sa' ix xuk a lem chap-cho-Ø-Ø wi' (x)-b'a(a)n b'alamq'e kutan
kach'in ki-Ø-kana
Part Part Prep E(3s) corner Dm mirror grab-Prt-Pres-A(3s) Part E(3s)-RN PN
clear little Inf-A(3s)-remain
only inside the corner of that mirror, where (it was) held by B'alamq'e, a little
clarity remained

aran na-Ø-eek'a[a]n k'a'-aq r-u
there Pres-A(3s)-move what-NS E(3s)-RN
there something moves

17c. **a'an-eb' chan-Ø-Ø**
Dm-Plr say-Pres-A(3s)
'it is them', he says

tikto ki-Ø-x-chap ix puub'-che'
Part Inf-A(3s)-E(3s)-grab E(3s) gun-tree
immediately he grabbed his blow-gun

ki-Ø-x-ka'ya
Inf-A(3s)-E(3s)-look
he looked through it

ki-Ø-x-jayali
Inf-A(3s)-E(3s)-take_direction
he aimed it

ki-Ø-x-choy raj ix metz'e[e]w r-e ix tz'o(b')-b'al-eb' r-ik'in
Inf-A(3s)-E(3s)-finish CF E(3s) strength E(3s)-RN E(3s) blow-Nom-Plr E(3s)-RN
he finished (used up) all his strength in order to blow them with it

yal jun (x)-kub'-ik chi jun-il k'aj ik sa' ix xol-ol sa' ix b'eele-b'a[a]l musiq'
Part one E(3s)-ower-Nom Prep one-Abs piece chilli Prep E(3s) throat-Abs Prep E(3s) transport-Nom breath
at once there is the lowering of all the pieces of chilli into his throat, into his wind-pipe

na[a]-Ø-jiq'
Pres-A(3s)-choke
he wheezes

na-Ø-ojob'ak
Pres-A(3s)-cough
he coughs

na-Ø-paq'-e'
Pres-A(3s)-suffocate/choke-Psv
he is choked

na-Ø-t'an-e(')
Pres-A(3s)-fell-Psv
he falls

na-Ø-x-tolk(')osi r-ib'
Pres-A(3s)-E(3s)-knock_over E(3s)-Rflx
he is knocked down

chan kam-enaq ki-Ø-kana
Comp dead-Prt Inf-A(3s)-remain
like one who has died he remained

chi (j)[u]o'-kan x-Ø-tikla li jiq'
Prep Part-Dm Perf-A(3s)-originate Dm cough
like this originated coughing

18. **najt t'an-t(')o-Ø-Ø chi jo'-ka'in**
long fell-Prt-Pres-A(3s) Prep Part-Dm
(for a) long-time he remained fallen like this

kaq-r(ah)-il ki-Ø-k'ulun ix ch'ool
red-pain-Abs Inf-A(3s)-arrive E(3s) heart
envy/anger/pain came to his heart

(x)-laj-ik ki-Ø-x-mol k'a r-ib'
E(3s)-finish-Nom Inf-A(3s)-E(3s)-gather ? E(3s)-Rflx
(at its) end he gathered himself

chi ra chi sa ki-Ø-xaqli b'i('') chik
Prep pain Prep pleasure Inf-A(3s)-stand_up Part Part
with difficulty he stood up again

ink'a' chik jultik r-e x-b'aan ix maatan-il
Neg Part remember E(3s)-RN E(3s)-RN E(3s) gift-Abs
no longer did he remember the gift he received (i.e. his daughter?)

ki-Ø-x-b'oq r-ikan qaawa' kaaq r-e ix kamsink-il chi xerim-b'il-Ø-Ø aj eelel
chi x-kab'-ichal-eb'
Inf-A(3s)-E(3s)-call E(3s)-uncle SD thunder (=PN) E(3s)-RN E(3s) kill-Nom
Prep proportion-Prf-Pres-A(3s) SD fugitives Prep E(3s)-two-root-Plr
he called her uncle Lord Thunder in order to kill into pieces the two fugitives
together

toj a'an ink'a' ki-Ø-r-aj
Part Dm Neg Inf-A(3s)-E(3s)-want
but he didn't want to (kill her)

a'an (x)-rab'in li tzuultaq'a
Dm E(3s)-daughter Dm PN
(for) she (was) the daughter of Tzuultaq'a

toj ak ki-Ø-x-ch'olob'aak chi r-u ix na'-leb'-eb'
Part Part Perf-A(3s)-E(3s)-explain Prep E(3s)-RN E(3s) know-Nom-Plr
but when he had explained to him their characters/deeds:

k'a'ru x-Ø-e'x-b'aanu r-e qaawa' tzuultaq'a jo'-nim-al ix yib'ob'-b'aal i r-u
ki-Ø-uxk r-e x-b'aan-eb'
what Perf-A(3s)-E(3p)-do E(3s)-RN SD PN Part-large-Abs E(3s) ugly-Nom Dm
E(3s)-RN Inf-A(3s)-occur E(3s)-RN E(3s)-RN-Plr
what they had done to Lord Tzuultaq'a, (and) how great was the ugliness that
occurred to him because of them

jo'-ka'in ki-Ø-x-sume
Part-Dm Inf-A(3s)-E(3s)-accept
then he agreed

19. **qaawa' kaaq ki-Ø-x-xok ix maal**
SD thunder Inf-A(3s)-E(3s)-gather E(3s) axe
Lord Thunder grabbed his axe

ki-Ø-x-b'at r-ib' sa' q'eq-i-choql
Inf-A(3s)-E(3s)-wrap E(3s)-Rflx Prep black-SF-cloud
he wrapped himself in black clouds

naa-Ø-rumluk
Pres-A(3s)-go_quickly
he rushes (constantly)

naa-Ø-replok
Pres-A(3s)-flash
he flashes (constantly)

naa-Ø-pumluk
Pres-A(3s)-crash
he crashes (constantly)

a ix xik-ik[a] chi r-ix-eb' sa' iq'
Dm E(3s) go-Nom Prep E(3s)-RN-Plr Prep wind
(like this) is his going behind them in the wind

20a. **najt ak wan-k-eb' qaawa' b'alamq'e r-uchb'een ix po**
far Part be-Pres-A(3p) SD PN E(3s)-RN SD moon
already far are Lord B'alaamq'e accompanied by Moon

ak ewu(u)k r-e
Part become_evening E(3s)-RN
already it has become evening

hu[u]lak-eb' r-e chi r-e palaw
arrive-Plr E(3s)-RN Prep E(3s)-RN lake/sea
already they have arrived at the edge of the sea

yoo-k-eb' r-ab'ink-il kaamel jo' wi' r-il-b'al x-rep-om kaaq sa' q'eq-i-choql yoo-Ø-Ø chi nach'ok
be-Pres-A(3p) E(3s)-hear-Nom hailstone Part Part E(3s)-see-Nom E(3s)-make_
lightening-Nom thunder Prep black-SF-cloud be-Pres-A(3s) Prep approach
they are hearing the wind (hurricane), as well as seeing the lightning-flashes of thunder in black clouds (which) are approaching

ak naq(k) r-e[e] hab'
Part begin E(3s)-RN rain
already it has started to rain

20b. **anaqwan x-oo-oso' chan-Ø-Ø ix po**
now Perf-A(1p)-be_finished say-Pres-A(3s) SD moon
'now we are finished', says Moon

l-in yuwa' ki-Ø-x-taqla li w-ikan qaawa'-chi(i)n kaaq chi qa-kamsink-il
Dm-E(1s) father Inf-A(3s)-E(3s)-send Dm E(1s)-uncle SD-Hnr thunder Prep
E(1p)-kill-Nom
'my father must have sent my uncle Lord Thunder to kill us'

ix ye-b'al b'ar ta t-o(o)-ok
E(3s) say-Nom where IR Fut-A(3p)-enter
her saying 'wherever could we enter?'

b'ar ta to-Ø-qa-muq q-ib' chi r-u sa' yam-yo
where IR Fut-A(3s)-E(1p)-hide E(1p)-Rflx Prep E(3s)-RN Prep flat-Prt
'wherever could we cover ourselves on its barren face?'

r-ech-k'ul-b'al-eb' r-ib' r-ik'in jun chi ib'oy jo' wi' jun chi kok chi[k] r-e u(l) ul palaw
E(3s)-companion-receive-Nom-Plr E(3s)-Rflx E(3s)-RN one Prep armadillo Part
Part one Prep turtle Prep E(3s)-RN surface sea
they friend-received themselves with (encountered) an armadillo, also (with) a turtle at the edge of the surface of the sea

junpaat x-Ø-e'x-patz' r-ix a xul chi too'
quickly Perf-A(3s)-E(3p)-ask E(3s)-RN Dm animal Prep lend
quickly they asked these animals to lend (their shells)

sa' aanil x-Ø-e'x-kuj r-ib' chi (x)-sa'
Prep run Perf-A(3s)-E(3p)-place E(3s)-Rflx Prep E(3s)-RN
quickly they put themselves inside it

qana' po sa' r-ix ib'oy
SD moon Prep E(3s)-RN armadillo
Lady Moon (was) inside the shell of the armadillo

qaawa' b'alamq'e sa' r-ix kok
SD PN Prep E(3s)-RN turtle
Lord B'alamq'e (was) inside the shell of the turtle

jo'-ka'in ut an ix b'aanunk-il
Part-Dm Part Dm E(3s) do-Nom
like this was it done

21. **jun chik nim-la-xaml na-Ø-rep[r]ot jun r-u choxa**
one Part large-SF-fire Pres-A(3s)-light one E(3s)-RN sky
another large fire lit up the sky

ki-Ø-x-kut ix maal qaawa' kaaq
Inf-A(3s)-E(3s)-throw E(3s) axe SD thunder
Lord Thunder threw his axe

kaw na-Ø-tenlok
strong Pres-A(3s)-strike
forcefully he strikes

kaw na-Ø-chaq'ok ix yaab' chi r-u tzuul
strong Pres-A(3s)-respond E(3s) sound/cry Prep E(3s)-RN mountain
forcefully responds (echoes) his sounds from the mountain

22. **ix po sa' r-ix ib'oy**
SD moon Prep E(3s)-RN armadillo
Moon (was) inside the shell of the armadillo

maa-wa' aj numx
Neg-be SD swim
she is not a swimmer

ki-Ø-ta'li x-b'aan (x)-maal kaaq
Inf-A(3s)-be_found E(3s)-RN E(3s)-axe thunder
she was found by the axe of thunder

b'ok' xuj ki-Ø-xer-e' x-b'een u(l)ul
little piece Inf-A(3s)-proportion-Psv E(3s)-RN surface
little pieces (of her) were divided on the surface (of the sea)

kaq kaq ki-Ø-kub'e['] ix kik'-el sa' x-b'een ha' palaw
red red Inf-A(3s)-be_lowered E(3s) blood-Abs Prep E(3s)-RN water sea
red-red was lowered (flowed) her blood on top of the water (of the) sea

23. **qaawa' b'alamq'e sa' r-ix kok**
SD PN Prep E(3s)-RN turtle
Lord B'alamq'e (was) inside the shell of the turtle

ki-Ø-x-tolk(')osi r-ib' sa' palaw chi x-kol-b'al r-ib' sa' muq-a[a]l
Inf-A(3s)-E(3s)-roll E(3s)-Rflx Prep sea Prep E(3s)-save-Nom E(3s)-Rflx Prep
hide/bury-Abs
he rolled himself into the sea in order to save himself by hiding (in the depths)

ki-Ø-chup saq'e
Inf-A(3s)-be_extinguished sun
the sun was extinguished

q'ojyi[i]n ki-Ø-kub'e chi r-u(u) chi ch'och'
darkness Inf-A(3s)-be_lowered Prep E(3s)-RN Prep ground
darkness lowered on the earth

24a. **toj hu[u]laj sa' r-el-ik qaawa' b'alamq'e sa' palaw aran ki-Ø-r-il ix kik'-el ix**
ra-hom jo' wi' x-k(')aj ix tz'ejwal jo' x-mul ha'
Part tomorrow Prep E(3s)-leave-Nom SD PN Prep sea there Inf-A(3s)-E(3s)-see
E(3s) blood-Abs E(3s) love-Nom Part Part E(3s)-piece E(3s) body Part E(3s)-
trash water
in the morning, at the leaving of Lord B'alamq'e from the sea, there he saw the
blood of his loved-one, as well as the pieces of her body like flotsam of the water

ak yoo-k-eb' kok' kar r-ik'in aj mulum ix t'uplenk-il r-e ix w['']a(')[x]-b'al
Part be-Pres-A(3p) small fish E(3s)-RN SD trash E(3s) tear-Nom E(3s)-RN E(3s)
eat-Nom
already the small fish along with the tepocates (cat sharks) are tearing it up in
order to eat it

ra sa' ix ch'ool
pain Prep E(3s) heart
(there is) pain inside his heart

24b. **ki-Ø-x-b'oq aj tuulu(x)[k] (tuulux: aguja del diablo, libelula, dragonfly)**
Inf-A(3s)-E(3s)-call SD dragonfly
he called the Aj Tuulux

mol-om-aq-Ø ke a x-mul ha' jo(')[b'] aj wi' rek' rek' ta ch-Ø-ee-lek chi jun-il
a kik' chan-Ø-Ø
gather-Prf-NS-A(3s) cold Dm E(3s)-trash water Part Part Part good good IR Opt-
A(3s)-E(2p)-collect Prep jun-Abs Dm blood say-Pres-A(3s)
'gather that cold water's flotsam, also collect all the blood very well', he says

aj tuulux x-Ø-e'x-ch'utub' r-ib' r-e ix b'aanunk-il
SD dragonfly Perf-A(3s)-E(3p)-gather E(3s)-Rflx E(3s)-RN E(3s) do-Nom
the Aj Tuulux gathered themselves in order to do it

lek lek as yoo-k-eb' chi lekok
SE SE ? be-Pres-A(3p) Prep collect
splish splash they are collecting

lek lek ix b'ut'-b'al sa' kuk
SE SE E(3s) fill-Nom Prep jar
splish splash (they are) filling jars

junpaat x-e'-raq-e' r-ik'in
quickly Perf-A(3p)-finish-Psv E(3s)-RN
at once they were finished with it

ox-laju kuk ki-Ø-nujak (x)[c]-b'a(a)n-eb'
three-ten jar Inf-A(3s)-be_filled E(3s)-RN-Plr
thirteen jars were filled by them

24c. **a'an x-e'-ix-k'ojob' sa' ix mu kab'l sa' r-ochoch jun tix-il ixq wan-Ø-Ø wi' chi r-e palaw**
Dm Perf-A(3p)-E(3s)-place Prep E(3s) shadow house Prep E(3s)-house one old-Abs woman be-Pres-A(3s) Part Prep E(3s)-RN sea
he places them under the eaves (house's shadow) of the house of an old woman, which is located on the edge of the sea

wa[a]n-k-Ø wan-Ø-Ø aran chan-Ø-Ø qaawa' b'alamq'e r-e aj eechal kab'l
be-Pres-A(3s) be-Pres-A(3s) there say-Pres-A(3s) SD PN E(3s)-RN SD owner house
'there (it is that) they are', says Lord B'alamq'e to the owner of the house

toj sa(') ox-laju kutan in chaq chi r-il-b'al
Part Prep three-ten day A(1s) Part Prep E(3s)see-Nom
'but in thirteen days I (will be) here to see them'

25. **toj maa-najti[i]nk ix xik-ik qaawa' sa' eb' a' kuk ut k'a'-aq r-u ki-Ø-yo'la**
Part Neg-distance E(3s) go-Nom SD Prep Plr Dm jar Part what-NS E(3s)-RN Inf-A(3s)-be_born
but not long after the going away of Lord (B'alamq'e), inside of those jars something was born

yoo-Ø-Ø chi eek'a[a]nk
be-Pres-A(3s) Prep move
it is moving

timil ki-Ø-tikla
slow Inf-A(3s)-begin
slowly it starts up

na-Ø-t'io-t'ok
Pres-A(3s)-Rdp-poke
it kicks (and stomps)

na-Ø-k'ob'-k'ot
Pres-A(3s)-Rdp-bite
it picks (and bores)

hu[u]laj hu[u]laj na-Ø-kawu ix yaab'
tomorrow tomorrow Pres-A(3s)-become_stronger E(3s) voice/cry
each day its cries become stronger

na-Ø-tzochak
Pres-A(3s)-rattle
it rattles

na-Ø-xujluk
Pres-A(3s)-break
it breaks

na-Ø-k'atzlok
Pres-A(3s)-crack
it cracks

na-Ø-pojlok
Pres-A(3s)-make_noise
it bangs

na-Ø-rumluk
Pres-A(3s)-crash
it crashes

na-Ø-jochlok
Pres-A(3s)-scratch
it scratches

chi (x)-sa' jo' e[e]lk na-Ø-r-aj
Prep E(3s)-RN Part leave Pres-A(3s)-E(3s)-want
from inside (of the jars) how (much) it wants to leave

26. **kach'in-aq ix ch'ool aj eechal kab'l**
    small-NS E(3s) heart SD owner house
    the owner of the house is timid (her heart is small)

na-Ø-xuwak
Pres-A(3s)-be_scared
she is scared

toj-a' ki-Ø-num-e' ox-laju kutan ki-Ø-r-il na-Ø-nach'ok qaawa' b'alamq'e
Part-Dm Inf-A(3s)-pass-Psv three-ten day Inf-A(3s)-E(3s)-see Pres-A(3s)-near
SD PN
when thirteen days had passed, she saw Lord B'alamq'e approaching

ki-Ø-x-japi r-e
Inf-A(3s)-E(3s)-call E(3s)-RN
she called to him:

Ø-seeb'a-Ø aaw-i[i]b'
Imp-hurry-A(3s) E(2s)-Rflx
'hurry up!'

t-Ø-aaw-isi l-a(a) yib' aj kuk sa' junpaat
Fut-A(3s)-E(2s)-remove Dm-E(2s) ugly SD jar Prep quickly
'you will remove your ugly/evil jars quickly'

k'a'ru x-Ø-aa-k'e w-e chi k'uula[a]k chi r-u k'i(i)-la-kutan jo' wi'
q'ojyi[i]n
what Perf-A(3s)-E(2s)-give E(1s)-RN Prep guard Prep E(3s)-RN much-SF-day
Part Part darkness
'what did you give to me to guard for so many days and nights?'

ink'a' chik x-Ø-kub'e l-in wara x-b'aan l-in xiw
Neg Part Perf-A(3s)-be_lowered Dm-E(1s) sleep E(3s)-RN Dm-E(1s) fear
'no longer do I sleep because of my fear'

27. qaawa' b'alamq'e ki-Ø-ok x-mu kab'l
SD PN Inf-A(3s)-enter E(3s)-shadow house
Lord B'alamq'e entered the corridor

tikto ki-Ø-x-te x-b'e(e)n kuk r-e x-ch'u(u)[n]kink-il chi (x)-sa'
Part Inf-A(3s)-E(3s)-open E(3s)-RN jar E(3s)-RN E(3s)-look-Nom Prep
E(3s)-RN
immediately he opened the first jar in order to look inside

junes k'anti(') ki-Ø-r-il
Part snake Inf-A(3s)-E(3s)-see
only snakes he saw

i(q)[k]'b'olay r-ech-ha' tzojtzoj o(o)to'[o]y aj t'upuy saq b'a'anqnal
fer-de-lance (barba amarilla) E(3s)-companion-water (mazaquate?), cascabel,
tamagas, SD ribbon, white ?
fer-de-lances, mazaquates (?), rattlesnakes, pit-vipers, ribbon-snakes (coral snakes?), white (snakes of some sort)

junes aj ti'on-el aj sachon-el
Part SD bite-Nom SD destroy-Nom
only those which bite, those which destroy

ki-Ø-te[e]h-e' ix kab' chi kuk ix b'a(a)n
Inf-A(3s)-open-Psv E(3s) two Prep jar E(3s) RN
the second jar was opened by him

junes yib' aj xul wan-Ø-Ø chi (x)-sa'
Part ugly/evil SD animal be-Pres-A(3s) Prep E(3s)-RN
only nasty animals were in it

alal milmich' tolokok per(e)'maal sele'may ch'ujchuj
salamander ? lizard chameleon ? ?
salamanders, ?, lizards, chameleons, ?, ?

chi junpaat seeb' ki-Ø-x-tz'ap wi' chik
Prep quickly fast Inf-A(3s)-E(3s)-close Part Part
very quickly he shut it again

jo'-ka'in (k)i-Ø-x-kub'si r-ox ix kaa r-o' chi kuk
Part-Dm Inf-A(3s)-E(3s)lower E(3s)-three E(3s) four E(3s)-five Prep jar
like this he lowered the third, fourth, and fifth jar

x-junes aj ti'on-el wan-Ø-Ø chi (x)-sa'
E(3s)-Part SD bite-Nom be-Pres-A(3s) Prep E(3s)-RN
only those things which bite are inside

yal-aq k'a' chi ch'ub' honon lem-saq'e kantb'olay k'ojote poj ch'ub' aj xaml
Part-NS what Prep wasp bees mirror-sun (a type of wasp?) ? ? pus wasp SD fire
(xamxul: type of bee)
all kinds of wasps, bees, sun-mirrors, ?, ?, pus-wasps, and fire-bees

wan-Ø-Ø aj am k'otz'eb'aq k'is-pek aj xook' hay x-tz'i'n kok(') chupil chajal
be-Pres-A(3s) SD spider ? (k'otz: bite/sting) fart-rock (k'ix: thorn) SD scorpion
wormE(3s)-? small worm worm
there are spiders, ?, ?, scorpions, hay-worms, ?, small and numerous chupil-worms, and chajal-worms

jo'-ka'in kab-laju chi kuk
Part-Dm two-ten Prep jar
like this (were) twelve of the jars

28. **ut l-ix po maak'a' x-b'aan naq li po yoo-Ø-Ø chi x-muq-b'al r-ib'**
Part Dm-SD moon not_exist E(3s)-RN Comp Dm moon be-Pres-A(3s) Prep
E(3s)-hide-Nom E(3s)-Rflx
and Moon is not there because the moon is hiding herself

ink'a' na-Ø-hu[u]lak chi r-u na(q) li saq'e raj l-ix b'e(e)lom
Neg Pres-A(3s)-arrive Prep E(3s)-RN Comp Dm sun CF Dm-E(3s) husband
it does not please her that the sun could be her husband

maa-jaruj tana chik t-Ø-w-il r-u in-ra-hom chan-Ø-Ø
Neg-how_much AF Part Fut-A(3s)-E(1s)-see E(3s)-face E(1s)-love-Nom say-
Pres-A(3s)
'never again perhaps will I see the face of my loved-one', he says

sa' ix te-b'al li r-ox-laju ix putix ut toj aran tz'aqal jun ki-Ø-el qana' po
Prep E(3s) open-Nom Dm E(3s)-three-ten E(3s) ? Part Part there true/exact/com-
plete one Inf-A(3s)-leave SD moon
in the opening of the thirteenth but there was the true one (and) out came Lady Moon

lemtz'un r-ix
reflective E(3s)-cover
brillant (is) her covering

saq saq ix tz'ejwal
white white E(3s) body
so white (is) her body

sa' chi jun-il ix ch'in-a-us-il-al ix chaab'il-al
Prep Prep one-Abs E(3s) small-SF-good-Abs-Abs E(3s) good-Abs
everything about her is beautiful and good

29a. **jun aj num-al b'e aj si'in-el ki-Ø-b'oq-e' chi ten(q')[k]a[a]nk chi ix b'e(e)n ix yamtesink-il mu kab'**
one SD pass-Abs road SD cut-Nom Inf-A(3s)-call-Psv Prep help Prep E(3s) RN E(3s) clear-Nom shadow house
a traveller, (a) woodcutter was called to help to clear out the corridor (above all, foremostly)

eb' a kuk a'an chi jun tz'eq sa' palaw
Plr Dm jar Dm Prep one trash Prep sea
'those jars are for trash (a toss) into the sea'

chi maa-wa['] t-at-ch'uuki[i]nq chi (x)-sa' cha-Ø-Ø 'an r-e
Prep Neg-time Fut-A(2s)-look Prep E(3s)-RN say-Pres-A(3s) Dm E(3s)-RN
'not once will you look inside', he says to him

29b. **a wi[i]nq ki-Ø-x-k'am r-iiq**
Dm man Inf-A(3s)-E(3s)-carry E(3s)-cargo
that man carried his cargo (of jars)

ti-Ø-x-naw raj k'a'-aq r-u na-Ø-eek'ank chi (x)-sa'
Fut-A(3s)-E(3s)-know CF what-NS E(3s)-RN Pres-A(3s)-move Prep E(3s)-RN
he would like to know whatever is moving inside (the jars)

ma(a) ho'on ta n-in-il-e' iho'on chan-Ø-Ø sa' ix ch'ool
Neg now Neg Pres-A(1s)-see-Psv now say-Prep-A(3s) Prep E(3s) heart
'not now will I be seen', he says inside his heart

timil [i]x-Ø-(x)-kuj r-u'uj r-uq(') x-taqsink-il ka[']ch'in-aq['] ix tz'ap-b'al r-e
slowly Perf-A(3s)-E(3s)-put E(3s)-tip E(3s)-hand E(3s)-raise-Nom small-NS E(3s) close-Nom E(3s)-RN
slowly he put in his finger to raise a little the top (of the jar)

ssst jun chi nim-la i(q)[k]'b'olay ki-Ø-el
SE one Prep large-SF barbamarilla Inf-A(3s)-leave
ssst! a large barbamarilla went out

na-Ø-num-e' ix b'een ix telb'
Pres-A(3s)-pass-Psv E(3s) RN E(3s) arm
it passes over his arm

jay ki-Ø-x-chaj r-e (x)-b'a(a)n ix xiw
Interj Inf-A(3s)-E(3s)-yell E(3s)-RN E(3s)-RN E(3s) fear
'jay!' he yelled because of his fear (yelled his mouth?)

o rum chi ch'och(')
? throw Prep ground
(and throws it) onto the ground

29c. **jun jor-b'al jun puk'-b'al li r-iiq**
one break-Nom one burst-Nom Dm E(3s)-cargo
(there is) a breaking, a bursting (of) his cargo

na-Ø-t'oroxin k'aj b'uj sa' b'e
Pres-A(3s)-scatter piece ? Prep road
many pieces are scattered onto the road

nek-e'-aalinak
Pres-A(3p)-run
they run

nek-e'-purik
Pres-A(3p)-fly
they fly

nek-e'-b'atz'-(b')atz(')n[']ak
Pres-A(3p)-Rdp-play
they scamper

nek-e'-mili[l]nak
Pres-A(3p)-?
they undulate

nek-e'-saapan
Pres-A(3p)-?
they jump

nek-e'-re[x]b'ak
Pres-A(3p)-tongue_flick
they flick their tongues

nek-e'-soyb'ak
Pres-A(3p)-roll_up
they coil

sa' ix wakli(j)[k]i(k)[j] l-aj ti'on-el xul nek-e'-jat(z)[c]'ak
Prep E(3s) raise-Nom Dm-SD bite-Nom animal Pres-A(3s)-hold_ rancor /look_
askance
at their awakening, the biting animals are angry

x-jek'-b'al-eb' r-ib' jun r-u(u) chi ch'och' ix maak li wi[i]nq
E(3s)-distribute-Nom-Plr E(3s)-Rflx one E(3s)-RN Prep ground E(3s) RN Dm
man
their distributing themselves (all over) the earth (was) the fault of the man (of man)

ink'a' (k-)Ø-ix-pa(a)b' r-aatin qaawa' b'alamq'e
Neg Inf-A(3s)-E(3s)-believe E(3s)-word SD PN
he did not obey the words of Lord B'alamq'e

30a. **ab'an a ak' po wi' ki-Ø-yo'la wi' chik**
Part Dm new moon Part Inf-A(3s)-be_born Part Part
however that new moon was born again

maak'a' ix ch'in-a tz(')ejwal wan-Ø-Ø r-e
not_exist E(3s) small-SF body be-Pres-A(3s) E(3s)-RN
she doesn't have the small body (she used to have)

jo'-ka'in qaawa' b'alamq'e ki-Ø-x-yokob' a po sa' ix ya[a]n(q) tzuul chi r-u taq'a
Part-Dm SD PN Inf-A(3s)-E(3s)-lay Dm moon Prep E(3s) RN mountain Prep E(3s)-RN valley
because of this Lord B'alamq'e caused this moon to lie down in-between the mountains and before a valley

ki-Ø-x-q'unb'es li yuk r-e sa' aanil na-Ø-numsi
Inf-A(3s)-E(3s)-soften Dm goat E(3s)-RN Prep run Pres-A(3s)-pass
he persuaded the goat to quickly pass by

x-Ø-(x)-k'e r-ib' chi r-ix r-e x-te[e]-b'al toon r-a' li po r-e ix te-b'al jun chik hopol-al
Perf-A(3s)-E(3s)-give E(3s)-Rflx Prep E(3s)-RN E(3s)-RN E(3s)-open-Nom horizontal E(3s)-leg Dm moon E(3s)-RN E(3s) open-Nom one Part hole-Abs
it put itself behind her (it gave itself to help) in order to spread open the moon's legs, in order to open another hole

jo'-ka'in i x-Ø-(x)-b'aanu
Part-Dm Dm Perf-A(3s)-E(3s)-do
like this he did it

yoo-Ø-Ø r-il-b'al qaawa' b'alamq'e
be-Pres-A(3s) E(3s)-see-Nom SD PN
Lord B'alamq'e was watching

yal kach'in aj wi' ki-Ø-x-te
Part small Part Part Inf-A(3s)-E(3s)-open
(but) only a little he opened it

30b. **yoo-Ø-Ø ix b'oq-b'al l-ix kej r-e x-te-b'al ix hopol-al l-ix sa'**
be-Pres-A(3s) E(3s) call-Nom Dm-E(3s) deer E(3s)-RN E(3s)-open-Nom E(3s) hole-Abs Dm-E(3s) stomach
he was calling his deer to open her belly's hole

xiw xiw naq ki-Ø-x-paab' mare t'ilq (x)-toq-b'al r-oq chi (x)-sa'
fear fear Comp Inf-A(3s)-E(3s)-obey/believe perhaps stick E(3s)-break-Nom E(3s)-leg Prep E(3s)-RN
(it was) very scared (for) it believed that it might get stuck (and) break its leg inside

ki-Ø-pisk'ok
Inf-A(3s)-jump
it jumped

ki-Ø-x-yak sa' ix yanq r-a' po (yeq'ok: patear, have sex with)
Inf-A(3s)-E(3s)-negotiate Prep E(3s) RN E(3s)-leg moon
it negotiated in-between the legs of (the) moon

ki-Ø-x-nimob'resi r-u chi us
Inf-A(3s)-E(3s)-enlarge E(3s)-face Prep good
it enlarged its face well

chanchan li k'i(i)-la atz'um l-ix sununk-il
Part Dm many-SF flower Dm-E(3s) smell-Nom
its smell was like that of many flowers

ki' ki' x-Ø-el ix woqx
sweet sweet Perf-A(3s)-leave E(3s) froth/spray
sweet sweet went out its spray

30c. **maa-min ki-Ø-hu[u]lak chi r-u qaawa' b'alamq'e**
Neg-Part Inf-A(3s)-arrive Prep E(3s)-RN SD PN
in no way was Lord B'alamq'e pleased

toj ki-Ø-x-k'e li ch'o chi (x)-sa' li po
Part Inf-A(3s)-E(3s)-give Dm rat Prep E(3s)-RN Dm moon
but when he placed the rat inside the moon

ut li ch'o aran ki-Ø-chu'uk
Conj Dm rat there Inf-Ø-urinate
and the rat peed there

jo'-ka'in ki-Ø-usa
Part-Dm Inf-A(3s)-improve
then it improved

30d. **us anaqwan chan-Ø-Ø qaawa' b'alamq'e**
good now say-Pres-A(3s) SD PN
'now it's good', says Lord B'alamq'e

ki-Ø-x-chap r-uq' qana' po r-e ix k'am-b'al sa' choxa jo'-ixaqil
Inf-A(3s)-E(3s)-take E(3s)-hand SD PN E(3s)-RN E(3s) carry-Nom Prep sky Part
E(3s)-wife
he grabbed the hand of Lady Moon to take her into the sky as his wife

31. **chalen a'an yoo-k-eb' r-il-b'al jun r-u(u) chi ch'och'**
Part Dm be-Pres-A(3p) E(3s)-see-Nom Num E(3s)-RN Prep ground
since then they have been watching all over the earth

qaawa' saq'e chi kutan
SD sun (=PN) Prep day
Lord Sun during the day

qana' po chi r-u q'ojyi[i]n
SD NP Prep E(3s)-RN night
Lady Moon during the night

chi jo'-kan eb' li wi[i]nq naq nek-e'-b'eek k'am-ol b'e chi r-u eb' li ixq
Prep Part-Dm Plr Dm man Comp Pres-A(3p)-walk carry-Abs road Prep E(3s)-RN
Plr Dm woman
because of this, it is men that walk as leaders in front of women

References

Adams, Richard N. 1965. *Migraciones internas en Guatemala: Expansión agraria de los indígenas Kekchiés hacia el Petén*. Guatemala City: Centro Editorial 'José de Pineda Ibarra'.

Adams, Richard N. and Arthur J. Rubel 1967. 'Sickness and social relations', in Manning Nash (ed.), *Social anthropology*, pp. 125–50. Austin: University of Texas Press.

Agha, Asif 1998. 'Stereotypes and registers of honorific language', *Language in Society* **272**: 151–93.

Allen, N. J. 1985. 'The category of the person in Mauss', in M. Carrithers, S. Collins, and S. Lukes (eds.), *The category of the person: Anthropology, philosophy, history*, pp. 26–45. Cambridge: Cambridge University Press.

Ameka, Felix 1992. 'Interjections: The universal yet neglected part of speech', *Journal of Pragmatics* **18**: 101–18.

Aristotle 2001. 'Politics', in Richard McKeon (ed.), pp. 1210–33. *The basic works of Aristotle*. New York: The Modern Library.

Austin, J. L. 2003 [1955]. *How to do things with words*. Cambridge, MA: Harvard University Press.

Averill, James R. 1980. 'A constructivist view of emotion', in R. Plutchik and H. Kellerma (eds.), *Emotion: Theory, research, and experience*, pp. 305–40. New York: Academic Press.

Bakhtin, M. M. 1981. *The dialogic imagination*. Austin: University of Texas Press.

  1990. *Art and answerability*. Austin: University of Texas Press.

Berinstein, Ava 1985. *Evidence for multiattachment in Kekchi*. New York: Taylor and Francis.

Berlin, Brent and Paul Kay 1969. *Basic color terms, their universality and evolution*. Berkeley: University of California Press.

Bloomfield, Leonard 1984 [1933]. *Language*. Chicago: University of Chicago Press.

Boas, F. 1989a [1889]. 'On alternating sounds', in G. W. Stocking Jr. (ed.), *Franz Boas Reader*, pp. 72–7. Chicago: Midway Reprints.

  1989b [1910]. 'Psychological problems in anthropology', in G. W. Stocking Jr. (ed.), *Franz Boas Reader*, pp. 243–54. Chicago: Midway Reprints.

Bourdieu, Pierre 1977 [1972]. *Outline of a theory of practice*. Cambridge: Cambridge University Press.

Brandom, Robert 1994. *Making it explicit: Reasoning, representing, and discursive commitment*. Cambridge: Cambridge University Press.

Brentano, Franz 1995 [1874]. *Psychology from an empirical standpoint*. New York: Routledge.

Brown, Gillian and George Yule 1983. *Discourse analysis*. Cambridge: Cambridge University Press.

Brown, Penelope 1994. 'The INs and ONs of Tzeltal locative expressions: The semantics of static descriptions of location', *Linguistics* **32**: 743–90.

Bühler, Karl 1990. *Theory of language: The representational function of language*, D.F. Goodwin (trans.). Amsterdam & Philadelphia: John Benjamins Publishing.

Bull, William E. 1960. *Time, tense, and the verb*. Berkeley and Los Angeles: University of California Press.

Bybee, Joan 1985. *Morphology*. Amsterdam and Philadelphia: John Benjamins.

Carter, William E. 1969. *New lands and old traditions: Kekchi cultivators in the Guatemalan lowlands*. Gainesville: University of Florida Press.

Chappel, Hilary and William McGregor (eds.) 1996. *The grammar of inalienability: A typological perspective on body part terms and the part-whole relation*. Berlin & New York: Mouton de Gruyter.

Chen Cao, Ernesto, *et al.* 1997. *Diccionario Q'eqchi'*. Antigua, Guatemala: Proyecto Lingüístico Francisco Marroquín.

Conklin, Beth, and Lynn M. Morgan 1996. 'Babies, bodies, and the production of personhood in North America and a native Amazonian society', *Ethos* **24**: 657–94.

D'Andrade, Roy 1995. *The development of cognitive anthropology*. Cambridge: Cambridge University Press.

D'Atri, A. 1995. 'The theory of interjections in Vico and Rousseau', in L. Formigari and D. Gambarara, *Historical roots of linguistic theories*, pp. 115–27. Amsterdam & Philadelphia: John Benjamins.

Dixon, Robert M. W. 1994. *Ergativity*. Cambridge: Cambridge University Press.

Du Bois, Jack W. 1980. 'Beyond definiteness: Trace of identity in discourse', in Wallace Chafe (ed.), *The Pear stories*, pp. 203–74. Berkeley: University of California Press.
   1987. 'The discourse basis of ergativity', *Language* **63**: 805–55.

Duncan, S. 1973. 'Towards a grammar for dyadic conversations', *Semiotica* **9**: 29–46.

Durkheim, Emile 1947 [1912]. *The elementary forms of religious life*. New York: Free Press.

Ehlich, Konrad 1986. *Interjektionen*. Tübingon: Niemeyer.

Estrada Monroy, Austín 1990. *Vida esotérica Maya-K'ekchí*. Guatemala: Edición Cultural.

Evans-Pritchard, E. E. 1940. *The Nuer: A description of the modes of livelihood and political institutions of a Nilotic people*. Oxford: Oxford University Press.

Freeze, Ray A. 1970. *Case in a grammar of K'ekchi' Maya*. Unpublished Ph.D. dissertation, University of Texas, Austin.

Frege, Gottlob 1997 [1892]. 'On Sinn and Bedeutung', in Michael Beaney (ed.), *The Frege reader*, pp. 151–71. Oxford: Blackwell Publishers Ltd.

Friedrich, Paul 1979. 'The symbol and its relatively non-arbitrariness', in Anwar S. Dill, *Language, context, and the imagination: Essays by Paul Friedrich*, pp. 1–61. Stanford: Stanford University Press.

Friestad, M. and P. Wright 1995. 'Persuasion knowledge: Lay people's and researchers' beliefs about the psychology of advertising', *Journal of Consumer Research* **22**: 62–74.

Gardner, D., P.L. Harris, M. Ohmoto, and T. Hamazaki, 1988. 'Japanese children's understanding of the distinction between real and apparent emotions', *International Journal of Behavioral Development* **11**: 203–18.

Gillen, Jack 1948. 'Magical fright', *Psychiatry* **11**: 387–400.

Givón, Talmy 1980. 'The binding hierarchy and the typology of complements', *Studies in Language* **52**: 163–93.

Goffman, Erving 1981a. 'Footing', in *Forms of talk*, pp. 124–59. Philadelphia: University of Pennsylvania Press.

   1981b. 'Replies and responses', in *Forms of talk*, pp. 5–77. Philadelphia: University of Pennsylvania Press.

   1981c. 'Response cries', in *Forms of talk*, pp. 78–123. Philadelphia: University of Pennsylvania Press.

Greenberg, Joseph H. 1963. 'Some universals of grammar with particular reference to the order of meaningful elements', in J.H. Greenberg (ed.), *Universals of language*, pp. 58–90. Cambridge, MA: MIT Press.

   1966. *Language universals*. The Hague: Mouton de Gruyter.

   1980. 'Universals of kinship terminology: Their nature and the problem of their explanation', in Jacques Maquet (ed.), *On linguistic anthropology: Essays in honor of Harry Hoijer*, pp. 9–32. Malibu: Undena.

Grice, Paul 1989a. 'The causal theory of perception', in *Studies in the ways of words*, pp. 224–47. Cambridge, MA: Harvard University Press.

   1989b. 'Utterer's meaning and intention', *Studies in the ways of words*, pp. 86–116. Cambridge, MA: Harvard University Press.

   1989c. 'Logic and conversation', in *Studies in the ways of words*, pp. 22–40. Cambridge, MA: Harvard University Press.

Griffiths, Paul E. 1997. *What emotions really are*. Chicago: University of Chicago Press.

Haiman, John 1985. *Natural syntax*. Cambridge: Cambridge University Press.

Hanks, William F. 1989. 'Elements of Maya style', in W. F. Hanks and D. S. Rice (eds.), *Word and image in Maya culture: Explorations in language, writing, and representation*, pp. 92–111. Salt Lake City: University of Utah Press.

   1991. *Referential practice*. Chicago: University of Chicago Press.

   1993. 'Metalanguage and the pragmatics of deixis', in J. Lucy (ed.), *Reflexive language: Reported speech and metapragmatics*. Cambridge: Cambridge University Press.

Haugeland, John 1998. 'The intentionality all-stars', in *Having thought: Essays in the metaphysics of mind*, pp. 127–70. Cambridge, MA: Harvard University Press.

Haviland, John 2003. 'Comments on interjections', *Current Anthropology* **44**(4): 480–1.

Hawkins, John A. 2004. *Efficiency and complexity in Grammars*. Oxford: Oxford University Press.

Heidegger, Martin 1988. *The basic problems of phenomenology*. Bloomington: Indiana University Press.

Herder, Johann Gottfried 1966. 'On the origin of language', in A. Gode (trans.), *On the origin of language: Two essays*, pp. 84–166. Chicago: University of Chicago Press.

Heritage, John and Geoffrey Raymond 2005. 'The terms of agreement: indexing epistemic authority and subordination in talk-in-interaction', *Social Psychology Quarterly* **68**: 15–38.

Hill, Jane H. and Bruce Mannheim 1992. 'Language and world view', *Annual Review of Anthropology* **21**: 381–406.

Hofling, Charles Andrew 1993. 'Marking space and time in Itzaj Maya narrative', *Journal of Linguistic Anthropology* **32**: 164–84.

Holland, Douglas 1992. 'Cross-cultural differences in the self', *Journal of Anthropological Research* **48**: 283–300.

Horn, L.R. 1984. 'Towards a new taxonomy for pragmatic inference: Q-based and R-based implicature', in D. Schiffrin (ed.) *Georgetown University round table on languages and linguistics*, pp. 11–42. Washington, DC: Georgetown University Press.

Howard, M.C. 1975. *Ethnicity in Southern Belize: The Kekchi and the Mopan.* Columbia, MO: Curators of the University of Missouri, Museum Brief No. 21.

Jackendoff, Ray 2003. *Foundations of language.* Oxford: Oxford University Press.

Jakobson, Roman 1990a. 'Shifters and verbal categories', in L.R. Waugh and M. Monville-Burston (eds.), *On language*, pp. 386–92. Cambridge, MA: Harvard University Press.

  1990b. 'The speech event and the functions of language', in L.R. Waugh and M. Monville-Burston (eds.), *On language*, pp. 69–79. Cambridge, MA: Harvard University Press.

James, William 1893. *The principles of psychology.* New York: Holt.

Jaynes, Julian 1976. *The origin of consciousness in the breakdown of the bicameral mind.* Boston: Houghton Mifflin.

Jespersen, Otto 1965. *The philosophy of grammar.* New York: W.W. Norton and Company.

Johnson, Mark 1987. *The body in the mind.* Chicago: University of Chicago Press.

Kant, Immanuel 1964 [1781]. *Critique of pure reason.* New York: St. Martin's Press.

King, Arden R. 1974. *Coban and the Verapaz: History and cultural process in northern Guatemala.* New Orleans: Tulane University.

Klein, Wolfgang 1994. *Time in language.* London: Routledge.

Kockelman, Paul 1998. 'Legend of the Suns: Reproducing the production of a Nahuatl text', *Estudios de Cultura Náhuatl*, 28: 219–39.

  1999a. 'The collection of Copal among the Q'eqchi'-Maya', *Research in Economic Anthropology* Vol. 20: 163–94. Edited by B. Issac. Greenwich, CT: JAI Press Inc.

  1999b. 'Poetic function and logical form, ideal languages and forms of life', *Chicago Anthropology Exchange* Vol. XXIX: 34–50.

  2002. 'Minding language and measuring labor: Stance and subjectivity in the context of neoliberal globalization'. Unpublished Ph.D. dissertation, University of Chicago.

  2003. 'The interclausal relations hierarchy in Q'eqchi'-Maya', *International Journal of American Linguistics* **69**(1): 25–48.

  2004. 'Stance and subjectivity', *Journal of Linguistic Anthropology* **14**(2): 127–50.

  2005a. 'The semiotic stance', *Semiotica* **157**(1): 233–304.

  2005b. 'Psychological depth is the internalization of dialogical breadth: Modal clitics and mental states in Q'eqchi'-Maya', *Language and Communication* **26**: 55–116.

  2006. 'Representations of the world: Memories, perceptions, beliefs, plans, and intentions', *Semiotica* **162**(1): 72–125.

  2007a. 'Enclosure and disclosure', *Public Culture* **19**(2): 303–5.

  2007b. 'From status to contract revisited: Modality, temporality, circulation, and subjectivity', *Anthropological Theory* **7**(2): 151–76.

  2007c. 'Agency: The relation between meaning, power, and knowledge', *Current Anthropology* **48**(3): 375–401.

2007d. 'Number, unit, and utility in a Mayan community: The relation between use-value, labor-power, and personhood', *Journal of the Royal Anthropological Institute* **13**(2): 401–17.

2009. 'Inalienable possession as grammatical category and discourse pattern', *Studies in Language* **33**(1): 25–68.

Kroeber, Alfred 1909. 'Classificatory systems of relations', *Journal of the Royal Anthropological Institute* **39**: 77–84.

Lamb, Sarah 1997. 'The making and unmaking of persons: Notes on aging and gender in North India', *Ethos* **25**: 279–302.

Levinson, S. C. 1983. *Pragmatics*. Cambridge: Cambridge University Press.

1994. 'Vision, shape, and linguistic description: Tzeltal body-part terminology and object description', *Linguistics* **32**: 791–855.

2000. *Presumptive meanings: The theory of generalized implicature*. Cambridge, MA: MIT Press.

Levinson, S. C. and David P. Wilkins 2006. *Grammars of space: explorations in cognitive diversity*. Cambridge: Cambridge University Press.

Lillard, A. 1998. 'Ethnopsychologies: Cultural variations in theories of mind', *Psychological Bulletin* **1231**: 3–32.

Linton, Ralph 1936. *The study of man*. New York: Appleton, Century, and Crofts.

Lucy, John A. 1992a. *Grammatical categories and cognition*. Cambridge: Cambridge University Press.

1992b. *Linguistic relativity*. Cambridge: Cambridge University Press.

1993a. 'Reflexive language and the human disciplines', in John A. Lucy (ed.), *Reflexive language: Reported speech and metapragmatics*, pp. 9–32. Cambridge: Cambridge University Press.

1993b. *Reflexive language: Reported speech and metapragmatics*. Cambridge: Cambridge University Press.

Lutz, Catherine A. 1988. *Unnatural emotions*. Chicago: University of Chicago Press.

Malinowski, Bronisław 1936. 'The problem of meaning in primitive languages', in C. K. Ogden and A. I. Richards (eds.), *The meaning of meaning*, pp. 296–336. New York: Harcourt, Brace.

Mauss, Marcel 1954. *The gift*. Glencoe, IL: Free Press.

1979. 'A category of the human mind: The notion of person, the notion of "self"', in Ben Brewster (trans.), *Sociology and psychology: Essays by Marcel Mauss*, pp. 57–94. London: Routledge & Kegan Paul.

McVeigh, Brian 1996. 'Standing stomachs, clamoring chests and cooling livers: Metaphors in the psychological lexicon of Japanese', *Journal of Pragmatics* **26**: 25–50.

Meng, Katharina and Susanne Schrabback 1999. 'Interjections in adult-child discourse: The cases of German HM and NA', *Journal of Pragmatics* **31**: 1263–87.

Montes, Rosa Graciela 1999. 'The development of discourse markers in Spanish: Interjections', *Journal of Pragmatics* **31**: 1289–319.

Müller, Max 1862. *Lectures on the science of language*. New York: Charles Scribner.

Munn, Nancy 1992. *The fame of Gawa*. Durham: Duke University Press.

Nichols, Johanna 1992. *Linguistic diversity in space and time*. Chicago: University of Chicago Press.

Norman, W. M. 1980. 'Grammatical parallelism in Quiche ritual language', in *Proceedings of the sixth annual meeting of the Berkeley Linguistic Society*, pp. 387–99. Berkley: Berkley Linguistics Society.

O'Nell, Charles and Henry Selby 1968. 'Sex differences in the incidence of susto in two Zapotec pueblos: An analysis of the relationships between sex role expectations and a folk illness', *Ethnology* **7**: 95–105.

Padley, George A. 1976. *Grammatical theory in western Europe 1500–1700*. Cambridge: Cambridge University Press.

Pedroni, Guillermo 1991. *Territorialidad Kekchi: una aproximación al acceso a la tierra: la migración y la titulación*. Guatemala City: FLACSO.

Peirce, Charles S. 1955. 'Logic as semiotic: The theory of signs', in Justus Buchler (ed.), *Philosophical writings of Peirce*, pp. 98–119. New York: Dover Publications.

1931–35. *Collected papers of Charles Sanders Peirce*. Charles Hartshorne and Paul Weiss (eds.). Cambridge, MA: Harvard University Press.

Reichenbach, Hans 1947. *Elements of symbolic logic*. New York: Macmillan.

Rips, L. J. and F. G. Conrad 1989. 'Folk psychology of mental activities', *Psychological Review* **96**(2): 187–207.

Rousseau, Jean-Jacques 1966. 'On the origin of language', in A. Gode (trans.), *On the origin of language: Two essays*, pp. 1–83. Chicago: University of Chicago Press.

Sacks, H., E. Schegloff, and G. Jefferson 1974. 'A simplest systematics for the organization of turn-taking for conversation', *Language* **50**: 696–735.

Sahlins, Marshall 1972. 'On the sociology of primitive trade', in *Stone age economics*, pp. 185–230. Hawthorne, NY: Aldine de Gruyter.

1976. 'Colors and cultures', *Semiotica* **16**: 1–22.

Sapir, Edward 1921. *Language*. New York: Harcourt, Brace & Co.

1985 [1927]. 'The unconscious patterning of behavior in society', in David G. Mandelbaum (ed.), *Selected writings in language, culture, and personality*, pp. 544–59. Berkeley: University of California Press.

Sapper, Karl 1985. *The Verapaz in the sixteenth and seventeenth centuries: A contribution to the historical geography and ethnography of northeastern Guatemala*. Los Angeles, CA: UCLA Press.

Saussure, Ferdinand de 1983 [1916]. *Course in general linguistics*. La Salle, Illinois: Open Court Press.

Schieffelin, B., K.A. Woolard, and P.V. Kroskrity (eds.) 1998. *Language ideologies: Practice and theory*. Oxford: Oxford University Press.

Schiffrin, Deborah 1987. *Discourse markers*. Cambridge: Cambridge University Press.

Searle, John 1983. *Intentionality*. Cambridge: Cambridge University Press.

Secaira, Estuardo 1992. *Conservation among the Q'eqchi'-Maya: A comparison of highland and lowland agriculture*. Masters Thesis, Department of Conservation Biology and Sustainable Development. University of Wisconsin, Madison.

Sedat, Guillermo 1955. *Nuevo diccionario de las lenguas K'ekchi' y Española*. Chamelco, Alta Verapaz: Summer Institute of Linguistics.

Sharer, Robert J. 1994. *The Ancient Maya*. Stanford University Press.

Sherzer, Joel 1993. 'Pointed lips, thumbs up, and cheek puffs: Some emblematic gestures in social interactional and ethnographic context'. Paper read at Symposium about Language and Society, Austin Texas (SALSA).

Shweder, Richard and Edmund Bourne 1984. 'Does the concept of person vary cross-culturally?', in Richard Shweder and Robert LeVine (eds.), *Culture theory: Essays on mind, self, and emotion*, pp. 158–99. Cambridge: Cambridge University Press.

Silverstein, Michael 1979. 'Language structure and linguistic ideology', in R. Cline, W. Hanks, and C. Hofbauer (eds.), *The elements: A parasession on linguistic units and levels*, pp. 193–247. Chicago: Chicago Linguistic Society.

1981. 'The limits of awareness', *Sociolinguistic Working Paper* **84**. Southwest Educational Development Laboratory, Austin.

1993. 'Of nominatives and datives: Universal grammar from the bottom up', in Robert D. Jr. Van Valin (ed.), *Advances in role and reference grammar*, pp. 465–98. Amsterdam & Philadelphia: John Benjamins.

1995 [1976]. 'Shifters, linguistic categories, and cultural description', in Ben G. Blount (ed.), *Language, culture, and society: A book of readings*, pp. 187–221. Prospect Heights, Illinois: Waveland Press.

Sperber, Dan and Diedre Wilson 1986. *Relevance: Communication and cognition*. Hoboken, NJ: Blackwell.

Spiro, Melford 1993. 'Is the Western conception of the self "peculiar" with the context of the world's cultures?', *Ethos* **21**: 107–53.

Stewart, Stephen O. 1980a. *Gramática Kekchí*. Guatemala: Editorial Académica Centro Americana.

1980b. 'Tense/aspect in Kekchi', *Georgetown University Papers on Languages and Linguistics* **17**: 72–90.

Stoll, Otto 1896. *Die Maya-Sprachen der Pokom-Gruppe, Die Sprache der K'e'kchi-Indianer*. Leipzig: K.F. Köhler's Antiquarium.

Strathern, Marilyn 1988. *The gender of the gift*. Berkeley: University of California Press.

Talmy, Leonard 2000. *Towards a cognitive semantics: Volume I: Concept structuring systems*. Cambridge, MA: The MIT Press.

Taylor, Charles 1985a. *Human agency and language*. Cambridge: Cambridge University Press.

1985b. 'The person', in M. Carrithers, S. Collins, and S. Lukes (eds.), *The category of the person: Anthropology, philosophy, history*, pp. 257–81. Cambridge: Cambridge University Press.

1989. *Sources of the self: The making of modern identity*. Cambridge: Cambridge University Press.

Taylor, John R. 1995. *Linguistic Categorization*. Chicago: University of Chicago Press.

Thompson, Sandra A. and Anthony Mulac 1991a. 'A quantitative perspective on the grammaticization of epistemic parentheticals in English', in Elizabeth Traugott and Bernd Heine (eds.), *Grammaticalization II*, pp. 313–39. Amsterdam: John Benjamins.

1991b. 'The discourse conditions for the use of complementizer that in conversational English', *Journal of Pragmatics* **15**: 237–51.

Tomasello, Michael 1999. *The cultural origins of human cognition*. Cambridge, MA: Harvard University Press.

Tomasello, Michael and Josep Call 1997. *Primate cognition*. New York: Oxford University Press.

Turner, Terence 1980. 'The social skin', in J. Cherfas and R. Lewin (eds.), *Not work alone*, pp. 112–40. Beverly Hills: Sage Publications.

Van Valin, Robert D. Jr. and Randy J. LaPolla 1997. *Syntax: Structure, meaning and function*. Cambridge: Cambridge University Press.

Van Valin, Robert D. Jr. and David P. Wilkins 1993. 'Predicting syntactic structure from semantic representations: remember in English and Mparntwe Arrernte', in Robert D. Jr. Van Valin (ed.), *Advances in role and reference grammar*, pp. 499–534. Amsterdam & Philadelphia: John Benjamins.

Vendler, Zeno 1967. *Linguistics in philosophy*. Ithaca: Cornell University Press.

Vygotsky, L. S. 1978. *Mind and society: The development of higher psychological processes*. Cambridge, MA: Harvard University Press.

Wagner, Regina 1996. *Los Alemanes en Guatemala, 1828–1944*. Guatemala City, Afanes, S.A.

Wallace, A. F. and M. T. Carson 1973. 'Sharing and diversity in emotion terminology', *Ethos* **1**: 1–29.

Weiner, Annette B. 1985. 'Inalienable wealth', *American Ethnologist* **12**: 52–65.

1992. *Inalienable possessions*. Berkeley: University of California Press.

Wellman, H. M. 1990. *The child's theory of mind*. Cambridge, MA: Bradford Books.

Wellman, H. M. and D. Estes 1986. 'Early understanding of mental entities: A reexamination of childhood realism', *Child Development* **57**: 910–23.

Wellman, H. M. and A. K. Hickling 1994. 'The mind's "I": Children's conceptualization of the mind as an active agent', *Child Development* **65**: 1564–80.

Whorf, B. L. 1956a. 'Grammatical categories', in John B. Carroll (ed.), *Language, thought, and reality: Selected writings of Benjamin Lee Whorf*, pp. 87–101. Cambridge, MA: The MIT Press.

1956b. 'The relation of habitual thought and behavior to language', in John B. Carroll (ed.), *Language, thought, and reality: Selected writings of Benjamin Lee Whorf*, pp. 134–59. Cambridge, MA: The MIT Press.

1956c. 'Some Verbal categories of Hopi', in John B. Carroll (ed.), *Language, thought, and reality: Selected writings of Benjamin Lee Whorf*, pp. 112–24. Cambridge, MA: The MIT Press.

Wierzbicka, A. 1988. *The semantics of grammar*. Sydney: Academic Press.

1992. 'The semantics of interjections', *Journal of Pragmatics* **18**: 159–92.

Wilk, Richard R. 1991. *Household ecology: Economic change and domestic life among the Kekchi Maya in Belize*. Tucson: University of Arizona Press.

Wilkins, David 1992. 'Interjections as deictics', *Journal of Pragmatics* **18**: 119–58.

Willett, Thomas 1988. 'A cross-linguistic survey of the grammaticalization of evidentiality', *Studies in Language* **12**(1): 51–97.

Wilson, Michael R. 1972. *A highland Maya people and their habitat: The natural history, demography and economy of the K'ekchi'*. Ph.D. dissertation, University of Oregon, Department of Geography.

Wilson, R. 1995. *Maya resurgence in Guatemala*. Norman, OK: University of Oklahoma Press.

Wimmer, H. and J. Perner 1983. 'Beliefs about beliefs: Representation and constraining function of wrong beliefs in young children's understanding of deception', *Cognition* **13**: 103–28.

Zwicky, Arnold M. 1985. 'Clitics and particles', *Language* **61**(2): 283–305.

Index

agency, 189, 195, 197, 199, 201
Agha, 36
animator, 1–2
Aristotle, 187
aspect, 66, 90, 105
Austin, 5, 12, 39, 127, 170, 189, 191, 208
Averill, 200

Bahktin, 82, 90
baptism, 43–45
Berlin and Kay, 3
Bloomfield, 13, 26, 164, 166, 167, 186, 194, 203
Boas, 189
Bourdieu, 193
Brandom, 4, 39
Brentano, 4, 54
Brown, 27
Bühler, 168
Bull, 90
Bybee, 65, 66

care, 37, 112
Chappel and McGregor, 22
commitment event, 1–2, 10, 67, 106, 124, 127, 203
complement-taking predicates, 3, 45–9, 52, 159, 163, 191, 200, 202
content event, 202, 204
counterfactive status, 1–2, 10, 76, 122
covert categories, 22, 61, 193, 197

D'Andrade, 62, 199
de Saussure, 203
deontic events, 67, 203
desire, 2, 73, 112, 139, 148, 153, 154
diachronic process, 13, 62
diagrammatic iconicity, 52, 204
disclosure, 45, 51, 55, 82
discourse pattern, 14, 27–35
displacement, 82, 168, 189, 202, 203, 204
Dixon, 30

DuBois, 28, 30
Durkheim, 6, 127

emblemeticity, 6, 23, 35, 39, 54, 81, 162, 203
emotion, 11, 37, 78, 117, 130, 139, 150, 164, 184, 187, 188, 192, 195, 199
empathy, 42, 51, 78, 137
enclosure, 55, 82
epistemologies of the everyday, 83
estrangement, 41, 47, 79
Evans-Pritchard, 43, 202
evidentiality, 3, 10, 66, 67, 95, 103, 136, 159, 202

form-functional domain, 12, 65, 164, 186, 200
Frege, 207
Friedrich, 179
fright, 45–9, 145

gifts, 43–5
Givón, 52, 53, 204
Goffman, 1, 124, 172, 180, 187, 189, 194, 203
grammaticalization, 2, 62, 67, 160, 203
Greenberg, 3, 22, 30, 65, 204
Grice, 4
Griffiths, 192

Hanks, 23, 110, 115, 168, 193
heart, 11, 37, 68, 73, 144
Heidegger, 42
Herder, 187

implicational universals, 63
implicature, 10, 126, 133, 160, 170, 204
inalienable possessions, 2, 10, 14, 109, 112, 117, 133, 137
inalienable wealth, 49
intensionality, 82, 207
intention, 2, 148
intentional horizons, 85, 107, 116, 118, 163

intentionality, 4–7, 54, 62, 81
interclausal relations, 52, 97
interjections, 3, 135
internalization, 128, 143, 183
intersubjectivity, 42, 85, 204

Jakobson, 1, 12, 13, 88, 90, 124, 170, 173,
    186, 189, 202, 207
joint attention, 170, 204

Kant, 120
Klein, 90
Kroeber, 3

Levinson, 3, 27, 172
lexicalization, 81
Linton, 5
Lucy, 3, 13, 39, 161, 189, 194, 207, 208
Lutz, 187

Malinowski, 173
marriage, 43–5
Mauss, 49
memory, 74
meta-language, 13, 81, 120, 193, 194, 207
meta-stance, 161
mode event, 202, 204
motivation, 41, 118, 129

narrated event, 1–2, 23, 67, 90, 124
natural constructions, 12, 201
Nichols, 22
Norman, 110, 115

participant roles, 1–2, 68, 111, 118, 121, 158, 203
Peirce, 12, 52, 82, 169, 179, 194, 204
personhood, 11, 42, 48, 50, 120, 161
positive status, 133, 141, 145
principle, 1–2
projection, 81, 200
propositional content, 80
propositional mode, 80
psycholocation, 11, 37, 68, 73, 158

reference event, 90, 97, 100, 101, 103, 104,
    105, 106
reflexivity, 14, 39, 41–3, 51, 54, 161, 164, 206

Reichenbach, 90
relations between relations, 14, 164, 201, 202
Rousseau, 187

Sachs, 172
Sahlins, 43, 200
Sapir, 186
Schieffelin, 193
Schiffrin, 166
script, 11, 55
Searle, 4, 54
Sherzer, 187
Silverstein, 13, 39, 52, 127, 189, 191, 193, 208
social kinds, 12, 201
social role, 4–7
social status, 4–7
source events, 67, 160, 203
speech acts, 4–7, 205
speech event, 1–2, 11, 23, 67, 90, 111, 124,
    202
Sperber, 127
stance, 7, 62, 161, 162
status, 3, 67, 106, 120, 202
Stewart, 9, 15, 92, 167
Strathern, 187
subjectivity, 50, 120, 158, 203

Talmy, 193
Taylor, 39, 49, 50, 161, 207
temporal adverbs, 92
theories of mind, 200, 207
thinking, 11, 77, 109, 133, 143
tightness, 52, 55, 66, 82, 203
Tomasello, 3, 39, 206
Turner, 36

value, 41–3, 80
Van Valin, 52, 53, 63, 65, 191, 204
Vendler, 52
Vygotsky, 194

Weiner, 49
Whorf, 61, 189, 197
Wierzbicka, 186, 191, 194
Wilkins, 3, 166, 191
Wilson, 86, 127

Zwicky, 166